THE MODERN LANGUAGE ASSOCIATION OF AMERICA

GENERAL SERIES

FRENCH REALISM: THE CRITICAL REACTION
1830-1870

Approved for publication in the General Series of the Modern Language Association of America

Ronald S. Crane
Joseph E. Gillet
George L. Hamilton
Eduard Prokosch
Hyder Rollins
Karl Young

Committee on Research Activities

Published under a grant awarded by the American Council of Learned Societies from a fund provided by the Carnegie Corporation of New York

FRENCH REALISM: THE CRITICAL REACTION, 1830-1870

BY

BERNARD WEINBERG

NEW YORK: MODERN LANGUAGE ASSOCIATION OF AMERICA
LONDON: OXFORD UNIVERSITY PRESS

1937

PRINTED BY THE GEORGE BANTA PUBLISHING COMPANY, MENASHA, WISCONSIN

FOREWORD

THE subject of this study was suggested to me by Professor Algernon Coleman and Professor E. Preston Dargan of the University of Chicago. The work was written under the direction of Professor Coleman; to him I wish to express my gratitude for his unfailing interest and for countless valuable suggestions. To Professor Dargan, who assisted me on the Balzac chapter and who kindly read and corrected the entire work, I am also grateful. Likewise, I am indebted to Professor W. Scott Hastings of Princeton University and to Professor Thomas R. Palfrey of Northwestern University for their kindness in reading the manuscript. To Mr. W. H. Royce, for his help on Balzac bibliography, thanks are also due. Without the aid, finally, of the trustees of the American Field Service Fellowships for France, who enabled me to pursue a year of reading at the Bibliothèque nationale, the project would have been impossible of achievement. To them, and to the Institute of International Education, I should like to express my sincere appreciation.

B. W.

Chicago, August, 1937

v

TABLE OF CONTENTS

INTRODUCTION

O F THE literary controversies that arose in France in the last century, those relevant to Romanticism and to Realism were by far the most considerable. Romanticism, in recent years, has been studied carefully by literary historians, whose interest has centered both about the development of the movement and about its reception by the public. Although Realism came but shortly after Romanticism, from which it sprang, and although its advocates made equally positive assertions, it has provoked less debate on the part of contemporaries and of later critics. This we may explain by several facts. On the one hand, many of the liberties demanded by Realism had already been solicited, if not won, by the earlier school, and public opinion was naturally less aroused by the reiteration of these demands. In a word, the cleavage between Realism and Romanticism was less considerable, in many respects, than that between Romanticism and the antecedent tradition. On the other hand, there existed for Realism no body of theory comparable in unity of purpose and in scope to the credos and manifestoes of the romanticists. Hence we find that while scholars have made many studies of individual realists, they have given less attention to the general movement, to its gradual development of an artistic method and to the reception accorded the method by contemporaries.[1] In the present study, I shall examine the second of these problems—the critical reaction to French Realism from 1830 to 1870.

Each of the terms in this formulation of the problem—the critical reaction to French Realism from 1830 to 1870—demands elucidation.

In the first place, *whose* critical reaction? I have already indicated that my interest focused on "the reception accorded the method by contemporaries," on the reaction of contemporaries to the realistic movement. But practical considerations necessitated a restriction of the term *contemporary:* restriction to the contemporary who lived in France, and who wrote and published his opinions in Parisian journals or in books. For the study of memoirs and letters as a means of ascertaining "public" opinion yielded, in most cases, meager results indeed; when literary comments did appear in these sources, they were usually of an anecdotal nature. Hence the mass of opinions consulted were "professional," the writings of literary critics proper.

In order that these opinions might approximate the general attitude of the period, I have included a very large number of critical articles.

1

These I discovered by examining nearly all the Parisian reviews and journals which contained literary materials and which appeared within the time limits adopted.[2] Materials found there were supplemented by articles in two daily newspapers, *Le Constitutionnel* and *Le Journal des débats,* both of which I studied for the whole period; by items in *Figaro* up to the time it became a daily newspaper (1866); by other newspaper articles to which I had specific references; and by non-periodical works such as biographies, collections of essays, histories of literature, and prefaces. It is to be noted that the study is based only on this limited group of representative materials, and that the conclusions are valid only for these materials. I hope, however, that they will be found typical of the entire mass of journalistic writing in this period.

From these various sources, I gathered more than a thousand pertinent items. Many of these had not previously been mentioned in historical studies, and therefore constitute a contribution to the bibliography of the subject.[3]

In the second place, critical reaction *to what?* To French Realism, to the movement in nineteenth-century literature known by that name. For critics, however, this "movement" would take the form of specific works and specific statements of theory. Any work, then, which was regarded by a contemporary as an example of the realistic tendency should be considered a realistic work, and any such criticism should be eligible for inclusion in the materials of this study. But, again, limitations of time and of space made a selection necessary. Thus I have omitted all critical discussion of the realistic dramatists, and have included only those novelists who were consistently related to the movement, for reasons adequately stated by the critics. And here another problem presented itself. For while affiliations of works and authors with Realism were clear enough after 1850, when the term *réalisme* had become current, how was one to determine what works before that date belonged to the new tendency? Once more, the materials were allowed to speak for themselves. For in the writings which deal with the realists proper, the critics named the principal forerunners of the school and described the traits which merited that designation. On the basis of contemporary opinion, therefore, I have studied the reaction to Stendhal, Mérimée, and Balzac as precursors of the school: Stendhal and Mérimée as isolated figures with partly realistic tendencies; Balzac as the earliest complete expression of a realistic system in the novel and as the fountain-head of the subsequent literary movement. The chapter on criticism of Balzac is, indeed, the longest in the study; for over one-third of the total number of articles consulted dealt with the author of the *Comédie humaine.* In a second group came Champfleury and

Murger, who prepared the way for the realistic group proper—Flaubert, Feydeau, and the Goncourts. Several minor authors, Monnier, Charles de Bernard, About, Dumas *fils* as author of *Affaire Clémenceau,* have been studied in their appropriate groups.

There are good reasons for including so large a number of writers. It is possible to discover the contemporary reaction to Realism as such only by examining the reaction to all the important writers participating in the movement. Thus, by eliminating individual differences, one may determine how realistic practices in general were received by the critics. Moreover, the critical judgments of authors who are as different from one another as those enumerated will indicate fully the critical standards and attitudes of the period.

In addition to the works, the statements of theory; in addition to the judgments of given novels, the remarks on the body of realistic doctrine and on the general tendencies of the school. A large number of special articles, and many passages in other articles, contained statements of the critical attitude towards Realism, taken as a general term designating a complex of literary practices. These statements, and the formulations of literary theory which they upheld or controverted, I have included in a chapter called "Theory and Opposition." It became manifest, however, that such statements were usually relevant not only to literature, but also to painting; that in the estimation of the critics, the two arts were closely connected during the realistic period. Hence I have included a chapter on the criticism of realistic painting (from 1840 to 1860 especially). If the chapter on painting precedes that on theory, it is because realistic theory and the reaction to it first crystallized about the work of the painters, and the same attitudes were later transferred to literary discussion.

In the third place, critical reaction *at what time?* The realistic movement had obscure beginnings before the nineteenth century, and still continues. Within this span of time, it was necessary to select a limited period for study; the selection was again made on the basis of the materials themselves. Critics pointed to Balzac and Stendhal as the chief precursors of the school. Now Balzac's earliest work as a realistic novelist came in 1830, which was also the date of Stendhal's *Le Rouge et le Noir* and of Monnier's *Scènes populaires.* Thus the famous date of the triumph of Romanticism would seem to mark the beginning of a second, realistic phase of that movement, and I have taken it as the *terminus a quo* for this study. Similarly, certain facts pointed to 1870 as the *terminus ad quem:* the publication of Flaubert's *L'Education sentimentale* and the beginnings of Zola's ambitious naturalistic sequence (both in 1869), and, in 1870, the death of Jules de Goncourt, which marked the close of the joint authorship of the Goncourts. Both termini, furthermore, were dates of political significance, and critics frequently spoke of them as influencing literary trends; Realism proper may be said to extend from the Revolution of July to the fall of the Second Empire.

The principle of organization of the materials has already been suggested: I have classified the critical opinions according to the works (or authors) criticized, or with respect to statements of realistic theory. Each chapter (or part of a chapter) presents the criticism of a single author from the beginning of his career as a realist until 1870; the arrangement is chronological within each chapter. In some cases, I have been able to treat separately the reaction to each of the successive novels of a writer; in others, it has been necessary to group the criticisms within larger periods, on the basis of the points discussed in the critical remarks. Again, the chronological principle directs the ordering of the various chapters: the realists are taken up in approximately the sequence in which they presented themselves to contemporaries, the chapters on painting and theory also occupy an approximate chronological place. Throughout, I have tried to quote the most representative pronouncements, and to give references to all other passages offering similar opinions. The references, for the sake of brevity, give only the index-number of the item as it appears in the Bibliography, the author's name, and the page. Each chapter has been prefaced by a chronology of those works of the author which were published during the period, and which aroused critical comment of a pertinent character; these chronologies are thus partial rather than complete.

Through the examination and classification of the materials, I have tried to answer a number of questions inherent in the problem. What did contemporaries think of the realistic movement? Were they essentially sympathetic or antagonistic towards it? What aspects of realistic writing attracted them, what repelled them? What did they mean by *réalisme*, by *réaliste?* Was there any change, any evolution in their attitudes? Is it possible to determine the general criteria of the period as applicable to the literature of any school?

In answering these questions, I have been led to what I might call a statistical approach. I have tended to subordinate the critic's personality, to consider his contribution as merely another manifestation of the general spirit. So too I have been very democratic: the dictum of an anonymous writer may have just as much weight in my analysis as the expert statement of a Sainte-Beuve or a Taine. In a word, I am concerned with the general attitude towards Realism, and with the successive phases of that attitude.

I make no attempt at writing a history of Realism. Such a history would study sources, the advances made by individual writers, the development of the technique, the formulation of theory, personal relationships. With these I am occupied only in so far as they explain new or different responses from the critics. I treat rather the converse of the problem, the critical judgments elicited by the constituent elements of Realism as these were embodied in the work of one realist after another.

---

[1] The most prominent general studies are Bouvier's *La Bataille réaliste* (Paris: Fontemoing, 1913) and Martino's *Le Roman réaliste sous le Second Empire* (Paris: Hachette, 1913).

[2] See Appendix A for a list of the periodicals examined.

[3] A complete bibliography of the materials used, arranged chronologically according to the authors criticized, will be found in Appendix B.

THE PRECURSORS

CHAPTER I

STENDHAL AND MÉRIMÉE

Chronologies
[Stendhal]

1830: *Le Rouge et le Noir*
1838: *Mémoires d'un Touriste*
1839: *La Chartreuse de Parme*
1842: Stendhal's death
1853-1855: *Œuvres complètes*

[Mérimée]

1829: *Chronique du règne de Charles IX*
1830: *Théâtre de Clara Gazul* (2nd ed.)
1833: *Mosaïque*
       La Double Méprise
1835: *Notes d'un voyageur dans le midi de la France*
1840: *Colomba*
1844: *Arsène Guillot*
1845: *Carmen*
       Reception at the Académie française
1850: *Les Deux Héritages*
1852: *Nouvelles*

DURING the romantic period, in the decade of the 1820's, Stendhal and Mérimée distinguished themselves from their associates by qualities which were one day to be recognized as realistic. They were, even at that early date, isolated figures whose work evidenced varied and sometimes conflicting impulses: the "classical," the "romantic," the "realistic." As they progressed in their literary careers, it was perhaps the realistic aspect that gained the ascendency in their writings; at any rate, it was this aspect which, in the eyes of the succeeding generations, identified them as predecessors of a new literary manner. Because of these traits, readily described as realistic, and because they were both linked, in the later years, with the realistic movement, I have chosen to study their literary fortune between 1830 and 1870 as a prologue to the study of the critical reaction to the realists themselves.

When, in 1840, Henri Beyle announced to Honoré de Balzac that he "had not expected to be read before 1880," he was expressing a conviction that appears frequently in his writings.[1] This conviction had a

9

double source: it sprang first from Stendhal's sense of his maladjust-
ment to the tastes of contemporary readers, and secondly from his
experiences with the critics. With judgments on his work prior to 1830
I am not here concerned; but it is significant to note that from that date
to the time of his death, there appeared (or at least I have been able to
discover) but thirty critical discussions of his novels. The years from
1842 to 1870 added scarcely fifty more. The total is indeed small. It is
especially small when we realize that the same periodicals examined for
Stendhal yielded, in the case of Balzac, some four hundred items.
Beyle's statement was at once a recognition of fact and a presentiment.

For our purposes, criticism of Stendhal began with the appearance
of *Le Rouge et le Noir* in 1830. That year and the following saw a relatively large number of critical articles. A second peak came between
1838 and 1840, with the appreciations of *Mémoires d'un Touriste* and
of *La Chartreuse de Parme;* a third between 1842 and 1847, comprising
the notices following Stendhal's death; and a fourth between 1853 and
1855, when the publication of his complete works was stimulating critical comment. From that time to 1866 (the date of my last item) discussions were scattered and sporadic.

1830 TO 1831

Le Rouge et le Noir appeared during the week of November 13,
1830; for about four months it received a certain amount of attention
from the critics. Then came a complete silence. Short as this space was,
however, and limited in number as were the items, they were still numerous enough to record a fairly unified body of attitudes; disapproval by
the critics was the principal unifying element. The various reactions
find their most typical and perhaps their most complete expression in
an article by Jules Janin in the *Journal des débats* of December 26,
1830.[2]

Janin gives a long summary of the novel, with intercalated critical
remarks. He defines Stendhal's purpose to "peindre la société telle que
l'avait faite le jésuitisme de la Restauration." Passing on to the character of the hero, he says:

Dans ce personnage, si cruellement exact, il n'y a pas un mouvement de
jeune homme, pas un mot naïf, pas un transport naturel. . . . Si c'est là
de la vérité, c'est une vérité bien triste; si c'est là de la nature, c'est une
horrible nature. On ne saurait imaginer combien souvent je me sens
déchaîné contre ces esprits méthodiques et inflexibles, qui considèrent le
moral avec une loupe, qui se posent là comme sur un cadavre, disséquant
scalpel en main les recoins les plus hideux de cette nature sans vie.

Follow attacks on Stendhal's blackened portrayal of provincial life, and
on his anti-bourgeois and anti-Jesuit prejudices. Then:

Sous sa plume, tout se flétrit sans retour, le plus beau jour, le plus beau sol, les plus heureux sentiments. Il promène avec un admirable sang-froid son héros, son monstre, à travers mille turpitudes, à travers mille niaiseries qui sont pires que des turpitudes. Singulier plaisir que s'est donné cet écrivain de réunir en bloc toutes les criailleries, toutes les misères, toutes les dissimulations, tous les mensonges, toutes les super-stitions, toutes les cruautés de notre état social. . . .

Arriving at the end of his résumé, Janin condemns the dénouement as artificial, and then proceeds to a summary statement:

Si le dernier roman de M. de Stendhal est, avec de si graves invraisem-blances et si peu morales, un ouvrage remarquable, vif, colère, plein d'intérêt et d'émotions, s'il mérite d'être lu, même dans le grand oubli de la littérature contemporaine, M. de Stendhal est autrement digne d'être étudié. M. de Stendhal est un de ces écrivains à plusieurs noms, à triple visage, toujours sérieux, dont on ne saurait trop se méfier. C'est un observateur à froid, un railleur cruel, un sceptique méchant, qui est heureux de ne croire à rien, parce qu'en ne croyant pas, il a le droit de ne rien respecter et de flétrir tout ce qu'il touche. Un auteur ainsi fait, corps et âme, s'en va sans inquiétude et sans remords, jetant son venin sur tout ce qu'il rencontre; jeunesse, beauté, grâces, illusions de la vie; les champs même, les forêts, les fleurs, il les dépare, il les brise. . . . jamais on n'aimera l'auteur qui vous aura gâté toutes vos illusions, qui vous aura montré le monde trop laid, pour que vous osiez désormais l'habiter sans pâlir.

And he closes with an objection to Beyle's excessive use of the para-dox, which constitutes, with "cet invincible besoin de tout peindre en laid," the principal element of his literary approach.

I may summarize thus Janin's objections: Stendhal gives a false portrait of society, and his hero and situations are exceptional; his de-parture from truth is always in the direction of the ugly; the general effect of his book, since he has the cynical outlook of a scientist, is to sadden and disillusion the reader. These objections, I hardly need insist, are essentially non-literary in character; they are concerned with the philosophy and, still more definitely, with the moral attitude of the author. This tendency to raise a moral objection to *Le Rouge et le Noir* is prevalent in criticisms of these years. An anonymous writer of *La Revue de Paris* calls the book "une dénonciation en forme contre l'âme humaine, une sorte d'amphithéâtre où on le voit occupé à la disséquer pièce à pièce, pour mieux mettre en relief la lèpre morale dont il la croit rongée"; it is a "satire des mœurs contemporaines," in which the desire for vivid portrayal, leading to exaggeration and caricature, de-prives the work of naturalness.[3] Again, *L'Artiste* characterizes it as "de l'algèbre sur le cœur humain,"[4] and *La Gazette de France* as an "honteuse production."[5] Even for Mérimée, Beyle's intimate friend,

Julien is true, but horrible—art must not treat this side of human nature[6]—and for Balzac the novel is the "conception d'une sinistre et
froide philosophie."[7] La Gazette littéraire, in an ironic review, mocks
at the "manie . . . de faire des mœurs et des passions" and at Stendhal's
attempt to make common life "distinguished" by multiplying minute details.[8] Even a satirical song, entitled Le Rouge et le Noir, calls Stendhal "un sceptique désenchanté," and continues:

> Il hait l'honneur pusillanime
> Et, dans son sot égarement,
> N'accorde un cœur un peu sublime
> Qu'à l'homme qui tue et qui ment.[9]

By contrast with these adverse opinions, Amédée Pichot finds in the
work a penetrating and faithful depiction of society; he considers the
events (whose historical source he indicates) and the hero true, and
he sees in Julien a representative of the youth of his time.[10] Alexis de
Saint-Priest exclaims: "Voilà de la vérité! voilà de l'exactitude!"[11]

For expressions on the formal, literary aspects of the work we must
turn to other passages. A tribute to the plot and its interest is paid by
La Revue de Paris;[12] but its opinion is contradicted by La Gazette
littéraire, which finds the narrative capricious and without logical sequence:[13] everywhere, except in the laudable treatment of the love of
Julien and Madame de Renal, the author strains for originality, and as
a result his style, his characterizations, his descriptions, are uneven.
The most favorable review of all appears in Figaro: its author finds
that certain of the figures are without individuality; but Julien and
Mathilde are original creations, and the handling is generally superior;
especially is the style "jeune, frais et plein de couleur."[14] However, this
is not the opinion of L'Artiste, which notes an abuse of the unexpected
("l'imprévu") and a monotony of plot; only the "esprit" and the
"choses vues et décrites à la loupe" are praiseworthy.[15]

In general, then, the novel was rejected by the critics, chiefly because
they disapproved on moral and philosophical grounds of the subject-
matter and the author's cynicism, and also because they found structural deficiencies. None of the writers, indeed, was sufficiently impressed by the literary qualities of the work to comment upon them
extensively.

1838 to 1840

After seven years of an almost absolute silence—I find only a passing compliment to the description in Le Rouge[16] and an allusion to its
immorality[17]—we come to the Mémoires d'un Touriste in 1838 and to
La Chartreuse de Parme in 1839. The former is only incidentally of

interest to us, since it is not a novel; but certain remarks on Stendhal's general method are worthy of note. Such, for example, is Francis Wey's mockery of "la feinte banalité des observations, les niaiseries simulées," of "ces détails si vrais, si naturels; le *vrai seul est aimable,*" of the "ineffable simplicité," and of the "profonde connaissance de la classe la plus nombreuse des lecteurs." He speaks lightly of Stendhal's "profondes pensées politico-théo-philosophiques."[18] More significant is the judgment of Frémy in *La Revue de Paris:*

> . . . l'auteur a compris que la première qualité du voyageur comme de l'historien était d'être vrai; il n'a donc voulu rien déguiser, rien farder, il a tenu avant tout à raconter les choses telles qu'elles se sont passées, telles qu'elles existent.

He finds a certain charm in the conscious simplicity and naïveté; but the lack of transitions is fatiguing. Beyle's style, although sometimes affected in rhythm, has real originality, and he avoids the abuse of description. He sees things in a true, albeit a sad light; above all, he is absolutely sincere.[19] Chaudes-Aigues, who speaks of *Le Rouge* as one of the finest contemporary novels, lauds the naturalness of the new book and the presence of "ces qualités étouffées par l'emphase de certains écrivains modernes"—obviously an allusion to romantic excesses, of which he believes Stendhal to be free.[20] Eugène Guinot, in a review of the *Mémoires,* also praises *Le Rouge* since it "paints well the world and the heart."[21] Finally, Forgues—like many later critics—compares Stendhal to Diderot and comments, incidentally, on his excessive use of detail.[22]

Early in 1839, before the appearance of *La Chartreuse,* Amédée Duquesnel gave a belated appreciation of *Le Rouge et le Noir,* which he termed "singulièrement remarquable par la profondeur des observations et la contexture nerveuse de l'ensemble." Like his predecessors he blamed the dénouement and the disenchanting moral conclusion. But he was obliged to declare: "mais quelle science de la vie! quelles peintures de la haute société parisienne et de cet égoïsme brillant qui la ronge!"[23]

The reception of *La Chartreuse de Parme,* although extremely limited in scope, was on the whole favorable: not that the criticisms were all laudatory, nor that its enthusiasts found nothing deprecatory to say; but in general the balance swung towards praise rather than towards blame. We may again consult Frémy for such a statement of mingled praise and blame; he begins his article by scoring Stendhal's narrative technique:

> On peut faire plus d'un reproche à la *Chartreuse de Parme:* la manière de raconter de l'auteur est étrange, elliptique, et il est même douteux qu'il soit avantageux de l'imiter. Il fait entrer ses personnages

en scène; puis une fois introduits, il les laisse parler, se mouvoir, se conduire à leur guise et sans qu'il y ait de sa part presque aucune participation directe. . . . Les situations sont indiquées à peine; l'action voltige, se déplace, s'interrompt, coupe sa marche, et tout cela au hasard, sans motif apparent, avec l'intention formelle d'éluder le point où elle serait tentée de se cristalliser en scène. . . . On se surprend plus d'une fois à se demander si cette histoire est inventée, ou bien si elle n'a pas été prise sur le fait, calquée fidèlement sur la réalité.

These deficiencies of the technique, however, are to be attributed to a fundamental unsuitability of the subject, as well as to the author's inclination to adore reality: "du moment où il entre dans une époque ou une contrée quelconque, on sent qu'il tient avant tout à en réfléchir les moindres détails, à réunir les plus subtils fragments de mœurs et de particularités locales." Frémy advises Stendhal rather to enter into "cette vaste arène poétique où il n'y a plus de limite de mœurs, de lois ni de conventions, où le poète crée tout, même le terrain et la contrée de ses personnages." In spite of these inherent faults, the author has excelled through his wit, his detachment, his talent in the delineation of characters and in certain narrative passages—above all the treatment of the battle of Waterloo. By fleeing excessive description he has avoided the fault of "ces histoires d'à présent qui n'ont littéralement d'autre but que de clouer des tapisseries, d'analyser des boiseries et des murailles, et d'épousseter de vieux meubles"—a manifest thrust at Balzac's manner. Beyle's style is free of bombast and exaggeration, and the reproach of Voltairianism is unfounded. In conclusion, Frémy urges him to give his next novel a French setting.[24]

Balzac, in the famous *Revue parisienne* article of 1840, agrees with Frémy in condemning Beyle's handling of plot. A narrative which follows the disorder of life, he says, is unsatisfying artistically:

M. Beyle a bien disposé les événements, comme ils se sont passés ou comme ils devraient se passer; mais il a commis dans l'arrangement des faits la faute que commettent quelques auteurs, en prenant un sujet vrai dans la nature qui ne l'est pas dans l'art. En voyant un paysage, un grand peintre se gardera bien de copier servilement, il nous en doit moins la Lettre que l'Esprit. Ainsi, dans sa manière simple, naïve et sans apprêt de conter, M. Beyle a risqué de paraître confus.[25]

On the other hand Cherbuliez, in a sympathetic review, opposes this criticism, stating that "autant le fond du récit est simple et peu compliqué, autant les détails, les incidents et les aventures du héros sont nombreux et enchaînés avec art, de manière à soutenir constamment la curiosité du lecteur."[26] Both Balzac and Cherbuliez agree with Frémy in singing the praises of the Waterloo episode,[27] but they disagree with him when they condemn the style, which constitutes for Balzac the

principal weakness of the work, whereas Cherbuliez finds fault mainly
with certain vulgarities and grammatical mistakes. What appeals to the
latter above all is the depiction of Italian society and manners.[28] Balzac, in consonance with the statement quoted above, points out the lack
of unity in La Chartreuse; but he defends Stendhal brilliantly as a
proponent of "la littérature des idées," as well as for his characterization and for the profound sentiment underlying his work.[29]

In this sketch of criticism of La Chartreuse, I have omitted from
consideration an article published by Théodore Muret in La Quotidienne,[30] since it approaches the novel from a purely moralistic standpoint; in this respect it is an echo of the criticism pertaining to Le Rouge
et le Noir. Like his predecessors, Muret calls Stendhal "un esprit
positif, sceptique et railleur, qui va impitoyablement chercher le fond
sous la forme"; with Frémy, he accepts the style, and for similar reasons; but the rest of the opinion in negative. He would admit Beyle's
subject and manner if the writer had drawn from them a moral conclusion:

. . . mais . . . le caractère dominant, chez M. Beyle, c'est le scepticisme :
il est voltairien en 1839, rôle tant soit peu arriéré. M. Beyle a su prendre
à l'auteur de Candide la limpidité de son style, la finesse de sa touche,
le mordant de son expression; mais il lui a pris aussi, en plus d'un endroit, sa moquerie pour les choses saintes, pour les idées que, sans distinction d'opinion, chacun est tenu de respecter au moins chez autrui.
C'est chose rare aujourd'hui que ce style exempt de boursouflure, de
manière, d'affectation de pittoresque; aussi se laisserait-on aller avec
un plaisir sans mélange au récit amusant et spirituel de M. Beyle, sans
ce vieux et étroit philosophisme peu digne d'un écrivain distingué.

This moral censure makes more striking the absence of similar opinions
among the items of 1838-1840. The other critics, though few in number,
came to the work with a more definitely literary attitude; they blamed it
for its lack of unity and transitions, sometimes for its subject, for the
incorrectness of its style; they praised it for its characterization, for
certain narrative portions, and occasionally for its fidelity to the realities
represented.

1842 TO 1847

On March 25, 1842, two days after Stendhal's death, several newspapers printed short and inadequate necrologic notices. It was not until
the first of April, with an article by E. D. Forgues in Le National, that
a literary discussion was devoted to the deceased writer.[31] From that
time until 1847, some fifteen articles took up the man and his work.
Despite the fact that these included a large variety of opinions, it is
nevertheless possible to discern in them a certain unity of approach.

Most of the writers, whether they approved of the fact or not, pointed out that Stendhal was primarily a student of objective reality. For example, the statement of Albert Aubert:

... l'art n'est pour lui que l'expression vive et pure de la réalité. ... Beyle laisse, pour ainsi dire, la vie se moquer d'elle-même; son livre est un miroir où passent tour à tour les belles images et les laides, les objets gais ou tristes, admirables ou risibles. Quant à la moralité de ces divers tableaux, peu lui importe vraiment ...[32]

Similarly, Gobineau remarks that "Il aime la réalité avant toutes choses, mais ce n'est pas pour la reproduire telle qu'elle est; il faut toujours qu'il s'en empare et qu'il la transforme d'une manière particulière."[33] Comments on this devotion to reality are also found in the reviews by Bussière and by Babou.[34] Certain critics object, however, that Stendhal's reality is incomplete; so an anonymous writer in the *Feuilleton mensuel*,[35] and especially Aubert in a discussion of Balzac, where he points out incidentally that Stendhal's *petits faits vrais* are insufficient, and that in art the ideal is essential.[36]

Recognizing that Beyle's work is in the realm of the real rather than of the imagined, the critics comment on the persistence and the excellence of his powers of observation. As Bussière says,

... comme l'objet unique de ses pensées a été une science d'observation, toutes ses visées, toute son ambition, toute sa gloire, tout le fruit de sa vie, sont restés attachés au renom d'observateur pénétrant et de logicien rigoureux.[37]

In the writings of Forgues, of Aubert de Vitry, of Colomb, of Albert Aubert and of Ducoin we find additional comments on Stendhal's faculty of observation.[38] Closely related to this—indeed merely another aspect of it—is the novelist's attention to detail. This attention constitutes, for Albert Aubert, the key to Stendhal's talent: "Des petits faits vrais sur une passion, sur une situation de la vie, voilà comme il comprenait le roman, le traité de morale ou de philosophie."[39] In two different studies, Ducoin singles out Stendhal's use of details as his principal merit, especially in *Le Rouge;*[40] he here echoes an earlier statement of Bussière to the same effect.[41]

This acuity of observation might, of course, manifest itself in any phase of the novel, in character depiction as well as in descriptive detail. Gobineau, studying Beyle's technique of characterization, applauds the reality of the Duchesse de Sanseverina, and his skill in delineating complex personages.[42] Romain Colomb and Aubert see the hand of a master in the character portrayals, even though Colomb rejects Julien as a "triste exception."[43] Babou, too, considers all the people in *Le*

Rouge et le Noir convincingly true.[44] Again, as a result of his scientific approach, Beyle is said to arrive at a complete and faithful representation of society, whether it be that of contemporary France (Colomb)[45] or of eighteenth-century Italy (Gobineau) : "c'est l'état d'une société et d'une époque que Stendhal a prétendu nous faire connaître."[46]

The more penetrating critics were not long in tracing this concern with reality to Stendhal's general philosophical attitude. What strikes them as most noteworthy is the logical cast of his mind. Not only do his works show, chronologically, an orderly progression towards their climax in *La Chartreuse* (Gobineau, Bussière),[47] but the individual novel is rigorously planned and executed : "Stendhal n'est pas entraîné par ses émotions ; la réflexion chez lui fait tout, dirige tout, place tout, et, ayant sans cesse la conscience de ce qu'elle produit, n'abandonne rien au hasard prophétique."[48] According to Aubert, "il ne se livre jamais, il se contient et se réserve."[49] Whether it be a cause or a result of this intellectual habit, the dominant element in his philosophy is unquestionably materialistic. Forgues calls him "le plus spirituel parmi les derniers champions de la philosophie matérialiste," and likens him again to Diderot ;[50] in the *Feuilleton mensuel* we hear echoes of earlier critics in the phrase "esprit éminemment sceptique, railleur, fin et spirituel" ;[51] Stendhal's friend Louis Crozet sees in his materialism abundant reason for withholding certain works from reedition :

. . . les fondements de ses écrits sont assis sur la philosophie des sensations, sur le pur matérialisme, et sur un mépris hautement affiché, je dirai même sur une haine de l'esprit religieux qui sont parfaitement opposés aux idées du moment et qui sont injustes même philosophiquement parlant.[52]

In this connection I might note that Stendhal is now frequently associated by critics with the philosophers of the eighteenth century and the "Idéologues" : with Montesquieu and Voltaire,[53] with Diderot for his ideas and his style,[54] with Destutt de Tracy for his metaphysics, with Cabanis.[55] Evidences of his materialism are his physiological approach to character and passion ; on this compare the assertion of Bussière : "Il pose comme base de la connaissance de l'homme la physiologie : il veut connaître l'homme, il étudie donc la physiologie . . ."[56] Aubert, in his article on Balzac, declares that Beyle and Balzac resemble each other in their cold, analytical approach to the study of the passions ; the general affinity which he discerns between them was to be loudly asserted in the following years.[57] Another evidence of Beyle's materialism is the concreteness of his expression : "Nous savons quelle est l'horreur de M. de Stendhal pour les choses abstraites. C'est ce qu'il appelle le vague. Il réduit, il ramène toujours le style à l'expression concrète, les pensées à un fait, les ensembles de faits à des noms propres."[58]

The critics of these years agree, therefore, in emphasizing the overwhelming rôle of reality and of positivism in Stendhal's work, whether in the subject-matter, or in the treatment, or in the author's philosophy. On the question of literary composition, too, they are in essential agreement; they point to Stendhal's attention to *fond* rather than to *forme* as a reason for the carelessness, the negligence of his style. They complain of his lack of transitions, of his tendency to be elliptical and confusing. Balzac, who maintains his enthusiasm of 1840, nevertheless writes: "il n'a pas assez soigné *la forme:* il écrivait comme les oiseaux chantent et notre langue est une espèce de Dame Honesta qui ne trouve rien de bien que ce qui est irréprochable, ciselé, léché."[59] The same reproach is made by Forgues, Bussière, Aubert de Vitry, Gobineau, Colomb.[60] Albert Aubert sees these defects, but justifies them:

... le passage d'une idée à l'autre y est souvent un peu brusque, les transitions y font fréquemment défaut, et l'on y sent une recherche de concision, de vivacité, qui obscurcit parfois la pensée; mais, du moins, vous ne voyez là aucune de ces bizarreries de forme, de ces excentricités d'idée, de ces digressions capricieuses et fantasques, à la manière de Sterne et de Byron . . . Non, ici encore, l'originalité de Beyle n'est pas dans la forme, mais dans le fond même; n'est pas dans les mots, mais dans les choses; et il faut étudier de près ses livres pour apercevoir la vive personnalité de l'écrivain, pour reconnaître l'indépendance et la nouveauté de son talent.[61]

This appreciation of Stendhal's originality is repeated by other critics (especially one in the *Feuilleton mensuel* and Aubert de Vitry);[62] still others agree with Albert Aubert in ranking *La Chartreuse de Parme* as Beyle's best book.[63]

It would seem, then, that the criticism of the years following Stendhal's death was fairly unified in tendency; it pointed out that objective reality—treated scientifically—constituted the *fond* of his writings, and that his almost exclusive attention to this *fond* accounted for the impression of negligence in his *forme*. I may indicate other features of this body of criticism. In the first place, it is less concerned than were earlier articles with evaluation, with the business of praise and blame, and more directly interested in explanation. It attempts to discover Beyle's method and approach, his philosophy, to explain the one by the other when possible. In the second place, it is more judicious than earlier comments had been; the reproach of immorality scarcely appears. There is no hostility, but at the same time there is no exaggerated praise; there is, rather, a fair amount of study and unimpassioned examination.

1853 TO 1855

When we come to the articles occasioned by the Michel-Lévy edition of Stendhal's works between 1853 and 1855, we find an entirely different note, a change in emphasis as well as a change in tone. It becomes evident immediately that the general attitude, from one of tolerant impartiality, has developed into one of frank animosity. There is, first, a protest against Stendhal's recent vogue, which the critics deem unwarranted.[64] Then a number of specific objections are made to one phase or another of Stendhal's work; among the most frequently recurrent is that of artificiality. Beyle's originality is feigned rather than genuine, and his striving for it pierces through to annoy the reader. The simplicity of his style, the very disorder of his presentation, all these are counterfeit. This point is made by Ratisbonne, Sainte-Beuve, Despois, Caro, Barbey d'Aurevilly;[65] I quote the first of these:

Il veut à tout prix être original, faisant profession d'être simple et ayant des recherches de simplicité infinies, courant après le naturel sans l'attraper, après l'humour et le dépassant pour tomber dans l'affectation, échappant à l'emphase sans éviter toujours le galimatias, hâché et sans suite...

The comment of Despois is particularly interesting, since he is the first critic (I believe) to characterize Beyle's approach as "Bélisme," which he defines thus:

... une absence complète d'abandon, et souvent une raideur doctorale, une sorte de pédantisme mondain, qui affecte de traiter avec une légèreté extrême les choses sérieuses, et réserve toute sa gravité pour des niaiseries de société. Tout y semble calculé, jusqu'à l'imprévu.

Paul Boiteau, however, in the liberal *Artiste,* declares that the author of *De l'amour* possessed real originality of the best French type, and that therefore his works would endure.[66]

More persistent even than the cry of artificiality was that of immorality, lack of ideal, cynicism, and the related philosophical vices. In this respect, at least, the body of criticism now under discussion resembles the criticism of *Le Rouge et le Noir* in the early years of our period. Perhaps the objection is now more violently formulated. Some of the testimony, indeed, is somewhat invalidated by the strong bias lying behind it; but it gains significance as its elements recur in other critics. Even Sainte-Beuve takes exception to the character of Fabrice, who is "fort laid, fort plat, fort vulgaire; il ne se conduit nulle part

comme un homme, mais comme un animal livré à ses appétits. . . .
Aucune morale, aucun principe d'honneur."[67] Barbey d'Aurevilly, link-
ing Stendhal again with the eighteenth-century *philosophes,* discerns
in him a quintessence of their negation, their impiety, their dissolving
analysis.[68] Small wonder, then, that other critics—Emile Chasles, Ulbach, Caro[69]—charged Stendhal with these philosophical misdemeanors,
and from them proceeded (in the cases of Ulbach and Caro at least) to
a general condemnation of his work.

Inevitably, the problem of truth arises again, either as connected with
these philosophical traits or as dissociated from them. In the early
posthumous appreciations, as we have seen, this problem served as a
focal point for much of the criticism. Now, with *le réalisme* a definite
part of the literary vocabulary and with the new school prominent in
artistic discussion, Stendhal's exact portrayal of society promptly enters under the new denomination. An anonymous writer in *L'Athenaeum
français* (1854) is the first to establish the analogy:

> Beyle avait entre autres qualités celle d'être véridique, et il portait le
> paradoxe, non dans l'erreur, mais dans la recherche de la vérité. De
> même que dans ses ouvrages d'imagination, il péchait plutôt par un
> réalisme exagéré, de même dans ses descriptions des lieux, dans ses
> jugements sur les arts, sur l'histoire, sur les mœurs, il se complaisait à
> mettre en évidence le côté vrai, exact, fidèle des choses.[70]

Again, a few months later, Babou refers to Stendhal's particular brand
of romanticism as "une sorte de réalisme largement compris."[71] Aside
from these statements, Stendhal is not as yet explicitly associated with
the realistic movement; yet much of the debate continues to center about
his attitude towards external reality and his treatment of it.

One of those who had inveighed against the immorality of Stendhal,
Elme-Marie Caro, interprets his novels not as reflections of the world
without, but as mere demonstrations of his theories. The people are
personified abstractions without any life of their own, and they move
confusedly through impossible actions; the society they live in is distorted, imaginary, unreal. But even if these materials were real, they
would not be acceptable for the novel; the functions of the historian
and the creative writer are distinct.[72] We may take this opinion as fairly
typical of the 1853-1855 period. Sainte-Beuve, for one, agrees with Caro
that the *dramatis personae* are automata:

> . . . il forme ses personnages avec deux ou trois idées qu'il croit justes et
> surtout piquantes . . . Ce ne sont pas des êtres vivants, mais des automates
> ingénieusement construits; on y voit, presque à chaque mouvement,
> les ressorts que le mécanicien introduit et touche par le dehors.[73]

On the accuracy of Beyle's *tableaux de mœurs* opinions differ. Most of the writers recognize that such portrayals are one of the author's principal aims; but while Monselet, Ulbach, and E. Chasles admit the fidelity of the representation,[74] Castille, Sainte-Beuve, and Caro tend to find it unsatisfactory.[75] For Sainte-Beuve, "le tableau des partis et des cabales du temps [in *Le Rouge et le Noir*] . . . manque aussi de cette suite et de cette modération dans le développement qui peuvent seules donner idée d'un vrai tableau de mœurs."[76]

The difficulty is not in the lack of observation, for critics such as Ratisbonne and Chasles concede that this is Stendhal's primary faculty, and others find it entirely adequate.[77] Rather, his world is unconvincing because of the philosophical prejudices entering into its depiction, and because of stylistic and structural excentricities.

Beyle ne compose jamais, il note toujours et suit en écrivant les fantaisies d'un tempérament d'esprit extrêmement mobile; il n'a pas la robuste constitution intellectuelle des hommes de premier ordre. Génie incomplet, il apporte dans le travail de la pensée le coup d'œil d'un philosophe, les allures d'un sceptique, l'esprit de comparaison d'un voyageur actif; il aura jeté une lumière vive sur l'âme humaine sans avoir fait un livre définitif, et sa réputation restera celle d'un *observateur*.

The opinion is that of Emile Chasles;[78] it is corroborated, for both the structural and the intellectual aspects, by Sainte-Beuve and Caro.[79] As for style, we have already seen the adverse attitude of Ratisbonne; Sainte-Beuve found it lacking in color, poetry, progression, vigor;[80] and for Monselet it was "plat comme un paysage de la Beauce."[81]

Are we then to conclude that the critics found nothing admirable in Stendhal's work? Obviously not. We have already seen certain points defended by individual writers; others made further concessions. Sainte-Beuve, as if to temper the severity of his judgment, pointed to the charm of certain descriptive passages;[82] Monselet regarded Beyle's "science complète de la vie" as giving him a real superiority;[83] Barbey d'Aurevilly justified his novels by their forcefulness and vigor: characters, style, observation, language, all attest to a real power and virility.[84] But more significant than these, perhaps, is the recognition of Stendhal's historical importance. Says Emile Chasles:

Reportez-vous . . . à l'époque où il écrivait, vous le verrez se détacher de toute cette littérature qui faisait rimer *gloire* avec *victoire* et *lauriers* avec *guerriers*. Il s'isole pour réclamer la liberté littéraire, ou la liberté civile des femmes, avant Victor Hugo et Georges Sand, pour exercer une analyse profonde de la société, avant Balzac.[85]

Louis Ulbach, too, places Beyle with Balzac as one who was instrumental in initiating the second, analytical phase of romanticism.[86] And Babou links his romanticism with realism:

Il [his romanticism] ne comportait aucun des styles en vogue: musical, pittoresque, sculptural, diamanté, ciselé, vaporeux, splendide. Beyle voulait un style net, ferme, direct, plein et concis; et pour nous résumer en un mot, "le romantisme sans phrase!"

Il était, par une exception singulière, le seul libéral qui fût romantique, ou le seul romantique qui fût libéral. . . . Ecrire selon le goût et les mœurs de la société où l'on vit, tel est le romantisme de Beyle.[87]

As in several of the above passages, so in many other critics Stendhal is now frequently likened to Balzac. We shall see later that these are years of enthusiasm for Balzac; but already we may note that in these comparisons Stendhal is usually considered inferior. The two novelists are studied for similarities in descriptive technique, in the analytical approach to character, or they are contrasted in style and in thought. If any superiority is accorded to Balzac, it is largely because of the idealism which is attributed to his work, but which is found completely absent from Stendhal's. "Balzac," remarks Monselet, "domine Stendhal de toute la hauteur de sa bonne foi."[88] "Balzac," says Ulbach, "est bien supérieur et a bien mieux compris les conditions de l'analyse. Dans les autopsies les plus vives, on voit comme une lueur au bout de son scalpel, et il fait pénétrer un rayon d'or au fond des entrailles qu'il met à nu."[89] Emile Chasles gives a more extended summary of their relationship:

Ces écrivains se touchaient par quelques côtés et, sans le savoir, appartenaient au même mouvement littéraire. Tous deux, en étudiant avec persévérance la vie sociale de l'Europe moderne, en peignant les figures inquiètes d'une époque de civilisation raffinée, ont donné au roman une profondeur et une importance nouvelles. Sans les comparer autrement, on peut dire que la littérature du dix-neuvième siècle eut en chacun d'eux un observateur, un écrivain original et surtout un audacieux éclaireur.[90]

These repeated juxtapositions of the two writers cannot be fortuitous; evidently the epoch saw in them, if not a unity of approach, at least some points of contact which made comparison possible. Both, in the last analysis, are now to be identified with the realistic group.

It is this attempt to place Stendhal historically in his century and to relate him to the general literary movement that constitutes the real originality of criticism during these few years. The reiterated reproach on moral and philosophical grounds, the discussion centering about the problem of reality as related to Stendhal's novels, had appeared earlier in criticism of him, and their recurrence here merely shows the persistence of a point of view—with, of course, the changes brought by the passage of time.

1856 TO 1866

During the next ten years (1856-1866) there are but few articles devoted specifically to Stendhal; most of the criticisms—some fifteen in all—are allusions found in discussions of other writers. They continue, in the main, the tradition of the preceding period. Thus Barbey d'Aurevilly and Poitou in 1857 draw comparisons between Beyle and Balzac;[91] Barbey unites them as "les seuls romanciers d'invention et d'observation de ce siècle"; Poitou condemns them jointly for their moral and philosophical ideas, their scientific method, their similar literary practices. Thus Barbey, again, in 1860 calls Stendhal "ce père de tous les réalistes, qui cravacherait ses bâtards," and reproaches him with his wilful dryness.[92] But perhaps the general tone is more favorable. Thulié (1856) admires him for the vivacity of his characters;[93] Watripon (1857) insists especially on the moral function of *Le Rouge et le Noir*, which he considers unsurpassed by any subsequent novel;[94] Barthet (1859) goes so far as to term *Le Rouge* and *La Chartreuse* the most remarkable novels of the nineteenth century.[95]

In an article of 1862 on Delécluze, Sainte-Beuve again discusses Stendhal at some length, and restates most of his earlier opinions.[96] The lack of ensemble and composition, the constant effort to suppress imagination and poetry in style and subject, are Beyle's principal failings. He does seek truth, particularly by restricting himself to contemporary *mores;* but even here he leans too strongly in the direction of the reprehensible, and is apt to be misunderstood. This article is, on the whole, much less significant than two discussions which Taine devoted to Beyle, in 1863 and 1864 respectively. As early as 1856, Taine had pointed to Beyle's preeminence as a psychologist and to the qualities of his style.[97] Now, in the Introduction to the *Histoire de la littérature anglaise,* he develops these ideas;[98] Stendhal, alone, has undertaken the work of explaining the individual by analysis:

Un seul homme, Stendhal, par une tournure d'esprit et d'éducation singulière, l'a [ce travail] entrepris, et encore aujourd'hui la plupart des lecteurs trouvent ses livres paradoxaux et obscurs; son talent et ses idées étaient prématurés; on n'a pas compris ses admirables divinations, ses mots profonds jetés en passant, la justesse étonnante de ses notations et de sa logique; on n'a pas vu que sous des apparences de causeur et d'homme du monde, il expliquait les plus compliqués des mécanismes internes, qu'il mettait le doigt sur les grands ressorts, qu'il importait dans l'histoire du cœur les procédés scientifiques, l'art de chiffrer, de décomposer et de déduire, que le premier il marquait les causes fondamentales, j'entends les nationalités, les climats et les tempéraments; bref, qu'il traitait des sentiments comme on doit en traiter, c'est-à-dire en naturaliste et en physicien, en faisant des classifications et en pesant des forces. A cause de tout cela on l'a jugé sec et excentrique, et il est demeuré isolé, écrivant des romans, des voyages, des notes, pour lesquels il souhaitait et obtenait vingt lecteurs. Et cependant, c'est dans ses livres qu'on trouvera encore aujourd'hui les essais les plus propres à frayer la route que j'ai tâché de décrire. Nul n'a mieux enseigné à ouvrir les yeux et à regarder, à regarder d'abord les hommes environnants et la vie présente, puis les documents anciens et authentiques, à lire par delà le blanc et le noir des pages, à voir sous la vieille impression, sous le griffonnage d'un texte, le sentiment précis, le mouvement d'idées, l'état d'esprit dans lequel on l'écrivait.

The next year, in an "Etude sur Stendhal," Taine expands these principles still further. Stendhal's approach is primarily psychological, and he therefore disdains the attention to externals which is characteristic of other writers such as Balzac. His is a higher form of art, and the particular province of literature; description is the function of the painter, and is admissible only as it throws light upon character. His people are superior, but not bizarre; the logical consistency of their various traits and of their actions endows them with naturalness and *vraisemblance*.

Ils sont réels, car ils sont complexes, multiples, particuliers et originaux comme ceux des êtres vivants; à ce titre ils sont naturels et animés, et contentent le besoin que nous avons de vérité et d'émotion. Mais, d'autre part, ils sont hors du commun, ils nous tirent loin de nos habitudes plates, de notre vie machinale, de la sottise et de la vulgarité qui nous entourent.[99]

Stendhal's ideas are true and universal; his style is perfect since it disappears as a separate element, and serves merely as an expression of the idea.

These articles form, as it were, the apotheosis of Stendhal in our period. Not that the ideas are entirely new: we have seen them scattered here and there throughout preceding articles. But they attain here a synthesis, an eloquence of expression, a compactness which give them unprecedented authority. We readily understand Taine's enthusiasm, realizing as we do the conformity of Stendhal's aesthetic practice with Taine's aesthetic doctrine, and the influence of the one upon the other. From 1864 to 1870, criticism has little to say about Beyle. I might mention Sarcey's tribute to his powers of analysis and sobriety of taste,[100] Barbey's repeated condemnation of his morality and his crudity,[101] Claretie's appreciation of *Le Rouge* as a masterpiece of analysis,[102] Bougy's ranking of Beyle with Balzac.[103] I might indicate, too, that in these last few years, Stendhal becomes a standard of comparison for other authors; this is especially evident in the articles on Dumas *fils' Affaire Clémenceau* in 1866.[104]

In its totality, the criticism of Stendhal shows a certain unity as well as a certain progression. Throughout, although in varying proportions, the critics censure his work for moral deficiencies and philosophical errors. Throughout, and again in a varying degree, they see in him a painter of reality, an artist whose principal interest is in the depiction of the true and the observable. To this in itself they have no objection. But when they compare Stendhal's reality with that of the world about them or, more specifically, with the conception that they themselves have formed of the world, they find Stendhal's universe unduly ugly and discouraging. It is their own persistent 'idealism' which makes Stendhal's 'realism' objectionable. As for the purely structural aspects of his work, these too are found deficient. Composition, order, unity, appropriateness—Beyle has none of these. The 'classicism' of these criteria is immediately evident. The critics applying them are not romantics who would delight in freedom of form as well as of subject-matter; they are rather the descendants of a long line of critics whose judgments were based on fixed literary standards. Whatever artistic unity Stendhal's work may have had within its own kind escaped them.

Yet there was an evolution in these opinions. Not on the moral question, where changes were erratic and independent, it would seem, of any logical progression. But on the formal side a movement is discernible—a movement which gradually admits Stendhal's eccentricities of style and of characterization, of plot and of description, and which culminates, for Taine at least, in a synthesis of the new art for which Stendhal is responsible.

The relationship of the whole of the criticism of Stendhal to the criticism of realism will shortly be manifest. We need only bear in mind the debate centering about the depiction of reality, the question as to whether an exact portrayal of life is moral or admissible in art, the conclusion that such an attempt must end in exaggeration of the ugly; and remembering these we shall perceive, as we come to other authors and to the general discussion of realism, the resemblance between these problems and the ones which were constantly raised in the criticism of realism.

If Stendhal differed from his contemporaries largely because of his progressive realistic tendencies, Mérimée's departure was in the opposite direction of classicism. Although his literary production included a wide variety of works—short stories and plays, translations and novels, travel impressions—critics of the entire forty-year period concurred in finding a remarkable unity of method and of spirit in his writings. The seventy articles upon which the following pages will be based repeat the same comments throughout, with practically no change from year to year. Essentially, the critics accepted and admired Mérimée as a classical writer, typically French in all his practices. They applauded his restraint and his moderation, his *mesure*, his avoidance of excess of any kind. His works, they said, were simple in matter and in form, severe in outline, and he concentrated—as his classical predecessors had done —on the study of the inner man. Hence description was subordinated to the analysis of character, and his whole manner was dramatic rather than novelistic. Finally, his style was pure, concise, chaste. These observations, I repeat, constitute the burden of criticism of Mérimée during the entire period.

At the same time, critics pointed to certain elements of Mérimée's work which they and others considered as realistic. These involved, in large part, the subject-matter which he chose to treat and his attitude towards that material. Mérimée's principal realistic trait, according to the commentators, was his constant preoccupation with truth. This is the one aspect of his writing upon which there is almost unanimous assent; some thirty articles make specific statements relevant to Mérimée's *vérité*, and others allude in some form or other to this truthfulness. Charles de Rémusat quotes the well-known verses of Musset on the artist:

> L'un, comme Caldéron et comme Mérimée,
> Incruste un plomb brûlant sur la réalité,
> Découpe à son flambeau la silhouette humaine,
> En emporte le moule, et jette sur la scène
> Le plâtre de la vie avec sa nudité.[105]

J.-J. Ampère, as early as 1830, points to this quality of reality as a promising feature in Mérimée's art: "on ne peut nier que ce ne soit une direction positive du talent, un cachet de réalité qui, dans ce moment, ait le plus de chance d'avenir et qui résiste le mieux à l'épreuve du passé."[106] Sainte-Beuve, the following year, declares that "il a . . . aimé s'en tenir à ce qu'il y a de plus certain, de plus saisissable dans le réel"; he speaks of "chaque réalité serrée de près et rendue avec une exactitude sévère."[107] Also in 1831, Cs. defines Mérimée's "complète vérité" and demonstrates its harmony with the spirit of the times:

A force d'artifices et de pompe oratoire, nous sommes revenus au goût de la vérité nue, non plus de cette vérité d'emprunt, que Diderot cherchait à mettre en honneur, mais d'une vérité fondée sur l'observation et présentée sans voiles. Il y a aussi dans le talent de M. Mérimée quelque chose de positif, de sagace et d'inexorable qui nous convient éminemment. Il a banni de son drame toute illusion; ses caricatures sont bien réelles; elles vivent encore . . .[108]

For Cuvillier-Fleury "il est, dans le roman, le peintre un peu rude de la vérité."[109] The principal element of his genius, for Molènes, is "ce sentiment cruel de réalité."[110] And I might multiply the examples and the quotations.[111]

But it would perhaps be more instructive to consider the critics' opinions on Mérimée's choice of 'real' objects. Clearly, he is not indiscriminate or all-inclusive in his subject-matter. Unlike those who garner 'truth' at every street-corner, he establishes definite conditions:

... il voit si dans le sujet qui s'offre à lui, il se trouve assez de poésie préexistante pour n'être pas obligé de faire à lui seul tous les frais; il se prend de prédilection à la peinture des mœurs méridionales ... parce que dans ces mœurs la poésie est chose courante.[112]

He seeks countries and climates in which truth itself is poetic and passionate, and thus he may remain scrupulously exact without being banal.

There is somewhat less agreement among the critics with respect to Mérimée's intention and achievement as a *peintre de mœurs*. For some, *La Double Méprise* was primarily a study in contemporary manners.[113] But in the other novels and stories, according to most critics, this element of social portrayal was secondary. Not that the author of *Carmen* was inferior in the depiction of local customs: Etienne, to cite only one, compliments Mérimée on the fidelity and the vigor of his tableaux.[114] But the novelist regarded these tableaux as accessory parts of a story, subordinate to character and plot. I quote Planche's judgment to this effect:

... il ne sépare jamais la peinture des temps et des lieux de la peinture de l'homme, et c'est par là surtout qu'il se détache de l'école poétique de la restauration. La couleur locale, la couleur historique, dont il comprend toute l'importance, ne sont pas pour lui la loi suprême de l'art. Il a trop de bon sens et de goût pour ne pas mettre l'homme au–dessus des temps et des lieux, c'est-à-dire pour ne pas placer la philosophie au-dessus de l'histoire.[115]

Whether the materials be people or things or customs, however, Mérimée is preeminent in reproducing them because of the care and the accuracy of his observation. Just as the journalists regard later realists as primarily "observateurs" and realism as an "école d'observation," so too they emphasize the importance of this faculty in Mérimée. Sainte-Beuve characterizes him as an "esprit positif, observateur, curieux et studieux des détails, des faits, et de tout ce qui peut se montrer et se préciser."[116] For Cs., "sa conception est toute d'observation terrestre, sociale, naïve, sans aucun rapport avec cette idéalisation de la vie humaine, qu'on nomme poésie."[117] A contributor to *Bagatelle* speaks of "cette observation fine et judicieuse que l'on pourrait appeler la philosophie expérimentale du cœur humain. . . ."[118] Asseline points to "les milles petites observations très fines qui n'appartiennent qu'à lui" as his chief merit.[119] And I cite but a few of many such remarks.[120]

Impersonality is a function of this method of observation. The author limits himself to reporting what he sees, without comment or criticism, and the result is an exact copy of the original. *Figaro* gives a noteworthy appreciation of this approach:

M. Mérimée . . . se borne à narrer les faits avec le plus de précision, de calme, de froideur, sans interprétation ni réflexion aucune, rapportant les paroles, décrivant les gestes seulement de ses personnages, et s'abstenant sur leur compte de tous développements intérieurs où il se verrait contraint d'appliquer sa méthode personnelle, psychologique et morale. C'est uniquement à l'art de conteur qu'il se propose d'atteindre. Cette abnégation du moi écrivain, a de grands avantages. Les faits dépouillés de tout alliage étranger parlent mieux à l'esprit du lecteur, et l'espèce de froideur avec laquelle il dit les catastrophes les plus poignantes, en fait encore mieux ressortir le côté passionné.[121]

After a comparison of this with Balzac's analytical method of characterization, which seems to him less natural, he goes on to say of *Mosaïque:* "Vous eussiez été témoin du fait raconté, c'eût été à peu de chose près comme le livre de M. Mérimée." *La Gazette littéraire,* Sainte-Beuve, Cs., make other remarks on this quality of impersonality.[122]

Critical judgments on Mérimée's realistic subject-matter and approach thus form a fairly consistent body: Mérimée is an artist primarily concerned with a truthful representation of reality—although a restricted reality—and he attains it, whether it be of individuals or of social milieux, by persistent observation.

Certain opinions falling outside of this unified corpus merit attention. These are mixed, favorable and unfavorable, but they all stress distinctive features of Mérimée's work. The remark, for example, that the writer was an "esprit positif" and a sceptic is in harmony with the earlier statements on Mérimée's impersonality and observation; yet it serves to link him even more closely with the other novelists we are studying, on whom the same comment was usually made. Vattier gives us an expression of this point of view, found in some ten critics:

M. Mérimée se montre rarement ému, il est net et positif comme un fait, mais trop distingué, trop artiste pour jamais être brutal. . . . il a de l'opérateur le sang-froid, la perspicacité du coup d'œil, la fermeté de la main, il a aussi—la répétition est obligée—le scepticisme à l'égard des choses qui échappent à l'observation matérielle.[123]

It is significant that, in the case of Mérimée, this is not a reproach; commentators merely point to it as one of his traits. Some, like Clément de Ris, go so far as to explain by it certain of the writer's outstanding qualities.[124] Related to this is the blame, in *La Revue européenne,* of Mérimée's failure to deduce a moral lesson from *La Double Méprise,*[125] and the accusation of positive immorality by Asseline.[126] But this accusation is infrequent as compared with the similar charge brought against Stendhal and all the later realists.

Yet Mérimée was one of the earliest novelists to whom the term *réaliste* was applied. In 1846, in an article on Balzac, Castille declared that Balzac's work was less realistic than Mérimée's since the former presented exceptional rather than typical people; at the same time he spoke of Mérimée as "illustrating" the realistic school.[127] Later critics were equally careful to distinguish the realism of "Clara" from that of other writers. Merlet denies that his method was realistic, since there was no attempt to debase nature.[128] Vattier, too, pointed to his adherence to the "rights of the imagination" as a trait differentiating him from the realists.[129] For Claveau, he differs from Flaubert in that he includes the beautiful in the real, and in that he depicts the psychological as well as the physical side of man; his is therefore a special type of realism.[130]

Of what, then, does his realism consist? First, of the elements already mentioned above, of his various approaches to the problem of truth. In addition, it consists of his photographic method—Asseline, Enault, and Merlet speak of him as "daguerreotyping" his characters[131] —and of his scientific method of analysis. "Ce qu'on pourrait lui reprocher avec justice," says Planche, "c'est d'avoir plus d'une fois dans ce récit [*Chronique*] envisagé l'amour comme une maladie, d'en avoir décrit les symptômes avec une précision qui appartient à la science médicale, et qui étonne chez un poète."[132] In the third place, it consists of his preference for "low" subjects. His people are frequently picturesque, but they come from the lower spheres of society and their background is popular. *La Revue de Paris* reproaches him with treating certain "passions honteuses et brutales."[133] Pontmartin blames him for giving, in *Arsène Guillot,* another example of 'rehabilitation' literature.[134] Barbey d'Aurevilly, finally, speaks of his "réalité poignante et basse," which he derives from Stendhal.[135] This article of Barbey is the fiercest attack on Mérimée during our period, and counts as one more blow in the critic's unrelenting battle against the realists.

It is noteworthy, however, that other constant objectors to realism gave Mérimée full amnesty. Planche, Pontmartin, Merlet, to cite a few cases, did not extend to Mérimée their prejudices against realism.[136] Those prejudices, indeed, were based on idealism, and apparently the critics found in the author of *Carmen* enough of the idealistic to satisfy their needs. Or if they did find a lack, they thought it compensated by other qualities which they considered essential to art—composition, order, unity, appropriateness. Whatever philosophical failings Mérimée may have had, whatever errors he may have committed in the choice of subject-matter or in descriptive method, all of these were to be pardoned because of the aesthetic excellence of his art, whether viewed from a classical or a realistic standpoint. People and places, themes and plots which would probably have been condemned if treated in the way of Balzac or of Stendhal, were here admitted as justified by artistic handling. This fact is revelatory of the literary temper of the period.

---

[1] Letter of October, 1840: "La Véritable Lettre de Stendhal à Balzac," *Revue d'histoire littéraire,* xxiv (1917), 537-559; cf. *Souvenirs d'égotisme,* ed. Le Divan, p. 88, and *Vie de Henri Brulard,* ed. Champion, i, 242.

[2] *80,* Janin.   [3] *77,* Anon., pp. 258-259.   [4] *83,* Anon.

[5] *85,* Anon.   [6] *87,* Mérimée.   [7] *81,* Balzac, p. 168.

[8] *78,* Anon., p. 4.   [9] *86,* Béranger (?).   [10] *84,* Pichot, pp. 357-359.

[11] *88,* Saint-Priest.   [12] *77,* Anon., p. 259.   [13] *78,* Anon., pp. 3-4.

[14] *79,* Anon.   [15] *83,* Anon.   [16] *245,* Anon., p. 244.   [17] *287,* Berthoud.

[18] *90,* Wey.   [19] *93,* Frémy, pp. 209-215.   [20] *94,* Chaudes-Aigues, p. 262.

[21] *95,* Guinot.   [22] *89,* Forgues.   [23] *96,* Duquesnel, pp. 200-201.

[24] *99,* Frémy, pp. 51-63.   [25] *104,* Balzac, p. 334.

[26] *98,* Cherbuliez, p. 111.

[27] *104,* Balzac, p. 335; *98,* Cherbuliez, p. 112. Cf. *97,* Balzac, and *103,* Balzac, p. 82.

[28] *104,* Balzac, p. 338; *98,* Cherbuliez, pp. 111, 113.

[29] *104,* Balzac, pp. 335, 278, 338.   [30] *100,* Muret.

[31] *105,* Forgues.   [32] *115,* Aubert.   [33] *111,* Gobineau, p. 10.

[34] *107,* Bussière, p. 254; *116,* Babou, p. 372.   [35] *106,* Anon., p. 49.

[36] *443,* Aubert.   [37] *107,* Bussière, p. 254.

[38] *105,* Forgues; *110,* Aubert de Vitry, p. 173; *113,* Colomb, p. 57; *115,* Aubert; *117,* Ducoin, p. 193.

[39] *115,* Aubert.   [40] *117,* Ducoin, p. 192; *118,* Ducoin, p. 345.

[41] *107,* Bussière, p. 292.   [42] *111,* Gobineau, pp. 11, 13.

[43] *113,* Colomb, p. 74; cf. *115,* Aubert.   [44] *116,* Babou, p. 377.

[45] *113,* Colomb, pp. 75, 77.   [46] *111,* Gobineau, p. 11.

[47] *111,* Gobineau, p. 8; *107,* Bussière, p. 293.   [48] *111,* Gobineau, p. 8.

[49] *115,* Aubert.   [50] *105,* Forgues.   [51] *106,* Anon., p. 48.

[52] *108,* Crozet, p. 105.

[53] *110,* Aubert de Vitry, p. 173; *107,* Bussière, pp. 282-283.

[54] *105,* Forgues; *115,* Aubert.   [55] *107,* Bussière, pp. 258-259.

[56] *107,* Bussière, p. 258.   [57] *443,* Aubert.

[58] *107,* Bussière, p. 283; cf. *115,* Aubert.   [59] *114,* Balzac, pp. 491-492.

[60] *105,* Forgues; *107,* Bussière, p. 254; *110,* Aubert de Vitry, p. 173; *111,* Gobineau, p. 14; *113,* Colomb, p. 77.

[61] *115,* Aubert.   [62] *106,* Anon., p. 48; *110,* Aubert de Vitry, p. 173.

[63] *115,* Aubert; *107,* Bussière, p. 293; *111,* Gobineau, p. 8; *116,* Babou, p. 346.

[64] *119,* Ratisbonne; *122,* Ulbach, p. 662.

[65] *119,* Ratisbonne; *123,* Sainte-Beuve, p. 335; *130,* Despois, p. 15; *131,* Caro, p. 215; *132,* Barbey d'Aurevilly, p. 50.

[66] *124,* Boiteau.   [67] *123,* Sainte-Beuve, pp. 333-334.

[68] *132,* Barbey d'Aurevilly, p. 44.

[69] *120,* E. Chasles, p. 1002; *122,* Ulbach, p. 663; *131,* Caro, p. 215.

[70] *126*, Anon. [71] *127*, Babou. [72] *131*, Caro, pp. 209-241.

[73] *123*, Sainte-Beuve, p. 330.

[74] *121*, Monselet, p. iv; *122*, Ulbach, p. 664; *128*, Emile Chasles, p. 526.

[75] *490*, Castille, p. 314; *123*, Sainte-Beuve, p. 335; *131*, Caro, p. 215.

[76] *123*, Sainte-Beuve, p. 330. [77] *119*, Ratisbonne; *120*, E. Chasles, p. 1002.

[78] *Ibid.* [79] *123*, Sainte-Beuve, p. 330; *131*, Caro, p. 211.

[80] *123*, Sainte-Beuve, pp. 317-318. [81] *121*, Monselet, p. vii.

[82] *123*, Sainte-Beuve, p. 334. [83] *121*, Monselet, p. iv.

[84] *132*, Barbey d'Aurevilly, p. 53.

[85] *120*, E. Chasles, p. 1003. Chasles borrows this mockery from Stendhal himself, Preface of 1842 to *De l'amour*, ed. Champion, p. 7.

[86] *122*, Ulbach, p. 663. [87] *127*, Babou. [88] *121*, Monselet, p. vi.

[89] *122*, Ulbach, p. 663. [90] *128*, E. Chasles, p. 526.

[91] *882*, Barbey d'Aurevilly, p. 62; *522*, Poitou, pp. 113-114.

[92] *967*, Barbey, p. 231. [93] *724*, Thulié, p. 23. [94] *740*, Watripon, p. 249.

[95] *749*, Barthet, p. 76. [96] *134*, Sainte-Beuve, pp. 111-118.

[97] *133*, Taine. [98] *135*, Taine, pp. xlv-xlvi. [99] *136*, Taine, p. 204.

[100] *918*, Sarcey, p. 498. [101] *198*, Barbey, p. 329.

[102] *1002*, Claretie, p. 172. [103] *137*, Bougy.

[104] Cf. *970*, Jouvin, 1st article; *971*, Pradal; *972*, Bernard, p. 26.

[105] *172*, Rémusat. Cf. Musset, "La Coupe et les lèvres: Dédicace," *Œuvres complètes*, Paris: Charpentier, 1879, I, 246.

[106] *142*, Ampère, p. 533. [107] *145*, Sainte-Beuve, pp. 282-283 n.

[108] *146*, Cs. [109] *188*, Cuvillier-Fleury. [110] *174*, Molènes, 2nd article.

[111] Cf. *141*, Anon., p. 166; *143*, Anon., p. 743; *148*, Planche, p. 580; *149*, Anon.; *151*, Pichot, p. 226; *152*, Anon.; *157*, Anon., p. 371; *158*, Planche, p. 710; *161*, Anon.; *164*, Girault, p. 89; *165*, Anon.; *167*, Cherbuliez; *168*, Sainte-Beuve, p. 470; *180*, Labitte, p. 741; *186*, Enault; *187*, Sainte-Beuve, p. 388; *193*, Planche, p. 1210.

[112] *141*, Anon., p. 166; cf. *147*, G. P.; *151*, Pichot, p. 226.

[113] *153*, Saint-Michel, p. 186; *154*, Anon., p. 308; *155*, Anon., p. 21.

[114] *175*, Etienne; cf. *146*, Cs.; *164*, Girault, p. 89.

[115] *193*, Planche, p. 1209; cf. *141*, Anon., p. 166; *167*, Cherbuliez; *170*, Cherbuliez, p. 160; *171*, Cassou, p. 543; *190*, Delessert, p. 715.

[116] *145*, Sainte-Beuve, p. 282 n. [117] *146*, Cs.

[118] *155*, Anon., p. 21. [119] *169*, Asseline, p. 108.

[120] Cf. *143*, Anon., p. 743; *147*, G. P.; *186*, Enault; *192*, Clément de Ris, p. 101; *197*, Vattier, p. 40.

[121] *149*, Anon.

[122] *143*, Anon., p. 743; *145*, Sainte-Beuve, p. 282 n.; *146*, Cs.; *150*, Rémusat, p. 498; *168*, Sainte-Beuve, p. 472.

[123] *197*, Vattier, p. 42; cf. *145*, Sainte-Beuve, p. 282 n.; *146*, Cs.; *147*, G. P.; *156*, Desessarts, p. 411; *321*, Anon., p. 129; *191*, Ulbach, p. 790.

[124] *192*, Clément de Ris, p. 101. [125] *157*, Anon., p. 371.

[126] *169*, Asseline, p. 109. [127] *435*, Castille, p. 367. [128] *196*, Merlet, p. 142.

[129] *197*, Vattier, p. 42. [130] *902*, Claveau, p. 648.

[131] *169*, Asseline, p. 108; *186*, Enault; *196*, Merlet, p. 127.

[132] *193*, Planche, p. 1218. [133] *141*, Anon., p. 167; *142*, Ampère, p. 536.

[134] *185*, Pontmartin, p. 170.

[135] *198*, Barbey d'Aurevilly, p. 329; cf. *143*, Anon., p. 743.

[136] *158*, *193*, Planche; *183*, *185*, *189*, Pontmartin; *196*, Merlet.

CHAPTER II

BALZAC

Chronology

1829 : *Les Chouans*
    Physiologie du mariage
1830 : *Scènes de la Vie privée*
1831 : *La Peau de chagrin*
    Romans et contes philosophiques
1832 : *Contes bruns*
    Contes drolatiques
    Scènes de la Vie privée (2nd ed.)
    Nouveaux Contes philosophiques
1833 : *Louis Lambert*
    Le Médecin de campagne
1834 : *Etudes de mœurs au dix-neuvième siècle*
    Scènes de la Vie de province
    Eugénie Grandet
    La Recherche de l'absolu
1835 : *Père Goriot*
    Etudes philosophiques
    La Fille aux yeux d'or
    Le Contrat de mariage
    Séraphita
1836 : *Le Lys dans la vallée*
1837 : *La Vieille Fille*
    Illusions perdues (I)
1838 : *Les Employés*
    César Birotteau
    La Maison Nucingen
    Splendeurs et misères des courtisanes (I)
1839 : *Le Cabinet des antiques*
    Illusions perdues (II) :
        Un Grand Homme de province à Paris
    Une Fille d'Eve
1840 : *Vautrin* (drama)
    Revue parisienne
1841 : *Ursule Mirouet*
    Le Curé de village
1842 : *Mémoires de deux jeunes mariées*
    Ressources de Quinola (drama)
    Albert Savarus
1842-1846 : *La Comédie humaine* (ed. Furne)
1843 : *La Rabouilleuse*
    Monographie de la presse parisienne

> *Paméla Giraud* (drama)
> *La Muse du département*
> 1844: *Honorine*
> *Modeste Mignon*
> *Un Début dans la vie*
> *Splendeurs et misères* (II)
> *Les Paysans*
> 1846: (*Comédie humaine* completed)
> *Béatrix* (III): *La Lune de miel*
> *Cousine Bette*
> 1847: *Cousin Pons*
> 1848: *La Marâtre* (drama)
> 1850: Balzac's death
> 1851: *Mercadet* (drama)
> 1859: *La Marâtre* (revival)
> 1863: *Quinola* (revival)
> 1868: *Mercadet* (revival)

HONORÉ DE BALZAC was not only the "most prolific novelist of the century," he was also probably the most discussed, the most attacked and the most lauded. Indeed, with novels and stories appearing incessantly over a period of twenty years, it is not surprising that a great number of critical pronouncements (my bibliography contains some two hundred and seventy-five entries) were published during his lifetime. What is more noteworthy is the fact that in the twenty years following his death, discussion never died down, the balance never ceased to swing between praise and blame. I have some one hundred and twenty-five items for this period. This interest in Balzac was kept alive not only by the republication of his works and the constant dramatization of his novels, but more especially by the growing concern with his literary progeny, the realists. In a sense, therefore, the criticism of Balzac may be taken as a touchstone of the criticism of realism between 1830 and 1870: each new development in realism, and each consequent critical reaction, had repercussions in the attitude towards Balzac.

In this mass of opinion on one writer, it is difficult to distinguish any clear-cut periods. Literary historians have discovered a similar difficulty in the treatment of 'movements': as evidence accumulated, divisions which seemed clear to them in the light of fewer facts lost their distinctness and their sharpness of outline, and it became evident that no exact delimitations of literary periods could be made. So in the present instance: the relatively sparse materials on Stendhal, for example, have enabled me, in his case, to make fairly clear divisions between critical periods; but with Balzac the problem is by no means so simple. As a matter of convenience, however, and without violating the evidence any more than was necessary, I have divided criticism of Balzac into four periods: (1) an early period, extending between 1830 and 1839, the year of *Un Grand Homme de province à Paris;* (2) a second, largely unfavorable period, running from 1839 to 1845; (3) a third period, continuing from 1846, when the publication of the first edition of *La Comédie humaine* was completed, and when a definite swing in Balzac's favor is apparent, to 1856, and including the numerous posthumous articles; (4) a final period, 1856-1870, mixed in nature, but in which a general progression from condemnation to acceptance is discernible.

In treating the first period, I shall discuss the criticism of Balzac in some detail. In subsequent sections I propose to summarize the situation at a given time, largely by comparing each period with the one preceding. That is, I shall be concerned with indicating any change, any disturbance in the balance of opinions as stated in the first section; or, as may frequently happen, any persistence of that balance.

1830 TO 1839

Balzac's first two collections of stories were called, respectively, *Scènes de la Vie privée* and *Romans et contes philosophiques.* These titles are important. They not only foreshadow two of the larger divisions of the later *Comédie humaine,* but they also indicate two of Balzac's principal innovations in the field of the novel. They state his intention to study—in a genre which had hitherto been mainly preoccupied with the telling of tales—conditions of contemporary society and the effect of philosophical conceptions on the life of the individual. Critics of the time perceived these intentions (or pretentions, as they called them) as characterizing Balzac's work, and much of the nonaesthetic discussion centered about two questions: first, does Balzac really have philosophical ideas, and if so what is their validity? Secondly, is his representation of society accurate and acceptable?

Almost immediately upon the appearance of *La Peau de chagrin,* both pretentions were denied by the critics. Let us first examine the situation with regard to the moral and philosophical ideas. There are a few critics who discern, as does Charles de Bernard, "une haute et grave pensée" in Balzac.[1] In 1832, a writer of the *Revue européenne* comments on the "pensée morale fortement suivie" of *L'Auberge rouge,* and finds that in *Louis Lambert* "la pensée vaut peut-être mieux que la forme."[2] The following year, a critic in *Bagatelle* remarks: "M. de Balzac est de tous nos jeunes écrivains celui qui a le mieux compris l'alliance de la littérature et de la philosophie; ses nombreuses productions portent l'empreinte d'une haute pensée philosophique, et concourent à un même but."[3] The same appreciation appears in an article of Desessarts of 1835: "Dans chacun de ses écrits se révèle une pensée philosophique, chose remarquable à cette heure où les conteurs donnent tant au hasard et ne s'inquiètent de rien."[4]

But aside from these statements and a few passing remarks the evidence is negative. Most commentators deny Balzac all capacity to handle ideas. *La Vérité* styles him a "philosophe hebdomadaire" and states humorously that "la philosophie balzachienne a le mérite d'être la plus aimable, la plus bouffonne et la plus répandue."[5] More seriously, I. C. T. in the *Constitutionnel* blames his novels for their lack of general significance: "Que si après les avoir lus, on se posait la question: 'Qu'est-ce que cela prouve?' d'abord pour l'ensemble, puis pour chaque caractère isolé, on aboutirait presque toujours à la conclusion que rien n'est prouvé, si tant est que l'auteur ait voulu prouver quelque chose."[6] Perhaps the most typical statement of this kind is found in an article of Emmanuel Gonzalès (1836):

En traitant ainsi pendant plusieurs années M. de Balzac comme un simple romancier remarquable par la fécondité de ses ouvrages, et non comme un philosophe qui cherchait seulement à trouver dans le roman la formule et l'expression dramatique d'un système sérieux, la critique n'avait pas pris le change, ainsi que l'ont proclamé nombre d'admirateurs exclusifs de cet auteur. M. de Balzac a débuté par le roman sans aucun but arrêté. Rien dans ses premières conceptions ne saurait faire supposer un plan général . . . Il serait facile de prouver qu'il n'est pas même arrivé par le roman à doter son œuvre d'une pensée. . . . nous doutons qu'il ait parfaitement compris le but, la conclusion et les résultats de ce travail.[7]

Gonzalès, then, proceeds to declare that Balzac's sole glory is that of a painter, his only function descriptive. And this was the constant assertion of the other critics who took lightly his pretentions to a philosophical system. On the whole, whereas there are opinions on both sides of this question, it would seem that the negative side was much more amply supported.[8]

Consistent with Balzac's determination to treat ideas in fiction was his desire to exploit, for his materials, various special fields of knowledge which had not before been so used; this we have come to call his encyclopedic intention. In order that his depiction of society might be complete, it was necessary that he present people from all occupational levels, and hence that he give a clear picture of those occupations themselves. Philarète Chasles, as spokesman for Balzac, predicts what this investigation will include:

On le verra changer les couleurs de sa palette, et de nuance en nuance, d'existence en existence, de mode en mode, parcourir tous les degrés de l'échelle sociale et montrer tour à tour le paysan, le mendiant, le pâtre, le bourgeois, le ministre . . . Il ne reculera pas même devant le roi et le prêtre . . .[9]

There is never any doubt raised concerning Balzac's skill in these matters; the critics recognize the facility with which he handles the special vocabulary of each trade, the particular concepts of each profession. Edouard Charton's statement of 1832 is a good example:

Devant un paysage, il décrit en géologue, en astronome, en physicien, les accidents de terrain, les lueurs du ciel, les caprices du vent et des nuages. Devant une maison, il médite, comme ferait un architecte, un sculpteur ou un mouleur, sur la forme du toit, sur les contours des portes et fenêtres; et regardant curieusement à travers les vitraux dans l'appartement, il devient aussitôt décorateur, ébéniste, ciseleur . . .; s'il entre près de la personne assise dans la chambre, le voilà anatomiste, physiologiste plus que physiologue, modiste, camariste . . .; c'est un protée; il a toujours le terme technique, le geste analytique . . .[10]

But opinion on the appropriateness of these materials in the novel is by no means unanimous. Rather do the objectors far outnumber the approvers. One critic will cry out against the large dose of political economy in *Le Médecin de campagne*,[11] another against the alchemy in *La Recherche de l'absolu*,[12] a third against the medecine in *Père Goriot*,[13] a fourth against the law in *Le Contrat de mariage*,[14] and so forth. Or a writer will condemn the whole process of introducing these matters into art, as does I. C. T. in the *Constitutionnel*:

Mais ces hommes d'imagination et de poésie, demain si vous ne les contenez, demain, aujourd'hui même, ils seront partout: vous souffrez qu'ils soient économistes; ils seront géomètres, géographes, géologues, philologues, astronomes, chimistes . . . Si cet exemple devenait contagieux; si, après le roman physiologique, philosophique, psychologique, drolatique, épileptique, maritime, intime, etc., nous devions rencontrer le roman scientifique, nous déclarons d'avance que nous serions impitoyables.[15]

Thus Balzac's effort to make of the novel a medium for demonstration as well as for narration was constantly opposed during the years 1830-1839. As to the practical philosophy manifested in the characters, their actions and their speeches, the critics condemned it as being frankly materialistic and sceptical. The reproach of scepticism appears earlier. Charles de Bernard, in 1831, speaks of Balzac's "cold, sceptical, bitter philosophy";[16] *La Revue européenne* sees in him an expression of the contemporary tendency, in which "l'indifférence religieuse et le scepticisme philosophique mènent les esprits au fatalisme."[17] So too Charles de Bernard, later in the same year, explains Balzac's scepticism as merely a manifestation of a feeling universal in contemporary society.[18] In these statements, reproach is always inherent; it becomes overt in such a criticism as that of Hains:

Chez les écrivains qui ont été le plus avant dans le cœur de l'homme, la vérité a l'aspect dur et sévère, mais cette rude enveloppe recèle des trésors d'espérances. L'écorce dorée dont M. de Balzac a paré la sienne cache au contraire une amertume profonde. Cette poésie lymphatique et toujours plaintive, sans énergie même dans le blasphème, et dont toute la force est dans l'élégance de la forme, toute la portée dans le choix du mot, laisse l'âme du lecteur triste et vide. . . . M. de Balzac n'est en dépit du feu de sa phrase, qu'un froid élève de l'école de Voltaire, il possède tout au plus la force de détruire.[19]

Hains also blames Balzac for his materialism; in general, this accusation of materialism gains currency towards the middle of the decade. It is implicit in the article of Louise Ozenne, who points to Balzac's tendency to "materialize" description and to his awkwardness in handling the ideal,[20] and in the article of *L'Artiste*, which considers him capable of treating only trivial reality, not the "beau moral."[21] Nevertheless, this reproach is far from attaining the development and the vigor which it was to acquire in subsequent periods.

To these charges of materialism and scepticism was linked, almost inevitably, that of positive immorality. It was written into the book of realism in the earliest days and it was never effaced. So we find it inscribed against Balzac from the beginning and reiterated constantly as the supreme condemnation of his work. Rarely does a critic defend him, as does Saint-C. because of his admiration for *Eugénie Grandet*;[22] rarely does another, like Al. de C., justify his immorality as a mere reflection of contemporary society.[23] But these are exceptions; the bulk of the evidence is on the other side. We find that certain works were brushed aside completely for their "immorality." That this should have happened to the *Contes drolatiques* and *La Fille aux yeux d'or* is perhaps not surprising; but we can appreciate less readily the proscription as applied to *Père Goriot,* where old Goriot's connivance in the adulterous affairs of his daughters was deemed scandalous. The general attitude towards Balzac in this respect is adequately phrased by M. B.:

. . . [ses] nombreuses productions paraissent avoir été conçues dans une sorte d'insouciance systématique sur l'effet bon et mauvais qu'elles peuvent produire; il en résulte que ses ouvrages, à l'insu de l'auteur sans doute, servent presque tous à cette œuvre de démoralisation que notre littérature dramatique, lyrique et romantique poursuit journellement au milieu d'une société qui ne demanderait pas mieux que de se refaire. En mettant de côté toute espèce de but moral, M. de Balzac croit peut-être affranchir son talent, il ne fait que le fausser et l'appauvrir.[24]

Similarly Louise Ozenne describes his manner as "un certain apprêt musqué, sous lequel circule une chaude dépravation";[25] and Amédée Duquesnel calls him to task for neglecting to consider the moral consequences of a given subject or action.[26] There are, besides, numerous references to moral indifference or immorality as illustrated in one novel or another; to these I can merely direct the reader, without attempting to summarize their content.[27]

For most of these writers, the immediate proof of Balzac's literary depravity was his marked preference for vice, his willingness to condone the most reprehensible passions. This is what Louise Ozenne describes as "l'instinct qui le pousse de préférence à crayonner les traits du mal."[28] This is what the *Constitutionnel* opposes in the following passage: ". . . l'auteur me dira que pour corriger, autant que possible, les vices, il suffit de les peindre dans toute leur laideur; sans doute, mais il ne faut pas s'en faire le poète dithyrambique, y mettre tant de verve et n'avoir rien à opposer à ces tableaux-là."[29] Hains, M. B., Cherbuliez, and Sainte-Beuve supply us with additional statements on this point.[30]

There can thus be but little doubt that Balzac's adventures into theoretical philosophy, his attempt to expand the limits of the novel to include non-fictional materials, and his own *Weltanschauung* as indicated by his writings were almost completely condemned by critics of this early period. But when we come to the other aspect of his literary program, to his intention to depict contemporary society as it was, we discover the opposite to be true. Nearly all of the critics attest, in one form or another, the verity of his social portraiture, the accuracy of his observation, the fineness of his detail, the penetration of his psychological analysis. Opinion was not unanimous, by any means; but those who found deficiencies in any of these fields were decidedly in the minority.

The prerequisite for adequate social depiction is the faculty of observation; and that this faculty is present in Balzac to an eminent degree is admitted by practically all of the critics. The Comte de C. . . . calls it "une exquise délicatesse d'observation,"[31] an anonymous writer recognizes that Balzac is the only French "observer" since Molière,[32] Janin declares that "il est impossible de pousser l'observation plus loin."[33] Even those who condemn him on every other score are forced to admit his superiority here. D'Izalguier, for example, sees this method as responsible for Balzac's poor composition; but he cannot deny the efficacy of the method itself:

M. de Balzac n'imagine pas, n'invente pas; il observe avec une rare perspicacité et reproduit la réalité avec scrupule. Quand il essaie l'invention, quand il tente d'idéaliser, il échoue indubitablement. La fidélité du calque, voilà son mérite et toute la portée de son talent. Or, se résoudre à traduire exactement l'observation, quand on a un œil exercé et une plume patiente, c'est être sûr de donner à l'œuvre ainsi faite tout l'intérêt de la réalité; mais aussi c'est se soumettre au délaiement, au décousu, à l'éparpillement de la vie réelle . . .[34]

Numerous other critics hold the same opinion with regard to Balzac's powers of penetration;[35] indeed, it is the one point upon which there is an approximate unanimity of sentiment.

This science of observation might be applied either to external, physical reality or to a study of intellectual and emotional processes. As applied to material reality it results, with Balzac, in the accumulation of much minute detail; and on this score there was much controversy among the critics. While most of them admitted Balzac's virtuosity in this line, many believed that he carried the exploitation of detail to an excessive degree, to a point where it began to exist only for itself and out of all relation to the progress of the narrative. Let us consult first some of the passages which express admiration for Balzac's treatment of "le monde extérieur":

Si nous parlons de la peinture des détails, il faut louer leur charme et leur vérité, la délicatesse des nuances, la variété des teintes. Il se trouve dans les *Illusions perdues* des traits d'observation d'une ténuité telle qu'on dirait que la vue la plus perçante n'a pu suffire pour les découvrir, et qu'ils ont dû être révélés par une sorte d'intuition.[36]

This statement is by Fontaney in the *Revue des deux mondes;* I quote another by Jules Janin, apropos of *Eugénie Grandet:*

Quels détails! vous voyez toute la maison . . . et ces détails qui sont tirés des entrailles même de l'histoire que l'auteur raconte. . . . M. de Balzac excelle dans ces détails; si même il a un défaut, c'est de ne rien oublier. En effet, il ne vous fait grâce de rien, ni d'un carreau fêlé, ni d'une vitre raccommodée avec du papier, ni d'une mouche qui salit le baromètre. . . . il a fort bien compris que ces détails étaient le fond de son tableau . . .[37]

Even in this praise, however, there is an element of blame: Balzac leaves nothing out. So it is that we find a number of lists of humorous objects accumulated to caricature his minuteness of detail. Al. de C., for example, remarks: "Il montre une ride qui creuse le sillon d'une autre ride, un cil de paupière qui fait ombre, une fraction impalpable de sentiment qu'il décompose encore."[38] Thus Balzac ceases to be a novelist and becomes a mere "commissaire-priseur," preparing "des inventaires et . . . des états de lieux."[39] But even critics who make this reproach are apt to consider it of minor importance. Mennechet, for one, goes on to say that "it is by virtue of his details that Balzac surpasses his rivals."[40]

On the other hand, we find a group of journalists who definitely will not condone Balzac's 'inventorial' practices. Their principal argument is that these details obscure or arrest the development of the story. Such is the fault perceived by the Abbé Juin:

On a dit que M. de Balzac excellait dans les petits détails; mais bien souvent il pousse trop loin cette manie, et malgré l'art avec lequel il sait relever, colorer, et animer chaque chose, on trouve qu'il laisse bien des fois languir le sujet principal; on l'oublie, ou l'on s'impatiente de le voir sans cesse vous entraîner dans de nouvelles routes qui vous éloignent de celle que vous deviez suivre . . .[41]

Cherbuliez believes that this "manie des détails" has irreparably spoiled the two volumes of *César Birotteau*,[42] and Muret declares that the subject of *Père Goriot* is so obscured by minute description as to be frequently indiscernible.[43] He argues that while such depiction of physical objects is appropriate and successful in painting (of the Flemish school, for example), it cannot possibly have any efficacy in literature, where words are the only medium of expression.

Still another group of objectors to this method attack it on different grounds. They hold that it represents an inferior type of literary practice since it supplants the study of human beings by that of inanimate objects: this is the reproach of 'externality.' In the words of I. C. T., "M. de Balzac . . . est un poète excentrique et descriptif, se prenant aux formes extérieures, les épuisant à force de les détailler, ne creusant rien, mais habile à reproduire les surfaces. . . ."[44] The same critic remarks, a year later, that "la perception des choses extérieures lui est acquise, il n'aura jamais celle des choses profondes."[45] According to Nettement, Balzac is neither a moralist nor a philosopher, neither a proponent nor an antagonist of social ideas, but exclusively a painter.[46] Another statement comes from Gonzalès:

Il a peint pour peindre. La peinture est fidèle le plus souvent, le coloris est devenu de plus en plus éclatant, la gloire du peintre de plus en plus rayonnante, mais voilà tout. N'ayant pas le loisir d'étendre sa pensée sur une vaste toile, de forger une encyclopédie philosophique, il est retombé de ces hauteurs sur les détails de la vie. La mise en scène a dès lors envahi l'idée; la préoccupation matérielle a tué la synthèse intellectuelle.[47]

Such statements, of course, are directly related to the question of Balzac's philosophical achievement, discussed above. Those critics who considered him weak in the realm of ideas were apt—if they conceded him any merit at all—to admit an excellence in the depiction of physical reality. The whole attitude is summarized in Hains's ironic remark: "C'est l'Homère des infiniment petits; il inventorie la nature plutôt qu'il ne la peint, il s'est fait le commissaire-priseur de l'humanité."[48]

We have seen, in brief, the opinion of the critics on Balzac's capacity as an observer of nature, and on that capacity as applied to physical reality. Let us now examine the attitude towards this faculty as it operated in the field of intellectual and emotional processes, towards Balzac's psychological analysis—always, of course, basing our conclusions on the evidence of this early period, 1830-1839.

Here, again, we discover that the general impression was a favorable one. No sooner had the *Scènes de la Vie privée* appeared than a critic of *Figaro* applied to Balzac a phrase which was to be linked constantly with his name: "une grande connaissance du cœur humain."[49] Amédée Pichot used it again in 1831—"sa connaissance profonde du cœur humain"[50]—the Comte de C. in 1832;[51] it appeared in somewhat modified form in Paul Lacroix,[52] and intermittently throughout criticism of Balzac. That this was more than a catch-word applied unthinkingly to the author of *Père Goriot* is evidenced by certain more extended expressions on the subject. In *La Quotidienne*, a writer asserts that "Balzac est l'historien, le seul vrai historien des passions humaines; il est profond dans la matière. Moraliste, il a porté l'investigation jusque dans les replis les plus secrets du cœur. . . ."[53] Louise Ozenne, who, as we have seen, condemns Balzac for his immorality, nevertheless grants him a positive superiority here:

. . . il possède une grande connaissance des hommes, une perspicacité merveilleuse, une vue fine et déliée, qui voit clair jusqu'au fond du cœur, et peut compter les battements des moindres fibres . . . Sous ce rapport, son talent, que nous avons accusé de mensonge, quant aux beautés du style, et quant aux prétentions à la moralité, atteint à une vérité frappante.[54]

One special aspect of this insight into human nature was Balzac's interest and skill in the study of feminine nature. We remember Sainte-Beuve's declaration, in 1834, that much of Balzac's popularity might be explained by his attention to women;[55] but the idea had appeared earlier in other critics. Saint-C., for example, remarked in 1832 that "Vous verrez toujours dans les compositions de M. de Balzac une pensée cachée sous la forme dramatique, une révélation intime d'un cœur de femme."[56] Janin, in 1835, speaks of Balzac as "l'infatigable historien des *misères inconnues de la femme*."[57] The tendency is satirized by Al. de C.:

Elles [les femmes] se demandaient si ce flatteur de leurs péchés se tairait toujours, et s'il n'avait plus en réserve quelques douzaines de femmes de trente ans, adorables, discrètes, rêveuses, enveloppées de blondes, ornées de fleurs, faibles et coquettes, parant de vertu leurs charmantes faiblesses, ornant de sensibilité leurs délicieuses coquetteries, poussant leurs fautes de jeunesse jusqu'aux derniers confins de l'automne, effeuillant avec une élégance élégiaque les dernières roses de cette saison mélancolique, et philosophant sur l'erreur avec une grâce et une expérience merveilleuses. M. de Balzac est le Marivaux de l'époque . . .[58]

Thus it is apparent, from this and other statements,[59] that Balzac is rapidly becoming the "inventor of the woman of thirty"; as *Le Constitutionnel* says, in 1838, "La femme de trente ans est une création de M. de Balzac."[60] These remarks are important, not only because they recognize a tendency and a vogue, but because most of them accord to Balzac a real superiority in the study of feminine character.

As far as the technique of this psychological analysis is concerned, it amounts—as was the case with physical reality—to a search for and a discovery of the minute detail. Balzac is an anatomist, who dissects with the aid of the microscope and the scalpel: the analogy to medical science is constantly made. In 1831: "Comme le monde est disséqué par cet homme! Quel analyste!"[61] In 1832: "Le voilà . . . analysant la pensée à l'alambic, et examinant à la loupe jusqu'au signe qu'un héros portera sous l'ongle. Décrire comme fait souvent M. de Balzac, ce n'est pas décrire, mais disséquer en anatomiste"; the same writer speaks of him as "décomposant le sentiment et la passion."[62] Again in 1832, we find a reference to his "physiologie des passions" and to his "anatomie morale la plus complète de la femme."[63] Later, in 1855, Al. de C. says: "Il y a de l'homéopathie dans son système de physiologie et de nosologie intellectuelle."[64] And I might continue the accumulation of such passages almost indefinitely.[65]

But it will be more profitable to consider various estimates of the results given by this scientific technique. Some of these effects must be discussed later, when I consider (under formal criticism) Balzac as a creator of character. Plainly, the problem is double. First, there are those considerations of internal proportion, of consistency, of harmony, which concern the development of a character once its essential nature has been stated: it is the treatment of these considerations that I propose to postpone. Second, there is the question of conformity of the character to real, observable human nature—essentially a non-aesthetic consideration, and one which we may now take up.

In general, the critics concede that Balzac's people are truly observed and depicted; thus the Comte de C. remarks after enumerating Balzac's qualities:

. . . Il possède en outre une qualité, la plus importante et celle à laquelle vos jeunes auteurs accordent peut-être le moins; je veux parler de l'entente des caractères. Il me paraît impossible que l'imagination puisse suppléer à la vérité de l'observation, reproduire avec exactitude et précision ces nuances si variées, si délicates des passions humaines. . . . Je ne prétends pas que M. de Balzac soit tout à fait en dehors de cette voie commune [i.e., of purely imaginative writers], mais je trouve qu'il s'en éloigne souvent et tend à l'observation; je ne saurais oublier, par exemple, le caractère si exactement vrai de cet usurier de l'une des *scènes de la vie privée*. . . . vous ne pouvez vous empêcher de reconnaître une grande sagacité et une exquise délicatesse d'observation dans la plupart des ouvrages de notre auteur.[66]

The *Nouvelle Bibliothèque des romans* speaks of the truthfulness of each of the characters in *Eugénie Grandet,* and of the life with which they are endowed.[67] Of the same novel, A. D. L. says: "Il n'y a . . . pas un personnage supposé, pas un caractère pris en dehors de la vie réelle,"[68] and Al. de C. admits that "les caractères sont souvent vrais, nouveaux, bien observés."[69] Béranger admires the naturalness of his characters in *Père Goriot.*[70] Louise Ozenne, who finds most of Balzac's people reprehensible morally, nevertheless recognizes the "couleurs vraies" in which they are depicted.[71] Then there are certain writers who single out individual characters as examples of Balzac's fidelity to the real world: Pichot's praise of Mademoiselle de Verneuil,[72] the eulogy of Madame Claës in the *Chronique de Paris,*[73] Cherbuliez's admiration of César Birotteau,[74] may be cited as examples.

But not all the critics were disposed to recognize in Balzac's people representatives of existing types. Many of them, on the contrary, insisted that his heroes were exceptional or that, even when they had roots in common humanity, they were exaggerated to the point of becoming monsters. This reproach, it should be noted, is absent in the earliest years, and does not appear until the publication of *Eugénie Grandet.* It is then that Janin calls attention to the exceptional nature of the avaricious Grandet:

. . . cet avare Grandet va si loin, il est si terrible et si hors de la nature, même de la nature des avares, que ce n'est plus même un avare, c'est un fou. . . . Le père Grandet de M. Balzac, après avoir été un monstre assez accompli, finit par n'être plus qu'un objet de dégoût.[75]

With the appearance of *Père Goriot* in 1835, the cry becomes more general; old Goriot's character is inconceivable to most of the critics and it is to him that they refer—even much later—when they use the term *monstre.* "Le père Goriot," says J. in *Le Voleur,* "c'est l'amour paternel dans son paroxysme, un paroxysme continu, une fièvre, un délire, une monomanie. . . . c'est une malheureuse exception à laquelle un écrivain qui se respecte ne doit pas donner droit de bourgeoisie dans nos mœurs."[76] Hains phrases his opinions thus:

Je cherche partout l'homme dans ses œuvres, et je n'y rencontre que des natures épuisées, ou des anomalies bizarres. . . . Quant à ces passions éphémères qui se développent à certaines conditions et meurent avec les causes accidentelles dont elles sont nées, elles sont curieuses à étudier peut-être, mais leurs débris servent mal à reconstruire l'histoire de l'humanité. Ce sont les monstres de l'espèce, leur place est à la marge du siècle auquel elles ont appartenu. . . . il est au fond de l'âme humaine des mystères qui sont dans la main de Dieu. Prétendre les sonder est presque un sacrilège, je ne vois pas d'ailleurs ce que l'art y ait jamais gagné.[77]

This passage calls into question not only the final product of Balzac's psychological analysis, but the principle of that analysis itself. The same question is later raised by Chaudes-Aigues; he complains of the perpetual exaggeration of character in *Eugénie Grandet,* of the caricaturing of the miser who becomes a "grimacing and impossible creature." Old Goriot he considers as one of the "monstruosités morales qu'on doit laisser dans l'ombre, surtout quand on se propose d'être le peintre vrai d'une époque et l'historien des mœurs d'un pays."[78] Similar statements are to be found in Nettement ("ses héros, si énergiquement conçus, tournent trop au géant")[79] and in Cherbuliez ("Lez femmes . . . sont des êtres exceptionnels, des individus isolés qui ne sauraient passer pour des types, pour des représentants du sexe entier").[80] From these statements it is clear that, just as in the case of physical reality, there was here considerable opposition to Balzac's method of minute analysis, and to the characters produced by that method.

This dual approach, pictorial and analytic, had as its total product Balzac's depiction of contemporary society, his *tableaux de mœurs.* How, we may now ask, did the critics estimate Balzac's portrayal, as compared with the world as they themselves saw it?

It is hardly necessary to indicate that Balzac's contemporaries, even in this early period, were fully cognizant of his intention to present a complete picture of contemporary life. He himself, in the titles of his stories and of collected works, in his prefaces, in certain introductory passages, made this abundantly clear. Yet it is instructive to see what portions of this program his critics considered as accomplished. As early as 1832, *La Quotidienne* called attention to Balzac's rôle in the literary revival following upon the Revolution of 1830:

M. de Balzac, tout le premier, est venu avec ses *Scènes de la vie privée.* Homme habile, M. de Balzac a compris cette réaction vers la vie intérieure et l'a heureusement tentée. Il a reconstitué nos salons, renoué toutes les relations sociales, effacé toutes les antipathies, restitué le sourire sur les lèvres crispées; il a repris sa physiologie des passions. . . . il a embrassé la société entière: la société dans ses misères et ses plus grandes joies, dans ses mystères et son éclat de grand jour, au boudoir, au bal, dans l'intimité de la vie privée et du tête-à-tête; toujours dans sa réalité avec son vide, ses mensonges, ses illusions, ses fluctuations de vice et de vertu ; la société enfin, telle que l'ont faite les arts, la pensée, l'éducation et la loi ; et sa brillante imagination lui a fourni des cadres et des formules pour toutes les existences.[81]

A. in 1834 notices his preoccupation with aristocratic circles in the *Treize*,[82] A. D. L. comments on his study, in *Eugénie Grandet,* of provincial life.[83] Somewhat later (1835), in a review of contemporary literature, Louis de Carné sees two tendencies in the modern novel, the historical and the democratic. The latter is responsible for the interest in contemporary and especially popular manners. Balzac's special domain, here, is the bourgeoisie—not only in Paris, but in the provinces as well.[84] A still more significant statement comes from "The Reviewer":

Il était réservé à notre époque si hétérogène, si multiple, si confuse, de voir un romancier aborder successivement toutes les thèses morales, les définir avec netteté et profondeur, se lancer dans les spéculations métaphysiques, reproduire dans des récits fictifs les passions les plus réelles, les angoisses infinies qui déchirent le plus douloureusement les entrailles de la société, dire les mœurs ternes, prosaïques, grisâtres, de la province et l'éblouissant papillotage du dandysme parisien. Pour comprendre cette étrange comédie du dix-neuvième siècle, il suffit de se reporter un moment à celle que son propre auteur surnomma *la divine,* et qui résume pour nous le moyen âge.[85]

Then, after a comparison of contemporary society with that of Dante : "C'est cette société mobile, bigarrée, sceptique, insaisissable, que M. de Balzac a voulu peindre sous toutes ses faces." The effort to portray such a society, continues "The Reviewer," will necessarily preclude the possibility of creating a unified and synthesized group of novels ; but unity and synthesis may be sacrificed :

Nous sommes de ceux qui acceptons pleinement et entièrement M. de Balzac ; et c'est parce que nous croyons à la vérité et à la durée du monument qu'il construit pièce à pièce, que, bien loin de nous étonner et de nous irriter follement, comme des enfants gâtés, du manque d'unité, du défaut de concision, de l'absence du rythme, nous cherchons à tout expliquer, à tout comprendre.

Even Nettement, always severe towards Balzac and later a ruthless adversary, admits that the author merits a high place in contemporary letters as a "peintre de mœurs et de caractères," and exclaims : ". . . que d'occasions . . . où il a pris notre société sur le fait et où il a fait toucher du doigt ses plaies !"[86]

These statements, however, do little more than recognize an intention and its accomplishment. Aside from them we find, as we should expect, numerous passages which express definite approval or disapproval of these *tableaux de mœurs.* For most of the critics, Balzac's world was a true representation of contemporary society : the bulk of the evidence on this point is favorable to Balzac. First, there were those writers who admitted without reserve all of the Balzacian universe. And the admission came very early, as early as 1830: "c'est le monde vrai, et une jeune fille qui aura lu ce livre [*Scènes de la Vie privée*], connaîtra le monde aussi parfaitement que si elle le fréquentait depuis dix ans."[87] Of the same collection Emile Deschamps remarks in 1831: "Notre époque se reflète dans ces historiettes fantastiques, avec ses inconséquences et ses contrastes, son prosaïsme poétique, son incrédulité superstitieuse et fataliste, avec ses velléités de vertu et son égoïsme profond, seule base de l'édifice social actuel . . ."[88] Again, *Le Littérateur universel* states that "Les conceptions de M. de Balzac . . . sont en général toutes vraies au point de départ: on sent qu'il a vu les personnages qu'il met en scène, qu'il les a bien approfondis et que le peintre n'est qu'un habile et savant artiste copiant, avec le génie d'une patience infinie, un spectacle qu'il a eu devant les yeux."[89] A number of other statements bear witness to the reality of Balzac's world.[90]

All the critics, however, do not accept the whole of Balzac's portrayal. Some of them comment only on one phase of society as he presents it, others single out one aspect as good or bad. Thus at the time of *Eugénie Grandet* we find several tributes to his understanding of provincial life, which Stendhal for one admires in *Le Curé de Tours*.[91] For Sainte-Beuve, his greatest achievement is in the depiction of "private life," as exemplified by the *Scènes de la Vie privée*.[92] With the appearance of *Père Goriot*, attention is directed to Balzac's skill in the analysis of Parisian manners;[93] *César Birotteau*, again, elicits the same criticism.[94] These distinctions, of course, are the ones made by Balzac himself in the titles of his various collections. There are a few critics, however, who would make another division on the basis of the levels of society involved; thus I. C. T. deems him particularly expert in the handling of aristocratic circles, for which his novels are especially written.[95] With this opinion, Janin is entirely at variance; he says:

Tant qu'il est peuple, bourgeois, étudiant, observateur de la rue, tant qu'il est M. Balzac, il est excellent, naïf, amusant, bonhomme, gai, observateur, et même quelquefois écrivant bien. . . . mais une fois que M. Balzac devient ou redevient M. de Balzac, une fois qu'il se fait grand seigneur et marquis, alors ma foi! ce n'est plus le même homme. Il est raide, il est guindé, . . . car il ne sait pas ce que veut dire ce langage à part, tous ces petits mots qui ont un sens à part.[96]

In the long run, it was Janin's opinion that prevailed;[97] many later critics pointed to Balzac's deficiencies in the presentation of aristocracy.

It was only natural, of course, that the critics should emphasize Balzac's intention or achievement as an analyst of contemporary life. The tendency was a new one, and Balzac was in large part its founder. Hence many commentators remark upon the 'actuality' of Balzac's novels, on the fact that these works depict a contemporary situation, and that they derive their excellence from this contemporaneity. For one writer, Grandet is Harpagon brought up to date: "C'est l'Avare de Molière, avec plus d'*actualité,* avec ces détails du dix-neuvième siècle qui rafraîchissent un vieux chef-d'œuvre."[98] The comment of Al. de C. is wider in scope:

Si le siècle n'aimait pas Balzac, il serait ingrat: il a fait Balzac, il a créé ce peintre de l'égoïsme . . . , cet écrivain, qui dans un monde social incomplet, ne créé rien de terminé, de simple et de complet, ne forme aucun grand système, n'achève rien et prodigue les études admirables. Copiste d'une société sans Dieu, sans foi, sans but, mais non sans passions, sans art, ni sans lumières, Balzac restera comme l'interprète de ce monde vacillant, qui n'est que grains de sable, et qui fuit sous nos pas.[99]

We have already noted a similar conclusion on the part of "The Reviewer," and we may now call attention to additional appraisals by Nettement and Sainte-Beuve in which his qualities and defects are traced to the spirit of the century.[100]

Finally, in this study of the critics who accepted Balzac's representation of society as real, I might cite several passages which derive this reality from the novelist's impersonality. For their authors, it is only because Balzac is willing to treat any subject, any phase of any question, that he arrives at an accurate *vue d'ensemble.* Thus Charles de Bernard: "Parmi tous les éloges auxquels a droit M. de Balzac, nous en offrons un à cette vigoureuse impartialité qui, peu soucieuse des suffrages de coterie ou de parti, frappe indistinctement, partout où elle trouve un vice ou un ridicule."[101] And Nettement, who speaks of "les types variés que l'auteur a successivement décrits avec une impartialité qui tient de l'indifférence; car tout devient une étude pour ce paysagiste de la pensée . . ."[102] In the article of D'Izalguier, however, we have the best expression of this point of view:

. . . pour arriver à cette vérité du calque, l'auteur a dû se préserver de toute vue systématique, et, pour respecter les exigences de son lecteur, se garder de toute conclusion. Il considère moins son œuvre comme une profession de foi, comme une appréciation des faits, que comme la constatation de ces faits par une copie exacte et impartiale qui en facilite l'examen au lecteur et le mette à même d'y porter son jugement. . . . Cette neutralité d'ailleurs vaut mieux que les mille faussetés que chaque jour les romans accréditent. Dans ce temps de philosophie hasardée et de jugements équivoques, il y a du mérite, nous dirions presque du courage, à se contenter de dresser procès-verbal de la société, s'attachant exclusivement à bien compter et fidèlement décrire.[103]

Thus it is evident that a large number of critics were disposed to accept Balzac's world as a faithful portrayal of their own; that still others admired the accuracy of one phase or another of that world; that they attributed this fidelity and this accuracy not only to Balzac's gift of observation, but also to his essential concern with the present and to his impartiality. This, I might repeat, was the dominant judgment during the period 1830-1839. But it would be erroneous to suppose that it was the only judgment; for there were certain critics who rejected the world of the *Comédie humaine* in no equivocal terms, and for various reasons. We may now consider the case of the opposition.

The objections of these opposing critics were based on one of two premises: either that Balzac's novels were the product of imagination rather than of observation, or that his observation itself was incomplete or faulty. In either situation, clearly, the result would be a *tableau de mœurs* inconsistent with reality. Writers who took the first stand were comparatively few, and usually they merely pointed to an admixture, in Balzac, of the fantastic and the real. Such a comment is N.'s, which calls *La Peau de chagrin* "ce mélange de merveilleux et de vie positive."[104] Such another is Pichot's, which describes the same novel as "un conte fantastique sans aucune moralité," and with only a pretention at social depiction; the rest of Balzac's work (with the exception of the *Scènes de la Vie privée*) he defines as "une fabrication presque mécanique de tableaux sans vérité et sans profondeur."[105] Emile Deschamps, too, finds that the stories, however real they may be, are always "seasoned with an indescribable, cabalistic marvelous,"[106] and Cherbuliez insists that his subjects are drawn from without the realm of the existent.[107] Even Sainte-Beuve remarks that Balzac frequently abandons his delicate observations for "de fantastiques essais comme pour l'alchimie du genre."[108] The objection is developed most completely by Lecler:

> ... il a quelquefois un bonheur d'observation remarquable; mais si l'on en excepte quelques détails, tout s'empreint d'une couleur étrange d'hallucination et de magnétisme; tout est fantastique: histoire, description, métaphysique, psychologie; non pas fantastique à la manière moqueuse et pleine de persiflage de Voltaire, ni à la manière bouffonne, capricieuse, dévergondée, mais souvent profondément philosophique d'Hoffmann ... C'est quelque chose de mystérieusement métaphysique, d'obscurément et vaguement senti, d'emphatiquement rendu...[109]

The second stand, that Balzac's representation was faulty or incomplete, was taken by a much larger group of critics. Some of them merely insisted that his world was unreal, without stating what error in method produced that unreality. Several such remarks occur in the article of Hains, who first declares that "de cette nature microscopique à la vérité, la distance est incommensurable," then that Balzac's mixture of materialism and sentimentality is "bizarre and monstrous," next that his world is too subtle and too refined to be convincing, finally that his concern with the exceptional in character precludes all possibility of treating general human traits.[110] So, too, Chaudes-Aigues finds that as a historian of manners Balzac is flagrantly false, and that he looks at life through a gigantic microscope.[111] Finally, Sainte-Beuve asks: "Des mœurs telles qu'elles ressortent de ces prétendues peintures du jour, sont-elles réelles? Elles sont du moins vraies en ce sens, que plus d'un, aujourd'hui, les rêve."[112]

But most of the commentators were much more explicit in their objections. Many traced Balzac's falseness of depiction to the fact that he chose only the ugly side of nature: the *Constitutionnel*,[113] the *Nouvelle Bibliothèque des romans*,[114] the *Chronique de Paris*,[115] Janin in the *Débats*,[116] were all of this opinion. Guéroult phrased the same attitude thus:

M. de Balzac intitule ses livres: *Etudes de mœurs au dix-neuvième siècle*. Eh bien! en vérité, il y a des choses vraies au dix-neuvième siècle qui ont été vraies, je crois, dans tous les siècles, et qu'il ne convient nullement d'aller déterrer; il est des choses qu'il ne faut pas savoir . . .[117]

M. B., writing on *César Birotteau*, apologizes for his previous neglect of Balzac on the ground that earlier works had been too exclusively devoted to the bad and the vicious.[118] So stated, this objection is tantamount to the one we have already encountered in the discussion of Balzac's morality—that of preference for vice—and we may refer to the same passages as relevant to the present point.[119] The objection is akin, too, to that of incompleteness: the ugly is only a part of the whole world, and to single it out for treatment is to falsify the picture. Other critics made this broader reproach of incompleteness: D'Izalguier on *La Vieille Fille*,[120] Janin on *La Recherche de l'absolu*,[121] Louise Ozenne on Balzac's general practice,[122] point out that his sphere of activity is a restricted one, and that the reader must not take his books as giving a full knowledge of society.

Still other writers rejected the France of Balzac because of its exaggeration. I have already indicated that this was one of the strictures made on his characters: they tended to be magnified beyond the bounds of human possibility. As applied to his total portraiture, the objection involves descriptive detail as well as character, plot as well as morality. We may take as an example the definition, by I. C. T., of Balzac's principal weakness:

Ce défaut est l'exagération. Le premier trait de l'auteur est vrai, il est pur; mais il le charge ensuite tellement, que la figure grimace. La

première description est satisfaisante; continuée ainsi, elle resterait irréprochable; mais il la fatigue et l'épuise. L'abus de tout, du bien comme
du mal, voilà ce qui caractérise M. de Balzac.[123]

Pichot uses almost identical terms in speaking of *La Peau de chagrin*,[124]
and one "De Blanzac" styles "De Balzac" as "le poète, qui n'abandonne
une idée qu'après l'avoir triturée, délayée, allongée; qu'après l'avoir
teinte de toutes les enluminures connues, qu'après l'avoir courbée,
redressée, grossie, amincie, selon les caprices de sa fertile plume."[125]
The evidence of some ten other critics on Balzac's exaggeration indicates that it was a fairly widespread censure, not a chance opinion.[126]

The total estimate of Balzac's social depiction might be summarized
thus: in his favor, a prodigious faculty of observation, operating alike
in the fields of character and of physical background, and producing
in the ensemble a satisfactory representation of contemporary society;
against him, the tendency to abuse this faculty by excessive minuteness
of detail or over-subtle analysis, to produce exaggerated situations and
people verging on caricatures, and the kindred tendency to choose for
portrayal the undesirable aspects of life. Quantitatively, the favorable
criticisms are, in this first period (1830-1839), decidedly in the majority, although a slight movement towards adverse judgment is noticeable in the later years.

In the first period, too, criticism that attempted to evaluate Balzac's
philosophical ideas and the veracity of his depiction, such as I have discussed so far, was predominant, and aesthetic or formal criticism was
decidedly secondary. Nevertheless, there was a definite body of opinions
on Balzac as an artist. It was, on the whole, unfavorable to Balzac:
plainly, critics of these years were interested primarily in the sociological aspects of his work and discovered his principal merit therein;
his artistic qualities went unheeded or stimulated only adverse comment.

If the critics, at this time, accorded any artistic talent to Balzac, it
was as a narrator, a "conteur." Indeed, all through this period Balzac
is frequently considered as a spinner of tales, as one who possesses to
the highest degree the art of conducting a narrative. If, in certain cases,
critics disapprove of his adventures into philosophy and sociology, it is
because they see him abandoning this narrative strain. Janin, among the
first, placed him "au premier rang de nos conteurs" for his achievement
in *La Peau de chagrin*.[127] Then Chasles, also in 1831, defined him both
as "un conteur, un amuseur de gens" and as "un homme de pensée et de
philosophie."[128] As soon as *Le Médecin de campagne* appeared, however, several journalists protested against the new genre. M. F., in the
Echo de la Jeune France, deplores the concern with moral problems and

the consequent sacrifice of narrative interest. "Que M. de Balzac fasse des contes," he says, "qu'il ait soin de les finir aussi bien qu'il les commence, sa place est assurée à la tête des conteurs de notre temps; cela vaut bien mieux que d'être un romancier de la force de M. Ricard."[129] H. de V., in *Bagatelle*, discards all of the economic and political materials, admitting however that "deux ou trois des épisodes du *Médecin de campagne* rappellent le beau talent de narration qui fit surtout admirer M. de Balzac dans ses *Scènes de la Vie privée;* là comme toujours, quand M. de Balzac veut être seulement le grand conteur de notre caravane européenne, nul peut-être ne peut lui être préféré."[130] In the same article (1833), H. de V. coined the phrase, "Monsieur de Balzac, si vous vous souvenez, encore un de ces beaux contes que vous contez si bien."[131] This became rapidly famous and was adopted as a *cri de guerre* by a number of the critics.[132] Exactly what this narrative talent of Balzac's was they did not say; they merely attested to his power to hold the interest of the audience and to stir up an emotional response.[133]

Several writers explained this attraction of Balzac's stories by their essentially dramatic character: Pichot, Philarète Chasles, Sainte-Beuve, and an anonymous writer in *L'Artiste* may be cited as examples.[134] The last of these affirms: "En prenant ainsi et du premier bond une place à côté de ces conteurs formidables ou gracieux [Voltaire and the author of *Les Mille et une nuits*], M. de Balzac a prouvé une chose qui n'était pas démontrée encore, à savoir que le drame qui n'était plus possible aujourd'hui sur le théâtre, était encore possible dans le conte . . ." A few others—but very few—commented on the quality of the plot of one novel or another: Souvestre on the compression of *Eugénie Grandet*, Chaudes-Aigues on *Père Goriot* and on *Le Lys dans la vallée*, give the only significant statements in this connection.[135] Most critics, instead, condemn Balzac's plots for their poor construction, the number of digressions they suffer, their lack of balance. These points I shall take up directly in the section on composition. I might note here, however, that in several passages Balzac is indicted for the "invraisemblance" of his action. A. D. L., Chaudes-Aigues, and Sainte-Beuve are the chief accusers.[136]

For most of the evidence on action, we must turn to general statements regarding Balzac's composition. Here the materials are abundant. Again and again, the critics insist that Balzac's composition is bad; the point is one of those most frequently made during the period. By bad composition, of course, many things may be implied, and these critics made their objection under several specific forms. In the first place, and most often, they submitted that while Balzac's stories began brilliantly, they tended to become obscure as they progressed, and to end poorly if they ended at all. The *Revue des deux mondes* opened the assault against this particular weakness:

. . . il persiste à ne rien achever; . . . c'est en général le défaut de ces nouveaux contes comme celui de leurs aînés. *Maître Cornélius* et *l'Auberge rouge* commencent à merveille. L'auteur nous introduit convenablement dans ces deux histoires; mais de ce riche et spacieux vestibule où il nous a fait entrer, nous voulons monter aux appartements; après être demeurés si longtemps sur le seuil, nous voudrions le franchir; nous voudrions voir le reste de la maison. Par malheur, l'architecte a oublié de la finir. Il n'y a qu'un vestibule.[137]

M. F. made the same complaint: an excellent beginning, with a growing interest on the part of the reader; then a gradual falling off of that interest with the increasing platitude of the tale.[138] A. suspected Balzac of having no fixed plan when he began to write, but of following his fancy wherever it led him.[139] From Sainte-Beuve, a similar disapproval:

Dans l'invention d'un sujet, comme dans le détail du style, M. de Balzac a la plume courante, inégale, scabreuse; il va, il part doucement au pas, il galope à merveille, et voilà tout d'un coup qu'il s'abat, sauf à se relever pour retomber encore. La plupart de ses commencements sont à ravir; mais ses fins d'histoire dégénèrent ou deviennent excessives. Il y a un moment, un point où malgré lui il s'emporte. Son sang-froid d'observateur lui échappe.[140]

And Janin and Cherbuliez, Guinot and Gonzalès, and a host of others say the same thing in practically the same words.[141] In the second place, the critics disliked the numerous digressions (or what they considered digressions) which interrupted the progress of the story to discuss irrelevant matters. I. C. T. is one of these: "il a délayé trop souvent des pages dramatiques ou coquettes dans des digressions demi-descriptives, demi-philosophiques."[142] Bourjot addresses the reader as "vous qui vous êtes tant de fois perdu au milieu des digressions sans fin, quelquefois sans but, de l'auteur des études philosophiques."[143] In the third place, the critics stress a failing related to the second—the tendency to dwell too long on certain points, even when these were entirely pertinent, and thus to fall into "longueurs." We have already noticed this objection as it bore upon Balzac's use of minute detail. In addition, we might take cognizance of passages in *La Revue de Paris,* in *L'Indépendant,* in Muret (who speaks of "diffusion" and "délayage");[144] also of a statement by Deschamps which justifies such "longueurs" on the basis of the contribution that they make to the general understanding of the novel.[145]

A few writers defended Balzac against these attacks; thus A. D. L.

on the unity and simplicity of *Eugénie Grandet,* and *L'Indépendant* on
the sustained art of *Les Chouans.*[146] More important than these, however, are two statements which attempt a complete justification of
Balzac's "lack of form" on the basis of the appropriateness of that form-
lessness to the materials which he handled. That is, they proposed that
in adapting the novel to its new functions, Balzac was obliged to change
or to disregard the conventions of novelistic writing. I have already
quoted the first of these, by "The Reviewer," on the comparison between
Dante and Balzac; one additional passage is significant: ". . . dès l'abord,
l'unité manquant au modèle et la foi au peintre, ni l'une ni l'autre ne
peuvent se rencontrer dans le tableau: ainsi point de synthèse. L'absence
d'unité exclut toute concision . . ."[147] D'Izalguier provides the other
statement:

> . . . se résoudre à traduire exactement l'observation, . . . c'est être sûr
> de donner à l'œuvre ainsi faite tout l'intérêt de la réalité; mais aussi
> c'est se soumettre au délaiement, au décousu, à l'éparpillement de la vie
> réelle: le détail envahit l'ensemble, le portrait remplace l'action, la
> vérité descriptive dissout l'intérêt dramatique. Les intrigues savantes,
> bien nouées, bien graduées, croissantes et heureusement résolues, que
> l'imagination peut combiner dans les sphères idéales, ne se rencontrent
> pas dans la vie réelle telle qu'elle se manifeste au sein de notre société.
> Là, tout marche par soubresauts, d'une façon inégale, sans préparation
> logique, sans suite probable; le drame ne va jamais où il tend, mille
> choses soudaines le font dévier et se perdre . . . Dans le milieu de la
> réalité, la combinaison dramatique est faible, l'intrigue irrégulière,
> l'action intermittente. Mais le portrait des individualités est ressemblant,
> et par cela même intéresse; on se complaît à l'analyse, qui dit vrai, à la
> description de la vie prise sur le fait.[148]

Whether or not this constitutes a valid aesthetic justification it is not
my province to decide; but the passages are indicative of a tendency,
on the part of at least a few people, to reconsider artistic conventions in
the light of a new purpose, and to find Balzac's performance entirely
satisfactory on this basis.

As against this fairly general disapproval of Balzac's composition, we
find that his treatment of character was usually accepted as excellent.
And by treatment of character I mean here only the artistic processes
involved in stating and developing a personage. In some cases, the
critic merely comments on a specific character: so Pichot on Mademoiselle de Verneuil, Latouche on Raphaël, the *Constitutionnel* on the
Marquise de Listomère, the *Chronique de Paris* on Madame Claës, A. on
Madame Claës and Marguerite, Chaudes-Aigues on all the characters of
Père Goriot, especially Vautrin.[149] These portrayals are admired for a
certain breadth of outline, a sharpness of definition, an entirely distinctive quality. The same aspects are mentioned by others who appre-

ciate Balzac's general talent in character creation; thus Charles de Bernard speaks of "des caractères largement dessinés d'un seul trait."[150] Only one critic, Muret, seems to have realized the importance of Balzac's description of physical background as an element in characterization; he remarks on it in two separate reviews, of which I quote the second:

On sait que le grand mérite de M. de Balzac est surtout cet art de préparations avec lequel il vous initie, avant même de les introduire sur la scène, à la vie, aux habitudes, au caractère de ses personnages. Aucun d'eux n'a encore paru devant vous, et déjà, grâce à la description *parlante,* qui vous transporte dans les lieux où ils demeurent, vous avez un avant-goût de leur figure et de leur personne.[151]

One other phase of Balzac's technique, the indication of psychological traits through physiognomy, is noted by Gonzalès: "le masque extérieur lui sert de guide; il flaire l'âme aux odeurs du corps, la pensée aux plis et aux creux du visage."[152] In connection with character, still another point is worthy of note, the early dislike of Balzac's use of reappearing characters. Balzac introduced the practice in *Père Goriot,* in 1834; it was not until 1837, however, when he had already applied it in several works, that it came in for adverse criticism. Again, the *Revue des deux mondes* sets the example:

Jusque dans les romans qu'il présente comme neufs de tout point, vous le voyez replacer, dans des rôles pareils, nombre de personnages et de caractères par lui précédemment employés. Cette perpétuelle rumination embarrasse et décontenance beaucoup les enthousiastes les plus déterminés de M. de Balzac.[153]

Next came Pichot, who expressed an immense boredom at seeing the same people doing the same things, and never concluding anything.[154] Finally, Sainte-Beuve phrased the objection thus:

Les acteurs, qui reviennent dans ces nouvelles, ont déjà figuré, et trop d'une fois pour la plupart, dans des romans précédents de M. de Balzac. Quand ce seraient des personnages intéressants et vrais, je crois que les reproduire ainsi est une idée fausse et contraire au *mystère* qui s'attache toujours au roman ... Grâce à cette multitude de biographies secondaires qui se prolongent, reviennent et s'entrecroisent sans cesse, la série des *Études de Mœurs* de M. de Balzac finit par ressembler à l'inextricable lacis des corridors dans certaines mines ou catacombes. On s'y perd et l'on n'en revient plus, ou, si l'on en revient, on n'en rapporte rien de distinct.[155]

Despite this objection, however, Balzac's handling of character was on the whole found to be laudable.

As in characterization, so also in description Balzac was recognized as superior. His descriptive passages, as I have already noted, were sometimes blamed for the inclusion of excessively minute details, sometimes for interrupting the march of the narrative. But in themselves, as pieces of prose writing and evocative media, they were usually regarded in the highest light. They are described as "fort belles de style et de couleurs,"[156] as "d'une richesse éblouissante."[157] A. D. L. speaks of "l'agrément des descriptions,"[158] Sainte-Beuve remarks that "il sait vous émouvoir et vous faire palpiter dès l'abord, rien qu'à vous décrire une allée, une salle à manger, un ameublement,"[159] Janin insists that "personne n'entend la description comme M. de Balzac."[160] "C'est chose étonnante," according to Nettement, "que la finesse d'aperçus que M. de Balzac déploie dans de pareilles peintures, chose plus étonnante que la délicatesse de ses lignes et la vérité de ses couleurs."[161] Nettement, too, calls Balzac a "peintre inimitable"; he is one of the first so to describe Balzac's talent as pictorial rather than literary. Philarète Chasles does so again in 1838,[162] and "De Blanzac" in 1839.[163] In connection with Balzac as a descriptive artist and as a "painter" it is important to note that very early his style is assimilated to that of the Flemish and Dutch masters. Later in realistic criticism, much is made of this similarity; in fact, the attitude towards Flemish painting contributes significantly to the reception of French realism in painting and in literature.[164] In 1833, *La Revue des deux mondes,* discussing *Le Médecin de campagne,* speaks of "une vieille femme, dont on dirait les rides comptées par le pinceau de Gérard Dow";[165] Muret, in 1835, makes the comparison to a "tableau flamand,"[166] Cherbuliez (1835) likens Balzac to Gerard Dow and Teniers.[167] There were soon others to repeat and expand the notion.[168]

In almost every extended statement on Balzac's literary technique, there is some appreciation of his style. Taking into account only the most significant of these, we find that they total, nevertheless, some fifty passages that give a negative or a positive evaluation of Balzac's prose. We find, too, that numerically at least the balance of pluses and minuses is almost perfect. On this point of Balzac's style—always a moot problem—the period from 1830 to 1839 seems to have reached no distinct decision. At best, I may point out the nature of the appraisal in each case. First, the defence: the principal arguments in Balzac's favor were the picturesqueness and the richness of his prose, its flexibility which adapted it to every idea and every situation, its originality. *La Revue de Paris* comments on the last of these:

Son style . . . a un caractère. Ce n'est pas le style de ses émules, de ses rivaux; il lui est propre, il lui appartient. C'est un style fort d'études, fort de mots, d'expressions scientifiques arrachées à leur sens propre; d'images toutes jeunes ou qu'il rajeunit avec puissance, en les déplaçant de leurs emplois connus. Il y a là dedans un instinct de nouveauté qui mérite qu'on s'y arrête un moment.[169]

On the flexibility or the variety of his style, there were more numerous and more enthusiastic remarks. *Le Littérateur universel* supplies such a statement:

... sa phrase brillante varie sans cesse, elle a toutes les formes comme tous les reflets; tantôt souple, languissante et gracieuse, elle se développe avec une noble lenteur; tantôt serrée, concise et ferme, elle se hâte pour s'arrêter encore, pour entrer dans quelque minutieuse subtilité qu'elle dépeint sans efforts.[170]

Another appreciation comes from Legoyt, who compares Félix Davin to Balzac; the disciple, he thinks, imitates the master in "cette phrase concise, énergique, compréhensive, et souvent imagée qui détache chaque idée en relief et la présente rapidement à l'esprit du lecteur sans effort de sa part, sans embarras d'intelligence."[171] Gonzalès speaks of the admirable adaptation of style to subject-matter in such works as *Le Lys dans la vallée, La Peau de chagrin, Eugénie Grandet.*[172] Most numerous of all, however, were the praises of what the critics called Balzac's "richesse," his "profusion," his "brillant." They speak of his style as "éblouissant" and "prestigieux,"[173] of his "magie de pinceau,"[174] of his manner as "éclatant, taillé à facettes, incorrect quelquefois, coloré toujours."[175] It was this phantasmagoric quality, this oriental luxuriance associated usually with *La Peau de chagrin,* that explained for them Balzac's domination of his reader and his palpitating interest.

On the other hand, there was the opposition: it was violent in its attack, and brought a number of accusations. Balzac, it said, was negligent and incorrect, pretentious and bombastic, confused, endeavoring to be forceful and arriving only at a dissipated and amorphous style. What it most objected to was perhaps Balzac's sins against grammar and syntax, his cultivation of "barbarismes" and "solécismes." Hence it produced such statements as E. C.'s:

Le plus grand défaut de son style est de n'être pas français. Il n'est plus question de syntaxe, ni de grammaire; toutes ces vieilles entraves étaient trop pesantes, il a fallu les secouer. A la place, nous avons des inversions continuelles, les néologismes les plus bizarres, une langue nouvelle en vérité et qui n'est ni facile, ni harmonieuse. Le vocabulaire de toutes les sciences est mis à contribution pour peindre les mouvements de l'âme.[176]

For similar reasons, "L'Indépendant" described *La Femme supérieure* as "un amas de barbarismes, de locutions triviales, de comparaisons ridicules, d'aphorismes ignobles, le tout enveloppé dans une obscurité d'expressions mirobolantes, de tournures inusitées, dédale véritablement infernal, où le diable lui-même ne saurait se reconnaître."[177] Even the distinguished lawyer, Chaix d'Est-Ange, in his plea for *La Revue de*

Paris in the suit against Balzac, took it upon himself to make damning remarks about the literary character of Balzac's work, and most of these bore upon details of style; or, as he phrased it, of "ce langage, que personne ne comprend."[178] Others of the opposition blamed Balzac for his negligence, as they called it; they probably had in mind something akin to the incorrectness just discussed.[179] This type of reproach reaches its climax in those who hold that Balzac has no style at all, that "il ne soupçonne pas les plus simples secrets du style."[180] On a somewhat different basis, certain critics object that Balzac is prolix, overabundant, and consequently confused in his expression. His pen, according to Al. de C., is "diffuse, épisodique, vagabonde, prolixe, abandonnée, pleine de mots inutiles, bavarde, amusante par le détail, fatigante par l'abondance des minuties."[181] Louise Ozenne sees a decline from his early manner, when he wrote relatively well, to that of *Le Lys,* where his former merit is "étouffé sous les caprices de style les plus étranges, sous un amas d'images et d'expressions empruntées au langage technique des ordres de choses les plus divers et pressées, entassées, confondues dans la même phrase de manière à produire l'effet le plus incohérent, le plus fatigant et le plus obscur."[182] For Sainte-Beuve, his style "ressemble souvent au mouvement brisé d'une orgie, à la danse continuelle et énervée d'un prêtre de Cybèle."[183] These are drastic condemnations indeed, but they are equalled by several others in which Balzac's style is rejected because of its pretentiousness. We might take, as an example, Stendhal's sly remark: "Je suppose qu'il fait ses romans en deux temps, d'abord raisonnablement, puis il les habille en beau style néologique, avec les *pâtiments* de l'âme, *il neige dans mon cœur,* et autres belles choses."[184] Or Pichot's complaint upon completing a parody of Balzac: ". . . plaignez-moi, moi qui, pour vous plaire, ai consenti à transcrire, ainsi et mot à mot, plus de non-sens, plus de niaiseries, plus de fadeurs sans esprit, plus de prétentieuses extravagances et plus de fautes de français, que je n'en ai entendu dire et rêver en toute ma vie."[185]

Before leaving the question of style, it is necessary to call attention more directly to the reaction towards Balzac's use of neologism and scientific vocabulary. We have already seen several indications of this reaction in the preceding paragraphs. In addition, it might be said that the neologisms especially caused much comment, which was unfavorable in all cases except two.[186] Equally unfavorable was the attitude towards the use of technical and scientific words introduced into fiction. Thus this aspect of Balzac's program, which he himself considered so important, did not usually meet with the approval of the critics.[187]

Related to the problem of style is that of Balzac's general manner, his treatment of all the elements constituting an artistic whole. Such reflections were not numerous, since a critic's point of view was usually stated apropos of some specific trait. But there were, for example, some dozen statements on the "recherché" effect of his novels, their tone of over-refinement and subtlety. The most complete of these comes from one of Louise Ozenne's articles: '

Rien de naturel, rien d'abandonné, pas une étincelle de véritable verve; aucunes traces de jeunesse; on sent le calcul dans tous les effets de style, et ces effets n'ont qu'un éclat trompeur comme celui des diamants faux; . . . pas un tour vraiment éloquent, pas une pensée neuve et salutaire; pas une image vraiment grande, quoiqu'au premier abord vous ayez cru entrevoir tous ces mérites. En y regardant de près, vous ne trouvez plus que recherche et que manière . . .[188]

On the contrary, there were some critics who commented on the simplicity of Balzac's studies—of *Eugénie Grandet* as a whole, of the plot in *César Birotteau* or in *Le Lys dans la vallée,* of such fragments as the soldier's narrative in *Le Médecin de campagne.*[189] These remarks, applied to given novels, are restricted in scope; but they indicate that the critics did recognize Balzac's virtuosity in widely different manners. Also in the line of general considerations were the very frequent remarks on his ability to awaken the interest of the reader and to stir him emotionally; these we have seen in connection with one detail or another, and it is hardly necessary to insist upon them further. But we have not yet touched on one criticism—of a personal as well as of a literary nature—which was regularly made: that of overfecundity. To this vice were traced Balzac's negligence in style, his poor plot construction, the episodic character of his stories, their lack of unity.[190] To the same vice, also, was attributed the 'decadence' of his talent, a reflection which critics just begin to make in this first period, and which is to gain marked development in the second.[191]

Opinion on Balzac's literary technique, then, was divided in tendency. More than elsewhere, it depended upon the nature of the specific novel studied; all of the excellencies, for example, might be ascribed to *Eugénie Grandet,* and all of the failings to *Séraphita.* In a general way, the formal criticism recognized in Balzac a high merit in the creation of the short story, in the handling of character and description, and a relatively low degree of performance in plot construction and composition. On style, opinion was hesitant, with the negative statements perhaps better supported by example and citation than the vague assertions of superiority.

By way of epitomizing the whole of the criticism of Balzac during the period 1830-1839, I shall outline the content of three articles which Philarète Chasles devoted to *César Birotteau* in the *Journal des débats* for January 30, March 5, and August 16, 1838.[192] These constitute the most representative single judgment of Balzac during the period, and are especially interesting since they have hitherto escaped notice.

First article. Balzac's incontestable talent; its variety and scope; vastness and delicacy. His world as irregular; but numerous "moral" and virtuous characters; their contemporaneity. Exactness, detail, dissection, truth. Complication and subtlety. Madame Birotteau contrasted favorably with the affected women of aristocratic circles. Characterization of his "femme de trente ans." His weakness in treating aristocracy. *César Birotteau* a Flemish painting. Balzac's attention to minute detail, physical and psychological, and especially to the ugly. He is merely an observer; his philosophical pretentions are absurd. Complete depiction of contemporary society, whose traits are reflected in his style: materialism, exaggeration, coquetry, fine analysis. His fecundity.

Second article. Richness, variety, appropriateness of his prose style. Mixture of the real and the imaginary. Lack of direction, of a unifying philosophical principle, of a moral sense. Hence he goes from the extremes of mysticism to those of cynicism. Variety in his works.

Third article. Eugénie Grandet combines the real and the ideal. Intimate perception of human character. His double method: material analysis and psychological investigation. Great and varied production of unfinished stories; the excitement of interest. His comic genius, enhanced by its application to tragic situations. His essential materialism. Penetration into Parisian society and human character; its delicacy and truth, even when treating the exception or the false. His tendency to see and depict "la seule matière"; this is less acceptable in literature than in painting. His only legitimate successes are those in which the subject itself offers a combination and balance of the real and the ideal.

Without attempting to appraise the ensemble of criticism of Balzac for this period, we may say this about it: that it affords a very large number of opinions on Balzac's work (I have taken some one hundred and forty into account), and that these opinions relate to most of the novels and stories published during these ten years, when over half of the *Comédie humaine* was written; that in these opinions a fair attempt is made to judge the novelist—without prejudice for or against him— and that, as a consequence, there is an equitable distribution of praise and of blame. Thus we can hardly agree with Marcel Bouteron or with Mme de Korwin-Piotrowska when they affirm that Balzac's works were sooner and more judiciously appreciated abroad than at home.[193] Whether or not Balzac was popular in Parisian salons, whether or not he was regarded favorably as a person, whether or not he had many friends or enemies, are all considerations irrelevant to the problem of this study. On the basis, then, of the critical opinions themselves, it is evident that Balzac as a writer was discussed and evaluated in considerable detail, that his literary reputation was extensive, and that on the whole the judgments bore directly on the works themselves and gave in many cases an adequate appreciation of these works.

Not only was this appreciation adequate, but it was also in a sense prophetic. For critics of the first period evolved and formulated many of the salient judgments which were later to be pronounced on Balzac's work. They anticipated the arguments of Sainte-Beuve in 1850, of Taine in 1858, of Brunetière as late as 1906. Sainte-Beuve, for example, in his final article on Balzac,[194] commented on the latter's oriental style, on his attention to vice, on the physiological nature of his approach. Taine,[195] too, gave special mention to his cataloguing descriptions, to his use of technical vocabularies, to his peculiar treatment of virtuous characters. Brunetière,[196] finally, based his whole evaluation of Balzac on the excellence of social portrayal in the *Comédie humaine*. And like these, many other critics were to repeat and expand notions first developed in the earliest years of criticism of Balzac.

1839 TO 1845

During the period 1839 to 1845, critical articles on Balzac were marked by a tone of animosity and violence not discernible in the earlier years. This feeling had its source in *Un Grand Homme de province à Paris,* in which an attack upon the press in general and upon specific critics aroused the wrath of Parisian journalistic circles. Nor did Balzac's subsequent activities during the period contribute to pacify their wrath. In the same year, 1839, there was the Affaire Peytel; Balzac's intervention in behalf of the notary, guilty of murdering his wife and servant, was severely censured. His first incursion into the field of drama, with *Vautrin* (1840), provoked the resentment of dramatic and literary critics alike. Then came his editorship of *La Revue parisienne* (1840) with its challenge to the established journals and to prominent critics. *Les Ressources de Quinola* and the accompanying scandal of the ticket sale (1842) again brought opposition, even ridicule. Finally, in 1844, he launched the *Monographie de la presse parisienne,* hardly calculated to appease a well-nourished antagonism. This antagonism explains not only the general tone of criticism during these years and the predominance of adverse over favorable judgments, but it also makes more significant the change in attitude towards any specific point. The problem of the second period may be stated thus: given the intention of the critics to be severe towards Balzac's work, on what specific elements of his work will that severity be exercised?[197]

As in the first period, most critics in the second deny the validity of Balzac's philosophical pretentions.[198] They discover in his works no unifying idea or principle; instead, they regard his conceptions as

singular and as contradictory to one another, and his desire to exploit
them as injurious to his literary technique. A new aspect of this disapproval is its application to the idea of a *Comédie humaine;* the critics
insist upon the impossibility of studying all of society in the light of an
all-inclusive scheme, such as Balzac had proposed in the *Avant-
propos.*[199] Limayrac calls the *Comédie humaine* "cet immense imbroglio
qu'il donne pour un vaste poème, gigantesque Babel qu'il élève à la gloire
du siècle, et qui s'écroule à mesure."[200] Consequent upon the general rejection of Balzac's encyclopedic pretentions is the continued rejection of
his nonfictional materials—"ces détails de tailleur, de bottier, da fiacre,
de marchande de modes et de restaurateur," as Janin terms them.[201]
Chaudes-Aigues remarks that Balzac's novels replace lectures at the
Collège de France,[202] and Molènes that they compete with the *manuels-
Roret.*[203]

On Balzac's practical philosophy—his materialism, his apology for
vice, his general immorality—there is now a notable swing towards more
trenchant accusations. Especially on the score of materialism, which
had been barely mentioned in the first period. Francis Girault, for
example, classes Balzac in the *école des faits,* and condemns his work
as illustrating the tenets of that school:

. . . le théorie de l'*école des faits,* dans le roman, est abusive et infiniment
dangereuse en enseignant, lorsqu'il lui est impossible de déterminer
l'emploi des facultés libres de l'âme, l'exercice fatal de ces facultés dans
des circonstances données.

Tel est le vice radical de toutes les œuvres de M. de Balzac, qui ont
pour but, sous l'écorce apparente des faits, d'introniser une vaste idée
philosophique, embrassant notre société tout entière, idée qui tend à
matérialiser l'âme, en proclamant l'absolutisme des sens et en assujettis-
sant la volonté, le libre arbitre, à l'entraînement irrésistible des appétits
charnels.[204]

Seven other critics now make adverse statements on the same point.[205]
At the same time, insistence on Balzac's immorality is proportionately
more frequent and more considerable; the character of Vautrin especially is severely criticized on this score.[206] More than before, this
immorality is now regarded as intentional and malicious; Molènes calls
it "une sorte d'immoralité qui lui est particulière, et dont je le croirais
volontiers l'inventeur . . . C'est une immoralité pédante, érudite, presque
inconnue aux gens du monde. . ."[207] Gandonnière suggests that his work
be called *l'Orgie humaine.*[208] Concomitantly, the statement that Balzac
prefers and condones vice appears more often and is more lucidly made;
compare the opinion of Forgues:

. . . tandis que la vertu subit des faillites, vit de privations, blêmit
d'heure en heure, et entasse bévues sur bévues, le vice est alerte **et**

heureux; il a le parler bref et profond, il tire l'épée comme Saint-Georges, et se fait respecter par son courage quand il ne domine pas l'opinion par les admirables combinaisons d'une hypocrisie machiavélique . . .[209]

On the whole, then, critics of the second period were as little disposed as those of the first to admit Balzac's philosophical pretentions, and were increasingly categorical in their rejection of his materialism and his immorality.

In the judgments of social depiction in the *Comédie humaine* a change is again to be noted. It does not affect the attitude towards Balzac's powers of observation, which are still admired; the unanimity on this score indicated in the first period persists in the second, in which there are some twenty-five laudatory statements of the kind.[210] Nor does it affect the opinion that the author frequently abuses these powers by cultivating excessive detail; so Marc Fournier's quip that "Un [journal] a statué dans une assemblée de ses actionnaires, qu'on ne permettrait pas à M. de Balzac de mettre plus de trente clous à chacun des fauteuils qu'il lui plairait de mentionner."[211] Similarly, the earlier opinion on his observation as applied to character persists: we find a number of remarks, largely favorable, on his knowledge of the human heart,[212] with special attention called to his study and understanding of women.[213] The emphasis on the scientific qualities of his analysis is smaller,[214] but it is compensated for by more sweeping tributes to the delicacy of his treatment of the passions.[215] In his portrayal of the passions, says Francis Girault, "il ressemble à ces artistes patients qui veulent atteindre la perfection dans les lignes et les traits les plus imperceptibles, les moins accusés, et dont les ouvrages, étudiés à la loupe, arrivent à un fini minutieux."[216] Nevertheless, and perhaps surprisingly, there are very few comments on the truth of his characters,[217] and a proportionately larger number of claims that these are false or exceptional.[218]

It is in the estimates of Balzac's achievement in social portrayal that the change mentioned is most notable. There are, first, fewer commentaries on his intention to give a complete picture of society; this is natural enough, since the novelty of the innovation has now worn off. At least one critic, Molènes, protests angrily against the practice:

Je hais, et je hais profondément tous ces poèmes de l'existence parisienne que les romanciers de ce temps-ci ont maintes fois tenté d'écrire, le tableau des luttes de la conscience contre les mille misères de la vie, l'intervention de l'usurier chez l'écrivain, l'irruption des affreux spectres de la réalité parmi les doux fantômes de l'imagination . . .[219]

On the other hand, tributes to the truthfulness of his world are comparatively more numerous. If examined closely, however, these tributes are seen to be much less general than those of the former years, and to be restricted usually to some specific novel.[220] Cormenin, almost alone, emphasizes the artistic use of reality in Balzac's works: "M. de Balzac revêt ses peintures d'une teinte plus idéale [than does Henri Monnier], de sorte qu'elles rentrent à la fois dans le domaine de la vie réelle et dans le domaine de l'art. Jamais il ne manque à cette double loi de produire de grands effets à l'aide d'éléments restreints."[221] Besides, the critics single out for praise his treatment of bourgeois[222] and provincial life[223] rather than that of aristocratic circles. They are much less impressed with the contemporaneity of his writings,[224] and say nothing at all about his impersonality.[225] On the whole, these opinions on the truth of Balzac's world betray much less enthusiasm, much less wholehearted praise, than did those of the preceding period.

Concurrently, the emphasis on the falseness of his portrayal, which was already present to a considerable extent in the years 1830-1839, now is intensified. Critics insist, as we should expect, on the falseness of the journalistic world as shown in *Un Grand Homme de province à Paris.*[226] But others impugn his entire production, in such sweeping statements as Girault's: ". . . si le monde réel est copié d'après nature dans les romans dont nous parlons, il est, au fond, bien méprisable et bien hideux; mais, Dieu merci, il ne saurait en être ainsi."[227] Still others declare that his world is one of fantasy, with no relationship to reality; as Sainte-Beuve says, "Homme d'imagination et de fantaisie, il la porte trop aisément en des sujets qui en sont peu susceptibles, et il pousse, sans y songer, à des conséquences fabuleuses dont chaque œil peut redresser de lui-même l'illusion."[228] But these reproaches are overshadowed by one which now looms increasingly large, and comes to constitute the principal objection to the world of the *Comédie humaine,* the objection that Balzac treats only the seamy side of life. Sixteen critics in these years attack him for this tendency, and mostly in a tone of angry vituperation. Perhaps none was so violent as Janin:

. . . M. de Balzac excelle dans ces sortes de descriptions fangeuses, le bois pourri, l'eau stagnante, le linge lavé dans les cuvettes, étendu sur des cordes, digne lessive des lieux vicieux; l'odeur horrible du moisi, de la chaufferette, du hareng saur, les causeries des marchands et des marchandes, la gent trotte-menu des filles de joie . . . En un mot, tout ce cynisme public des personnes et des choses, tout cela monte à la tête de l'écrivain . . . Rien ne lui échappe, pas une ride, pas une croute gluante de cette lèpre immonde, c'est à faire soulever le cœur, et, malgré toute la puissance que doit avoir un écrivain pour en arriver là, l'on se demande quels plaisirs peuvent donc trouver les lecteurs de M. de Balzac à ces affreux détails?[229]

Janin's criticism, moreover, should not be considered as exceptional;

a number of others equalled it in vehemence. One new note in this censure is the insistence on Balzac's devotion to "crude" reality—"aux teintes les plus crues de la réalité."[230] Another is the attention directed to his excessive preoccupation with money matters—"ce bruit d'argent et cette horrible odeur de billon," as Janin puts it;[231] "la passion d'entasser milliards sur milliards dans ses livres," as Chaudes-Aigues says.[232] All of these remarks charge Balzac's depiction, more or less implicitly, with incompleteness, and certain writers make direct comments on this point.[233] The final argument against Balzac's world is that of exaggeration, and it continues in prominence during this period. "M. de Balzac," says Lucas, "a sur les yeux la loupe du romancier, loupe qui grossit considérablement les objets."[234] In its totality, then, the assertion that Balzac's world is false gains in vividness and definiteness, as well as in the number of its proponents, during this second period.

Coming now to the body of criticism regarding Balzac as an artist, we find that the attitude towards his literary technique also undergoes numerous changes. In the first place, he is no longer considered the bewitching "conteur"; there are now only two echoes of what was once a general cry.[235] Nor, in the second place, did the former claims of dramatic ability withstand the new light thrown upon them by Balzac's unsuccessful ventures in the theater. Almost unanimously, the critics concluded that his talent was unfit for the stage, and was essentially undramatic in the novel.[236] Hence the old condemnation of his plots, unmitigated by the earlier concessions to his narrative and dramatic ability, now becomes more severe. These plots, for Reybaud, "ont pour défaut essentiel celui qu'Horace caractérisait . . . en disant: *Desinit in piscem mulier formosa superne.*"[237] Edouard Thierry's dictum is even more categorical: "Jamais, dans ses romans, M. de Balzac n'a su conduire une action, l'exposer, la nouer, et la dénouer; il y a plus: jamais M. de Balzac n'a su faire une scène; car une scène est aussi une action tout entière."[238] On Balzac's composition in general, the negative evidence is much more considerable than before; there are seventeen discussions in all, and only one of them is favorable. I may cite the opinion of Chaudes-Aigues as typical:

. . . nous voulons parler de l'absence de proportions qui règne entre les diverses parties d'*Une Fille d'Eve,* de la confusion des scènes, des tiraillements en sens contraire auxquels l'action est soumise presque à chaque page, du manque de composition en un mot . . .[239]

The judgment of Molènes on *Mémoires de deux jeunes mariées* is also interesting:

Des rameaux échevelés, des plantes exubérantes, une végétation mons-trueuse, un fouillis de choses mauvaises, des herbes parasites et des bêtes rampantes, figurez-vous tout cela moins la majesté des grands arbres, le ciel qu'on voit à travers les branches, et vous aurez une idée de l'impression que ce livre laisse dans l'esprit.[240]

Naturally, the old complaint of the faulty dénouement reappears,[241] as well as that of unnecessary *longueurs;*[242] on the latter point, however, I might call attention to the article of Cormenin, which justifies these lengthy developments.[243]

On the subject of characterization, the critics are again well-nigh unanimous as to Balzac's excellence, as they are also on his powers of observation. There is rarely a dissenting voice on this score, and for many, as for Loménie, his characters constitute "la base la plus solide de l'édifice littéraire de M. de Balzac."[244] In addition to those who praise his general art of characterization, there are many who indicate individual portraits as excellent.[245] Nevertheless, critics are increasingly impatient with his use of reappearing characters, which is constantly condemned; nine statements between 1839 and 1845, as against three in the preceding years, indicate the growth of this feeling.[246] The talent of description, cognate to that of characterization, is still recognized as possessed by Balzac to a high degree; for some, indeed, the essentially descriptive nature of his genius is responsible for his failure in the drama; and for many his pictorial passages are incomparable.[247] He is a painter, an etcher, above all a descendant of the Flemish school; this analogy is now more fully developed, and we find long passages devoted to it. Such, for example, is the paragraph of Molènes:

Nous avons tous passé des heures entières dans les galeries du Louvre à contempler quelques-uns de ces merveilleux intérieurs de Van-Ostade, de Metzu ou de Gerard Dow, dans lesquels notre imagination pénètre, s'établit et s'amuse; M. de Balzac savait quelquefois donner à ses romans le genre d'attrait mystérieux que présentent ces tableaux . . . Le monde que M. de Balzac a reçu le don de comprendre et de reproduire, est le même que celui de ces peintures bourgeoises . . .[248]

Balzac's processes were likened to those of the daguerreotype as early as 1841[249] (Daguerre's discoveries were published in 1839); subsequently this comparison was often made.

On the question of style, still vigorously debated in the early years, opinion now swings definitely towards the censorious attitude; of thirty-nine expressions, two-thirds are distinctly unfavorable. The arguments employed on both sides are fundamentally the same as those analyzed above for the years 1830-1839. We may take Girault's statement as summarizing the affirmative:

Après Victor Hugo, c'est l'écrivain qui a sondé la langue française avec le plus de courage et de bonheur, et qui la plie le mieux aux besoins divers de la pensée. M. de Balzac marche en conquérant sur le terrain de la linguistique . . . M. de Balzac est un des littérateurs qui a rendu le plus de services à la prose du dix-neuvième siècle, en lui imprimant des allures vives, un tour spirituel et éminemment français, et en remontant, pour la faire valoir et la perfectionner, à la source de ses richesses primitives.[250]

Here is Loménie's as epitomizing the negative:

. . . on est stupéfait des incroyables licences que le célèbre romancier se permet en ce genre; maintes pages de lui resteront comme un modèle du genre baroque et rocailleux. Ce sont de longues phrases traînantes mal soudées, semées de néologismes bizarres, qui loin d'éclaircir la pensée la rendent inintelligible; ce sont des métaphores à faire dresser les cheveux; des images où se trouvent mêlés et tordus ensemble les trois règnes de la nature. . . . tous ces délits sont commis avec la circonstance aggravante de la préméditation.[251]

The old objection to neologisms, while it still appears in several of these articles, is now considerably less prominent.

As to Balzac's general manner, remarks are not so abundant on the whole. He is again indicted for affectation and obscurity,[252] although a few novels gain praise for their simplicity.[253] The numerous witnesses to the interest and the emotional reaction awakened in the reader no longer appear, except in very rare instances. On the contrary, the similarity of many of Balzac's stories to one another, plus the unpopular device of the reappearing characters, bring the complaint of monotony.[254] But among such general considerations, none is now as prominent as the idea of Balzac's decadence, of a rapid failing of his powers and a noticeable deterioration in his productions. As I have pointed out, this idea had barely been intimated in the first period; it now attains its fullest development.[255] The critics speak of Balzac as a "talent malade," of the "décroissance et désorganisation" in his mind, of his "bas-empire." Only one critic, Girault, raised his voice against this widespread notion,[256] although a few others claimed that the press was unfair and biased in its condemnation of the novelist.[257] Otherwise, the mass of critics was prone to look upon Balzac as a failing genius.

From this brief summary of criticism between 1839 and 1845 we may conclude that: (1) the animosity of the journalists expressed itself in an increased condemnation of Balzac's philosophical ideas, of his morality, of his social depiction as false, and in a growing rejection of his general scheme, of his reappearing characters, of his style, of his narrative manner in general; (2) they concluded from these deficiencies that his best work was in the past, and that his recent production showed a marked decadence; (3) in spite of their tendency to find fault, they continued to praise his faculties of observation, his technique of description and of characterization. On the whole, then, we find a decided movement in the direction of severity, but which failed to prevent the recognition of certain uncontested superiorities.

1846 TO 1856

In 1846, when Furne, Dubochet, and Hetzel published the sixteenth volume of the first edition of the *Comédie humaine*, there was a sharp, almost spectacular swing of opinion in Balzac's favor. The critics now had, for examination and study, practically all of Balzac's realistic writings in all but definitive form, and for the first time the unity and the imposing mass of his production broke upon them. To these collected works were now added, in a few years, two vigorous and successful novels—*La Cousine Bette, Le Cousin Pons*—and Balzac's first successful play, *La Marâtre*. Thus during the last four years of his life, Balzac gained recognition as a supreme and superior genius—as the Molière of the nineteenth century,[258] as the "most remarkable of contemporary novelists,"[259] as a "great man in the fullest sense of the word."[260] But this high praise was a mere prelude to the burst of panegyric which followed upon Balzac's death, and which continued almost uninterrupted until its culmination in Taine's article of 1858.[261] One critic claims that "il dépasse de toute la tête tous les romanciers, les peintres de mœurs, les physiologistes et les psychologistes qu'a eu la France. Pour moi, j'aimerais mieux laisser ce nom . . . que n'importe quel nom de la littérature actuelle."[262] For another, "M. de Balzac est non seulement le plus grand romancier qui ait été et qui sera probablement . . . ; mais encore nous ne connaissons pas d'historiens qui puissent lui être comparés."[263] The old taunt of "decadence" hardly appears[264]—there are even positive denials of it[265]—and in its stead comes the affirmation that Balzac progressed steadily until his death.[266] Even the most enthusiastic critics, however, discovered certain failings in Balzac's novels. Their adverse comments gain significance since they appear in a period which was ready to praise and accept Balzac. The problem in this third period of criticism (1846-1856), in contrast with the second, is to determine what elements of his work were thrown into a more favorable light as a result of this tendency to glorify Balzac, and what elements still resisted the good-will of the critics.

As a consequence of the new attitude, we note for the first time a trend favorable to Balzac's philosophical ideas and pretentions: some fifteen critics now declare Balzac a "philosophe," a "penseur," a "moraliste,"[267]—Louis Lurine speaks of "la plus puissante qualité de l'écrivain: *la pensée*"[268]—while only five continue to see an inferiority here.[269] But still more striking than this change, especially since it contrasts directly with the opinion of the preceding period, is the whole-hearted approval of the *Comédie humaine* as a unified and interrelated group of novels. As Amédée Achard says:

Ils se tiennent entre eux par l'esprit et encore par les personnages. Les héros naissent dans un livre et meurent dans un autre; l'action court de volume en volume; on n'en sait pas la fin. C'est en quelque sorte une petite société extraite de la grande société et délayée dans vingt romans. . . . Cette pensée d'une œuvre collective, il ne faut jamais l'abandonner, quand on veut étudier la manière de M. de Balzac. Lisez et analysez le volume, si vous voulez; mais ne faites pas abstraction du lien qui le relie à la *Comédie humaine:* là est la tendance, là est le but, là est la vérité.[270]

In the appraisal of Balzac's philosophy, several interesting new ideas appear—especially the notion that he disdains the humanity which he depicts,[271] and that he combines mysticism with his dominant material-ism.[272] The inevitable reproach of immorality still has almost as many proponents as it had in the second period,[273] but they are now contro-verted, for the first time, by a number of critics who either deny the accusation or justify whatever immorality they admit. The justification rests usually on the basis of artistic necessity—"chaque fois," says Cas-tille, "que M. de Balzac s'écarte du sens moral, on peut en accuser, neuf fois sur dix, son profond amour pour l'art"[274]—or of fidelity to the model portrayed:

. . . c'est encore son droit de présenter la réalité toute nue, dans sa beauté ou sa laideur; il peut se réfugier dans la maxime de l'histoire: *Scribitur ad narrandum,* et se reposer sur nous, lecteurs, du jugement qu'il faut porter des faits qu'il raconte, des vérités qu'il expose. Une peinture fidèle n'est donc de soi morale ni immorale; la seule excitation au vice, la seule exaltation du mal méritent d'être flétries; mais un portrait, si laid qu'il soit, doit être jugé seulement au point de vue de la ressem-blance.[275]

George Sand declares: "Nulle part, dans ses livres, je ne vois le mal réhabilité ou le bien méconnu pour le lecteur."[276] These same apologies, of course, were repeated in answer to the critics who continued to berate Balzac for his preference for vice.[277]

In the criticism of Balzac as a painter of contemporary society, there is now a general shift of opinion to a state approximating that of the first period, 1830-1839. Especially, the tributes to his powers of observa-tion increase far beyond their former development; forty-six of the ninety-five articles under consideration bear witness to Balzac's excel-lence in this province.[278] At the same time, the statements which re-proach him with excessive or over-minute detail continue to decrease markedly;[279] George Sand goes so far as to hold that his use of detail will constitute Balzac's principal interest for readers of the future.[280] We note a return, too, to the attention centered on Balzac's "connaissance du cœur humain," on the profundity and delicacy of his analysis of human passions. Thus Rolle, in *Le Constitutionnel*, remarks: ". . . tout en se renfermant plus particulièrement dans les mœurs contemporaines, sa sagacité et son génie analytique et pénétrant va en deçà et au delà et touche aux éternelles et immuables peintures du cœur humain dans tous les temps et sous toutes les latitudes."[281] Similarly, Desnoiresterres emphasizes this double rôle: ". . . il aura été et l'historien du cœur qui ne varie pas, et l'historien des mœurs qui sont essentiellement varia-bles."[282] Again, the critics now revive the earlier interest in Balzac's portrayal of women, for which, they say, this delicacy of psychological analysis equips him admirably.[283] More than ever before, they speak of him as the "analyst," as the one who penetrates profoundly into human motives and psychological arcana; they speak of his "seconde vue psychologique."[284] Of course, ever since the earliest years, the com-parison of Balzac's analytical method to that of the scientist and the doctor had been made, and we find it constantly reiterated in subsequent periods. On the reality of the characters produced by this method there are now surprisingly few comments; the emphasis, as we shall see, tends to be rather on the artistry of their portrayal than on the conformity to contemporary models.[285] In fact, as frequently as not the judges decide that the characters of the *Comédie humaine* are exceptional.[286]

The most remarkable shift of attitude during these years is that rela-tive to Balzac as a historian of contemporary society. In the first period, it will be remembered, critics pointed to this intention as an interesting novelty; in the second, they said very little about it. But now, recon-sidering the total mass of his works, they insist again and again on the fact that his principal merit was not that of a spinner of tales, but rather of a patient and encyclopedic historian—patient for the detail, en-cyclopedic for the ensemble. Forgues states Balzac's purpose thus:

[Balzac] a conçu l'idée de faire passer devant le même miroir, d'insérer dans le même cadre toute la société moderne, ses classes nouvellement reformées, ses institutions dont la vie de chaque individu reçoit forcé-ment l'empreinte; d'analyser les rapports complexes qui unissent, de nos jours, chacun avec tous, tous avec chacun; et l'effet de ces rapports qui se multiplient et changent, pour ainsi dire, d'année en année, sur les passions éternelles que le travail de vingt siècles paraît avoir laissé, à peu de chose près, les mêmes et qui, selon toute apparence, accompagne-ront l'humanité jusqu'au seuil de ses destins mystérieux.[287]

At the same time, the critics regard this analytical method as Balzac's own contribution to the development of the novel. Before him, they say, it was a light and frivolous *genre*, which he dignified by directing it towards serious study of character and of society.[288] Again, he wrote at a time when the "genre médiéval et cadavérique" was beginning to cloy upon the public, and his anti-romanticism was welcome.[289] For others, he initiated a second phase of romanticism; as Ulbach says, "Balzac a été l'initiateur tout-puissant de cette seconde révélation du romantisme. Il nous a débarrassés des souliers à la poulaine, et a ébréché les bonnes lames de Tolède."[290] This growing consciousness of Balzac's socio-historical rôle was accompanied, as we might expect, by the effort to associate him with the realistic school. Concerning this association, however, there was still much controversy. Castille, as early as 1846, first connected Balzac with the "école réaliste," but maintained that he departed from it in the exceptional nature of his characters.[291] Many others connected him with the movement, some giving him the title of "chef de l'école réaliste," others declaring that he was the founder of the group.[292] But there was a considerable group of critics who refused to admit this connection, either because they considered Balzac's fundamental idealism incompatible with the tenets of realism (as phrased by contemporary theorists), or because they regarded his realism as superior to that of the new writers.[293]

The claims that he was a realist were based not only on Balzac's dual method of physical observation and psychological analysis, but on the reality of the world produced as well. On this truthfulness of the Balzacian universe many more critics than ever before now comment favorably. I quote as examples the opinions of Achard—"M. de Balzac est resté, autant que la chose est praticable à un romancier, dans les limites du possible et du vraisemblable. . . . sa Comédie humaine est le monument qui donnera à la postérité l'idée la plus exacte de la France au dix-neuvième siècle"—and of George Sand—"Balzac . . . avait presque trouvé . . . la solution d'un problème inconnu avant lui, la réalité complète dans la fiction complète."[294] More than previously, too, commentators ascribed this impression of reality to the contemporaneity of Balzac's work, to its essential conformity with current manners and ideas; also, they saw in it an answer to the new demand for reality in art.[295] But, in spite of the benevolent attitude of most critics, there were still some who continued to insist that the world of the Comédie humaine was fundamentally false, and that it gave a distorted representation of the real world. Some few merely made a sweeping statement of this type,[296] while most writers attributed this falseness to an excess of imagination: Balzac, even when he started from reality, allowed his fancy to "run away with him," and fell into the absurd and the impossible. Castille defines his manner as "la réalité sans cesse démentie par le démon de la fantaisie," and Forgues characterizes him as "épris de son élaboration intérieure qui avait les prestiges du rêve des *theriakis*, les flamboyantes hallucinations, les excitations presque voluptueuses de l'état fébrile."[297] In this connection it is interesting to note the use of the term "voyant" to describe Balzac.[298] Other critics declared Balzac's world false because of its restriction to the ugly side of life; Jules Jolly's opinion is typical:

. . . Balzac affectionne particulièrement la peinture des imperfections, des faiblesses, des défauts, des vices de la nature humaine. . . . la société qu'il nous peint, avec ses vives et saisissantes couleurs, semble être un abîme sans issue, où le mal pénètre et s'infiltre par tous les pores; où la vertu délaissée s'étiole comme une fleur sans soleil; où se produit de tous côtés une fermentation dévorante de vice et de corruption.[299]

But there were soon a few writers to answer this accusation; Achard gives a typical statement:

Ces intelligences habituées à chercher le vrai en toutes choses, ne dénigrent pas leur époque, parce qu'elle n'est pas en tout point pareille à l'idéal monstrueux que rêvent les faiseurs d'utopies; elles acceptent le bien comme une aumône tombée du ciel, et se résignent au mal comme à une plaie incurable attachée aux flancs de l'humanité![300]

In these and other statements concerning the ugliness of Balzac's world, certain critics now emphasize the crudity and rawness of the depiction.[301] Both ugliness and crudity are by some ascribed to a fundamental lack of idealism in Balzac; "il manquait complètement," says Mazade, "d'un certain idéal élevé, d'une certaine règle supérieure capable de diriger, de contenir et de féconder son observation."[302] But these are few in comparison with a large number of critics who now insist that one of Balzac's principal merits is precisely the tempering of the real by the ideal. This emphasis on the completeness of Balzac's portrayal, its inclusion of the observable and the imagined alike, is a new and striking note in criticism of these years. It is one of the answers to the accusation of realism brought against Balzac; compare the statement of Ulbach:

L'école réaliste se donne aujourd'hui comme héritière de Balzac; parce qu'elle prend ses héros dans la même région, elle prétend à la même gloire; c'est là une illusion violente. . . . Quant à l'imagination, à l'idéal, à cet héroïsme, à ce je ne sais quoi de surhumain et d'inconnu qui nous ravit loin de ce monde, Balzac s'en faisait une religion. Ses plus réels personnages ont le reflet divin; et il sait rester vrai dans ses plus paradoxales inventions, sans jamais risquer d'être plat. L'école prétendue réaliste s'en tient, au contraire, à la platitude . . . [303]

On the formal, literary side of Balzac's work the criticism shows a much less marked development; there are, however, certain shifts, which I shall indicate briefly. As before, his plots are blamed for lack of unity and clearness;[304] but such censure is now answered by a group of critics who maintain that the simplicity of his plots is a virtue, or that—when they are complicated—the complexity serves all the more to give the "sense of life."[305] Eugène Maron, especially, speaks of his "péripéties plus émouvantes cent fois que les grands coups de foudre de certains de ses confrères." Furthermore, his dramatic ability, so contested in the earlier periods, is now generally admitted; the statement of Clément de Ris is here notable:

Il comprit et fit comprendre que le drame n'était pas à l'extérieur, mais à l'intérieur, qu'il pouvait se trouver autant de passion, autant de rage, autant d'ivresse et de douleurs dans l'âme d'un marchand de draps, d'une parfumeuse, d'un millionnaire, d'une duchesse ou d'un élégant, que dans celle d'un malandrin ou d'un page . . . [306]

On the other hand, the old reproach of poor composition, while reiterated somewhat less frequently, is as persistent as ever; plainly, the virtues of order, harmony, proportion, were not to be accorded to Balzac. In Pontmartin's opinion, he lacks "le goût, la proportion, la mesure, le naturel, l'art de s'arrêter à ce moment précis, unique, décisif, où l'effet s'altère en se grossissant, où la situation se gâte en se prolongeant . . ."[307] The emphasis is now rather on such broad "classical" considerations than, for example, on matters of excessive detail or of digression; indeed, the latter find more apologists than ever before.[308] That Balzac's technique of characterization is excellent is still generally admitted by the critics; on this particular superiority of the novelist, there seems to be no change from one period to another.[309] Yet there is now a growing realization that his descriptive technique is itself largely a means to characterization; "les types," says Lurine, "sont en même temps des corps, des sentiments, des vêtements, des ameublements, des choses et des idées."[310] At the same time, some writers begin to accept the device of reappearing characters. A number of critics still raise the old objection of monotony;[311] but almost as many now defend the scheme for its contribution to the unity of the *Comédie humaine,* and for the opportunity it gives of developing given characters in detail.[312] With regard to description, the general attitude is practically the same as that of the preceding period: a favorable disposition towards Balzac's technique,[313] frequently compared to that of the painter[314]—especially the Flemish painter.[315] Sainte-Beuve's attitude on this point is representative:

Lorsqu'il plaçait dans un roman ces masses d'objets qui, chez d'autres, eussent ressemblé à des inventaires, c'était avec couleur et vie, c'était avec amour. Les meubles qu'il décrit ont quelque chose d'animé; les

tapisseries frémissent. Il décrit trop, mais le rayon tombe en général là
où il faut. Même lorsque le résultat ne répond pas à l'attention qu'il a'
paru y donner, il en reste au lecteur l'impression d'avoir été ému. Balzac
a le don de la couleur et des *fouillis*. Par là il a séduit les peintres, qui
reconnaissaient en lui un des leurs transplanté et un peu fourvoyé dans
la littérature.[316]

The additional comparison of his method to that of the daguerreotype
is, however, more frequent.[317]

Finally, on the subject of style, we note the most important change
in aesthetic criticism during this period: for the first time, those who
approve of Balzac's style out-number and out-argue those who disapprove. The latter bring the customary objections: confusion, affectation,
incoherence, harshness of rhythm.[318] Against them, defenders of Balzac
cite the vigor and richness of his style, its delicacy of shading, its variety,
its appropriateness to every subject, its color and novelty. Even objectors of earlier years, such as Sainte-Beuve, are now won over, and some
critics go so far as to declare Balzac one of the masters of French
prose. I quote a more moderate statement by Babou:

. . . il est expressif, coloré, plein de curieux artifices, parsemé de tours
nouveaux et de rapprochements inattendus, prolixe et concis à la fois,
également propre à l'abstraction et à l'image, vivant et remuant comme
une fourmilière, tendu jusqu'à la roideur énigmatique et parfois aussi
d'une négligence toute féminine. Enfin, pour tout exprimer en une comparaison, c'est une de ces machines modernes hérissées de pointes et
d'engrenages, formées de mille pièces qui semblent tourner en sens
contraire, lourdes et presque monstrueuses d'apparence, mais admi-
rablement construites pour la fonction qu'elles remplissent et douées
d'une énorme puissance de mouvement.[319]

Thus the favorable disposition of the critics during the years 1846-
1856 results in the rejection of the old charge of decadence, and in
placing Balzac in a position preeminent among French novelists. In
detail, this means (1) a defence of his philosophical pretentions, of the
general scheme of the *Comédie humaine,* and even of his morality;
(2) a growing admiration for his powers of observation, both physical
and psychological, and for his truthful picture of contemporary society;
(3) the belief that this analytical method was responsible for directing
the novel away from romanticism and towards realism, and that Balzac
was the founder or the head of the realistic school; (4) the contention
that his great merit was in combining the real and the ideal; (5) on the
formal side, a continued tribute to his powers of characterization and
of description, and an increased acceptance of his plots and his style.
It is to be noted however that various aspects of his work—for example,
the ugliness and the incompleteness of his world, and his defects of

composition—are still blamed by the critics, and that many other points continue to breed controversy.

1856 TO 1870

The favorable attitude towards Balzac of the years 1846-1856 continues during the subsequent period; it motivates such glowing eulogies as Taine's article of 1858, Gautier's study of the same year, and the various tributes of Baudelaire and Barbey d'Aurevilly. It results, finally, in the acceptance of Balzac as a dramatist: the revivals of *La Marâtre* and *Mercadet* are highly successful, and these plays are hailed by the critics as marking a revolution in the drama. But the unanimity of the preceding years no longer prevails, and a controversial tone now pervades the discussion. For in November, 1856, Armand de Pontmartin publishes the first of two articles which constitute the most unsparing attack on Balzac of our entire forty-year period. This violent condemnation is answered by Duranty in December; but on the same day Eugène Poitou publishes an attack which almost equals Pontmartin's in vitriolic anger. Then Barbey d'Aurevilly, on New Year's Day, 1857, responds to Poitou. And so the battle continues, with brilliant sallies by the offensive and the defensive. Several reasons may be suggested for the sudden interjection of this belligerent element into criticism of Balzac. In the first place, it arose as a natural reaction against ten years of deification of the novelist; the critics voice a protest against so much praise.[320] In the second place, it came as an answer to the publication of *Madame Bovary*. The first instalments of Flaubert's novel appeared in the *Revue de Paris* in October, 1856; Pontmartin's articles appeared in the *Correspondant* on November 25 and December 25 of the same year; the coincidence in dates is striking. Besides, while Pontmartin makes no direct allusion to *Bovary,* he emphasizes constantly the influence of Balzac on contemporary literature, and concludes with the sentence: "Il y aura toujours contre M. de Balzac une satire plus sanglante que toutes les nôtres: c'est le spectacle que nous donnent ses héritiers et ses disciples."[321] Later, when *Madame Bovary* appeared "en librairie," the critics continually regarded it as an imitation of Balzac, and many of the unfavorable statements on the latter occur in reviews of Flaubert's novel. Plainly, the anger against the new writer was expressed in a fresh attack on what the critics considered his source, the example of Balzac.

As a result of this new attack, discussion now tends to center around three problems: (1) the morality of Balzac's work; (2) the reality of his world; (3) his connection with the realistic school. Other considerations, so prominent in the earlier periods—remarks on his powers of observation, or on his style, or on his composition—now are eclipsed by these larger issues; hence I shall in a measure depart from the plan followed in preceding sections, and examine first the materials on these three points.

The new opposition based its objections very largely on the immorality of Balzac's work. It claimed that not only were the works themselves immoral, but that they had contributed to the corruption of literature and even of public morals. So bad are the works, says Pontmartin (who always applies a moral criterion to literature), that it is impossible to discuss them, even to outline their subject or to give their titles:

On se trouve en présence de personnages, de mœurs, de peintures qui souillent de leur seul contact et de leur seul voisinage les imaginations honnêtes ou timorées . . . Il y a dans Balzac des immoralités incompréhensibles pour toutes les honnêtes femmes, et pour tous les honnêtes gens qui, n'étant pas confesseurs ou juges, médecins ou critiques, ne sont pas forcés d'approfondir la casuistique du vice . . . [322]

Pontmartin, too, claims that Balzac's work is taken as a justification by the realists in their treatment of vice:

Il prouve à leur profit qu'on peut se jouer froidement de tout sentiment moral, se complaire dans tout ce qui ravale et salit la nature humaine, caresser la matière dans toutes ses suggestions fangeuses, changer le monde et le roman qui le reflète en bourbier, en égout, et le fouiller sans cesse, et en aspirer les miasmes, et s'y plonger avec délices, et qu'on peut avec tout cela être un puissant inventeur et un conteur éminent . . . [323]

As for the novelist's influence, Elme-Marie Caro speaks at length of his contributions to current sensualism, cynicism, materialism:

Dans son ensemble . . . l'œuvre de Balzac est une œuvre malsaine d'inspiration, malsaine d'influence. Balzac est, à mes yeux, le plus grand corrupteur d'imaginations qu'ait produit le demi-siècle littéraire qui s'achève à sa mort. [324]

His characters are the impersonation of all the vices; they demonstrate the triumph of force and cupidity.[325] As usual, the critics accuse him of materialism,[326] and of magnifying vice while he minimizes virtue.[327] There were, of course, a few judges who defended Balzac's morality—Gautier called him a "moraliste austère"—and who protested against this growing wave of prudery, but they were a small minority indeed.[328]

Naturally, those critics who declared Balzac's portrayal immoral were unwilling to admit that it represented the real world with any degree of fidelity. For most of them, it was too exclusively devoted to the representation of the ugly,[329] too devoid of idealism,[330] too prone to show men as worse than they really were, to be considered faithful or acceptable. For some commentators, this falsification was wilful, and hence all the more to be condemned; for example, Poitou:

Où le danger commence, c'est quand, sous prétexte de la peindre, l'écrivain fausse et défigure la nature humaine; c'est quand il la montre sous des couleurs mensongères, et, en développant des idées fausses et des sentiments outrés, altère les sentiments vrais et obscurcit les saines notions de la conscience. C'est ce qu'a fait trop souvent M. de Balzac.[331]

On the other hand, there were journalists who declared the Balzacian universe unreal by virtue of an excess of imagination, which led to an exaggeration of the good as well as the bad, and to a complete loss of perspective. Thulié, in the militant journal *Réalisme,* is one of these:

Balzac est un enthousiaste, un exagérateur; le moindre fait, le moindre bonhomme, lui font entrevoir des événements formidables, un homme plus grand que nature. Il procède par bonds, par tirades, . . . il aime les gens extravagants, il a donné dans beaucoup d'utopies, beaucoup de superstitions, il a peint plutôt un monde qu'il a dans la tête que le monde réel.[332]

For a number of writers, however, it is this very quality of imagination which makes of Balzac an important novelist. He joins, they say, the qualities of a visionary to those of an observer,[333] and hence there is in his writing a marked idealization of the real world.[334] The equitable balance of the real and the ideal in his novels confers upon them an artistic as well as a historical value. Paul de Léoni summarizes this entire attitude:

On a dit, à propos de M. Flaubert, qu'il y avait entre lui et Balzac de grandes affinités littéraires. Nous n'en voyons aucune, si ce n'est de part et d'autre une même préoccupation: la vérité, le sentiment exact du réel. Seulement Balzac voyait autrement de haut que M. Flaubert. L'exactitude des faits n'excluait chez l'auteur de la *Comédie humaine* ni les combinaisons de l'imagination ni les exigences de l'idéal.[335]

Along with these critics, of course, went always a large group of writers who insisted on the truthfulness of the Balzacian portrayal.[336]

It was the critic's estimate of Balzac's idealism which determined, usually, his opinion on Balzac as a realist. If he regarded the novelist as lacking in idealism, or even in imagination, he was apt to class him as a realist, as the head or the founder of the new school; for many saw in realism merely the converse of idealism. Poitou declares:

L'idéal est la vie, il est l'âme même de l'art. Cette âme est absente chez M. de Balzac. Et voilà pourquoi nous avons été en droit de le signaler comme un des pères légitimes, comme un des chefs de cette triste école du réalisme . . . [337]

Contrariwise, those writers—and there were many of them—who attributed to Balzac a sense of the ideal objected vigorously to his inclusion among the realists. Such objections occur, usually, in discussions of Champfleury, or of Flaubert, or of Dumas *fils,* and the writer takes pains to indicate the superiority of Balzac to these authors on the very basis of his imaginative qualities. Gautier's contention may be taken as typical:

Ce serait peut-être ici le lieu de définir la vérité telle que l'a comprise Balzac; en ce temps de réalisme il est bon de s'entendre sur ce point . . . Balzac accentue, grandit, grossit, élague, ajoute, ombre, éclaire, éloigne ou approche les hommes ou les choses selon l'effet qu'il veut produire. Il est *vrai,* sans doute, mais avec les augmentations et les sacrifices de l'*art* . . . Balzac, que l'école réaliste semble vouloir revendiquer pour maître, n'a aucun rapport de tendance avec elle . . . [338]

In fact, even such writers as Pontmartin, who called Balzac a realist, admitted that his realism was different from that of the present day—and by all odds superior.[339]

Along with the special attention accorded to these three problems of morality, reality, and realism, there were of course the usual comments on other aspects of Balzac's work, aspects aesthetic or non-aesthetic. The balance favorable to Balzac's capacities as a philosopher, noted in the preceding period, now prevails generally, with striking tributes from Taine and the Goncourts. I quote the latter:

Personne n'a dit Balzac homme d'Etat, et c'est peut-être le plus grand homme d'Etat de notre temps, le seul qui ait plongé au fond de notre malaise, le seul qui ait vu d'en haut le déséquilibrement de la France depuis 1789, les mœurs sous les lois, les faits sous les mots, l'anarchie des intérêts débridés sous l'ordre apparent, les abus remplacés par les influences, l'égalité devant la loi annihilée par l'inégalité devant le juge, enfin le mensonge de ce programme de 89 qui a remplacé le nom par la pièce de cent sous, et fait des marquis des banquiers—rien de plus. Et c'est un romancier qui s'est aperçu de cela.[340]

Concurrently, the *Comédie humaine* as a general scheme meets with the approval of the judges.[341] Among matters relevant to social depiction, it is again Balzac's observation which calls forth the loudest chorus of acclaim, to which even the most recalcitrant critics lend their voices. Poitou, for example, despite all his moral prejudices, is obliged to admit that, "Se borne-t-il à observer, à copier la nature, il est supérieur."[342] The reproach of excessive detail, so prominent in earlier opinions on Balzac and in most later views on the other realists, now appears only infrequently.[343] On his psychological analysis we find again the usual remarks concerning his "knowledge of the human heart,"[344] his attention to women,[345] and his careful, scientific method of investigation.[346] With regard to his merit as a historian of manners, the critics now continue the trend of the preceding period, a trend which gradually pointed to this as his principal contribution. "Le titre de gloire sérieux, incontestable, de M. de Balzac, c'est la peinture de mœurs," says Poitou; "là est son génie, là est son originalité."[347] Many of these commentators indicated the introduction of these materials into the novel as Balzac's chief stimulus to the development of the modern genre. Caro's judgment is typical:

L'originalité de Balzac est d'avoir entièrement changé le point de vue du roman. Il a véritablement innové dans ce genre, à ses risques et périls. Jusqu'à lui, le roman était essentiellement œuvre d'analyse et de passion. A tort ou à raison, il a voulu faire tout autre chose, le résumé complet d'une époque, l'expression de la vie moderne, si raffinée et si complexe, l'histoire des mœurs au dix-neuvième siècle.[348]

Amid all these preoccupations with the materials and the methods of the *Comédie humaine,* there was surprisingly little said about aesthetic problems. A few critics made isolated remarks on the conduct of the plot,[349] a few others reiterated the familiar censure regarding composition.[350] Against them, Gautier defended Balzac's practices:

Ces éléments nouveaux introduits dans le roman ne plurent pas tout d'abord,—les analyses philosophiques, les peintures détaillées de caractères, les descriptions d'une minutie qui semble avoir en vue l'avenir, étaient regardées comme des longueurs fâcheuses, et le plus souvent on les passait pour courir à la fable. Plus tard, on reconnut que le but de l'auteur n'était pas de tisser des intrigues plus ou moins bien ourdies, mais de peindre la société dans son ensemble . . . [351]

Several others concurred with Gautier in justifying what were once called *longueurs.*[352] With respect to character, in addition to the customary assertions of Balzac's superiority,[353] there were several statements about his use of description as a means to character portrayal. Roqueplan, for example, attests a fine understanding of Balzac's method when he describes the close relationship between personality, milieu, and external detail.[354] Even more interesting are Taine's repeated allusions to the method, especially the passage (in the article on Stendhal) in which he asserts that "La maison du père Grandet lui convient et le représente, comme une coquille son limaçon."[355] We find, on the other hand, fewer items than ever before on reappearing characters.[356] The author's power in description itself came in for the usual laudatory comments,[357] although there were rare allusions to Balzac as a painter,[358] as a "Flamand,"[359] as a photographer.[360] On style, a change from the preceding period is to be noted: the enthusiasm of those years for Balzac's diction proved to be short-lived, and adverse opinions are now predominant.[361] However, there are several tributes to Balzac's prose, most eloquent of which is Taine's:

[Les beautés de son style]. D'abord la grandeur, la richesse et la nouveauté. Ce style est un chaos gigantesque; tout y est: les arts, les sciences, les métiers, l'histoire entière, les philosophies, les religions; il n'est rien qui n'y ait fourni des mots. . . . Vous êtes choqué d'abord; puis l'habitude vient, bientôt la sympathie et le plaisir. . . . Avec l'esprit, bientôt le cœur s'émeut; sous le fourmillement tumultueux de ces idées regorgeantes on sent une chaleur qui croît. Ces expressions violentes, ces images ramassées dans l'hôpital et dans le bagne, ces accouplements d'expressions inouïes, cette ardeur du style étouffé d'idées qu'il ne peut contenir annoncent un degré de souffrance, d'effort et de génie qu'on ne trouve point ailleurs. Il lutte contre la lourdeur de sa nature et l'encombrement de sa science. . . . La poésie orientale n'a rien de plus éblouissant ni de plus magnifique; c'est un luxe et un enivrement; on nage dans un ciel de parfums et de lumière, et toutes les voluptés des jours d'été entrent dans les sens et dans le cœur, tressaillantes et bourdonnantes comme un essaim tumultueux de papillons diaprés.

Evidemment cet homme, quoi qu'on ait dit et quoi qu'il ait fait, savait sa langue; même il la savait aussi bien que personne; seulement il l'employait à sa façon.[362]

Finally, as far as Balzac's general manner is concerned, we need note only a number of statements praising the "sense of life" which he bestows upon his people, his settings, his actions—upon the whole gigantic mass of the *Comédie humaine*.[363]

If one were to desire conclusive proof of the high esteem in which Balzac was held during this final period, one would need only to turn to articles on other writers. There, one would discover that he was regularly taken as a standard of comparison for the later realists. The excellence of Flaubert, of the Goncourts, of the minor novelists, is stated in terms of their similarity to Balzac. Thus Hugo writes to Flaubert himself: "Vous avez la pénétration comme Balzac, avec le style de plus";[364] and Léon Gozlan tells the author of *Madame Bovary:* "Je n'ai jamais tant pensé à Balzac qu'en vous lisant."[365] Again, Banville thinks that the heroine of *Renée Mauperin* is worthy of Balzac,[366] and Zola remarks that "On trouve dans le livre [*Germinie Lacerteux*] un souffle de Balzac et de Flaubert; l'analyse y a la pénétrante finesse de l'auteur d'*Eugénie Grandet* . . ."[367] There are many similar expressions: Balzac, by 1870, has become a classic.

From these varied and abundant materials on Balzac, what conclusions may be drawn for the entire forty-year period? What general movement may be discerned in opinions on his work? First, on philosophical and moral questions, the trend may be described thus: in the earliest years, a general disapproval of Balzac on the score of his philosophical pretentions, of his use of non-fictional materials, of his materialistic philosophy, of his immorality. In the second period, this disapproval is still more violently stated, and with it comes the rejection of the general scheme of the *Comédie humaine*. Later, in 1846-1856, and because of a wave of enthusiasm, the balance on all these matters swings in Balzac's favor: these are the only years in which Balzac's philosophy and morality are accepted. For in the subsequent period, the reproach of immorality regains some of its earlier vigor, while the approval of Balzac's philosophical tendencies is small-voiced and occasional. Hence, on the whole, Balzac the philosopher and Balzac the moralist are never the object of sincere or lasting admiration.

Secondly, on his depiction of society, the current of opinion is approximately as follows: in 1830-1839, the attitude towards Balzac's portrayal of contemporary society is essentially sympathetic, although a less favorable trend may be discerned in the later years. This trend becomes predominant in the second period, when critics no longer admit that the Balzacian universe is true, and point rather to the various senses in which it is false. Then, in the years of glorification, Balzac's world is once again fully accepted—not only because it is true, but also because its truth includes both the real and the ideal. Furthermore, Balzac's affiliation with the realistic school and his historical importance (precisely on grounds of social depiction in the novel) are now recognized. In the final period, the charge of unreality is again a consistent cry, but now it is not always a cry of condemnation: for the very idealism and imagination which contribute to creating an impression of unreality are considered praiseworthy; at the same time, these qualities are said to differentiate Balzac from the unpopular realistic school and to constitute one element of his superiority. Hence, in general, Balzac the *peintre de mœurs* and Balzac the *historien de son temps* are the essential Balzac for critics of these years: historically and intrinsically his importance and his merit lie here.

Third, in regard to aesthetic or formal considerations, the tendency is as follows: between 1830 and 1839, critics say very little (proportionately) about the purely aesthetic aspects of Balzac's work, and what little they say is markedly unfavorable. In the second period, this is even more clearly the situation. The third period, as we might expect, produces more numerous and more sympathetic commentaries on these artistic aspects. But in the fourth period we again return to the familiar situation of infrequent and unenthusiastic statements about Balzac's merit as an artist. This general tendency to condemn does not, however, include his technique in description and characterization. For here the critics admire Balzac's observation of physical reality and of character, rather than the purely literary elements of his presentation, and their praise is based essentially on sociological grounds. Hence, in general, Balzac the artist is at all times considered inferior to Balzac the historian and even to Balzac the philosopher.

Nevertheless it will be evident from the preceding pages that the fairly consistent censure of Balzac the philosopher and Balzac the artist is overbalanced by the continued and genuine admiration for the *peintre de mœurs*. In the last analysis, then, the total evaluation of Balzac by the critics of the whole period was manifestly in his favor.

---

[1] *209*, Bernard, p. 357; cf. *205*, Anon., p. 287.   [2] *234*, Anon., p. 369.

[3] *239*, Anon.; cf. *216*, Chasles, p. 18; *217*, Anon., p. 195; *219*, Anon., p. 96.

[4] *270*, Desessarts, p. 187; cf. *296*, Juin, p. 707; *325*, Bourjot, p. 109.

[5] *266*, Anon.   [6] *276*, I. C. T.   [7] *301*, Gonzalès, pp. 243-244.

[8] Cf. *211*, N.; *210*, Pichot, p. 328; *215*, E. C., pp. 282-284; *269*, Muret, p. 34; *294*, Accarias.

[9] *216*, Chasles, pp. 43-44.   [10] *226*, Charton, p. 685.

[11] *241*, H. de V., p. 544; *243*, Anon.; *246*, Desessarts, p. 414.

[12] *259*, I. C. T.   [13] *302*, Nettement, 1st article.

[14] *301*, Gonzalès, p. 245.   [15] *256*, I. C. T.   [16] *209*, Bernard, p. 357.

[17] *212*, Anon., p. 93.   [18] *220*, Bernard, p. 358.

[19] *300*, Hains, pp. 107-108; cf. *218*, Anon.; *247*, Anon., p. 214; *298*, Legoyt, p. 349; *330*, M. B.; *339*, Girault, p. 40.

[20] *314*, Ozenne, pp. 55-57.   [21] *319*, Anon., p. 221.

[22] *237*, Saint-C., pp. 282-283.   [23] *289*, Al. de C.   [24] *306*, M. B.

[25] *314*, Ozenne, p. 53.   [26] *338*, Duquesnel, pp. 176-177.

[27] *200*, Latouche; *201*, Janin; *212*, Anon., pp. 92-93; *269*, Muret, p. 35; *271*, Al. de C., p. 23; *272*, Anon.; *274*, D., p. 88; *285*, Gonzalès, p. 70; *328*, Ozenne, p. 87; *330*, M. B.

[28] *314*, Ozenne, p. 55.   [29] *218*, Anon.

[30] *300*, Hains, p. 111; *330*, M. B., *335*, Cherbuliez, pp. 310-311; *337*, Sainte-Beuve, p. 365.

[31] *235*, Comte de C . . ., p. 43.   [32] *321*, Anon., p. 129.   [33] *268*, Janin.

[34] *312*, D'Izalguier, col. 434.

[35] Cf. *211*, N.; *213*, Deschamps, p. 320; *215*, E. C., p. 285; *223*, Anon., p. 186; *231*, Anon.; *234*, Anon., p. 368; *245*, Anon., p. 244; *247*, Anon., p. 215 n.; *250*, Anon., p. 265; *253*, A., p. 129; *254*, A. D. L.; *257*, Lecler; *274*, D., p. 88; *275*, Béranger, p. 57; *282*, Janin; *285*, Gonzalès, p. 71; *300*, Hains, p. 111; *302*, Nettement, 1st article; *317*, Fontaney, p. 506; *326*, Chasles, 1st article; *332*, Lacroix; *333*, Sainte-Beuve, p. 351; *338*, Duquesnel, p. 176.

[36] *317*, Fontaney, p. 506.   [37] *268*, Janin.   [38] *271*, Al. de C., p. 23.

[39] *252*, Mennechet, p. 178.   [40] *Ibid.*   [41] *296*, Juin, p. 710.

[42] *324*, Cherbuliez, p. 13.   [43] *280*, Muret.   [44] *256*, I. C. T.

[45] *276*, I. C. T.   [46] *302*, Nettement, 2nd article.

[47] *301*, Gonzalès, p. 244.   [48] *300*, Hains, p. 112; cf. *335*, Cherbuliez, p. 310.

[49] *204*, Anon.   [50] *210*, Pichot, p. 325.   [51] *235*, Comte de C . . ., p. 43.

[52] *332*, Lacroix.   [53] *231*, Anon.   [54] *314*, Ozenne, p. 54.

[55] *265*, Sainte-Beuve, p. 441.   [56] *237*, Saint-C., p. 282.

[57] *268*, Janin.   [58] *289*, Al. de C.

[59] *311*, Chaudes-Aigues, p. 414; *320*, Lecomte, p. 21; *338*, Duquesnel, p. 176.

[60] *323*, Anon. At a later date, Sirtema de Grovestins (cf. *534*) entitles his chapter on Balzac "L'Inventeur de la femme de trente ans."

[61] *219*, Anon., p. 96.   [62] *223*, Anon., p. 186.

[63] *231*, Anon.   [64] *271*, Al. de C., p. 23.

[65] *290*, Guinot, 2nd article; *298*, Legoyt, p. 347; *300*, Hains, pp. 105-106; *313*, Brucker; *318*, Janin; *332*, Lacroix; *341*, "De Blanzac."

[66] *235*, Comte de C., p. 43.   [67] *250*, Anon., p. 264.   [68] *254*, A. D. L., p. 48.

[69] *271*, Al. de C., p. 24.   [70] *275*, Béranger, p. 57.   [71] *314*, Ozenne, p. 55.

[72] *203*, Pichot, p. 721.   [73] *261*, Anon., p. 183.   [74] *324*, Cherbuliez, p. 14.

[75] *268*, Janin.   [76] *279*, J.   [77] *300*, Hains, pp. 105-107.

[78] *311*, Chaudes-Aigues, p. 413.   [79] *302*, Nettement, 1st article.

[80] *335*, Cherbuliez, p. 310.   [81] *231*, Anon.   [82] *253*, A., p. 129.

[83] *254*, A. D. L.   [84] *288*, Carné, pp. 394-395.

[85] *292*, "The Reviewer," pp. 51-53. The passage, written in 1835, is also interesting for its anticipation of the title, *Comédie humaine,* and for its comparison of Balzac's work to Dante's.

[86] *302*, Nettement, 3rd article, p. 240.

[87] *204*, Anon.   [88] *213*, Deschamps, p. 318.   [89] *283*, Anon., p. 63.

[90] *216*, Chasles, pp. 43-46; *221*, Buchey, p. 191; *233*, Desessarts, pp. 216-217; *269*, Muret, p. 34; *301*, Gonzalès, p. 244.

[91] *322*, Stendhal; cf. *249*, Anon., p. 256; *250*, Anon., p. 260; *251*, Desessarts, p. 455; *267*, Anon.

[92] *265*, Sainte-Beuve, p. 448; cf. *271*, Al. de C., p. 23.

[93] *278*, Anon.; *284*, Cherbuliez, p. 80.   [94] *324*, Cherbuliez, p. 13.

[95] *255*, I. C. T.   [96] *282*, Janin.   [97] *280*, Muret; *328*, Ozenne, p. 87.

[98] *250*, Anon., p. 264.   [99] *291*, Al. de C., p. 313.

[100] *302*, Nettement, 1st article; *333*, Sainte-Beuve, p. 351; cf. *213*, Deschamps, p. 316; *231*, Anon.; *288*, Carné, pp. 394-395.

[101] *220*, Bernard, p. 358.   [102] *302*, Nettement, 2nd article.

[103] *312*, D'Izalguier, p. 436.   [104] *211*, N.   [105] *210*, Pichot, pp. 326, 328.

[106] *213*, Deschamps, p. 316.   [107] *284*, Cherbuliez, p. 80.

[108] *333*, Sainte-Beuve, p. 351.   [109] *257*, Lecler, p. 114.

[110] *300*, Hains, pp. 105, 106, 107, 111.   [111] *311*, Chaudes-Aigues, p. 415.

[112] *337*, Sainte-Beuve, p. 366.   [113] *218*, Anon.   [114] *250*, Anon., p. 266.

[115] *261*, Anon., p. 183.   [116] *268*, Janin.   [117] *286*, Guéroult, p. 190.

[118] *330*, M. B.   [119] Cf. above, pp. 37-38.   [120] *312*, D'Izalguier, col. 439.

[121] *318*, Janin.   [122] *314*, Ozenne, p. 56.   [123] *276*, I. C. T.

[124] *210*, Pichot, pp. 329-330.   [125] *341*, "De Blanzac."

[126] *211*, N.; *254*, A. D. L.; *274*, D., p. 88; *278*, Anon.; *283*, Anon.; *284*, Cherbuliez, p. 81; *311*, Chaudes-Aigues, p. 412.

[127] *214*, Janin, p. 18.   [128] *216*, Chasles, p. 12.   [129] *242*, M. F., p. 235.

[130] *241*, H. de V., p. 544.   [131] *Ibid.*, p. 545.

[132] *248*, Janin, p. 14; *261*, Anon, p. 184; *282*, Janin; etc.

[133] Cf. *219*, Anon., p. 96; *217*, Anon., p. 195; *249*, Anon., p. 256; *265*, Sainte-Beuve, p. 440.

[134] *203*, Pichot, p. 721; *216*, Chasles, p. 18; *219*, Anon., p. 96; *265*, Sainte-Beuve, p. 447; cf. *298*, Legoyt, p. 347; *301*, Gonzalès, p. 244.

[135] *310*, Souvestre, p. 126; *311*, Chaudes-Aigues, p. 414.

[136] *254*, A. D. L.; *311*, Chaudes-Aigues, p. 413; *333*, Sainte-Beuve, p. 351.

[137] *236,* Anon., p. 608.   [138] *242,* M. F., p. 233.   [139] *253,* A., p. 126.

[140] *265,* Sainte-Beuve, p. 449.

[141] *282,* Janin; *284,* Cherbuliez, p. 81; *290,* Guinot, 1st article; *301,* Gonzalès, p. 244.

[142] *255,* I. C. T.   [143] *336,* Bourjot, pp. 207-208.

[144] *249,* Anon., p. 256; *258,* Anon.; *269,* Muret, p. 34.

[145] *213,* Deschamps, p. 316.   [146] *254,* A. D. L.; *258,* Anon.

[147] *292,* "The Reviewer," p. 52; cf. above, p. 45.

[148] *312,* D'Izalguier, cols. 434-435.

[149] *203,* Pichot, p. 721; *206,* Latouche; *218,* Anon.; *261,* Anon., p. 183; *264,* A., p. 266; *311,* Chaudes-Aigues, p. 414.

[150] *209,* Bernard, p. 357.   [151] *280,* Muret; cf. *269,* Muret, p. 34.

[152] *301,* Gonzalès, p. 244.   [153] *317,* Fontaney, p. 505.   [154] *334,* Pichot, p. 229.

[155] *337,* Sainte-Beuve, pp. 364-365.   [156] *203,* Pichot, p. 721.

[157] *262,* Anon., p. 200.   [158] *254,* A. D. L.   [159] *265,* Sainte-Beuve, p. 448.

[160] *282,* Janin.   [161] *302,* Nettement, 3rd article, p. 231.

[162] *326,* Chasles, 2nd article.   [163] *341,* "De Blanzac"; cf. *301,* Gonzalès, p. 244.

[164] Cf. p. 106.   [165] *245,* Anon., p. 244.

[166] *280,* Muret.   [167] *284,* Cherbuliez, p. 80.

[168] Cf. *312,* D'Izalguier, col. 439; *318,* Janin; *326,* Chasles, 1st art.; *328,* Ozenne, p. 87; *332,* Lacroix; etc.

[169] *208,* Anon., p. 130; cf. *277,* Anon, p. 395; also *301,* Gonzalès, p. 244, for a negative opinion.

[170] *283,* Anon.   [171] *298,* Legoyt, p. 347.

[172] *301,* Gonzalès, p. 244; cf. *253,* A., p. 129; *254,* A. D. L.; *300,* Hains, p. 106; etc.

[173] *213,* Deschamps, p. 320.   [174] *210,* Pichot, p. 333.

[175] *256,* I. C. T.; cf. *234,* Anon., p. 369; *262,* Anon., p. 200; *276,* I. C. T.; *277,* Anon., p. 394; *292,* "The Reviewer," p. 56; *293,* Y., p. 3; *217,* Anon., p. 195; *218,* Anon.

[176] *215,* E. C., p. 285.   [177] *316,* "L'Indépendant."

[178] *304,* Chaix d'Est-Ange, p. 50; cf. *309,* Second, p. 378; *321,* Anon., p. 129.

[179] Cf. *203,* Pichot, p. 722; *264,* A., p. 266.

[180] *224,* Anon., p. 635; cf. *230,* Anon., p. 718, and *275,* Béranger, p. 57, for a more moderate statement.

[181] *271,* Al. de C., p. 23.   [182] *328,* Ozenne, p. 88.

[183] *337,* Sainte-Beuve, p. 366; cf. *338,* Duquesnel, p. 175.

[184] *322,* Stendhal.

[185] *305,* Pichot, p. 80; cf. *311,* Chaudes-Aigues, p. 412.

[186] *292,* "The Reviewer," p. 57; *293,* Y., p. 3.

[187] Cf. *207,* R . . . n, p. 571; *305,* Pichot, p. 68; *304,* Chaix d'Est-Ange, p. 50; *308,* A. C. T., pp. 621-622; *311,* Chaudes-Aigues, p. 415; *335,* Cherbuliez, p. 311.

[188] *314,* Ozenne, p. 53; cf. *215,* E. C., p. 285; *223,* Anon., p. 186; *249,* Anon., p. 256; *270,* Desessarts, p. 187; *282,* Janin; *295,* Lassailly; *300,* Hains, p. 108; *328,* Ozenne, p. 88; *336,* Bourjot, p. 208.

[189] Cf. *250,* Anon., p. 264; *254,* A. D. L.; *267,* Anon.; *296,* Juin, p. 707; *309,* Second, p. 378; *328,* Ozenne, p. 83; *324,* Cherbuliez, p. 13.

[190] Cf. *210,* Pichot, p. 325; *230,* Anon., p. 718; *243,* Anon.; *269,* Muret, p. 34; *271,* Al. de C., p. 23; *316,* "L'Indépendant."

[191] Cf. *241,* H. de V., p. 544; *242,* M. F., p. 232; *316,* "L'Indépendant."

[192] *326,* Chasles.

[193] Cf. Bouteron, *Le Culte de Balzac* (Paris, 1924), pp. 12-13; Korwin-Piotrowska, *Balzac et le monde slave* (Paris, 1933), pp. 141-144.

[194] *465,* Sainte-Beuve.

[195] *523,* Taine.

[196] Brunetière, *Honoré de Balzac, 1799-1850* (Paris, 1906).

[197] As I have already stated (p. 34) this and the following sections on Balzac will be shorter than the first, since they merely indicate briefly the changes in the situation described.

[198] *346,* Second; *364,* Reybaud, 2nd art.; *365,* Cherbuliez, p. 143; *371,* Girault, p. 231; *374,* Ladet, p. 404; *378,* Loménie, p. 33; *399,* Molènes, p. 403; *410,* Babou, p. 53; *412,* Molènes, p. 826; *419,* Forgues; *427,* Cherbuliez, p. 329; *430,* Chasles, p. 415; etc.

[199] *347,* Reybaud; *374,* Ladet, p. 404; *399,* Molènes, p. 398; *412,* Molènes, p. 823.

[200] *422,* Limayrac, p. 809.

[201] *342,* Janin; cf. *358,* Janin; *386,* Forgues; *399,* Molènes, p. 401.

[202] *373,* Chaudes-Aigues, p. 346.

[203] *412,* Molènes, p. 823.   [204] *371,* Girault, p. 231.

[205] *342,* Janin, p. 161; *365,* Cherbuliez, p. 142; *378,* Loménie, p. 34; *390,* Anon., p. 302; *391,* Molènes, p. 144; *414,* Saint-Marc Girardin, pp. 242-244; *420,* Asseline, p. 12.

[206] *359,* Y.; *361,* Anon., p. 82; *364,* Reybaud, 2nd art.; *365,* Cherbuliez, p. 143.

[207] *380,* Molènes, pp. 979-980.

[208] *400,* Gandonnière, p. 136; cf. *357,* Sainte-Beuve, p. 482; *376,* Berthoud, p. 31; *377,* Barthélémy Lanta, col. 560; *401,* Asseline, p. 61; *404,* Molènes, p. 994; *406,* Anon., p. 429; *412,* Molènes, p. 825; *419,* Forgues; *427,* Cherbuliez, p. 329.

[209] *418,* Forgues; cf. *342,* Janin, p. 175; *354,* Chaudes-Aigues, p. 36; *362,* A—e, 3rd art.; *365,* Cherbuliez, p. 142; *390,* Anon., p. 303; *400,* Gandonnière, p. 136.

[210] Cf. *344,* Anon.; *364,* Reybaud, 2nd art.; *367,* Sainte-Beuve; *368,* Montigny, p. 171; *372,* Anon., p. 71; *375,* Nicolle; *377,* Barthélémy Lanta, col. 560; *379,* Anon.; *382,* D—y; *384,* Janin; *388,* M . . .; *398,* Anon., p. 79; *399,* Molènes, p. 401; *401,* Asseline, p. 62; *403,* Cormenin, p. 147; *406,* Anon., p. 429; *411,* Belenet, p. 324; *412,* Molènes, p. 826; *419,* Forgues; *424,* Thomas, p. 430; *426,* Gobineau, p. 18; *428,* Limayrac, p. 490; *430,* Chasles, p. 413.

[211] *417,* Fournier, p. 236; cf. *342,* Janin, p. 161; *364,* Reybaud, 2nd art.; *378,* Loménie, p. 14; *400,* Gandonnière, p. 138; *403,* Cormenin, p. 147; *415,* Ottavi, p. 455; *430,* Chasles, p. 415.

[212] *389,* AE., p. 281; *409,* Janin; *416,* Berru.

[213] *364,* Reybaud, 2nd art.; *369,* Eyma and Lucy, p. 200; *376,* Berthoud, p. 32; *422,* Limayrac, p. 808; *424,* Thomas, p. 431.

[214] *366,* Anon.; *378,* Loménie, p. 14; *400,* Gandonnière, p. 138; *418,* Forgues.

[215] *366,* Anon.; *382,* D—y; *392,* Thierry, p. 44; *403,* Cormenin, p. 148.

[216] *371,* Girault, p. 236; cf. *354,* Chaudes-Aigues, p. 25, for a negative opinion.

[217] *403,* Cormenin, p. 148; *387,* Laverdant, col. 603.

[218] *364,* Reybaud, 2nd art.; *400,* Gandonnière, p. 137; *402,* Janin; *431,* Limayrac, p. 955; etc.

[219] *391,* Molènes, p. 137; cf. *344,* Anon.; *369,* Eyma and Lucy, p. 200; *392,* Thierry, p. 45; *399,* Molènes, p. 401; *403,* Cormenin, p. 148.

[220] *344,* Anon.; *347,* Reybaud; *366,* Anon.; *375,* Nicolle; *377,* Barthélémy Lanta,

col. 562; *378*, Loménie, p. 33; *411*, Belenet, p. 324; *412*, Molènes, p. 821; *426*, Gobineau, p. 18.

[221] *403*, Cormenin, p. 147.

[222] *403*, Cormenin, p. 148; *424*, Thomas, p. 430; *430*, Chasles, p. 413.

[223] *404*, Molènes, p. 997; *419*, Forgues.

[224] *344*, Anon.; *366*, Anon.; *378*, Loménie, p. 16; *403*, Cormenin, p. 148.

[225] Cf. *419*, Forgues, for an adverse opinion.

[226] *342*, Janin, p. 159; *346*, Second; *355*, Muret.

[227] *371*, Girault, p. 240; cf. *352*, Cherbuliez, p. 310; *358*, Janin; *423*, Limayrac; *429*, Thomas, p. 609.

[228] *350*, Sainte-Beuve, p. 469; cf. *345*, Dumartin, p. 203; *364*, Reybaud, 2nd art.; *392*, Thierry, p. 42.

[229] *342*, Janin, p. 161; cf. *345*, Dumartin, p. 203; *347*, Reybaud; *352*, Cherbuliez, p. 310; *354*, Chaudes-Aigues, p. 36; *361*, Anon., p. 81; *364*, Reybaud, 2nd art.; *376*, Berthoud, p. 31; *395*, L. O.; *399*, Molènes, p. 407; *400*, Gandonnière, p. 136; *401*, Asseline, p. 62; *419*, Forgues; *429*, Thomas, p. 609.

[230] *390*, Anon., p. 302; cf. *420*, Asseline, p. 12; *422*, Limayrac, p. 808.

[231] *342*, Janin, p. 148.

[232] *373*, Chaudes-Aigues, p. 345; cf. *391*, Molènes, p. 143; *392*, Thierry, p. 42; *419*, Forgues.

[233] Cf. *355*, Muret; *360*, Lucas, p. 215; *411*, Belenet, p. 324; *429*, Thomas, p. 611.

[234] *351*, Lucas, p. 55; cf. *345*, Dumartin, p. 203; *347*, Reybaud; *357*, Sainte-Beuve, p. 482; *363*, Karr, p. 29; *369*, Eyma and Lucy, p. 206; *413*, Babou, p. 132.

[235] *366*, Anon.; *368*, Montigny, p. 173.

[236] *361*, Anon., p. 81; *381*, Merruau; *388*, M . . .; *390*, Anon., p. 303; *392*, Thierry, p. 45; *396*, F. G., p. 248; cf. *377*, Barthélémy Lanta, col. 562 and *389*, AE., for more favorable judgments.

[237] *356*, Reybaud.

[238] *392*, Thierry, p. 45; cf. *373*, Chaudes-Aigues, p. 343; *371*, Girault, p. 236; *381*, Merruau; *399*, Molènes, p. 401; *403*, Cormenin, p. 147; *424*, Thomas, p. 430; also *376*, Berthoud, p. 31, and *408*, Berru, for favorable opinions.

[239] *354*, Chaudes-Aigues, p. 33; cf. *342*, Janin, p. 147; *347*, Reybaud; *356*, Reybaud; *358*, Janin; *361*, Anon., p. 82; *364*, Reybaud, 2nd art.; *373*, Chaudes-Aigues, p. 343; *371*, Girault, p. 236; *381*, Merruau; *387*, Laverdant, col. 604; *392*, Thierry, p. 45; *395*, L. O.; *424*, Thomas, p. 431; *430*, Chasles, p. 415; also *372*, Anon., p. 68.

[240] *380*, Molènes, p. 979.

[241] *345*, Dumartin, p. 203; *364*, Reybaud, 2nd art.; *403*, Cormenin, p. 147.

[242] *371*, Girault, p. 237; *400*, Gandonnière, p. 138.

[243] *403*, Cormenin, p. 147.

[244] *378*, Loménie, p. 20; cf. *344*, Anon.; *362*, A—e; *371*, Girault, p. 233; *374*, Ladet, p. 404; *376*, Berthoud, p. 31; *398*, Anon.; *399*, Molènes, p. 403; *403*, Cormenin, p. 147; *412*, Molènes, p. 816; *416*, Berru; *419*, Forgues; *422*, Limayrac, p. 808; *424*, Thomas, p. 431; *426*, Gobineau, p. 18. Also *347*, Reybaud, and *354*, Chaudes-Aigues, p. 25, for negative opinions.

[245] *356*, Reybaud; *405*, Forest, col. 2667; *412*, Molènes, p. 823; *416*, Berru; *421*, Gobineau, p. 33.

[246] *342*, Janin, p. 148; *354*, Chaudes-Aigues, p. 25; *364*, Reybaud, 2nd art.; *373*, Chaudes-Aigues, p. 343; *402*, Janin; *403*, Cormenin, p. 149; *410*, Babou, p. 53; *412*, Molènes, p. 823; *418*, Forgues.

[247] *356,* Reybaud; *392,* A—e; *364,* Reybaud, 2nd art.; *392,* Thierry, p. 45; *396,* F. G., p. 248; *403,* Cormenin, p. 147.

[248] *391,* Molènes, p. 147; *347,* Reybaud; *376,* Berthoud, p. 31; *378,* Loménie, p. 33; *403,* Cormenin, p. 147; *410,* Babou, p. 53; *415,* Ottavi, p. 454; *424,* Thomas, p. 431; *430,* Chasles, p. 413.

[249] *372,* Anon., p. 71.

[250] *371,* Girault, pp. 246, 249. Cf. *344,* Anon.; *359,* Y.; *362,* A—e; *368,* Montigny, p. 173; *370,* Anon., p. 103; *372,* Anon., p. 68; *376,* Berthoud, p. 31; *382,* D—y; *408,* Berru; *411,* Belenet, p. 327; *416,* Berru; *419,* Forgues.

[251] *378,* Loménie, pp. 25-26; cf. *342,* Janin, p. 173; *346,* Second; *352,* Cherbuliez, p. 310; *353,* Janin, p. 191; *354,* Chaudes-Aigues, p. 34; *364,* Reybaud, 2nd art.; *369,* Eyma and Lucy, p. 205; *380,* Molènes, p. 985; *385,* La Boullaye; *386,* Forgues; *399,* Molènes, p. 401; *401,* Asseline, p. 65; *403,* Cormenin, p. 146; *404,* Molènes, p. 997; *406,* Anon., p. 429; *410,* Babou, p. 59; *412,* Molènes, p. 822; *418,* Forgues; *420,* Asseline, p. 12; *421,* Gobineau, p. 31; *422,* Limayrac, p. 808; *423,* Limayrac; *424,* Thomas, p. 431; *426,* Gobineau, p. 23; *428,* Limayrac, p. 490.

[252] *358,* Janin; *367,* Sainte-Beuve; *378,* Loménie, p. 13; *403,* Cormenin, p. 147; *421,* Gobineau, p. 31; *430,* Chasles, p. 414.

[253] *379,* Anon.; *426,* Gobineau, p. 19.

[254] *342,* Janin, p. 145; *352,* Cherbuliez, p. 310; *354,* Chaudes-Aigues, p. 25; *400,* Gandonnière, p. 136.

[255] *346,* Second; *347,* Reybaud; *357,* Sainte-Beuve, p. 482; *358,* Janin; *360,* Lucas, p. 215; *365,* Cherbuliez, p. 143; *368,* Montigny, p. 171; *374,* Ladet, p. 404; *394,* Janin; *401,* Asseline, p. 65; *406,* Anon., p. 429; *410,* Babou, p. 61; *412,* Molènes, p. 819; *420,* Asseline, p. 12; *422,* Limayrac, p. 808; *424,* Thomas, p. 430; *430,* Chasles, p. 413; *431,* Limayrac, p. 955; *432,* Anon.

[256] *371,* Girault, p. 251.

[257] *403,* Cormenin, p. 150; *377,* Barthélémy Lanta, col. 561; *425,* Asseline, p. 76; *180,* Labitte, p. 739.

[258] *453,* Roux, p. 138.   [259] *435,* Castille, p. 368; *444,* Babou, p. 108.

[260] *798,* Baudelaire; cf. *436,* Anon.; *443,* Aubert.

[261] But see below, p. 74, for my reasons for interrupting this third period in 1856.

[262] *464,* Lecomte, p. 108; cf. *463,* Aubryet; *470,* Jouvin, p. 249; *485,* Ulbach, p. 379; *119,* Ratisbonne; *708,* Lerminier, p. 613.

[263] *466,* Desnoiresterres, 2nd article.

[264] *468,* Janin; *496,* Nettement, p. 254.   [265] *433,* Achard; *445,* Lerminier, p. 166.

[266] *433,* Achard; *348,* Weill; *443,* Aubert; *459,* Janin, p. 5; *465,* Sainte-Beuve, p. 458.

[267] *453,* Roux, p. 138; *436,* Anon.; *437,* Pelletan, p. 103; *443,* Aubert; *798,* Baudelaire, p. 171; *452,* Champfleury; *478,* Anon.; *479,* Lacroix, pp. vii, ix; *480,* Baschet, p. 104; *489,* Sand, p. 199; *492,* Clément de Ris, p. 328; *820,* Goudall, p. 2; *504,* Sand, p. 137; *510,* Champfleury, p. 3.

[268] *509,* Lurine, p. 280.

[269] *438,* Weill; *445,* Lerminier, p. 165; *483,* Dufaï, p. 113; *484,* L'Hôte; *501,* Fournel, p. 186.

[270] *433,* Achard; cf. *436,* Anon.; *439,* Chavigny, p. 380; *443,* Aubert; *444,* Babou, p. 114; *455,* Rolle; *458,* Hugo, p. 192; *466,* Desnoiresterres, 2nd art.; *480,* Baschet, p. 13; *706,* Lenoir, p. 289; *490,* Castille, p. 313; *707,* Cormenin, p. 832; *498,* Forgues, p. 253. Cf. *437,* Pelletan, p. 99; *462,* Mazade, p. 914; and *497,* Pontmartin, p. 308, for the opposition.

[271] *435,* Castille, p. 362; *443,* Aubert; *444,* Babou, p. 118; *445,* Lerminier, pp. 157-158.

[272] *121,* Monselet, p. vi; *492,* Clément de Ris, p. 300.

[273] *440,* Nettement, p. 33; *441,* Sainte-Beuve, p. 341; *468,* Janin; *474,* Loisne, p. 351; *475,* Planche, p. 1136; *483,* Dufaï, p. 115; *493,* Pontmartin, p. 297; *495,* Lucas, p. 229; *496,* Nettement, p. 252; *497,* Pontmartin, p. 305; *503,* Pontmartin, p. 196; *504,* Sand, p. 295.   [274] *435,* Castille, p. 364.   [275] *443,* Aubert.

[276] *489,* Sand, p. 211; cf. *439,* Chavigny, p. 380; *479,* Lacroix, p. ix; *480,* Baschet, p. 116.

[277] *435,* Castille, p. 366; *461,* Achard; *468,* Janin; *473,* Jolly, p. 36; *484,* L'Hôte; *501,* Fournel, p. 187.

[278] *433,* Achard; *585,* Fournier, p. 258; *438,* Maron, p. 336; *439,* Chavigny, p. 380; *442,* Maron, p. 241; *443,* Aubert; *444,* Babou, p. 96; *445,* Lerminier, p. 160; *798,* Baudelaire, p. 171; *448,* Chavigny; *449,* Rolle; *450,* Janin; *451,* Pontmartin, p. 815; *453,* Roux, p. 136; *458,* Hugo, p. 192; *459,* Janin, p. 3; *460,* Chasles; *461,* Achard; *462,* Mazade, p. 914; *463,* Aubryet; *465,* Sainte-Beuve, p. 445; *469,* Lireux; *470,* Jouvin, p. 249; *472,* Lireux; *473,* Jolly, p. 36; *474,* Loisne, p. 351; *478,* Anon.; *479,* Lacroix, p. vii; *484,* L'Hôte; *485,* Ulbach, p. 379; *487,* Barbey, p. 33; *119,* Ratisbonne; *492,* Clément de Ris, p. 320; *495,* Lucas, p. 231; *496,* Nettement, p. 238; *499,* Planche, p. 558; *820,* Goudall, p. 3; *501,* Fournel, p. 187; *502,* Mazade; *505,* Cauvain; *508,* Anon.; *509,* Lurine, p. 282; *512,* Jouvin.

[279] *434,* Maron, p. 336; *483,* Dufaï, p. 115; *491,* Hippeau, col. 329; *492,* Clément de Ris, p. 332; *497,* Pontmartin, p. 310.

[280] *489,* Sand, pp. 199-200.   [281] *455,* Rolle.

[282] *466,* Desnoiresterres, 2nd art.; cf. *449,* Rolle; *453,* Roux, p. 136; *454,* Janin; *462,* Mazade, p. 914; *470,* Jouvin, p. 249; *479,* Lacroix, p. vi; *706,* Lenoir, p. 289; *491,* Hippeau, col. 329.

[283] *448,* Chavigny; *449,* Rolle; *456,* Sainte-Beuve, p. 27; *466,* Desnoiresterres, 2nd art.; *473,* Jolly, p. 36; *479,* Lacroix, p. ix; *480,* Baschet, pp. 184, 196; *492,* Clément de Ris, p. 322; *495,* Lucas, p. 229.

[284] *451,* Pontmartin, p. 812; cf. *449,* Rolle; *458,* Hugo, p. 192; *461,* Achard; *462,* Mazade, p. 914; *469,* Lireux; *472,* Lireux; *485,* Ulbach, p. 399; *486,* Lireux; *496,* Nettement, p. 249; *500,* Ulbach, p. 63. Also *483,* Dufaï, p. 115; *492,* Clément de Ris, p. 321, for negative opinions.

[285] *453,* Roux, p. 136; *464,* Lecomte, p. 108; *465,* Sainte-Beuve, p. 458; *466,* Desnoiresterres, 3rd art.; *469,* Lireux; *470,* Jouvin, p. 249; cf. *497,* Pontmartin, p. 308, for an adverse opinion.

[286] *434,* Maron, p. 337; *435,* Castille, p. 367; *445,* Lerminier, p. 160; *462,* Mazade, p. 915; *468,* Janin; *497,* Pontmartin, p. 308.

[287] *498,* Forgues, p. 253; cf. *436,* Anon.; *439,* Chavigny, p. 380; *445,* Lerminier, p. 157; *461,* Achard; *462,* Mazade, p. 914; *465,* Sainte-Beuve, p. 443; *482,* Boyer and Banville, pp. 9-11; *489,* Sand, p. 199; *505,* Cauvain; *509,* Lurine, p. 276.

[288] *437,* Pelletan, pp. 102-103; *444,* Babou, p. 115; *447,* Champfleury; *456,* Sainte-Beuve, p. 33; *463,* Aubryet; *466,* Desnoiresterres, 2nd art.; *481,* Champfleury; *483,* Dufaï, p. 115; *485,* Ulbach, p. 399; *122,* Ulbach, p. 663; *706,* Lenoir, p. 289; *490,* Castille, p. 320; *128,* Chasles, p. 526.

[289] *444,* Babou, p. 115; *492,* Clément de Ris, p. 312.

[290] *500,* Ulbach, p. 61; cf. *820,* Goudall, p. 2.

[291] *435,* Castille, p. 368.

[292] *444,* Babou, p. 119; *800,* D—yes; *469,* Lireux; *480,* Baschet, pp. 83, 90; *706,* Lenoir, p. 289; *493,* Pontmartin, p. 294; *496,* Nettement, p. 249; *820,* Goudall, p. 2.

[293] *808*, Cuvillier-Fleury; *486*, Lireux; *707*, Cormenin, p. 832; *500*, Ulbach, p. 62; *508*, Anon.; *824*, Aubryet, p. 282.

[294] *461*, Achard; *489*, Sand, p. 200; cf. *433*, Achard; *437*, Pelletan, p. 105; *439*, Chavigny, p. 380; *442*, Maron, p. 242; *443*, Aubert; *450*, Janin; *453*, Roux, p. 138; *463*, Aubryet; *464*, Lecomte, p. 108; *466*, Desnoiresterres, 2nd art.; *853*, Clément de Ris, p. 181; *469*, Lireux; *470*, Jouvin, p. 249; *475*, Planche, p. 1135; *480*, Baschet, p. 91; *486*, Lireux; *490*, Castille, p. 313; *492*, Clément de Ris, p. 332; *499*, Planche, p. 558; *500*, Ulbach, p. 61; *504*, Sand, p. 136; *505*, Cauvain.

[295] *435*, Castille, p. 368; *440*, Nettement, p. 26; *442*, Maron, p. 242; *443*, Aubert; *460*, Chasles; *492*, Clément de Ris, p. 301; *493*, Pontmartin, p. 299; *496*, Nettement, p. 250; *500*, Ulbach, p. 61; cf. *444*, Babou, p. 120, for a curious negative opinion.

[296] *476*, Cuvillier-Fleury, p. 276; *493*, Pontmartin, p. 301; *497*, Pontmartin, p. 308.

[297] *435*, Castille, p. 368; *498*, Forgues, p. 253; cf. *444*, Babou, p. 119; *460*, Chasles; *465*, Sainte-Beuve, pp. 447, 450; *468*, Janin; *492*, Clément de Ris, p. 296; *493*, Pontmartin, p. 301; *501*, Fournel, p. 187.

[298] *460*, Chasles; *466*, Desnoiresterres, 3rd art.; *493*, Pontmartin, p. 301; *509*, Lurine, p. 276.

[299] *473*, Jolly, p. 36; cf. *435*, Castille, p. 362; *442*, Maron, p. 242; *443*, Aubert; *444*, Babou, p. 111; *460*, Chasles; *468*, Janin; *479*, Lacroix, p. vi; *491*, Hippeau, col. 329; *495*, Lucas, p. 228; *499*, Planche, p. 559; *509*, Lurine, p. 276.

[300] *461*, Achard; cf. *466*, Desnoiresterres, 2nd art.; *470*, Jouvin, p. 249; *480*, Baschet, p. 116.

[301] *434*, Maron, p. 336; *445*, Lerminier, p. 166; *449*, Rolle; *455*, Rolle; *456*, Sainte-Beuve, p. 33.

[302] *462*, Mazade, p. 915; cf. *442*, Maron, p. 241; *443*, Aubert; *477*, Sand, p. 2.

[303] *500*, Ulbach, p. 62; cf. *443*, Aubert; *444*, Babou, p. 101; *458*, Hugo, p. 192; *460*, Chasles; *461*, Achard; *469*, Lireux; *471*, Janin; *808*, Cuvillier-Fleury; *485*, Ulbach, p. 399; *122*, Ulbach, p. 663; *489*, Sand, p. 201; *707*, Cormenin, p. 832; *509*, Lurine, p. 277.

[304] *435*, Castille, p. 367; *449*, Rolle; *451*, Pontmartin, p. 813; *465*, Sainte-Beuve, p. 456; *492*, Clément de Ris, pp. 297, 332.

[305] *434*, Maron, p. 337; *443*, Aubert; *444*, Babou, p. 100; *445*, Lerminier, p. 160; *466*, Desnoiresterres, 2nd art.; *469*, Lireux; *509*, Lurine, p. 276.

[306] *492*, Clément de Ris, pp. 312-313; cf. *435*, Castille, p. 367; *469*, Lireux; also *451*, Pontmartin, p. 814.

[307] *493*, Pontmartin, p. 301; cf. *451*, Pontmartin, p. 815; *475*, Planche, p. 1135; *489*, Sand, p. 212; *494*, Delacroix, p. 255; *498*, Forgues, p. 253; and *444*, Babou, p. 100, for a defence of Balzac.

[308] *466*, Desnoiresterres, 2nd art.; *489*, Sand, p. 199; *498*, Forgues, p. 253.

[309] *434*, Maron, p. 337; *435*, Castille, p. 363; *438*, Weill; *439*, Chavigny, p. 380; *443*, Aubert; *444*, Babou, p. 102; *445*, Lerminier, p. 161; *454*, Janin; *455*, Rolle; *463*, Aubryet; *465*, Sainte-Beuve, p. 456; *466*, Desnoiresterres, 2nd art.; *474*, Loisne, p. 351; *480*, Baschet, p. 198; *492*, Clément de Ris, p. 332; *123*, Sainte-Beuve, p. 337; *493*, Pontmartin, p. 300; *495*, Lucas, p. 231; *509*, Lurine, p. 277; *512*, Jouvin.

[310] *509*, Lurine, p. 277; cf. *479*, Lacroix, p. x; *480*, Baschet, p. 90.

[311] *434*, Maron, p. 336; *437*, Pelletan, p. 99; *441*, Sainte-Beuve, p. 337 n.; *445*, Lerminier, p. 160; *462*, Mazade, p. 914; *497*, Pontmartin, p. 307.

[312] *433*, Achard; *436*, Anon.; *464*, Lecomte, p. 107; *480*, Baschet, p. 88; *489*, Sand, p. 213.

[313] *435*, Castille, p. 367; *445*, Lerminier, p. 161; *466*, Desnoiresterres, 2nd art.; *480*, Baschet, p. 215; *493*, Pontmartin, p. 300; *495*, Lucas, p. 231. Also *483*, Dufaï, p. 115; *491*, Hippeau, col. 329, for adverse criticism.

[314] *435*, Castille, p. 368; *473*, Jolly, p. 36; *474*, Loisne, p. 351; *480*, Baschet, p. 198; *496*, Nettement, p. 253.

[315] *445*, Lerminier, p. 161; *480*, Baschet, p. 93; *492*, Clément de Ris, p. 320; *496*, Nettement, p. 249.

[316] *465*, Sainte-Beuve, p. 455.

[317] *435*, Castille, p. 367; *453*, Roux, p. 136; *470*, Jouvin, p. 249; *512*, Jouvin.

[318] *433*, Achard; *442*, Maron, p. 241; *461*, Achard; *483*, Dufaï, p. 115; *489*, Sand, p. 212; *492*, Clément de Ris, p. 297; *493*, Pontmartin, p. 302; *498*, Forgues, p. 253; *499*, Planche, pp. 558-559.

[319] *444*, Babou, p. 104; cf. *437*, Pelletan, p. 107; *443*, Aubert; *453*, Roux, p. 136; *463*, Aubryet; *464*, Lecomte, p. 108; *465*, Sainte-Beuve, pp. 449, 456-457; *478*, Anon.; *479*, Lacroix, p. x; *480*, Baschet, pp. 77, 171; *495*, Lucas, p. 231; *509*, Lurine, p. 277.

[320] Cf. *514*, Pontmartin, p. 32; *516*, Poitou, p. 713; *532*, Caro, p. 6; *537*, Mouy, p. 318; *547*, Vapereau, p. 235.

[321] *514*, Pontmartin, p. 103.

[322] *Ibid.*, p. 36.

[323] *514*, Pontmartin, p. 33.

[324] *532*, Caro, pp. 260-267.

[325] Cf. *516*, Poitou, pp. 717, 733; *519*, Aubineau; *522*, Poitou, pp. 20, 114-115; *523*, Taine, p. 81; *528*, Ancelot; *534*, Sirtema de Grovestins, p. 101; *537*, Mouy, p. 318; *538*, Geoghegan, pp. 489-491; *544*, Delaborde; *119*, Nettement, p. 118; *556*, Ampère; *562*, Pontmartin, p. 82; *564*, Lucas.

[326] *514*, Pontmartin, p. 33; *516*, Poitou, p. 726; *522*, Poitou, p. 56; *523*, Taine, p. 90; *538*, Geoghegan, p. 490.

[327] Cf. *523*, Taine, p. 82; *535*, Anon., p. 194; *537*, Mouy, p. 319; *538*, Geoghegan, p. 490; *554*, Desraimes, p. 4.

[328] *524*, Gautier, p. 175; *526*, Babou, p. 244; *550*, Dollfus, p. 182; *555*, Luzarche; *563*, Boulé, p. 389.

[329] *514*, Pontmartin, p. 40; *516*, Poitou, p. 746; *522*, Poitou, p. 189; *523*, Taine, p. 49; *532*, Caro, p. 227; *537*, Mouy, p. 318.

[330] *514*, Pontmartin, p. 53; *522*, Poitou, p. 180; *523*, Taine, p. 49; *542*, Avond, p. 326.

[331] *516*, Poitou, p. 732; *523*, Taine, p. 61; *542*, Avond, p. 326; *554*, Desraimes, p. 4.

[332] *827*, Thulié, p. 56; cf. *514*, Pontmartin, pp. 40, 58; *516*, Poitou, pp. 723, 750; *521*, Sarcey, p. 2; *532*, Caro, pp. 253-256; *534*, Sirtema de Grovestins, p. 104; *539*, Sainte-Beuve; *545*, Sainte-Beuve, p. 161; *549*, Sainte-Beuve, p. 110.

[333] *524*, Gautier, p. 38; *528a*, Baudelaire, p. 168; *548*, Barbey d'Aurevilly, p. 6; *974*, Pontmartin, p. 66; *557*, Roqueplan; *562*, Pontmartin, p. 76.

[334] *579*, Desdemaines, p. 4; *519*, Aubineau; *829*, Révillon; *526*, Babou, pp. 237, 242.

[335] *927*, Léoni; cf. *515*, Duranty, p. 29; *578*, Aubryet, p. 242; *519*, Aubineau; *524*, Gautier, p. 140.

[336] *523*, Taine, p. 50; *530*, Sarcey, p. 187; *532*, Caro, p. 228; *536*, Delacroix, p. 304; *553*, Gastineau, p. 122; *555*, Luzarche; *565*, Cuvillier-Fleury.

[337] *516*, Poitou, p. 761; cf. *514*, Pontmartin, pp. 33, 40, 41 and *passim;* *530*, Sarcey, p. 193; *532*, Caro, p. 6; *538*, Geoghegan, p. 489; *553*, Gastineau, p. 125; *563*, Boulé, p. 388.

[338] *524,* Gautier, pp. 140, 142; cf. *515,* Duranty, p. 29; *519,* Aubineau; *886,* Weiss, p. 145; *829,* Révillon; *526,* Babou, p. 237; *554,* Desraimes, p. 4; *974,* Pontmartin, p. 66; *926,* Levallois; *927,* Léoni.

[339] Cf. *514,* Pontmartin, p. 63.

[340] *520,* Goncourt; cf. *523,* Taine, pp. 21-24; *542,* Avond, p. 326; *548,* Barbey d'Aurevilly, p. 16; *557,* Roqueplan; *563,* Boulé, p. 382. Also *516,* Poitou, p. 720; *827,* Thulié, p. 56; *532,* Caro, p. 30; *553,* Gastineau, p. 127, for unfavorable opinions.

[341] *523,* Taine, p. 24; *548,* Barbey, p. 16; *565,* Cuvillier-Fleury. Aubineau, *519,* disapproves.

[342] *516,* Poitou, p. 744; cf. *514,* Pontmartin, p. 63; *882,* Barbey, p. 62; *521,* Sarcey, p. 2; *529,* Fiorentino; *532,* Caro, p. 225; *524,* Gautier, p. 38; *535,* Anon., p. 192; *537,* Mouy, p. 317; *904,* Scherer; *119,* Nettement, p. 118; *548,* Barbey, p. 7; *552,* Reynald, p. 629; *557,* Roqueplan; *562,* Pontmartin, p. 76; *564,* Lucas.

[343] *519,* Aubineau; *525,* Delacroix; *535,* Anon., p. 195. Jouvin, *531,* p. 2, defends Balzac.

[344] *528,* Ancelot; *529,* Fiorentino; *542,* Avond, p. 327; *552,* Reynald, p. 629.

[345] *523,* Taine, pp. 55-57; *532,* Caro, p. 249; *553,* Gastineau, p. 124.

[346] *518,* Mazade, p. 218; *522,* Poitou, pp. 19, 114; *523,* Taine, pp. 16, 27; *524,* Gautier, p. 38; *533,* Gautier; *538,* Geoghegan, pp. 489-490.

[347] *516,* Poitou, p. 744; cf. *878,* Donis, p. 77; *524,* Gautier, p. 70; *529,* Fiorentino; *530,* Sarcey, p. 187; *531,* Jouvin, p. 2; *532,* Caro, p. 32; *533,* Gautier; *541,* Mazade, p. 243; *545,* Sainte-Beuve, p. 161; *546,* Roqueplan; *548,* Barbey d'Aurevilly, p. 10; *563,* Boulé, p. 382; *565,* Cuvillier-Fleury.

[348] *532,* Caro, p. 32; cf. *878,* Donis, p. 77; *886,* Weiss, p. 145; *528a,* Baudelaire, p. 176; *974,* Pontmartin, p. 66; *560,* Féval, p. 50; *566,* Scherer, pp. 68-73.

[349] *516,* Poitou, p. 719; *842,* Dusolier, p. 31; *566,* Scherer, p. 68.

[350] *514,* Pontmartin, p. 88; *516,* Poitou, p. 748; *532,* Caro, p. 251; *538,* Geoghegan, p. 489.

[351] *524,* Gautier, pp. 69-70.

[352] *523,* Taine, p. 20; *531,* Jouvin, p. 2; *551,* Lamartine, p. 356; *563,* Boulé, p. 388.

[353] *521,* Sarcey, p. 2; *523,* Taine, pp. 10, 20; *524,* Gautier, p. 39; *528a,* Baudelaire, p. 168; *531,* Jouvin, p. 2; *533,* Gautier.

[354] *557,* Roqueplan; cf. *523,* Taine, p. 20; *551,* Lamartine, p. 356.

[355] *136,* Taine, p. 197.

[356] *514,* Pontmartin, p. 88, disapproves; *523,* Taine, p. 24, approves.

[357] *516,* Poitou, p. 744; *523,* Taine, p. 16; *531,* Jouvin, p. 2; *904,* Scherer; *566,* Scherer, p. 69.

[358] *516,* Poitou, p. 745; *523,* Taine, p. 45.

[359] *521,* Sarcey, p. 2; *526,* Babou, p. 237.

[360] *534,* Sirtema de Grovestins, p. 103; *553,* Gastineau, p. 127.

[361] *514,* Pontmartin, p. 48; *516,* Poitou, p. 758; *532,* Caro, p. 256; *535,* Anon., p. 193; *542,* Avond, p. 326; *544,* Delaborde; *136,* Taine, p. 214; *566,* Scherer, p. 73.

[362] *523,* Taine, pp. 43-48; cf. *524,* Gautier, p. 135; *526,* Babou, p. 244; *527,* Goncourt.

[363] *516,* Poitou, p. 744; *524,* Gautier, p. 39; *528a,* Baudelaire, p. 168; *532,* Caro, p. 227; *533,* Gautier; *566,* Scherer, p. 73.

[364] *934,* Hugo.   [365] *868,* Gozlan, p. 313.   [366] *995,* Banville, p. 187.

[367] *1008,* Zola, p. 82.

CHAPTER III

MONNIER, CHARLES DE BERNARD

Chronologies
[Henri Monnier]
1830: *Scènes populaires*
1831: *Recréations*
1841: *Scènes de la ville et de la campagne*
1849: *Les Compatriotes*
1852: *La Grandeur et la décadence de M. Prudhomme*
1857: *Mémoires de Joseph Prudhomme*

[Charles de Bernard]
1838: *Le Nœud gordien*
       Gerfaut
1843: *Un Homme sérieux*
1855: *Œuvres complètes*

BOTH Henri Monnier and Charles de Bernard are writers of minor importance. But since both were connected with the realistic movement—Monnier as writer and actor, Charles de Bernard as an imitator of Balzac—it will be profitable to examine the critical reaction towards them. The statements that follow are based on representative rather than complete materials for the periods indicated.

Henri Monnier occupied public attention spasmodically for thirty years. From the very first he distinguished himself as one who studied individually the various social classes, particularly the people. In 1830, *Figaro* indicated this new tendency (giving examples from the romantics), and pointed out the danger of portraying the evil to the exclusion of the good; this the contributor believed Monnier to have done.[1] Still more interesting is a statement by L. B. in *L'Artiste* (1831) to the effect that "les mœurs comme les plantes ont leurs espèces et leurs variétés."[2] He proceeds to show how Monnier analyses these various species, and compliments him on the truth, the exactness, and the impersonality of his depiction. For practically every subsequent critic, it is this quality of truth, of reality, that is the characteristic trait of Monnier's talent. Cherbuliez, in 1838, states that Monnier's ability to "prendre la nature sur le fait" is superior to that of Balzac.[3] Balzac himself, in 1840, classes Monnier in the "Littérature des Idées" because of the "vrai de ses proverbes, . . . pleins de ce naturel et de cette stricte observa-

tion qui est un des caractères de l'école."[4] This reality is largely a product
of the use of much exact detail, of "ces moindres détails de nuances
fugitives qui échappent si facilement même aux observateurs les plus
attentifs."[5] It springs ultimately from a genius for observation.[6] In
Henri Monnier these capacities are coupled with a rare talent for the
depiction of character, which attains its zenith in the stage creation of
Joseph Prudhomme.[7] Finally, he has a superior gift for humor and
irony, and his people and situations are informed with real wit and
gayety.[8] It is perhaps this quality of humor that accounts for the toler-
ance of practices in Monnier which were violently opposed in other
artists, and for the moderation in the reproaches brought against his
work. These reproaches we may now examine.

They are, in miniature, the objections we have already seen in the
study of Balzac and of Stendhal, and which we shall see constantly in
the criticism of realism. First, the subject-matter, restricted to a middle-
class or popular reality, is doomed to be uninteresting. Cherbuliez, whose
articles are generally typical of current opinion, states this vehemently:

. . . le choix des sujets n'est pas heureux. L'originalité des personnages
n'est point assez marquée pour exciter beaucoup d'attention . . . Ce sont
des scènes auxquelles on assisterait volontiers un instant, mais qui
fatiguent bientôt par la monotonie d'un dialogue plein de naturel, sans
doute, mais d'un naturel très-plat, sans saillie ni esprit. . . . Cela ne nuit
point à la scrupuleuse exactitude de ses tableaux, qui reproduisent la
société avec une fidélité bien rare; mais on aimerait mieux qu'il eût
choisi des modèles plus attrayants.[9]

Secondly, and as the writer in *Figaro* had already intimated, Monnier
tended to select only the disagreeable aspects of this reality, to paint
the evil and the ugly; hence some critics charged him with a positive
misanthropy.[10] In literary terms, this meant producing caricatures
rather than faithful portraits of people.[11] Thirdly—and this was by
far the most serious stricture—the reality represented was exclusively
an external reality; Monnier reproduced the shell, he had no understanding of the being within. His was a process of photography, of
stenography, of facsimile. Aubryet sees this as Monnier's principal
vice, as the great obstacle between him and greatness: "A quelques
vigueurs près, qui sentent la main du peintre, c'est la fidélité goguenarde
du procédé Daguerre appliquée à la reproduction du ridicule ou de l'o-
dieux."[12] For Gautier, too, this strict adherence to reality is Monnier's
prime weakness:

Henri Monnier ne choisit pas, n'atténue pas, n'exagère pas et ne fait
aucun sacrifice; il se gardera d'augmenter l'intensité des ombres pour
faire valoir les jours. . . . Ce n'est plus de la comédie, c'est de la
sténographie.[13]

This, in the last analysis, is not art; for art must use nature only as a means, not as an end; it must make a choice among the objects of imitation; it must give some freedom to the fantasy of the artist.[14]

The criticism of Charles de Bernard was never controversial. In general, the critics were inclined to accept his work as adequate; but he aroused no great enthusiasm, nor (with one exception) any great antagonism. For us, he is interesting because he was regarded as an imitator of Balzac and as representing an attenuation of the master's tendencies. Essentially, the imitation consisted in applying the method of observation and analysis to the study of manners. The critics recognized that Bernard was both delicate and subtle. "L'observation y est parfaite dans sa finesse et sa subtilité," said Girault de Saint-Fargeau.[15] Lamarque spoke of it as "une rare finesse d'aperçus, une richesse inépuisable d'observation, une faculté brillante d'analyse."[16] This faculty he applied only to one branch of society, the polite world of the aristocracy, and in the study of this world he was expert. Louis Alloury testifies to this expertness:

... il se plaît à retracer les mœurs élégantes, raffinées et compassées du monde à la mode. M. de Bernard connaît à fond ce monde-là; il en a savamment étudié le langage, les goûts, les habitudes, les caprices, les petites passions, les petits vices, les petits ridicules. On sent bien que les grands traits, la profondeur, l'énergie des passions et des caractères ne sont point ici de mise; ces choses-là ne sont pas du bel air; tout cela choque l'élégance et le bon ton. C'est un monde à part où tout est bien, quand tout y est *charmant.*[17]

In the presentation of these materials Bernard is credited with a gracefully appropriate style, a talent for well-constructed plot and clearly defined character, a lightness of touch and of wit entirely in keeping with his subject-matter.[18] His weaknesses are a failure to derive conclusions from his social studies, a proneness to avoid the poetic, to observe external details rather than the passions.[19]

In spite of his conscious imitation of Balzac, Bernard never attained the vigor of his model. For one critic, Babou, this was an advantage. In an article remarkable for its theory of the analytical novel,[20] Babou pointed out that Balzac went much too far in the application of his method, that he accumulated too much detail, that he drifted imperceptibly into the realm of the fantastic. Bernard, more logically minded, avoided these various pitfalls and hence gave an example, in *Un Homme sérieux,* of the analytical novel at its best.[21] For other critics, however, this attenuation of Balzac's method was merely a sign of Bernard's inferiority. Thus for Forgues the novels of Bernard are merely Balzacian works "arrangés en vaudevilles de Scribe."[22] But the most devastating criticism of this type comes from Marc Fournier. Wittily and ironically, he describes Bernard's method of copying. Bernard, at the outset, made the discovery that Balzac's unique virtue was that of patience. Then:

Il se mit en train d'écrire, lui aussi, sa comédie humaine, et plus il avança, plus il s'émerveilla qu'on eût tant crié au miracle à propos des livres de M. de Balzac. En effet, quoi de plus facile à faire qu'un portrait fidèle et minutieux de la société? La société est là, devant vous, sous vos yeux; il ne faut que la regarder avec un peu d'attention, et y savoir mettre le temps. Tout le mystère se réduit à rendre ce que vous voyez.

Pour ce qui est de la forme et du langage, M. de Bernard pense que le meilleur style est celui qui exprime exactement ce qu'on veut dire. . . . M. de Bernard a eu beau chercher, il n'a rien trouvé dans le monde qui méritât d'être dit en un style très particulier. . . . c'est en vain que M. de Bernard a écarquillé les yeux, il n'a rien aperçu parmi les hommes que de très naturel et de parfaitement défini.

Fournier continues in this tone, showing that Bernard practices observation only in the most superficial sense. Thus he misses all that is great in man and in society, he eliminates all that is striking and superior in his model. In a word, "M. de Bernard, c'est Balzac mis à la portée de tout le monde."[23]

---

[1] 567, Anon.

[2] 570, L. B., p. 43.

[3] 335, Cherbuliez, p. 311.

[4] 104, Balzac, p. 276; cf. 571, Cherbuliez, p. 334; 572, Nicolle; 574, Eyma; 575, Janin; 576, Dufaï, p. 368; 577, Gautier; 579, Desdemaines, p. 6.

[5] 571, Cherbuliez, p. 334; cf. 570, L. B., p. 44; 574, Eyma.

[6] 104, Balzac, p. 276; 571, Cherbuliez, p. 334; 572, Nicolle; 574, Eyma; 575, Janin.

[7] 576, Dufaï, p. 368; cf. 571, Cherbuliez, p. 334; 574, Eyma.

[8] 567, Anon.; 568, Anon.; 569, Balzac, p. 139; 574, Eyma.

[9] 571, Cherbuliez, pp. 334-335.

[10] 568, Anon.; 569, Balzac, p. 139; 578, Aubryet, p. 241; 579, Desdemaines, p. 4.

[11] 567, Anon.; 576, Dufaï, p. 368.

[12] 578, Aubryet, p. 241.

[13] 577, Gautier; cf. 572, Nicolle; 403, Cormenin, p. 147; 575, Janin; 576, Dufaï, p. 368; 579, Desdemaines, p. 6.

[14] Gautier, loc. cit.; 403, Cormenin, p. 147; 578, Aubryet, p. 242.

[15] 583, Girault de Saint-Fargeau, p. 63.

[16] 584, Lamarque, p. 134.

[17] 582, Alloury.

[18] Cf. 582, Alloury; 583, Saint-Fargeau, p. 64; 584, Lamarque, p. 134; 708, Lerminier, p. 615.

[19] Cf. 580, C., p. 422; 321, Anon., p. 129.

[20] See below, pp. 119-120.

[21] 413, Babou, p. 132.

[22] 586, Forgues, p. 254.

[23] 585, Fournier, pp. 257-258.

TOWARDS REALISM

CHAPTER IV

CRITICISM OF REALISTIC PAINTING (1840-1860)

THE intimate relationship between realism in painting and realism in literature has long been recognized. The best-known example, especially of the influence of painting upon literature, has been the friendship of Courbet and Champfleury; this "amitié à la d'Arthez" and its fruits for the theory and practice of realism have been treated in detail by Bouvier.[1] But additional cases might be cited: for instance, the fact that the first article in the short-lived *Réalisme* was devoted, by its editor Duranty, to painting. Again, and more strikingly, a large number of the critics who wrote articles on realism in literature also wrote *salons* or commentaries on realism in painting. Baudelaire, Gautier, Zola, the Concourts, Clément de Ris, Planche, Houssaye, Champfleury, Enault, About, Duranty—to cite only a few—comprise an imposing list of critics of both forms. It is evident that, if we are to have a complete picture of the criticism of realism, we must include expressions of opinion on painting. Besides, as the following pages will show, realism was recognized as a "school" first in painting, and many of the objections later offered to realism in literature were first formulated with respect to realistic paintings.

I do not propose here to repeat the work done by Bouvier in the statement of the formation of realistic doctrine, and of the importance of the movement in painting as an influence on Champfleury and his group. I propose rather to indicate how the art-critics defined realism, what elements they conceived of as comprising the realistic doctrine, what objections they raised to that doctrine, how it conformed or failed to conform to their concept of art. As in other chapters, the approach is here entirely from the point of view of the critics of the period. I might say at the outset that the critical judgments were almost entirely adverse; and yet our conclusions must be based on these adverse judgments, for we find practically no formulations of a theory of realistic painting, and indeed very few defences of its practice. In a sense, then, we must turn to a single group of unfavorable articles for arguments on both the affirmative and the negative side of realism in painting.[2]

How, we may begin by asking, did successive critics *define* realism? Or, when they did not give a definition of the thing itself, how did they describe manifestations of it in one artist or another? To what was it

97

said to be equivalent? To what opposed? The following schedule will answer these questions. It contains, in chronological order, a number of definitions and descriptions of the new pictorial manner, extracted from articles of the years 1840 to 1860. The numbers in italics denote the articles as they are given in the Bibliography; an asterisk is used to indicate a few statements in which the word *réalisme* or *réaliste* is not used.

[1841]

588. Gautier: "l'imitation exacte de la nature telle qu'elle est."*

[1844]

595. Thoré: "La théorie de l'imitation de la nature."

[1846]

602. Houssaye: "la nature elle-même telle qu'elle est, sans mensonge et sans ornements." "reproduire la créature telle que Dieu l'a faite." "la nature elle-même." [*Réalisme* used interchangeably with *naturalisme.*] (pp. 162, 203)
604. Leboucher: [*école réaliste;* no definition.]
605. Guillot: "ceux qui, ne la sentant pas [i.e., la nature], ne sauraient la comprendre." [*réalistes* opposed to *idéalistes.*] (pp. 427-428)

[1847]

607. Calemard de Lafayette: "un réalisme essentiellement anti-poétique."
608. Vaines: "les *réalistes* (pardon du barbarisme) . . . méprisent toutes . . . les recherches de l'élégance." "Ce qu'ils aiment . . . c'est la rude et pauvre nature des champs et des montagnes." "plaisir de copier." (p. 255)
447. Champfleury: [uses *réalisme* to describe Spanish painting, without defining the term.] (p. 18)

[1848]

611. "Feu Diderot": "la vérité." "le triomphe de la nature." (p. 98)

[1849]

613. Lagenevais: "un sentiment des harmonies du monde physique." "une expression grossière, . . . une sorte de protestation brutale contre les anciennes traditions." [*réalisme, réaliste* used as equivalent to *matérialisme, naturaliste;* opposed to *rêverie, idéalisme.*] (p. 561)

[1850]

614. Champfleury: "le *réalisme dans l'art*" [without definition].

[1851]

615. Delécluze: "le naturel brut que l'on obtient . . . en prenant la nature sur le fait, et en la reproduisant telle qu'on l'a saisie."*
616. Peisse: "ce principe très faux: que l'art n'est que l'imitation de la nature."
617. Clément de Ris: "l'école réaliste." "le grand mérite de voir et de rendre la nature telle qu'elle est, par son côté plutôt vigoureux que séduisant, laissant à la poésie le soin de se dégager toute seule." (pp. 5-6)
619. Geofroy: "L'art, étant fait pour tout le monde doit représenter ce que tout le monde voit; la seule qualité à lui demander, c'est une parfaite exactitude." "la reproduction fidèle de l'objet le premier passant."* (pp. 928, 930)
622. Bonnassieux: "l'imitation stricte et exclusive de la réalité."* (p. 17)
623. Clément de Ris: "coloristes: ceux qui se préoccupent principalement d'étudier et de rendre la nature, la vie, le mouvement, la vérité, et qui laissent sur le second plan le style et la convention."* [coloristes used frequently by him and others, as equivalent to réalistes.]

[1852]

627. Peisse: "la nature prise sur le fait."
628. Planche: "école réaliste." "réalisme." [without definition.] (p. 672)
630. M. du Camp: "[reproduire] la nature telle qu'elle est." (p. 83)
632. Boyer and Banville: [représenter] la nature elle-même." "Faire vrai, ce n'est rien pour être réaliste:/C'est faire laid qu'il faut!" "vérité dans l'art." (pp. 14, 15)

[1853]

635. Clément de Ris: [Courbet called a coloriste, not a réaliste.]
636. Gautier: [réalisme opposed to fantaisie.]
637. Mazade: "le réalisme dans l'art" [without definition.]
638. Viel Castel: "la nouvelle école du laid."* (p. 535)
639. Delaborde: "la reproduction formelle de la réalité." [réaliste opposed to fantaisie.] (p. 1143)
640. Du Pays: "l'école du laid."* (p. 392)
642. Calonne: "reproduction matérielle de la nature." "copies serviles." "simples traductions." [école réaliste used as equivalent to école naturaliste.] (pp. 131-134)
643. Peisse: "l'art n'est que l'imitation de la nature ... Ce qu'on appelle le Réalisme n'est pas autre chose que ce principe, entendu dans son sens le plus grossier et le plus matériel." "imiter exactement la nature." "il ne voit dans les choses que leurs qualités et propriétés matérielles; il paraît ne tenir compte, dans le représentation qu'il en fait, que de leur composition physique. . . . Donner à chaque chose son caractère propre et spécifique comme matière est pour lui le but essentiel, et quand il y est

parvenu il croit avoir fait tout ce que peut et doit faire l'art."
[*réaliste* used as equivalent to *naturaliste*, and as opposed to
spiritualisme.]

644. Clément de Ris: "adeptes fervents de la couleur." "étude consciencieuse, . . . investigation attentive de la nature." "Ils traduisent fidèlement, mais servilement." "Amants soumis de la
nature." [Note that Clément de Ris, who has hitherto used
coloriste, now uses *réaliste*.] (p. 6)

[1854]

646. L'Hôte: "représentation commune et simple de la nature." "Tout
ce que l'homme calque ou copie est d'un réalisme triste, plat,
désespérant, souvent horrible à force d'être vrai." "la nature
prise sur le fait." [*réalisme* opposed to *idéalisme, fantaisie,
imagination*.] (pp. 184, 185)

[1855]

648. Mantz: [French *réalistes* comparable in tendency to English *préraphaélites*.] (p. 125)

649. Champfleury: "Tous ceux qui apportent quelques aspirations
nouvelles sont dits *réalistes*." "[observer et décrire] avec exactitude les mœurs de son époque." (p. 2)

650. Deleutre: "l'art n'est pas autre chose que la reproduction sincère
de la nature; il n'admet pas le choix dans l'art." "faire laid,
faire trivial."

651. Dubosc de Pesquidoux: "[ils] se moquent et rient de l'idéal, et
n'adorent que la réalité." "le culte effréné et absolu de la
matière."

652. Perrier: "l'expression sincère de la nature." "observation vulgaire." "interprétation exacte de la nature." "la nature se suffit
à elle-même." "la reproduction matérielle des objets." [*réalisme*
opposed to *idéal, poésie*.] (pp. 85, 86)

653. Dubosc de Pesquidoux: "l'imitation littérale de la nature. L'intelligence, la comparaison, le choix, tout ce qui constitue l'art,
enfin, sont proscrits." "la reproduction servile de ce qu'il voit
chaque jour." "système de l'imitation pure." "Le réalisme, c'est
l'idéal de la laideur."

654. About: "rendre la nature telle qu'elle est, sans l'embellir, mais
sans la rendre laide ou grotesque." (p. 207)

[1856]

656. Ratisbonne: "l'art est l'imitation de la nature." "reproduction
exacte et triviale de la nature."

[1857]

664. M. du Camp: "voir l'humanité telle qu'elle est, avec ses qualités
et ses vices, et l'interpréter sincèrement, sans réminiscence de
ceux qui ont vu autrement et sans travail retrospectif."* (pp.
161-162)

665. Gautier: "l'étude consciencieuse de la nature." (p. 36)
666. Perrier: [*réalisme* equivalent to *naturalisme.*]

[1858]

667. Clément de Ris: "une religion pittoresque nouvelle." "représentation scrupuleuse des objets extérieurs." "le contraire de l'idéal, . . . le choix et la reproduction des vulgarités ou des laideurs de la nature." [compares English *préraphaélites.*] (p. 118)
668. Delaborde: [compares French *réalistes* to English *préraphaélites.*]
669. About: "saisit la nature, non par les côtés les plus intimes, mais par les plus apparents." (p. 144)

[1859]

672. Cantrel: [*naturalisme* derived from *réalisme,* of which it is "la poésie."] (p. 53)
673. Baudelaire: " 'Je crois à la nature et je ne crois qu'à la nature . . . Je crois que l'art est et ne peut être que la reproduction exacte de la nature . . . Copiez la nature; ne copiez que la nature.' " "L'artiste, le vrai artiste, le vrai poëte, ne doit peindre que selon qu'il voit et qu'il sent." " 'Je veux représenter les choses telles qu'elles sont, ou telles qu'elles seraient, en supposant que je n'existe pas.' L'univers sans l'homme." [*réaliste* equivalent to *positiviste.*] (pp. 264, 321, 327)
674. Perrin: "cette prétendue réaction vers la nature et la vérité." "[proscrire] la beauté jusque dans l'exécution matérielle et la partie purement technique de l'art." "théorie du laid pour le laid." (p. 650)
676. Houssaye: "Aristote, dans son Traité de la Poétique, divise les arts d'imitation en trois séries: l'exagération en bien, la fidélité et l'exagération en mal,—ou plutôt l'idéal, la vérité et le réalisme." (p. 100)
677. Pérignon: "la représentation de ce que l'on peut choisir de plus laid." "amour du laid." "l'imitation plus ou moins bête, plus ou moins maladroite du laid." (p. 122)

[1860]

678. Delacroix: "l'imitation la plus parfaite." "le retour à la nature." [*réalisme* opposed to *idéal.*] (pp. 266, 269)

Since a number of the above critics use *naturalisme* as equivalent to *réalisme* and employ them interchangeably, I append below examples of *"naturalisme"* found in the criticisms of painting during the years 1840-1860.

[1841]

587. Rolle: [*l'école des naturalistes* applied to landscape and genre, but without definition.]

[1842]

591. Robert: "copient purement et simplement la nature." "adorateurs exclusifs de la forme." [*naturalistes* opposed to *idéalistes.*]

[1844]

594. La Faloise: [*naturalistes* equivalent to *matérialistes,* opposed to *spiritualistes;* no definition.]
596. Viardot: [*naturalisme* opposed to *idéalisme;* no definition.]
597. Thoré: "le naturalisme du laid." "une imitation grossière et basse."

[1845]

600. Houssaye: [*naturalisme* opposed to *beauté idéale.*]

[1847]

609. Thoré: "cette théorie absurde de l'imitation *matérielle.*"

[1848]

610. Mercey: "les *naturalistes* . . . s'attachent avant tout à reproduire la réalité. Ils aiment la nature toute nue et la traduisent plus littéralement que naïvement."

[1849]

613. Lagenevais: "l'imitation de la nature." [cf. above his definitions as given under *réalisme.*] (p. 561)

[1851]

615. Delécluze: "*naturalistes:* ceux qui, regardant l'imitation comme le but final de l'art, prétendent que tout, jusqu'au laid et à l'ignoble, peut et doit être représenté, sous la condition seulement que l'imitation sera fidèle."

[1852]

631. Delécluze: "ce système d'imitation purement matérielle."

[1859]

672. Cantrel: "La préoccupation de peindre vraie une touffe d'herbe ou une feuille d'arbre fait oublier la nécessité bien plus grande de peindre le tout vrai, vrai de lettre et surtout vrai d'esprit." (p. 52)
674. Perrin: "nier la recherche du sujet, le choix de la forme, le mérite de l'invention." [But *réalisme* goes farther than this; cf. his definition above.] (p. 650)

From these definitions we may derive a general statement of how critics of these years conceived of realism (and of naturalism, which for most of them was an equivalent). Realism is the exact imitation (literal translation, *calque,* copy) of nature as it is, without choice of subject, and without idealization or intrusion of the artist's personality;

it emphasizes the material rather than the spiritual aspects of nature; in matters of form, it disdains 'style,' 'elegance,' 'convention.' It is synonymous with *matérialisme* and *positivisme,* and directly opposed to *idéalisme, rêverie, fantaisie, poésie, imagination.* There is little if any change in this general attitude, except that from about 1852 the critics insist increasingly that realism is the "school of the ugly," and that it devotes itself primarily to depiction of the trivial and the *laid.*

Aside from these more or less formal definitions, there were numerous statements—whether on specific paintings or in the abstract—which showed what elements the critics conceived of as constituting the realistic doctrine. The most frequently mentioned of these were (1) the desire for truth, (2) the desire for contemporaneity, (3) the contention of the realists that all subjects are proper for art.

As for truth, the words *vérité, vrai* occur repeatedly in these articles. By them the critics mean that the artists give, or attempt to give, a faithful reproduction of what they have seen, that the imitation resembles the original. Thus Houssaye remarks of Paul Potter:

. . . c'est la nature elle-même qu'il a fixée sur sa toile comme dans un miroir. Il n'a pas attendu que le nuage qui passait dans son ciel fût éclairci ou doré par un rayon de soleil; il n'a pas recherché tel arbre ou tel feuillage; il a vu, il a peint. Aussi est-il toujours vrai, quelquefois trop vrai . . .[3]

Thus Mantz speaks of Leleux's "parti pris d'être simple et vrai en dépit de tout,"[4] and Champfleury of "la peinture espagnole d'un réalisme si saisissant, si vrai."[5] Of Courbet's manner Enault says: "le fait surpris et rendu avec toute la violence, le sans-façon et le parti-pris de la vérité."[6] And a great many critics make similar statements.[7] They recognize this search for truth as the fundamental tenet of the new school, although, as we shall soon see, they do not always approve of this tenet.

This truth might be obtained, first, by limiting oneself to the material, physical world, and portraying only what was present to the senses. Charles Perrier constitutes himself spokesman for the realists:

Le grand argument des réalistes est que la nature se suffit à elle-même. A les en croire, cette fine fleur de poésie que les artistes s'efforcent de lui imprimer dans la reproduction des objets, et que l'on nomme l'idéal, n'est et ne peut être qu'une vaine subtilité dont les résultats sont plus ou moins puérils, et qui, en somme, n'a rien à voir avec l'art.[8]

Or it might be obtained by an absolute sincerity on the part of the artist, a refusal to record stock impressions, to delude oneself as to the meaning or import of a given object, to juxtapose objects so as to give them an artificial beauty. In the formulation, this point is closely related to the preceding; for example, the paragraph of Chesneau:

De notre temps . . . on étudie plus sincèrement le réel et la nature; cependant le Réalisme a eu le tort des doctrines exclusives; il a affecté plus de dédain qu'il n'en fallait pour toute interprétation poétique de la réalité; il s'est tenu systématiquement à ras de terre. Néanmoins notre moderne école de paysage, que l'on peut entre toutes qualifier d'école naturaliste, doit à cette sincérité même des qualités exceptionnelles qui constituent son originalité et lui donneront une valeur durable. Un peintre naturaliste, selon la plus fréquente acception du mot, est donc celui qui s'en tient à l'imitation scrupuleuse de la réalité, de la nature proclamée, en ses moindres manifestations, supérieure à toutes les combinaisons que l'imagination de l'artiste peut enfanter, même en se servant des éléments naturels le plus fidèlement observés. En un mot, les peintres réalistes ou naturalistes contemporains veulent s'abstenir de composer leurs tableaux; ils se placent au premier coin venu, copient ce qui est devant eux avec une exactitude d'effet scrupuleuse, l'effet fût-il vulgaire ou plat; et leur œuvre est plus ou moins réussi selon qu'ils se sont moins ou plus écartés de la vérité de l'aspect qu'ils avaient sous les yeux.[9]

Above all, truth might be achieved by limiting oneself to contemporary, observable reality: one can portray truly and sincerely only what one sees.

Very early, the critics manifest a feeling similar to that expressed by Thoré in 1845: "nous avons voulu de *l'actualité* dans les arts. Nous avons tous, plus ou moins, crié depuis dix ans que l'art devait se tourner quelque peu vers la réalité contemporaine."[10] Towards 1850, this contention takes the shape of the quarrel over the use of contemporary costume in art, which continued throughout the period. "L'époque des plumets est passée," says Champfleury in 1850, "beaucoup regrettent les costumes de Van-Dyck; mais M. Courbet a compris que la peinture ne doit pas tromper les siècles futurs sur notre costume."[11] In 1855, he again treats the subject:

Ce que les artistes appellent *costume,* c'est-a-dire, mille brimborions (des plumes, des mouches, des aigrettes, etc.), peut amuser un moment les esprits frivoles; mais la représentation sérieuse de la personnalité actuelle, les chapeaux ronds, les habits noirs, les souliers vernis ou les sabots de paysans, est bien autrement intéressante.[12]

The argument for the affirmative is completely and eloquently stated by Duranty in the first article of *Réalisme* (July, 1856). He proceeds from the general statement that "les gens qui ont reculé devant leur propre époque, et qui s'imaginent qu'ils comprennent mieux le passé qu'ils n'ont pas vu, que le présent où ils vivent et se meuvent, ces gens-là ne peuvent être absous de leur inintelligence." After a defence of the modern costume as typifying the modern man, he demands: "Vous proclamez, tous, les Flamands sublimes, vos modèles valent les leurs:

travaillez."[13] His opinion is upheld by Gautier, Auguste de Belloy, Proudhon, and Chesneau.[14]

It is because of their prejudices against the classical nude and the romantic *costume*, prejudices derived from their insistence upon contemporary subject and dress, that the realists oppose both of these older trends. A general reaction in this sense is to be noted around 1850. Delécluze, for example, deplores the depictions of Romans, Greeks, Etruscans, Egyptians, the imitations of Watteau, the vogue of the *rococo* and the *moyen âge* which have characterized much of the French painting of the nineteenth century.[15] Henri de la Madelène, and later Duranty, include both romanticism and classicism in a general condemnation.[16] So does Maxime du Camp, who sees in the new tendencies an escape from the eternal "divinités" and "héros."[17] The neo-classical style seems to have aroused consistent opposition earlier than did the romantic; indeed, it had long before been opposed by the romanticists themselves. In 1845, for example, the *Moniteur des arts* welcomes the reaction against the "vaporeuse école de Thomas Lawrence" and the "peintres du temps de David."[18] Numerous other attacks follow, including the amusing remark of the Baronne Decazes: "lors du règne despotique du classicisme, M. Courbet, lui-même, eût été obligé de représenter, au lieu de ses *Demoiselles de village*, des vierges grecques ou romaines, dessinées comme des figures étrusques. . . ."[19] The movement against romanticism came somewhat later, although, if we are to believe Clément de Ris, it must have set in about 1840; he writes in 1853: "Voilà une quinzaine d'années qu'il se manifesta contre le moyen âge et le bric-à-brac en peinture une réaction représentée par une école. . . ."[20] Many critics, of course, saw in realism only a reaction against *l'idéal* in general, not against any specific idealistic school.[21]

In the third place, according to the critics, the realistic school maintains—as the pre-romantics and the romantics had maintained before it—that everything existing in nature is a proper subject for art. There are no specifically 'literary' or 'artistic' subjects; the ugly, the ignoble, the unpoetic are to be included as well as the beautiful, the noble, and the poetic. Duranty's article best states this theoretical standpoint:

L'idée de la forme, du beau est inintelligente et païenne, il ne faut plus que le beau ait toute la place mais seulement une place; le dix-neuvième siècle a affranchi l'ordinaire, le général, le vrai. La beauté ne veut rien dire sinon la beauté; le reste, l'ordinaire, le réel, est autrement complet et étendu; chaque visage d'homme ordinaire crie vice, passion, douleur, esprit, méchanceté. L'infinie variété de l'homme moral se traduit par des aspects où la géométrie a moins de part, aspects irréguliers du corps et du vêtement. Sous la grande harmonie de la lumière il n'y a rien que de beau et digne d'être contemplé. Dans la réalité rien ne choque; au soleil, les guenilles valent les vêtements impériaux. Le vrai embrasse tout ce qui vit et pense . . .[22]

Many other critics conceive of realistic subject-matter in much the same way, but as we shall see, only to condemn it.[23]

Before stating the objections raised to this tri-partite doctrine (truth, contemporaneity, completeness), I shall indicate briefly the painters who were claimed as predecessors of realism, the types of painting affected by it, and the men included as realistic painters. The most frequently cited source was, of course, the Flemish and Dutch schools.[24] But isolated critics pointed to other examples by which they believed the realists to have profited: Ribeira,[25] the Neapolitan school,[26] Chardin,[27] the Spanish school,[28] Michelangelo da Caravaggio,[29] Murillo,[30] Delacroix,[31] Lenain,[32] Valentin,[33] even the ancient Zeuxis.[34] The new movement was generally thought of as connected with landscape and genre painting,[35] rarely with portraiture.[36] On the other hand, critics point to a falling off in religious and historical work, both as to quantity and to quality, and to a concomitant progress of the other genres.[37] Numerous artists, one after another, were designated as belonging to the new school, or showing an affinity to it in one or another of their traits: I list them here, giving the date of their first appearance in these articles: Verboeckhoven (1841),[38] Delaberge (1841),[39] Meissonnier (1842),[40] Coignet (1844),[41] Gavarni (1845),[42] Leleux (1846),[43] Roqueplan, Guillemin and Fortin (1847),[44] Courbet (1849),[45] Bonvin (1849),[46] Fontaine (1849),[47] Rosa Bonheur (1853),[48] Hornung (1854),[49] Millet (1855),[50] Salmon, Delvaux and Lafond (1855),[51] Breton (1859),[52] and Legros (1862).[53] One sculptor, Barye, is mentioned (1857);[54] several writers (Gérard de Nerval, George Sand, Béranger); and one musician, Wagner;[55] these are alleged to have connections with realism. Balzac appears as equivalent to Gavarni in the production of *tableaux de mœurs*.[56] Finally, the English Pre-Raphaelites are likened to the French realists in their faithful rendering of minute detail.[57]

The objections raised to realism in painting affect only two elements of the realistic trinity, fidelity to external reality and complete representation of that reality. To the doctrine that art must be faithful to contemporary reality there is no opposition. The critics rejected the search for absolute fidelity or "truth" on three grounds: first, that such "truth" was impossible in art; second, that it was undesirable philosophically; third, that it was non-artistic. The major opposition, let it be said at the outset, was on the last of these grounds. We may now examine these three objections.

(1) A work of art, say the critics, cannot possibly represent exactly the object imitated; it cannot rival the image in a mirror, the photograph, the mould. The artist has a mind and a hand as well as an eye, and what he sees is inevitably altered in the process of reproduction. This explains why no two artists ever "see" an object in the same way. "La nature," says Peisse, "ne pose pas de la même manière pour tous les yeux; elle a autant de faces ou d'aspects qu'elle a de contemplateurs; et chacun de ses aspects est également vrai et réel, sinon également intéressant."[58] I quote a more complete statement from Delacroix:

Qu'est-ce que serait, en sculpture par exemple, un art réaliste? De simples moulages sur nature seraient toujours au-dessus de l'imitation la plus parfaite que la main de l'homme puisse produire: car peut-on concevoir que l'esprit ne guide pas la main de l'artiste et croira-t-on possible en même temps que, malgré toute son application à imiter, il ne teindra pas ce singulier travail de la couleur de cet esprit, à moins qu'on n'aille jusqu'à supposer que l'œil seul et la main soient suffisants pour produire, je ne dirai pas seulement une imitation exacte, mais même quelque ouvrage que ce soit?[59]

Thus the attempt to "substitute" the work of art for nature itself cannot possibly be successful.[60]

(2) Such a substitution, even if it were practicable, would not be desirable from a philosophical point of view. For reality is not truth (metaphysically speaking),[61] and to confuse the two is to fall into the grossest materialism. It is this reproach of materialism that constitutes the chief philosophical objection to realism; the two terms, it will be remembered, were frequently identified in the definitions quoted above. Speaking of Courbet, for example, Peisse remarks: "il ne voit dans les choses que leurs qualités et propriétés matérielles; il paraît ne tenir compte, dans la représentation qu'il en fait, que de leur composition physique."[62] Again, Perrier objects: "Le réalisme . . . est un système de peinture qui consiste à exalter et à outrer un des côtés *réels* de la nature, je parle de la matière, au détriment d'un autre non moins réel, qui est l'esprit."[63] Delaborde calls the realists "ceux qui ne demandent pas à la matière de penser, qui ne lui demandent que d'être,"[64] and numerous other commentators repeat the reproach of materialism.[65]

(3) The rejection on philosophical grounds springs largely from an aesthetic theory which regards art as something other than an imitation of physical, sensible reality. For the critics of realistic painting, exactness and fidelity were unsatisfying artistically. To understand why they were insufficient, it is necessary to discover the aesthetic doctrine of these critics. To that end, I give below the definitions of art found in their writings.

[1847]

609. Thoré: "l'art résulte de l'impression produite sur l'homme par la nature."

[1849]

611. "Feu Diderot": "n'oublions pas qu'Aristote a dit: 'L'art est l'interprétation de la nature'; et non comme ses disciples: 'L'art est l'imitation de la nature.' De l'imitation à l'interprétation il y a tout un monde." (p. 97)

613. Lagenevais: "Si ces deux éléments, naturalisme et rêverie, parviennent à se combiner dans une juste mesure, si le premier ne se développe pas de façon à absorber le second et à nous conduire, de dégradations en dégradations, jusqu'aux dernières extravagances du matérialisme hollandais, l'art moderne aura rencontré une formule durable et féconde." (p. 561)

[1851]

618. Enault: "L'art c'est le choix; c'est l'élection; c'est le discernement." [Then, in reference to Courbet:] "il n'y a rien là qui *idéalise,* qui *typise.*"

619. Geofroy: "l'art n'est pas la reproduction indifférente de l'objet le premier passant, mais le choix délicat d'une intelligence raffinée par l'étude. . . . sa mission est . . . de hausser sans cesse au-dessus d'elle-même notre nature infirme et disgraciée." (p. 930)

621. Richard: "celui qui sait unir à la vérité la belle nature et la poésie atteint seul la perfection et le vrai but de l'art."

[1852]

630. Du Camp: "l'artiste est celui qui découvre et rend palpable la part de lui-même que Dieu a mise en toute chose." (p. 83)

632. Boyer and Banville:
"Dans sa forme élégante et choisie,
L'art fut toujours un don comme la poésie;
Avec l'amour du beau son destin est lié."
(p. 15)

[1853]

639. Delaborde: "qu'est-ce qu'une œuvre d'art sinon une idée rendue sensible par une image?" (p. 1143)

640. Du Pays: "l'art ne peut être que l'idéalisation de la réalité, sans quoi on n'aurait que faire de lui, on s'en tiendrait à la réalité elle-même." (p. 392)

[1854]

646. L'Hôte: "l'art, c'est l'idéalisme." "L'art est une nature à part, un monde *sui generis;* l'art, c'est la nature transfigurée." "L'art c'est le mensonge."

[1855]

653. Dubosc de Pesquidoux: "L'intelligence, la comparaison, le choix, tout ce qui constitue l'art." "l'artiste doit . . . chercher autre chose que la reproduction servile de la nature! il a un but plus noble et autrement difficile à atteindre. Ce but, c'est l'effet moral qu'il doit produire sur le spectateur. . . . l'artiste doit rêver quelque chose de plus parfait que la réalité."

[1856]

656. Ratisbonne: "La reproduction de la nature entre tout au plus dans l'art comme élément; c'est son point de départ, rien de plus . . . l'art est l'imitation de la nature telle qu'elle se réfléchit dans le cœur, et non pas telle qu'elle se montre banalement aux yeux. Etudiez la nature et peignez l'idéal."

[1857]

664. Du Camp: "La recherche du beau et de l'idéal, l'aspiration vers une nature supérieure, la compréhension de cette part vivante que Dieu a mise de lui en toutes choses [these, as opposed to *le métier,* constitute *l'art*]. . . . dégager de cet être ou de cet objet [un être ou un objet créé] l'étincelle divine qui l'éclaire, et qui est l'âme et le sentiment, et la rendre palpable aux foules qu'elle étonne et ravit, c'est le fait d'un artiste." (p. 163)

[1859]

674. Perrin: "l'imitation comporte encore l'idéal, . . . l'art est une interprétation et non une traduction littérale." (p. 651)

From these quotations, we may formulate a general or composite definition in the following terms: Art is (a) an idealization [transfiguration, interpretation, generalization] of nature, (b) in which the sensible aspects of the object imitated serve merely as a point of departure; (c) to these, the artist adds his personal reaction or impression; (d) he proceeds by selection, (e) and arranges what he represents in a harmonious and beautiful form. All the aesthetic objections to realistic painting fall under one or another of the points stated in this definition, and we may consider them in the order given.

(a) *Art is an idealization of nature.* Realism, by definition and in practice, avoids all idealization. Hence the critics reject realism for its lack of the ideal. In addition to the statements quoted above, we find numerous applications of this thesis to specific paintings. Edouard L'Hôte, for example, condemns Courbet's *Casseurs de pierres* and Hornung's *Savoyards* for this reason, and contrasts them with other paintings:

Ce que nous aimons dans ce portrait de Rembrandt et de Rigaud, ce n'est pas non plus la nature prise sur le fait, ce n'est pas le réalisme; c'est une certaine âme ou intelligence de la nature, fixée pour ainsi dire sur la toile par le peintre, en passant par la pensée.[66]

Perrier discusses the matter on a theoretical basis, saying of the realists:

A les en croire, cette fine fleur de poésie que les artistes s'efforcent de lui imprimer [i.e., à la nature] dans la reproduction des objets, et que l'on nomme l'idéal, n'est et ne peut être qu'une vaine subtilité dont les résultats sont plus ou moins puérils, et qui, en somme, n'a rien à voir avec l'art. Que l'art et la poésie soient incompatibles, cela est, ce me semble, plus qu'une hérésie, cela implique, pour ainsi dire, contradiction dans les termes.[67]

(b) *The sensible aspects of the object imitated serve merely as a point of departure.* But realism goes no farther than the reproduction of these sensible aspects. 'Imitation,' for it, is an end—not, as it should be, only a means. Delécluze phrases the standpoint of the opposition as early as 1842: *"l'imitation est un moyen et non le but de l'art."*[68] Thus realism, failing as it does to go beyond the servile copy, fails also to fulfil one of the essential conditions of art. We may take the statement of Cordier as typical:

L'école soi-disant nouvelle, partant de l'imitation pure et simple de la nature, a posé en axiome que l'imitation et la seule imitation était le critérium de l'art. C'est prendre tout uniment le moyen pour le but, c'est proscrire à tout jamais la poésie, l'art, c'est à dire ce moi de l'artiste qui lui donne cette émotion, qui fait le vers chez le poëte et le tableau chez le peintre. . . . imiter pour imiter, c'est arriver au trompe-l'œil;— et tout compte fait, nous lui préférons encore la photographie.[69]

With Cordier, many other critics compare realistic painting to photography; some even see an influence of Daguerre's method on the technique of the realists. Baudelaire, expressing what he believes to be the credo of the realists, defines: "l'art, c'est la photographie."[70]

(c) *The artist adds his personal reaction or impression.* But this personal reaction, which is the means of departing from the real object to arrive at the idealized object, is forbidden to the realist. The indication of this lacuna in the realist's philosophy of art is one of the most frequently recurring strictures in the criticism of realistic painting. We have seen it in the passage cited from Cordier; we find it again in a *salon* of Delaborde:

En aucun cas . . . , et quel que soit le modèle qu'on se propose, il ne faut se contenter de rendre les attributs et le caractère matériels de ce modèle: il faut que l'imitation des objets laisse entrevoir l'intention secrète de celui qui les a reproduits et le sens dans lequel ils l'ont particulièrement affecté . . .[71]

For this failing, Thoré condemns the realistic doctrine, "qui supposerait d'abord le suicide de l'artiste et le néant de toutes choses; car il faudrait enlever du même coup l'âme du peintre et la vie incessamment mobile de l'être qu'il veut peindre."[72] From 1843 to 1866, the same reproach repeatedly appears.[73]

(d) *The artist proceeds by selection;* that is, he chooses carefully both the object of imitation and the parts of that object which he will treat in the work of art. On the contrary, the realist insists that all objects, and all aspects of each object, should be represented in art; this is one of the fundamental tenets of his theory. Obviously, this direct contradiction between the concepts of the realists and the critics must lead to condemnation of the realists. For examples, we may consult the opinion of Clément de Ris on Courbet's self-portrait:

Quel que soit notre amour pour la nature, et quelque poésie que nous trouvions dans la réalité, nous ne sommes cependant pas de ceux pour lesquels tous les sujets sont également indifférents, et qui pensent qu'il n'y a pas un choix à faire. Nous croyons que tout n'est pas bon à montrer, et que dans le représentation du masque de l'homme il faut savoir atténuer ce qu'il y a de trivial et ne rendre que son caractère élevé.[74]

Or Geofroy's remark on the *Enterrement à Ornans:* "Si M. Courbet avait daigné élaborer sa pensée, ajuster les diverses parties en élaguant ou dissimulant celles qui déplaisent au profit des motifs heureux qui pouvaient se rencontrer, il eût produit un bon tableau."[75] Most of the remarks are directed against the theory of 'completeness,' for the critics soon found—as we shall see—that the realists did make a choice, and that they chose the ugly as subject for their art.

(e) *The artist arranges what he represents in a harmonious and beautiful form.* This point of the critics' aesthetic doctrine is the one least completely formulated; but it is constantly discernible in the judgments they pronounce on given painters or works. They find that because the realist attends so strictly to detail, he neglects the general effect of his work.[76] He makes no effort to arrange his materials in other than their natural disposition; he is not preoccupied with 'beauty' or 'elegance.' Planche, speaking of Courbet, gives an example of these objections:

. . . il a gardé . . . toute son inaptitude pour la composition, et cette inaptitude est tellement évidente, que ses toiles sont tout bonnement des morceaux copiés et ne ressemblent pas à des tableaux. . . . C'est en effet le même mépris, le même dédain pour tout ce qui ressemble à la beauté, à l'élégance des formes. . . . Difformité du visage, violation de l'harmonie, profusion de tons criards, M. Courbet n'a rien négligé pour offenser, pour scandaliser le goût.[77]

However, the objections on a purely formal basis are in the minority throughout.

Thus we find that, because of an essential conflict between their own aesthetic opinions and those of the realists, the critics were obliged to reject as unartistic the 'truth' sought by the new school. We have already seen that they also rejected it as impossible and as unphilosophical. To the second member of the realists' trinity, contemporaneity, there was, as I have said, no opposition. But the third, completeness, again called forth the censure of the critics. Not only did the notion of exploiting all subjects in art contradict their own aesthetic beliefs [see point (d) above], but they found that in practice the realists were unfaithful to their doctrine, that they did make a choice, but that they chose the trivial, the brutal, the ugly aspects of nature. The reproach of 'ugliness' is the most consistently and the most violently expressed in all the articles on realistic painting.

In its mildest form, this reproach charges realism with presenting people of a lower social level, with deserting picturesque royalty, nobility, aristocracy, to treat only the humdrum bourgeoisie and peasantry. This movement is regarded as a decadence; Peisse expresses his opinion in these terms:

Comme expression des mœurs et de l'état social, le Genre semble, dans l'art, répondre à l'élément bourgeois, devenu prédominant dans les sociétés nouvelles. Il en reproduit l'esprit et en quelque sorte l'idéal, comme en littérature le roman.[78]

Champfleury, in his defence of Courbet, complains of this attitude: "M. Courbet est un factieux pour avoir représenté de bonne foi des bourgeois, des paysans, des femmes de village de grandeur naturelle. Ç'a été le premier point. On ne veut pas admettre qu'un casseur de pierre vaut un prince."[79] To this complaint Perrier gives an answer which in itself is significant:

Ce n'est point, comme il l'affirme, parce qu'il a peint des bourgeois et des paysans que M. Courbet est traité de factieux, mais parce qu'il les a présentés sous un aspect auquel la nature humaine répugne. Nous avons, avant tout, le sentiment de notre dignité. Qu'un casseur de pierres vaille, en fait d'art, un prince ou tout autre individu, c'est ce que personne ne songe à contester. La preuve en est, encore une fois, dans l'intérêt qu'inspirent tous les héros de George Sand. Mais, au moins, que votre casseur ne soit pas lui-même un objet aussi insignifiant que la pierre qu'il casse.[80]

That is, the peasant is admissible only when surrounded with a halo of romantic sentimentality—when he is no longer a peasant.[81]

In a more violent form, the reproach inveighs against the cultivation, by the realists, of "trivial" reality—the representation of objects unworthy of artistic treatment. *La réalité triviale, la vérité triviale* appear on page after page of these articles. "Ces détails prosaïques de marmite, de crémaillère, de table et de siège de bois," says Lagenevais, are truthfully reproduced, but "cette exactitude ne produit pourtant qu'une vérité triviale."[82] "Tout ce monde," says Enault of the *Enterrement*, "est commun, trivial, grotesque."[83] And Paul Deleutre defends this standpoint: "La trivialité n'existe pas dans la nature, c'est un produit de la société civilisée, comme la maladie."[84]

But by far the most significant aspect of this objection is the critics' claim that the realists treat only the ugly. In the definitions, we have seen realism called "l'école du laid"; now we shall see that, in at least a third of the articles under consideration, some allusion is made to the tendency of the realists to cultivate the ugly. The critics explain the tendency thus: the realists aim to depict only what they see; but they are prejudiced against the noble because of its association with the idealistic schools, and they find the commonplace lacking in color and interest; hence they are obliged to draw on the world of the exaggeratedly ugly. Boyer and Banville, in their *Feuilleton d'Aristophane,* speak for the proponents of the new school:

> Faire vrai, ce n'est rien pour être réaliste:
> C'est faire laid qu'il faut! Or, monsieur, s'il vous plaît,
> Tout ce que je dessine est horriblement laid!
> Ma peinture est affreuse, et, pour qu'elle soit vraie,
> J'en arrache le beau comme on fait de l'ivraie!
> J'aime les teints terreux et les nez de carton,
> Les fillettes avec de la barbe au menton,
> Les trognes de tarasque et de coquesigrues,
> Les durillons, les cors aux pieds et les verrues!
> Voilà le vrai.[85]

In a more serious tone, Dubosc de Pesquidoux attacks the practice:

> . . . il n'y a aucun rapport entre l'art tel que chacun le conçoit et ces brutales reproductions; et si la peinture ne doit servir qu'à affliger notre regard par les scènes lugubres ou ignobles qu'il ne rencontre que trop souvent dans la réalité, le plus grand service qu'on pût rendre à l'humanité serait de supprimer et de défendre cet art malfaisant. . . . l'école réaliste tombe dans le *faux* qu'elle a tant reproché à l'école rivale; seulement, au lieu d'être faux dans le beau, on est faux dans le laid, voilà toute la différence.[86]

These ideas are repeated, expanded, intensified by other critics, until they constitute the most crushing single accusation brought against the realistic school in painting.[87]

Realism in painting was, therefore, condemned on almost every score; and if it was so condemned, it was because the realists and the critics proposed diametrically opposite functions and methods for art. The realists held that art was to make no choice of subject-matter; it was to present whatever it saw (and only what it saw) and to present it exactly as seen. The critics, on the contrary, maintained that art must choose its materials among objects susceptible of idealization, it must practice imitation only as a means to ultimate idealization, it must give free reign to the personality and the ideal of the artist. There was, then, no possibility of agreement between the two groups. Certain critics, to be sure, admitted that the realists had a salutary influence in the reaction against stultified conventions, against mere prettiness and cheap sentimentality. But that was the only value conceded to the new school. For the rest, there was a continued storm of protest. Chronologically, one discerns little change in the objections raised; most of them appeared at an early date and reappeared constantly throughout the period studied. Indeed, in seeking to detect modifications in the current of opinion, one can point only to an increasing vigor and vivacity in the attacks of the critics as, little by little, the new school of painting became more prosperous and its canvases more prominent in the annual expositions.

Having thus studied the critical conception of realism in painting and the reaction to the new movement in art, we may now turn to the problem of realism in literature, to an analysis of the realists' theory as it presented itself to the public and of the consequent public reaction. This analysis will be the subject of the following chapter.

---

[1] 7, Bouvier, pp. 214-257.

[2] The period 1840-1860 has been chosen as including the emergence and gradual acceptance of the terms *réalisme, réaliste,* and the formation of the realistic doctrine. Some articles of the succeeding decade have been studied, since they show the continuation and further development of the earlier attitudes.

Isolated instances of the use of *réalisme* and *réaliste* before 1840 have been indicated. Gustave Planche, for example, used *réalisme* as early as 1835 to characterize the manner of Rembrandt, making it equivalent to "vérité humaine" and contrary to "idéalité poétique" ("Histoire et philosophie de l'art. VII. L'Ecole anglaise en 1835," *Revue des deux mondes,* 15 juin 1835, II, 675-676; cf. *22a,* Du Val, p. 63). But such cases are sporadic, and do not affect my statement that the terms were not in general use until after 1846. For the peculiar rôle of Planche in the history of these terms, see below, p. 118.

[3] 602, Houssaye, p. 203

[4] 603, Mantz.

[5] 447, Champfleury, p. 18.

[6] 624, Enault, p. 234.

[7] *608*, Vaines, p. 258; *611*, "Feu Diderot," p. 98; *612*, Peisse; *617*, Clément de Ris, p. 6; *621*, Richard; *623*, Clément de Ris, p. 82; *625*, Clément de Ris, p. 99; *627*, Peisse; *628*, Planche, p. 670; *639*, Delaborde, p. 1143; *643*, Peisse; *644*, Clément de Ris, p. 7; *645*, La Madelène; *650*, Deleutre; *652*, Perrier, p. 86; *657*, Duranty; *659*, Gautier, p. 190; *664*, Du Camp, p. 161; *673*, Baudelaire, p. 263.

[8] *652*, Perrier, pp. 85-86; cf. *666*, Perrier, p. 121.

[9] *685*, Chesneau; cf. esp. *664*, Du Camp, pp. 161-162.

[10] *597*, Thoré; cf. *598*, Anon., p. 97; *599*, Janin; *601*, X.; *645*, La Madelène.

[11] *614*, Champfleury.   [12] *649*, Champfleury, p. 2.   [13] *657*, Duranty.

[14] *662*, Gautier, p. 245; *671*, Belloy, p. 17; *684*, Proudhon, p. 203; *686*, Chesneau.

[15] *631*, Delécluze.   [16] *645*, La Madelène; *657*, Duranty.

[17] *664*, Du Camp, p. 161.   [18] *598*, Anon., p. 90.

[19] *626*, Decazes; cf. *611*, "Feu Diderot," p. 97; *623*, Clément de Ris, p. 82; *686*, Chesneau.

[20] *644*, Clément de Ris, p. 6; cf. *614*, Champfleury; *642*, Calonne, p. 132; *649*, Champfleury, p. 2; *650*, Deleutre.

[21] Cf. *590*, Delécluze; *591*, Robert; *632*, Boyer and Banville, p. 13; *646*, L'Hôte, p. 184; *651*, Dubosc de Pesquidoux; *657*, Duranty.   [22] *657*, Duranty.

[23] Cf. *602*, Houssaye, pp. 162, 175; *615*, Delécluze; *619*, Geofroy, p. 929; *621*, Richard; *625*, Clément de Ris, p. 99; *645*, La Madelène; *649*, Champfleury, p. 2; *659*, Gautier, p. 190; *666*, Perrier, p. 121; *674*, Perrier, p. 650; *684*, Proudhon, p. 203.

[24] *592*, Luthereau, p. 95; *593*, Anon., p. 34; *596*, Viardot; *598*, Anon., 2nd art; *602*, Houssaye; *612*, Peisse; *613*, Lagenevais, p. 561; *614*, Champfleury; *649*, Champfleury, p. 2; *653*, Dubosc de Pesquidoux; *657*, Duranty; *681*, Pelloquet, p. 260; *683*, Ad. Viollet-le-Duc.

[25] *611*, "Feu Diderot," p. 98; *643*, Peisse.

[26] *611*, "Feu Diderot," p. 98; *681*, Pelloquet, p. 260.

[27] *612*, Peisse; *613*, Lagenevais, p. 577.

[28] *615*, Delécluze; *681*, Pelloquet, p. 260.

[29] *643*, Peisse; *668*, Delaborde, p. 260.   [30] *643*, Peisse.

[31] *644*, Clément de Ris, p. 6.   [32] *Ibid.*, p. 7.

[33] *668*, Delaborde, p. 260.   [34] *656*, Ratisbonne.

[35] On landscape, cf. *587*, Rolle; *591*, Robert; *593*, Anon., p. 33; *610*, Mercey; *644*, Clément de Ris, p. 6; *657*, Duranty; *664*, Du Camp, p. 161; *672*, Cantrel, p. 52; *673*, Baudelaire, p. 327. On genre, cf. *587*, Rolle; *593*, Anon., p. 33; *612*, Peisse; *613*, Lagenevais, p. 561; *629*, Peisse; *644*, Clément de Ris, p. 6; *664*, Du Camp, p. 161; *671*, Belloy, p. 17; *673*, Baudelaire, p. 327.   [36] *598*, Anon., p. 90.

[37] Cf. *589*, Luthereau; *593*, Anon., p. 34; *636*, Gautier, p. 136; *664*, Du Camp, p. 161; *673*, Baudelaire, p. 327.   [38] *587*, Rolle.   [39] *588*, Gautier, p. 268; *595*, Thoré.

[40] *592*, Luthereau, p. 95.   [41] *595*, Thoré.   [42] *599*, Janin; *601*, X.

[43] *603*, Mantz; *604*, Leboucher; *608*, Vaines, p. 257; *613*, Lagenevais, p. 575; *617*, Clément de Ris, p. 5; *644*, Clément de Ris, p. 7; *654*, About, p. 208; *665*, Gautier, p. 36.   [44] *608*, Vaines, p. 257.   [45] Practically all items after *611*.

[46] *612*, Peisse; *613*, Lagenevais, p. 577.   [47] *613*, Lagenevais, p. 577.

[48] *639*, Delaborde, pp. 1142-1143; *666*, Perrier, p. 123.   [49] *646*, L'Hôte, p. 184.

[50] *654*, About, p. 206; *664*, Du Camp, p. 163; *665*, Gautier, p. 33; *670*, Belloy, p. 5; *674*, Perrin, p. 654.

[51] *654*, About, pp. 206-207.   [52] *670*, Belloy, p. 6; *674*, Perrin, p. 652.

[53] *679*, Fillonneau, p. 24.   [54] *666*, Perrier, p. 124.

[55] *649*, Champfleury, p. 2; also *644*, Clément de Ris, p. 6, and *652*, Perrier, p. 88, on Sand.   [56] *601*, X.

[57] *648*, Mantz p. 125; *667*, Clément de Ris, p. 118; *668*, Delaborde.

[58] *643*, Peisse.

[59] *678*, Delacroix, pp. 266-267; cf. *609*, Thoré; *656*, Ratisbonne; *667*, Clément de Ris, p. 118.

[60] Cf. *609a*, Gautier; *591*, Robert.   [61] *616*, Peisse; *633*, Delacroix, p. 92.

[62] *643*, Peisse.   [63] *652*, Perrier, p. 85.   [64] *668*, Delaborde.

[65] Cf. *589*, Luthereau; *597*, Thoré; *598*, Anon., p. 90; *611*, "Feu Diderot," p. 97; *613*, Lagenevais, p. 561; *616*, Peisse; *624*, Enault, p. 234; *638*, Viel Castel, p. 534; *653*, Dubosc de Pesquidoux.

[66] *646*, L'Hôte, p. 185; cf. *612*, Peisse; *616*, Peisse; *618*, Enault; *680*, L'Hôte, p. 145.   .

[67] *652*, Perrier, p. 86; cf. *664*, Du Camp, p. 163; *674*, Perrin, p. 651; *683*, Ad. Viollet-le-Duc; *685*, Chesneau.   [68] *590*, Delécluze.

[69] *682*, Cordier, p. 407; cf. *611*, "Feu Diderot," p. 98; *615*, Delécluze; *656*, Ratisbonne; *658*, Planche, p. 553.

[70] *673*, Baudelaire, p. 264; cf. *588*, Gautier, p. 268; *590*, Delécluze; *591*, Robert; *592*, Luthereau, p. 95; *615*, Delécluze; *622*, Bonnassieux, p. 17; *653*, Dubosc de Pesquidoux; *659*, Gautier, pp. 190-191; *684*, Proudhon, p. 30; *683*, Ad. Viollet-le-Duc; *690*, Du Camp, p. 711.   [71] *639*, Delaborde, p. 1143.   [72] *609*, Thoré.

[73] *593*, Anon., p. 33; *598*, Anon., p. 90; *615*, Delécluze; *625*, Clément de Ris, p. 99; *646*, L'Hôte, p. 184; *652*, Perrier, p. 86; *653*, Dubosc de Pesquidoux; *656*, Ratisbonne; *664*, Du Camp, p. 163; *672*, Cantrel, p. 52; *673*, Baudelaire, p. 327; *680*, L'Hôte, p. 145; *683*, Ad. Viollet-le-Duc; *690*, Du Camp, p. 711.

[74] *620*, Clément de Ris, p. 34.

[75] *619*, Geofroy, p. 929; cf. *615*, Delécluze; *621*, Richard; *625*, Clément de Ris, p. 99; *650*, Deleutre; *653*, Dubosc de Pesquidoux; *678*, Delacroix, pp. 267-268.

[76] *666*, Perrier, p. 121; *672*, Cantrel, p. 52; *678*, Delacroix, p. 267.

[77] *628*, Planche, p. 671; cf. *592*, Luthereau, p. 95; *616*, Peisse; *632*, Boyer and Banville, p. 15; *685*, Chesneau.   [78] *629*, Peisse.

[79] *649*, Champfleury, p. 2.   [80] *652*, Perrier, p. 88.

[81] Cf. on this subject *598*, Anon., p. 90; *612*, Peisse; *613*, Lagenevais, p. 575; *616*, Peisse; *624*, Enault, p. 234; *633*, Delacroix, p. 18; *653*, Dubosc de Pesquidoux; *677*, Pérignon, p. 122; and the caricatures of Cham, *647*.

[82] *613*, Lagenevais, p. 578.   [83] *618*, Enault.

[84] *650*, Deleutre; cf. *616*, Peisse; *620*, Clément de Ris, p. 34; *622*, Bonnassieux, p. 18; *624*, Enault, p. 234; *640*, Du Pays, p. 392; *656*, Ratisbonne; *666*, Perrier, p. 122; *683*, Ad. Viollet-le-Duc.

[85] *632*, Boyer and Banville, p. 15; allusions are to Courbet.

[86] *653*, Dubosc de Pesquidoux.

[87] Cf. *597*, Thoré; *608*, Vaines, p. 258; *615*, Delécluze; *619*, Geofroy, p. 931; *620*, Clément de Ris, p. 34; *622*, Bonnassieux, p. 18; *624*, Enault, p. 234; *625*, Clément de Ris, p. 99; *628*, Planche, pp. 670-671; *630*, Du Camp, p. 83; *631*, Delécluze; *635*, Clément de Ris, p. 129; *638*, Viel Castel, p. 534; *642*, Calonne, p. 132; *640*, Du Pays, p. 392; *643*, Peisse; *645*, La Madelène; *650*, Deleutre; *652*, Perrier, p. 86; *654*, About, p. 203; *655*, Banville; *656*, Ratisbonne; *666*, Perrier, p. 121; *667*, Clément de Ris, p. 118; *674*, Perrin, p. 650; *677*, Pérignon, p. 122; *679*, Fillonneau; *691*, Goncourt; also the caricatures of Cham, *634*, *641*, and *663*.

CHAPTER V

THEORY AND OPPOSITION (1840-1870)

TO STATE adequately the history of realistic theory, one would have to go back at least as far as the eighteenth century, to the formulations of Diderot. It would then be necessary to trace in romantic credos and manifestoes the development of certain contentions which eventually formed the basis of the realistic gospel. Special attention would need to be paid, for example, to the prefaces and critical pronouncements of Stendhal and Balzac, and to minor novels and novelists of the '20's and '30's. Such a study, however, is beyond the scope of my investigation. In the present chapter, as elsewhere, I shall consider the situation only as it affected the critics and the press during the period indicated. For statements of realistic doctrine, I shall use only such articles as were accessible to contemporaries (thus eliminating private correspondences and unpublished treatises), and I shall attempt an analysis of that doctrine only to show what it was that critics were opposing when they opposed realism. In the second place, I shall try to state the nature of the critical reaction to the new movement, as this reaction affected the movement in general rather than any specific author. I have chosen 1840 as a *terminus a quo,* since before that date there was no realistic school and no doctrine recognizable by contemporaries as such.

As a prelude to this study, it will be well to examine the history of the words *réalisme* and *réaliste* in their literary connections. As philosophical terms, both had long been known; but it was only during the nineteenth century that they were transferred to the vocabulary of aesthetics, and applied especially to painting and literature. It is impossible to say how early the transfer took place, for not all the relevant documents have been studied. Whatever statements I shall make with regard to this early history must therefore be taken as tentative, and as valid only for the materials examined. As early as 1834, Hippolyte Fortoul uses "réalisme" in a review of Antony Thouret's *Toussaint-le-Mulâtre;* after speaking of the "souffrances réelles" and the "passions actuelles" depicted in the work, he goes on to say:

M. Thouret a écrit son livre avec une exagération de réalisme, qu'il a empruntée à la manière de M. Hugo. Lorsqu'il l'applique purement à des descriptions extérieures, aux révélations des ténèbres de la police, aux réminiscences du cachot, aux souvenirs du journalisme, il donne vraiment à son matérialisme une verve et une chaleur originales.[1]

In 1835 and 1837, Gustave Planche uses the words in a number of articles appearing in the *Revue des deux mondes;*[2] for a time, indeed, they seem to be the property of this writer and this journal. Planche conceives of realism as an exact reproduction or imitation of nature, limited strictly to the physical aspects of observable things; he regards it as incompatible with beauty, with the ideal, with art. "Envisagé comme une réaction accidentelle et passagère contre la dégénérescence des formes convenues, il peut avoir son utilité; mais ce n'est tout au plus qu'un moyen; et s'en tenir au réalisme, c'est méconnaître d'emblée le véritable but de l'invention."[3] During the same period (1836), Hains speaks of Balzac as "quittant le sentier mystérieux qui sépare le réalisme du monde fantastique";[4] but this is probably only a misuse of the philosophical term, taken as meaning *réalité.* Again, in 1840, an anonymous critic of *Le Semeur* reviews Eugène Villard's *Idéalisme et réalité,* and asks: "Ce romancier avait-il à cœur de combattre le *réalisme* ou le *positivisme,* termes barbares qu'il faut employer pourtant, parce qu'ils expriment des idées pour lesquelles il n'y a pas de mots dans notre vieille langue française?"[5] Here, too, the meaning is philosophical rather than literary. But more distinctly literary uses of the words come in 1846. Then, in June, Marc Fournier applies *réalisme* to Charles de Bernard:

Il semble, à première vue, que ce grand cachet de réalisme, dont M. de Bernard a le mérite d'empreindre ses ouvrages, doive leur donner un certain tour pittoresque et original. Oui, si c'était le véritable cachet d'un véritable réalisme.[6]

In October, Hippolyte Castille speaks of Balzac and Mérimée as belonging to the *école réaliste,* of Balzac as losing *la physionomie réaliste* when he portrays exceptional rather than typical characters.[7] In connection with these early specific uses, several facts are significant: first, that the words are for a time used almost exclusively by the *Revue des deux mondes,* and that they then 'disappear' for almost ten years; second, that when they reappear, it is to become the property of writers in *L'Artiste.* For Fournier's article appeared in that journal, edited by Arsène Houssaye, and it was Houssaye's *Histoire de la peinture flamande et hollandaise* (published in January, 1846) that first gave the words any real prominence. As we shall see later, *L'Artiste* was instrumental in supporting the realists and in formulating their doctrine; its whole connection with the movement deserves careful and detailed study.

After 1846, the words *réalisme* and *réaliste* become increasingly prominent. Houssaye in 1847[8] and Thomas in 1848[9] (both writing in *L'Artiste*) are the next authors to use them.[10] It is not until 1851, however, that they gain any real currency, both in criticism of literature and of painting. In 1856, they attain a sort of consecration when Duranty founds his review called *Réalisme;* in 1857, Champfleury publishes his volume of essays called *Le Réalisme.* From that time onward, they appear in almost every literary discussion, applied—and misapplied— to the most diverse writers, definitely a part of current critical vocabulary.[11] For a long time, however, writers continue to italicize the term, which remains for them a neologism; cf. Janin in 1852, Champfleury in 1853, Pontmartin in 1855, Claude Vignon in 1858, Barthet in 1859, Reymond in 1860, Lefrançais as late as 1867, Laprade as late as 1868, and many others too numerous to list.[12] It is important to remark, too, that in this period *naturalisme* is used only rarely as a literary term equivalent to *réalisme,* and that even in these few cases its meaning is not demonstrably literary.[13] *Naturalisme* had long been an accepted term in painting, where *réalisme* was merely adopted as a new synonym; it had not previously been used in regard to literature, however, and had to await a later school to be adopted as a literary by-word.

How, we may now ask, did realism present itself to its contemporaries?

(1) In 1843, before the days of a realistic school, Hippolyte Babou gave a definition of the "roman d'analyse" which merits a place as our first statement of realistic doctrine. Speaking of Balzac and his school, and especially of Charles de Bernard, Babou outlined the conditions of what Bernard himself had called "la chimie morale." His terms, in some passages, are remarkably similar to those of Taine a number of years later.

C'est par l'énumération des détails que les analystes réussissent à donner une idée de l'ensemble. Ils saisissent sur les objets extérieurs et matériels les reflets des sentiments et du caractère de leurs personnages. A leurs yeux, une existence humaine n'est pas concentrée tout entière au foyer de la pensée. Elle se compose de milliers d'atomes épars autour d'elle; la forme et la disposition des meubles, la couleur du vêtement, les particularités de l'habitation, le degré de lumière qui entre par la croisée, mille autres petites choses imperceptibles, révèlent les mœurs et les instincts d'un individu, d'une famille. L'analyste consciencieux pousse la religion du détail aussi loin que l'antiquaire.

L'analyse avait été jusque-là [before Balzac] une action réglée par un talent spontané; elle devint alors une science: de là le mal. Toute science qui se constitue a besoin d'une nomenclature; la chimie morale eut la sienne. Les passions et les caractères furent désormais traités comme l'oxygène et l'hydrogène. Une technologie barbare, pédantesque, obscure, remplaça le langage ordinaire. Peu s'en fallut que la chimie morale ne nous donnât des oxides d'amour et des sulfures de haine, correspondants aux oxides de fer et aux sulfures de plomb de la chimie proprement dite . . . Ces manipulations qui avaient, il faut en convenir, un certain air de nouveauté, tendaient de plus en plus à changer en laboratoire le cabinet de l'écrivain. Le roman de mœurs échappait à la littérature pour entrer dans le domaine des sciences physiques et naturelles. Après avoir été chimiste, le romancier se faisait médecin. Il tâtait le pouls de ses personnages, au lieu d'interpréter les secrets mouvements du cœur. Les passions se transformaient en maladies, et les caractères en tics. Le monde matériel, que l'intelligence humaine avait semblé d'abord élever jusqu'à elle, réagissait à son tour et envahissait l'intelligence.[14]

These same ideas, as we shall see, appear often in later statements of realistic theory.

(2) Ten years later, 1853. Champfleury voices a *confession de foi* and a complaint in his "Lettre à M. Ampère touchant la poésie populaire":

L'art vrai, ce qu'on pourchasse aujourd'hui sous le nom de *réalisme* . . . , l'art simple, l'art qui consiste à rendre des idées sans "les faire danser sur la phrase" comme disait Jean-Paul Richter, l'art qui se fait modeste, l'art qui dédaigne de vains ornements de style, l'art qui creuse et qui cherche la nature comme les ouvriers cherchent l'eau dans un puits artésien, cet art qui est une utile réaction contre les faiseurs de ronsardisme, de gongorisme, cet art trouve partout dans les gazettes, les revues, parmi les beaux-esprits, les délicats, les maniérés, les faiseurs de mots, les chercheurs d'épithètes, les architectes en antithèse, des adversaires aussi obstinés que les bourgeois dont je vous ai donné un portrait.[15]

(3) April, 1854. Elme-Marie Caro, professed adversary of the realist group, states what he considers to be its point of view:

Nos jeunes réalistes du théâtre . . . annoncent hautement la prétention de donner à notre siècle la représentation du siècle lui-même exactement copié dans tous ses traits même les plus difformes, dans tous les éléments même les plus vulgaires de sa physionomie, dans les réalités les plus honteuses de son existence. Ils font de l'art, et ils s'en vantent, un trompe-l'œil; leur but n'est plus l'expression de l'idéal, c'est l'illusion du réel. Leur poétique a pour règle unique l'imitation; l'art véritable sera pour eux le plus exact plagiat de la nature. Produire sur la scène des hommes et des femmes comme ceux que vous rencontrez chaque jour dans les ateliers, dans les estaminets, dans la rue ou ailleurs, et jeter tous ces personnages de bas aloi dans le moule d'une action vulgaire, en leur donnant des mœurs de hasard et un langage brutalement vrai, c'est là une pratique destinée à remplacer les théories discréditées des romantiques et des classiques, la théorie d'*Hernani* aussi bien que celle d'*Athalie*. C'est ce qu'on appelle briser les formes usées de la vieille tragédie et renouveler l'aspect du romantisme épuisé.[16]

(4) May, 1854. Champfleury, in the *Revue de Paris*, publishes two articles on the "Aventurier Challes," an early eighteenth-century novelist whom Champfleury hailed as a precursor of realism. From the mass of anecdotic and biographical materials, we may isolate the following

critical theories. (a) The novel should proceed by the observation of minute details, not by "invention" or "imagination"; (b) limiting itself thus to reality and to truth, it is absolutely sincere; (c) at the same time, it must be contemporary, giving *peintures de mœurs* and *scènes de la vie habituelle;* (d) but this does not mean photography, for the author's personality everywhere prevents him from giving a mechanical reproduction; (e) choice, indeed, is necessary, and the artist must arrange and distribute his materials to make of them a work of art; (f) the style of the novel should be simple.[17]

(5) In December, 1855, in *L'Artiste,* the poet Fernand Desnoyers published the first deliberate manifesto of the school, entitled "Du réalisme," and beginning with "Cet article n'est ni la défense d'un client ni le plaidoyer pour un individu, il est un manifeste, une profession de foi." I quote the most important passages:

Le Réalisme est la peinture vraie des objets.

Il n'y a pas de peinture *vraie* sans couleur, sans esprit, sans vie ou animation, sans physionomie ou sentiment. Il serait donc vulgaire d'appliquer la définition qui précède à un art mécanique. . . .

Le mot réaliste n'a été employé que pour distinguer l'artiste qui est sincère et clairvoyant, d'avec l'être qui s'obstine, de bonne ou de mauvaise foi, à regarder les choses à travers des verres de couleur.

Comme le mot vérité met tout le monde d'accord et que tout le monde aime ce mot, même les menteurs, il faut bien admettre que le réalisme, sans être l'apologie du laid et du mal, a le droit de représenter ce qui existe et ce qu'on voit.

On ne conteste à personne le droit d'aimer ce qui est faux, ridicule ou déteint, et de l'appeler idéal et poésie; mais il est permis de contester que cette mythologie soit notre monde, dans lequel il serait peut-être temps de faire un tour.

D'ailleurs, on abuse de la poésie. . . . La poésie pousse comme l'herbe entre les pavés de Paris. Elle est rare . . . Quant à moi, je crois que cette poésie que chacun pense avoir dans sa poche, se trouve aussi bien dans le laid que dans le beau, dans le fantastique que dans le réel, pourvu que la poésie soit naïve et convaincue et que la forme soit sincère. Le laid ou le beau est l'affaire du peintre ou du poète: c'est à lui de choisir et de décider; mais à coup sûr la poésie, comme le Réalisme, ne peut se rencontrer que dans ce qui existe, dans ce qui se voit, se sent, s'entend, se rêve, à la condition de ne pas faire exprès de rêver. Il est singulier à ce propos qu'on se soit spécialement suspendu aux pans de l'habit du Réalisme, comme s'il avait inventé la peinture du laid. [All the great artists of the past have depicted evil and the ugly.] Que les réalistes jouissent de la même liberté! si les gens en paletot qui passent devant nos yeux ne sont pas beaux; tant pis! ce n'est pas une raison de mettre une redingote à Narcisse ou à Apollon. Je réclame le droit qu'ont les miroirs, pour la peinture comme pour la littérature.

[Mockery of the classicists and the romanticists.]

Enfin, le Réalisme *vient!*

C'est à travers ces broussailles, cette bataille des Cimbres, ce Pan-
démonium de temples grecs, de lyres et de guimbardes, d'alhambras et
de chênes phtisiques, de boléros, de sonnets ridicules, d'odes en or, de
dagues, de rapières et de feuilletons rouillés, d'hamadryades au clair
de la lune et d'attendrissements vénériens, de mariages de M. Scribe, de
caricatures spirituelles et de photographies sans retouche, de cannes, de
faux cols d'amateurs, de discussions et critiques édentées, de traditions
branlantes, de coutumes crochues et couplets au public, que le Réalisme
a fait une trouée.
[The noisy objections to its advent.]
Et tout cela pourquoi? parce que le Réalisme dit aux gens: Nous avons
toujours été Grecs, Latins, Anglais, Allemands, Espagnols, etc., soyons
un peu nous, fussions-nous laids. N'écrivons, ne peignons que ce qui
est, ou du moins, ce que nous voyons, ce que nous savons, ce que nous
avons vécu. N'ayons ni maîtres ni élèves! Singulière école, n'est-ce-pas?
que celle où il n'y a ni maître ni élève, et dont les seuls principes sont
l'indépendance, la sincérité, l'individualisme.[18]

(6) The first number of *Réalisme* (July, 1856) included, besides the
article of Duranty cited in the chapter on painting,[19] one other item of
interest for realistic theory. This was a review, by Jules Assézat, of
Auguste Vacquerie's *Profiles et grimaces,* attacking Vacquerie's romanticism:

Pour les romantiques, le but de la littérature était une chose fantastique: l'art; pour nous, c'est une chose réelle, existante, compréhensible,
visible, palpable: l'imitation scrupuleuse de la nature.
Pour nous, nous admettons le laid, parce qu'il est vrai; nous admettons
le beau, parce qu'il est vrai aussi; nous admettons le vulgaire comme
l'extraordinaire, parce que tous deux sont vrais; mais ce que nous n'admettons pas, et ce qui a tué le romantisme, c'est la manie exclusive du
laid-horrible et de l'extraordinaire-monstrueux.[20]

(7) August, 1856. Champfleury publishes, in *Figaro,* a letter from
one of his readers criticizing *M. de Boisdhyver;* to it he appends a reply,
which he terms "ma poétique":

Tout romancier sérieux est un être impersonnel qui, par une sorte
de métempsycose, passe de son vivant dans le corps de ses personnages.
Il serait dangereux de présumer de son tempérament, de ses vices
ou de ses vertus, de son caractère, par les personnages qu'il met en scène.
Tout homme qui ne se sentira pas assez de courage pour devenir une
sorte d'encyclopédiste, pour ne rien ignorer des tendances scientifiques
et morales de son époque, devra renoncer à faire du roman. Joignez à
ces études une attention profonde, une indifférence pour les actualités
politiques, artistiques et religieuses, une oreille fine, un regard profond,
une intelligence native, un travail absorbant, une volonté de fer dans
un corps robuste ou maladif, et vous aurez un type de romancier auquel
il est donné à bien peu d'atteindre.
Au-dessous de ces fortes intelligences se place le romancier personnel,
qui n'a qu'à se regarder au dedans, pour, à un certain âge, retrouver au

fond d'un tiroir les bouquets séchés de sa jeunesse, et, grâce à la réalité, laisser un livre curieux, quelquefois plus longuement vivace que les œuvres de cerveaux puissants. [e.g. *Adolphe, Manon Lescaut*.]

L'idéal, pour le romancier impersonnel, est d'être un protée souple, changeant, multiforme, tout à la fois victime et bourreau, juge et accusé, qui sait tour à tour prendre la robe du prêtre, du magistrat, le sabre du militaire, la charrue du laboureur, la naïveté du peuple, la sottise du petit bourgeois.

Par ses incarnations si diverses, l'auteur est obligé d'étudier en même temps le physique et le moral de ses héros; s'il endosse divers habits, il connaît diverses consciences.

Le romancier ne juge pas, ne condamne pas, n'absout pas.
Il expose des faits.[21]

(8) November, 1856. Xavier Aubryet, in *L'Artiste*, discusses Champfleury; incidentally, he states his own concept of the realist:

Qu'est-ce en effet et que doit être un réaliste? Un homme qui n'est d'aucun parti, qui n'a pas de préférence, qui réfléchit les êtres et les choses, sinon avec sévérité, du moins avec une exactitude impartiale; il peint l'humanité dans tous ses milieux et dans toutes ses sphères, il ne la parque pas dans un coin obscur. De l'homme du peuple au patricien, de la beauté à la laideur, de la détresse à l'opulence, de l'infirmité à la toute puissance, il passe sans indifférence, mais sans élection déterminée; au point de vue de l'art, il choisit,—car c'est là la condition de l'art,— mais au point de vue humain, il ne choisit pas; car sa nature de *réaliste* le force à reproduire la réalité telle qu'elle est; or, la *réalité* est aussi charmante qu'horrible, aussi délicate que grossière, aussi naïve que raffinée. [Balzac and Shakespeare are true realists.] Ils n'ont ni haine ni engouement; il y aurait là deux périls d'aveuglement; ils sont surtout *impersonnels, objectifs.*—Le *moi*, ce *moi humain* qui est le secret de tant d'œuvres, ne joue aucun rôle dans leurs créations; ils ont le don de ne *pas rester* eux-mêmes, non pas comme écrivains, mais comme observateurs.[22]

(9) December, 1856. Duranty, in the second number of *Réalisme*, summarizes—"pour ceux qui ne comprennent jamais"—the content of the first issue:

. . . il a été très-nettement établi:
Que le Réalisme proscrivait l'*historique* dans la peinture, dans le roman et dans le théâtre, afin qu'il ne s'y trouvât aucun mensonge, et que l'artiste ne pût pas emprunter son intelligence aux autres;
Que le Réalisme ne voulait, des artistes, que l'étude de leur époque;
Que dans cette étude de leur époque, il leur demandait de ne rien déformer, mais bien de conserver à chaque chose son exacte proportion;
Que la meilleure manière de ne pas errer dans cette étude, était de toujours songer à l'idée de représenter le côté *social* de l'homme, qui est le plus visible, le plus compréhensible et le plus varié, et de songer ainsi à l'idée de reproduire les choses qui touchent à la vie du plus grand nombre, qui se passent souvent, dans l'ordre des instincts, des désirs, des passions;

Que le Réalisme attribue par là à l'artiste un but philosophique pratique, utile, et non un but divertissant, et par conséquent le relève;

Que, demandant à l'artiste *le vrai* utile, il lui demande surtout le sentiment, l'observation intelligente qui *voit* un enseignement, une émotion dans un spectacle de quelque ordre qu'il soit, bas ou noble, selon la convention, et qui tire toujours cet enseignement, cette émotion, de ce spectacle en sachant le représenter *complet* et le rattacher à l'ensemble social, de sorte que par exemple les reproductions à la Henry Monnier, isolées, fragmentaires, doivent être rejetées de l'art et du réalisme bien qu'on ait voulu les y rattacher;

Que le public était juge définitif de la valeur *des sentiments* étudiés dans une œuvre, parce que la foule est tout aussi accessible à la pitié, au malheur, à la colère, etc., que l'écrivain qui s'adresse à elle . . .[23]

(10) In Numbers 2, 3, 5, and 6 of *Réalisme,* from December, 1856 to May, 1857, Henri Thulié published four articles on the novel, treating respectively character, description, action, and style.[24] These constitute the most important body of theoretical materials in the journal. We may summarize them briefly thus: (a) The character—the most important element in the novel—must be depicted as an individual, not as a type, and with all of the special traits springing from his rank and his environment; he must be typical only in the sense that he represents all the traits of his class; naturally, he must be contemporary, and drawn from any social level. (b) Description is valid only as a means to characterization: landscape and setting as influences on character, together with interiors, physiques and clothing as expressions of character, must be fully described as seen by the artist. (c) Action, too, is subsidiary to character; it arises from differences between the characters of the various actors, and exists only as a further explanation of these characters; hence it must be as simple as possible. (d) Style must be simple, clear, using only as many words as are necessary to express the idea, cultivating the *mot propre* always in preference to the periphrasis.

(11) August, 1857. Antonio Watripon writes, in *Le Présent,* an article called "De la moralité en matière d'art et de littérature," in which he insists on the necessity of truthful depiction:

Au fond, ce prétendu idéal de beauté, ce type primitif, n'est qu'une chose de convention et n'aboutit presque toujours qu'au *maniérisme.* . . . Aussi, les mœurs contemporaines ne tentent-elles que les écrivains vraiment observateurs et les artistes sérieux.

Ce sont précisément ces gardiens antédiluviens de la beauté primitive qui ont toujours à la bouche le *rappel au sens moral.*

. . . une littérature ne peut pas plus se passer d'observation que les rayons lumineux ne peuvent se passer de demi-teintes et d'oppositions. Or, l'observation n'est pas autre chose que la science; c'est la somme acquise des investigations d'une époque, aussi bien du laid que du beau, de ses croyances que de ses négations. Donc, littérature et science ne peuvent vivre, c'est-à-dire s'élever, qu'autant qu'elles expriment d'une façon générale les besoins, les aspirations et les mœurs, QUELLES QU'ELLES SOIENT, du temps qu'elles prétendent guider et éclairer.

L'œuvre du romancier est donc de peindre la vie comme elle est; il serait souverainement immoral et dangereux de la peindre autrement; ce serait induire en erreur une masse de lecteurs et conseiller implicitement l'hypocrisie.

Etre vrai avant tout! La vérité ne peut effrayer qui que ce soit; elle ne peut égarer personne.[25]

(12) Francisque Sarcey, in an attack on Champfleury (*Figaro*, February, 1859), defines "Réalisme et champfleurisme." For each statement on realism, he gives a parallel remark about Champfleury; I quote only the former here:

"Il ne faut peindre que ce que l'on a vu, et le peindre comme on l'a vu; en d'autres termes: il n'y a de véritablement bon dans les lettres, que ce qui est absolument vrai, et les romantiques ne sont pas vrais."

Le Réalisme peint des caractères: sous la variété infinie et toujours changeante des traits qui distinguent chaque individu et lui donnent sa physionomie propre, il cherche les traits immuables de l'espèce où rentre cet individu; il les fixe en un portrait, qui vit et ne doit plus périr.

Le réalisme jette ses personnages dans une action, qui a son commencement, ses progrès et sa fin. Il prend la peine de former ses drames, comme il a pris la peine de les ouvrir.

Le réalisme étudie les passions et les étale à nos yeux dans un relief puissant. C'est ainsi que le peintre fait jaillir, sous la surface unie de la peau, des muscles qui èchappent à la vue courte et inattentive du vulgaire.

Le monde est mêlé de bien et de mal; c'est ainsi que le réalisme l'a toujours représenté. Il met des vertus sublimes à côté de vices hideux, d'héroïques dévouements près de passions égoïstes ou furieuses.

Le réalisme ne remue ces misères que du bout du doigt et pour en inspirer l'horreur . . .

Le réalisme ne mourra point: au moment même où le faux, le convenu, le boursouflé, le grotesque triomphaient sous le couvert du romantisme, les trois grands maîtres du roman contemporain, Stendhal, Balzac et Mérimée, maintenaient avec des fortunes diverses les fortes traditions du réalisme. Ils ont laissé leur succession à de jeunes écrivains, qui la transmettront à d'autres.[26]

(13) 1863. Ernest Feydeau, in a "Préface" to *Un Début à l'Opéra*,[27] reopened the discussion of realism, especially in its relation to the moot question of morality; the preface excited much comment and controversy. Feydeau pointed out that the contemporary, materialistic public no longer demanded in fiction the *pittoresque,* but rather an exact representation of itself; hence realism was the only possible form of literature for the second half of the nineteenth century. Realism he defined as "le système qui consiste à peindre la nature (ou l'humanité) telle qu'on la voit." This portrayal involves choice, arrangement, and inter-

pretation of the materials, it includes the ideal as well as the real. If it represents corrupt manners, it is because society itself is corrupt; the novel derives from society, rather than being responsible for social corruption. Hence the reproach of immorality is nonsense.

These are the documents. They extend (if we exclude the first) over a period of ten years. They are the work of ardent realists, of no less ardent adversaries of realism, of critics and novelists, poets and journalists. They appear in the most conventional and in the most progressive of Parisian reviews. Nevertheless, they show a striking unity of conception: realism stating its case in "la bataille réaliste," stated it in approximately these terms: Romanticism and classicism, striving for an ideal beauty and seeking it mainly in the historical subject, arrive only at affectation and falseness. Realism, on the contrary, aims to attain truth. Now truth is attainable only by the observation (scientific and impersonal) of reality—and hence of contemporary life—and by the unadulterated representation of that reality in the work of art. Therefore, in his observations, the artist must be sincere, unprejudiced, encyclopedic. Whatever is real, whatever exists is a proper subject for art; this means that the beautiful and the ugly, the physical and the spiritual, are susceptible of artistic treatment; it does not imply that the artist refrains from choosing his subject and his detail, for choice is fundamental in art. The principal object of imitation is always man; description of the material world, construction of plot, are thus subsidiary and contributory to character portrayal. In setting down his observations, the artist must of course arrange and dispose his materials; but he avoids all possible falsification of them by practicing the utmost simplicity of style and form. The product of this method is moral in the highest sense— truth being the highest morality—and is eminently adapted to the needs of a materialistic, 'realistic' society.

Realism in literature, so conceived, differs in certain respects from realism in painting; these divergences are to be explained largely by the difference in the media of the two arts. The desire for truth, contemporaneity, and completeness, the insistence upon observation and impersonality, the reaction against romantic and classical convention, are common to both. But literary realism goes farther in proclaiming the priority of man and human character among the objects to be imitated, and in declaring that character must be approached by a scientific, analytical method of observation. Again, and unlike pictorial realism, it insists that the artist must choose and arrange his materials. This insistence, in all probability, was merely an answer on the part of the theorists to the attacks levelled previously at the practices of the painters and at the early manifestations of realism in literature. In spite of these differences, however, the doctrine of the realists is essentially the same in both arts.

This similarity is borne out more strikingly still when we consult the definitions of realism which appear in the criticisms of these years. "Calque de la réalité," "copie fidèle de la nature," "peinture exacte," "vérité dans l'art," these and similar phrases recur in practically all of the seventy odd definitions given by the critics. As in the definitions of realism in painting, *réalisme* is again contrasted with *fantaisie, idéalisme, spiritualisme*. These formulations, indeed, are almost monotonous in their similarity; very few of them go beyond some phrase such as those quoted, and it would hardly be profitable to list them all here. I cite only a few of the most representative:

[1846]

585. Fournier: "donner à tous ses récits comme à tous ses personnages les solides contours de la réalité." "rendre la société telle qu'il la voit." (p. 258)

[1847]

695. Houssaye: "ceux-là qui violent la vérité toute ruisselante encore sur la margelle de son puits."

[1851]

696. Poincelot: "culte de la vulgarité." "la reproduction infime et systématique de la réalité, sans élévation, sans aspiration vers l'idéal." "l'antithèse de l'*Idéalisme*." (pp. 118-119)

[1852]

480. Baschet: "le côté magnifique du Réalisme dans le roman. La vie réelle, la société telle quelle, le monde avec ses accessoires, la représentation des sentiments et des désirs." (p. 83)

[1853]

812. Mazade: "la minutieuse anatomie des choses qu'il entreprend de peindre et de décrire." "il suffit d'observer, quelle que soit la chose qu'on observe, pourvu qu'elle ait un caractère réel." "la reproduction minutieuse des vulgarités les plus crues." (p. 1222)

814. Villedeuil: "la vie réelle avec ses drames mesquins et ses catastrophes exiguës; . . . avec ses grandeurs et ses petitesses, ses misères et ses ridicules." (p. 338)

705. Rouquette: "[copier] la nature ligne pour ligne, contour pour contour." "la nature telle qu'elle est, mais non pas telle qu'elle paraît être." (p. 313)

[1854]

709. Caro: "sensualistes de la forme et de la couleur." "l'imitation brutale de nos mœurs, une sorte de contr'épreuve daguerrienne de la vie de chaque jour." (pp. 431, 432)

[1855]

713. Pontmartin: "le sentiment vrai ou excessif de la réalité se passant de toute poésie ou ne la cherchant qu'en lui-même." (p. 28)

821. Janin: "tout ce qu'il entend, il le répète; tout ce qu'il voit, il le raconte; il n'arrange rien, il ne déguise rien."

[1859]

892. Monpont: "peindre de préférence, avec le pinceau ou la plume, les scènes et les objets les plus grossiers, les plus vulgaires, dans ce qu'ils ont de plus vrai, de plus naturel, de plus saisissant, et même de plus repoussant, et ne pas sortir de là." (p. 28)

[1864]

917. Delaplace: "copier simplement la nature, et mettre son ambition suprême dans l'exactitude de la peinture, dans la perfection des détails." (p. 140)

[1868]

794. Laprade: "l'art sans idéal." "la reproduction aussi exacte, aussi directe que possible des qualités matérielles d'un objet, . . . la représentation de ce qui tombe sous les sens, de manière à tromper les sens eux-mêmes." "photographier en quelque sorte la nature, . . . reproduire le monde matériel avec toutes les qualités les plus saisissantes de la matière." (pp. 485, 489)

From the earliest years, realists and critics alike cast about for ancestors of the new school, for prototypes and examples in the past. Balzac, of course, was the most obvious choice. He had, since 1830, practiced in his works most of the teachings of the new group; in fact, his example had been a major factor in the development of the theory of realism.[28] Others sought farther afield. André Thomas, for instance, went back to Brantôme, Lesage, Prévost, Sterne, and Voltaire.[29] Jules Janin saw sources for the new Bohemian school, including Champfleury and Murger, in Diderot, Prévost, Restif de la Bretonne, and Musset.[30] Champfleury himself would include Challes, Lesage, Prévost, Diderot, Sorel, Furetière, and Vigny,[31] while Auguste de Belloy would elect Voltaire.[32] For Paul Boiteau, Rabelais, Pascal, and Molière are *réalistes*.[33] Even Homer was claimed by Sarcey,[34] and Goethe by Saint-René Taillandier.[35] Among nineteenth-century authors, Pontmartin traces a filiation from Hugo, through Balzac, Gautier, Musset and Karr, to Murger;[36] others see Eugène Sue and Paul de Kock as forerunners of the new school.[37] In considering the sources, it is interesting to note that many critics regarded realism as having derived rather from a new materialistic spirit in society, following upon the Revolution of 1848, than from any literary tradition. Camille de Chancel's attitude is typical:

Au moment où nous sommes du temps et de l'histoire, il n'est point étonnant que la réalité ait en littérature le dessus sur l'idéal. Dans l'ordre économique, les applications ont le pas sur les théories. La société que 1830 et 1848 ont couverte de philosophies, d'utopies, de religions, est en train, aujourd'hui que les grandes eaux fécondantes se sont abaissées, de s'assimiler petit à petit, par un travail silencieux et intime, mais actif et incessant, les débris de doctrines, les fragments de projets, les amas d'idées accumulés autour d'elles. Pour l'instant, l'attention est plus particulièrement aux améliorations immédiatement réalisables, aux aspirations qui peuvent se traduire en affaires, aux réformes qui peuvent se mettre en actions, aux progrès qui donnent des dividendes. Entre la tendance sociale aux choses pratiques et la tendance littéraire aux héros réels, il y a un certain parallélisme assez exact qui saute aux yeux.[38]

No less curious and varied than the sources suggested for the realists were the authors considered as belonging to the new movement. A mere listing of the names (with the dates when they first appeared in association with the movement) will indicate how carelessly and indiscriminately writers were attached to the group; it will indicate, too, how vacillating was the concept of the term *réalisme* for about a decade. Hugo, Thouret, and Dumas *père* were early called realists by Planche.[39] Novelists such as Stendhal, Mérimée, and Balzac were, from the earliest years, considered as having similar literary practices, and were promptly identified with realism when the new movement came into existence.[40] Henri Monnier was regarded as embodying the same principles both in writing and in acting.[41] With them, too, was linked Balzac's 'disciple,' Charles de Bernard.[42] Then, beginning with 1848, the following French authors were connected by the critics with the new realistic school:[43] Champfleury (1848),[44] Murger (1849),[45] Dumas *fils* (1852),[46] Dupont and Büchon (1852),[47] Reybaud (1852),[48] Barthet (1853),[49] Sand (1853),[50] Souvestre, Gautier, and Gozlan (1854),[51] Augier (1854),[52] About (1855),[53] Desnoyers (1855),[54] Barrière (1856),[55] Flaubert (1857),[56] Taine (1857),[57] Baudelaire and Renan (1858),[58] Feydeau (1858),[59] Thierry and Thiers (1859),[60] Malot and Gourdon (1859),[61] Perret and Deltuf (1860),[62] Vermorel, Kéraniou, and Scholl (1861),[63] Achard and Roux-Ferrand (1861),[64] Charles Bataille (1863).[65]

Returning now to the realistic doctrine as we have stated it, we may attempt to discover the reaction of the critics to the various constituent elements of that doctrine. First, the open opposition of the realists to the classical and the romantic approaches in literature. For most critics, realism was anti-romantic rather than anti-classical; surprisingly enough, for many of them this departure from the romantic was a welcome step. That is evident from statements such as Thomas's:

... ils [le cénacle qui se moque des bavards et des lyres éoliennes] rient au nez des ciselures, des guillochages, des arabesques, des contours, des mignardises, des crevés de satin, de l'oiseau Rock, du lapis-lazzuli et des fanfreluches de toute sorte que la flamme de l'oubli a brûlés d'un clin d'œil.[66]

We might compare Pontmartin's remark that "quand le réalisme se prend au sérieux, quand il se propose de ramener au réel et au vrai l'art que nous avions égaré sur les vagues hauteurs du romantisme, il mérite que l'on compte avec lui."[67] Only rarely do we find a critic who, longing nostalgically for the glitter and tinkle of romanticism, attacks the banishment of these ornaments by the realists.[68] A few critics see in realism an attempt to overthrow classical convention—similar in that respect to romanticism—and they, too, approve the effort. Witness the remark of Léon Gautier:

... nous n'avons pas été trop indignes de notre châtiment [le Réalisme]. Pendant plusieurs siècles, la périphrase a régné parmi nous; pendant plusieurs siècles, on s'est pudiquement efforcé de ne jamais écrire ou prononcer le mot propre.[69]

In this sharp turn from romanticism and classicism, the realists naturally proscribed what they considered to be the essential aim of those schools—the quest for the beautiful and the ideal. But on this point the critics were in violent opposition to the theorists. For the former, like their colleagues in the field of painting, conceived of art as an idealization of nature; their definitions merely reëcho those given in the preceding chapter. For example, that of Charles de Mazade: "le but essentiel de l'art, c'est de rechercher et de reproduire une certaine vérité générale dans la nature physique comme dans la nature morale, dans la combinaison des lignes comme dans la combinaison des sentiments et des caractères."[70] Likewise, Caro contends that art must be an aspiration of the intelligence towards immaterial beauty, that it must use nature only as a point of departure, that it must cultivate the ideal which is superior in every respect to the real.[71] Critics so disposed were apt to exaggerate the realists' disdain for the ideal, and to condemn their product as lacking in that ideal. This is one of the most persistent objections to the new tendency; indeed, there are so many good statements of this reproach that it is difficult to choose among them. Albert Aubert's is one of the most typical:

Le roman, quoi qu'en dise Stendhal, n'est pas "une suite de petits faits vrais"; l'idéal y doit bien aussi avoir sa part, l'idéal . . . un grand mot, difficile à définir, et dont on a trop abusé! . . . Il faut . . . que le roman, comme la poésie dont il est frère, nous arrache aux étroites limites du réel, et nous emporte à quelque distance du pauvre *moi,* l'hôte fastidieux du matin et du soir; il faut qu'il caresse la chimère que chacun de nous au-dedans de lui nourrit amoureusement, qu'il nous console de la vérité présente par une autre vérité plus haute et plus belle.[72]

Without the ideal, says another, a work of art is incomprehensible, for the real and the particular may never be understood by the reader.[73] Without the ideal, declares a third, people and things have no meaning, they are merely matter.[74] And a host of other reasons are given.[75]

Instead of this ideal, the realists would seek and incarnate in their art only the true, the observable, the verifiable. This, for the critics, is the salient feature of the doctrine; the Goncourts, for example, in their burlesque of a realist, make him declare: "je pense que le vrai, le vrai tout cru et tout nu est l'art."[76] Almost all the critical discussions of realism point to this as its *sine qua non;*[77] but none is as explicit as the celebrated passage of Sainte-Beuve on "la réalité":

. . . si, en ressouvenir de toutes ces questions de réalité et de réalisme qui se rattachent à son nom [Champfleury], on voulait absolument de moi une conclusion plus générale et d'une portée plus étendue, je ne me refuserais pas à produire toute ma pensée, et je dirais encore:
Réalité, tu es le fond de la vie, et comme telle, même dans tes aspérités, même dans tes rudesses, tu attaches les esprits curieux, et tu as pour eux un charme. Et pourtant, à la longue et toute seule, tu finirais par rebuter insensiblement, par rassasier; tu es trop souvent plate, vulgaire et lassante. C'est bien assez de te rencontrer à chaque pas dans la vie; on veut du moins dans l'art, en te retrouvant et en te sentant présente ou voisine toujours, avoir affaire encore à autre chose que toi. Oui, tu as besoin, à tout instant, d'être relevée par quelque endroit, sous peine d'accabler et peut-être d'ennuyer comme trop ordinaire. Il te faut, pour le moins, posséder et joindre à tes mérites ce génie d'imitation si parfait, si animé, si fin, qu'il devient comme une création et une magie à son tour, cet emploi merveilleux des moyens et des procédés de l'art qui, sans étaler et sans faire montre, respire ou brille dans chaque détail comme dans l'ensemble. Il te faut le *style,* en un mot.
Il te faut encore, s'il se peut, le *sentiment,* un coin de sympathie, un rayon moral qui te traverse et qui te vienne éclairer . . .
Il te faut encore, et c'est là le plus beau triomphe, il te faut, tout en étant observée et respectée, je ne sais quoi qui t'accomplisse et qui t'achève, qui te rectifie sans te fausser, qui t'élève sans te faire perdre terre, qui te donne tout l'esprit que tu peux avoir sans cesser un moment de paraître naturelle, qui te laisse reconnaissable à tous, mais plus lumineuse que dans l'ordinaire de la vie, plus adorable et plus belle,—ce qu'on appelle l'*idéal* enfin.
Que si tout cela te manque et que tu te bornes strictement à ce que

tu es, sans presque nul choix et selon le hasard de la rencontre, si tu te
tiens à tes pauvretés, à tes sécheresses, à tes inégalités et à tes rugosités
de toutes sortes, eh bien! je t'accepterai encore, et s'il fallait opter, je te
préférerais même ainsi, pauvre et médiocre, mais prise sur le fait, mais
sincère, à toutes les chimères brillantes, aux fantaisies, aux imaginations
les plus folles ou les plus fines . . . parce qu'il y a en toi la source, le fond
humain et naturel duquel tout jaillit à son heure, et un attrait de vérité,
parfois un inattendu touchant, que rien ne vaut et ne rachète.[78]

If Sainte-Beuve's enthusiasm for reality was shared by but few critics,
his objections to the pursuit of this goal in art were reiterated by many.
Some of these arguments we shall consider under the discussion of specific realistic tenets, others we may now examine briefly. In the first
place, this "truth" was unsatisfactory because it excluded the ideal: truth
was taken as meaning, in its strictest sense, reality, also taken as meaning, in its strictest sense, the material and the factual. Hence there was
no room for the ideal. I have already cited the objections of the critics
to the lack of idealism. In the second place, it was denied that truth was
identical with reality. For "truth," metaphysically speaking, is something
greater and more far-reaching than the world as we see it—even if we
see it completely. "La réalité," says Barbey d'Aurevilly, "est complexe;
c'est une implication qu'il faut fouiller pour en démêler les mélanges et
les profondeurs."[79] "La vérité," says Arnould, "n'est pas la réalité: la
vérité est éternelle, la réalité change comme la mode."[80] "La réalité,"
according to Montégut, "n'est vraie pour [le spectateur] que lorsqu'il la
rencontre dans sa propre expérience."[81] And so on down the line.[82] In the
third place, truth so conceived was regarded as unattainable; as A. de
Belloy phrases it:

. . . le réalisme a cela contre lui, que son principe, étant absolu, est par
cela même absolument inapplicable. . . . Dans l'art, tout est plus ou
moins de convention. Le trompe-l'œil même ne trompe que les yeux qui
consentent à l'être. Si simple que soit, en apparence, le programme des
réalistes, ils ne peuvent s'y conformer . . . [The necessary omission of
vulgar language, for example.] L'auteur répugne, je veux le croire, à
ce douloureux sacrifice; mais il faut bien qu'il s'y résigne, et, dès lors, il
n'est plus réel; il cherche un compromis, un moyen terme, un procédé; il
fait de l'art, je suis fâché de le lui dire.[83]

To attain the truth they desired, the realists advocated a careful observation of nature, an impersonal and scientific approach on the part of
the artist. The response to this demand for observation was complex.
The critics would admit of it in principle, but they found that in application it led to a multitude of vices. They would welcome it as an antidote
to the riot of romantic imagination, but at the same time they would condemn it as leading inevitably to an accumulation of meaningless, minute

details, and as tending to replace the study of man by that of inanimate objects. As to minute details, preoccupation with them was regarded by many as being the basis of realism. Baudelaire, for example, points out that *"réalisme . . .* signifie, pour le vulgaire, non pas une méthode nouvelle de création, mais description minutieuse des accessoires."[84] And George Sand, unwittingly placing herself in the "vulgaire," defines realism as "le simple nom de science des détails."[85] So defined, realism cannot but dethrone man and exalt things. As Jules Levallois says:

Le brin d'herbe, le moucheron, l'arbre, le chat, le chien, le perroquet, la batterie de cuisine, les fauteuils, le canapé, la couleur des rideaux, l'étoffe de la jupe et les rubans du corsage, voilà les éléments qui suffisent aux prétendus héritiers de Balzac pour construire aujourd'hui un roman de longueur raisonnable. Ils y mettent bien de temps en temps, par un reste d'habitude, quelques hommes et quelques femmes . . . , mais de l'âme humaine aucune nouvelle.[86]

Even when man is the object of study, it is his external rather than his psychological aspects that attract the attention of the novelist. Vapereau exclaimed against this practice: "Il est si commode de substituer la description des formes à l'analyse des sentiments, les scènes matérielles de la débauche aux orages intérieurs de la passion, les impressions brutales des sens aux charmes mystérieux de l'amour, en un mot, le corps à l'âme!"[87] Of the numerous other passages offering a similar complaint, I quote only that of Merlet in his definition of realism: "Le monde moral n'offrant à l'imitation ni la figure ni la couleur, l'imagination, qui n'a pas charge d'âmes, doit se renfermer dans le monde physique, comme dans un immense atelier peuplé de modèles qui tous ont la même valeur à ses yeux."[88] This amounts to saying that the realists are frankly materialistic. Their disdain for idealism pointed immediately to this conclusion, their desire for "reality" contributed to it, their method of observation now confirms it. *Réalisme, matérialisme:* the words are synonymous. The new school is an *école matérialiste;* it answers the "tendance toute *matérialiste* de notre époque."[89]

Realistic observation, as I have already said, must be impersonal and scientific in so far as possible. If we remember the response to "impersonality" in painting, the attitude of the literary critics will immediately be evident. For they, too, demanded that art be a reflection of reality against the temperament of the artist, and the definite program of realism to suppress such a reflection could not but be rejected. Few critics, in fact, pointed to impersonality as a plank in the realistic platform;[90] but many of them revolted against what seemed to them, in one realistic novel after another, the suppression of the artist. Among them, none was more eloquent than Clément de Ris:

En vertu même de la dénomination sous laquelle ils sont connus et qu'ils ont acceptée, ils semblent repousser non-seulement l'intervention de l'imagination, mais celle du goût, de la réflexion, du caractère. Copiez la réalité, transcrivez-la littéralement, telles sont les suprêmes conditions de l'art, tout le reste n'est qu'erreur ; c'est-à-dire ne sentez pas, ne pensez pas, ne réfléchissez pas, comprimez votre cœur, éteignez votre intelligence, étouffez votre goût, faites de votre cerveau un objectif de daguerréotype, et tout ira bien.[91]

Arnould is equally angry in his repudiation of realism on these grounds:

. . . le réalisme n'étant point de l'art, est simplement un procédé. Comme il ne demande ni goût, ni style, ni imagination, ni pensées neuves ou idées fortes, ni études préalables, comme c'est un travail mécanique exigeant de l'exactitude et de la patience, tout homme qui en connaît un autre peut devenir auteur. On regarde, on écoute, on transcrit. Au besoin, on se peut servir de modèle à soi-même, à condition toutefois qu'on ait une glace où se mirer.[92]

Of the many others who scoffed at realism for its elimination of the artist,[93] there were of course some who found a simple reason for this state of affairs: the realists had no talent, and were forced to invent an art which could dispense with genius. Many critics, too, compared the artist so reduced and so minimized to a photographic apparatus. For what difference is there between a writer who copies nature exactly as it is, without interpretation, and a sensitized plaque exposed momentarily to the light? Many critics saw none whatsoever. Hence article after article equates realism with photography, with a purely mechanical rendition of the object imitated, with the consequent absence of anything recognizable as 'art.'[94]

Along with impersonality, a scientific approach. An attempt at classification of the people studied, at discovering the motives and causes of their actions, at indicating influences of heredity, environment, circumstance on their personalities. This technique, applicable essentially to the study of character, was often commented upon by the critics; Babou's article of 1843[95] is the most striking example. Another is Auguste de Belloy's summary which, in 1857, foreshadows Zola's theory of the novel:

. . . si, à l'instar de la science actuelle, la littérature s'est faite expérimentale, empirique, si vous le voulez, il n'en pouvait arriver autrement, car tout s'enchaîne et se déduit plus rigoureusement qu'on ne le pense dans le cerveau d'un peuple bien organisé. Petit ou grand, chacun a son laboratoire, et là fait des expériences dont il publie les résultats sans s'occuper en aucune façon de les relier à un système, à une théorie quelconque. Tout le monde en agit plus ou moins ainsi.[96]

By 1860 the tendency towards the experimental and medical novel was so widespread that Ernest Bersot was moved to write, in the *Débats,* two articles called "De l'application de la médecine à la littérature."[97] Of the numerous references to this method, most were disapproving; critics believed such scientific analysis incompatible with art, they saw it as rapidly leading to the description of the rare bird and the exceptional case, they feared that it would replace the normal by the pathological.[98]

These various realistic techniques were applicable only to the contemporary world; indeed, they arose as means to the adequate study and portrayal of that world. The demand for contemporaneity, so important a part of the realists' doctrine, was only rarely discussed by the critics, and in those rare discussions it was heartily welcomed. For critics and public alike were surfeited with the exotic in time and in space, they were eager for a literature treating their own times.[99] The objections raised to the banal nineteenth-century costume by the critics of painting did not appear in the case of the novel: again a difference to be explained by the difference in the artistic medium.

Similarly, and for almost the same reasons, the insistence upon 'sincerity' met with no opposition. Who would not applaud a return from the forced lyricism, the artificial passion, the counterfeit heroics of the preceding period? Jules Levallois, for one, was delighted at such a return: "L'école sincère nous a débarrassés de la sentimentalité factice, de la hâblerie nuageuse, de l'exaltation à froid, de l'imagination déréglée."[100]

But on the broader question of the subject-matter of literature, the outburst of censure was violent, and the point of view of the realists was entirely repudiated. It will be remembered that the realists had declared all subjects proper for literary treatment; that is, they believed that all levels of society, all classes of people, might supply heroes for the novel. In the later years, largely in rebuttal of insistent criticism, they had maintained that a choice of people was to be made within each class, a choice of details within each object. But this secondary, *ex post facto* affirmation was never accepted by the critics, who persisted in blaming realism for its failure to select. The reasons for so blaming it will be obvious when we recall the definitions they gave of art. These reasons will be obvious, again, from such a statement as the following by Peytel:

Ce qui fait l'erreur de l'école réaliste actuelle, c'est qu'elle a pris pour axiome, qu'il suffit qu'une chose soit vraie pour qu'elle soit bonne à peindre ou à raconter; c'est que, dans l'intention d'affirmer plus énergiquement son principe, elle a choisi des sujets dépourvus de toute autre qualité que leur vérité, et qu'ainsi par une pente naturelle l'amour du réel est devenu le culte du laid. Les réalistes ont oublié que la copie, si elle est exacte, ne peut pas être plus intéressante que l'original. . . . c'est précisément la difficulté de trouver dans ce qui est sous nos yeux des sujets intéressants qui a introduit ce qu'on nomme l'idéal dans l'art et la littérature.[101]

The attitude is epitomized by Fournel: "qui dit art, dit choix, et le réalisme ne se croit pas libre de faire un choix."[102] On the other hand if the realists, theoretically, aimed at being all-inclusive, practically they did make a choice. But whereas the romanticists and the classicists had chosen the beautiful, the ideal, the grandiose, the realists—if we are to believe the critics—chose only the low, the trivial, the ugly. Commonness, triviality, ugliness: these three combine to make what is by far the most sweeping and the most vigorous denunciation of the realistic movement.

By 'lowness' and 'commonness' the critics meant the tendency of realistic writers to seek their subjects in the very lowest spheres of society. Say Gustave Merlet: "à les entendre, il n'y a dans le monde que des filles de joie plus ou moins déguisées; tous les cœurs ne battent que pour le vice; la société serait un lieu mal famé dont leur plume tient le registre."[103] Says Louis de Cormenin:

Lisez ses œuvres, voyez dans quels repaires il entre, quelles effronteries sociales il coudoie, quel cloaque de sentiments il remue,—des voleurs, des filles de joie, des consciences douteuses, des êtres avilis. Au lieu de faire lever de généreuses semences dans le cœur de l'homme, il en agite les souillures, et tenant à la main, non la lancette qui sonde les plaies pour les guérir, mais le scalpel qui les fouille pour les étaler, il se promène de l'amphithéâtre au charnier.[104]

Again, in a poem entitled *Réalisme* and purporting to exemplify realistic literature, Henri Dubellay presents a horrible "bouge" and the encounter of a man with a prostitute.[105] Charles Monselet, too, writes his *Poème réaliste,* dedicated to "Gustave Courbet, maître peintre":

> Mon tailleur me pressait pour un billet échu.
> Je n'avais pas les fonds. Grande était ma torture.
> Mon concierge railleur me donnait tablature,
> Vers mon seuil s'avançait l'huissier au pied fourchu.
>
> Un long voile timbré pesait sur la nature
> Et dans l'opinion je me voyais déchu.
> Donc, n'aimant pas à voir traîner ma signature,
> Afin qu'il m'obligeât j'allai voir Barbanchu.
>
> Il n'était pas chez lui. Ce n'était plus tenable.
> Je rêvais je ne sais quel fatal dénouement.
> Enfin, pour terminer ce drame à l'amiable,
> Je fis à mon tailleur un renouvellement.[106]

These and other passages show conclusively that the critics saw in realism an abasement of art through the choice of inferior objects of imitation; that they objected in each case to this abasement need hardly be indicated.[107]

By 'triviality' the critics designated the readiness of the realists to select as objects of imitation persons and things eminently unworthy of artistic treatment. This reproach is related to the preceding, but it is not identical. For here it envisages, first, things so insignificant in themselves as not to merit attention in a work of art; then, language and actions which by their vulgarity or even their obscenity rank as unfit for art; finally, people and problems entirely uninteresting in life, and hence all the more so in literature. A passage in which Aurélien Scholl parodies the method of the realists (with special reference to Champfleury) will demonstrate the current conception of realistic triviality:

Jean Chouyou, souffrances domestiques des porteurs d'eau

Chapitre premier.—Les personnes qui passent à huit heures du matin par la rue Grégoire de Tours, ont pu remarquer au pied d'un mur humide et lézardé qui se trouve sur la droite, un peu avant d'arriver à la rue de Buci, un bourrier dont l'observation ne manque pas d'intérêt. C'est un amas pittoresque de bouts de carottes, de cosses de pois, de feuilles de salade, d'arêtes de poissons et autres rebuts. A de certaines saisons, les côtes odorantes du melon et la peau fine et rouge de la tomate viennent augmenter l'attrait du coup d'œil. Les os y sont rares. On les vend jusqu'à trois sols la livre pour fabriquer du *noir animal,* denrée qui sert à raffiner le sucre. . . .
Un homme sale et mal mis, appartenant à la lie du peuple, s'arrêta devant le bourrier.
Cet homme, c'était Jean Chouyou, notre héros.
Il considéra le bourrier avec une attention pleine d'amour; puis, tout à coup, il pâlit horriblement.
—Mon Dieu, murmura-t-il sourdement, elle ne m'aime plus.
Cet homme aux larges épaules, aux cheveux roux, aux mains noires et velues, aimait éperduement une femme de journée qui faisait le ménage de M. Nourrichet, employé du Mont-de-Piété. Cette femme, nommée mademoiselle Porquin, avait coutume d'indiquer des rendez-vous à son amoureux par la disposition des morceaux de navets et par l'arrangement des cosses de pois.
C'est ce que les Orientaux appellent selam. . . .
Mademoiselle Porquin était une femme de quarante ans. Une petite moustache brune ombrageait sa lèvre, et un énorme bouquet de poils jaillissait d'une tache foncée placée sur sa joue droite. Elle portait un bonnet tuyauté, une espèce de bonnet acariâtre et grincheux qui lui avait été donné pour sa fête par M. Nourrichet.[108]

Hippolyte Babou uses a different image to express the same notion; desirous of discovering "What is realism?" he turns to the works of Champfleury:

Je me trouvais transporté dès la première ligne dans une société de Lilliputiens. Il me fallut regarder presque à terre pour examiner de près le monde microscopique où j'avais mis le pied. Tous ces êtres de convention étaient uniformément petits, maigres, mesquins, plats, secs, décolorés. Je les considérai à la loupe, afin de savoir si, dans leur petitesse, ils gardaient du moins forme humaine. Je m'aperçus très-vite qu'on avait bridé des oisons, habillé des poupées, suspendu des marionnettes, mais qu'en fait de créature humaine il n'y avait pas même un nain de Laponie dans cette collection de jouets d'enfants.[109]

He finally decides that *réalisme* should properly be called *rachitisme*. Again, we might consult the opinion of Fournel, who says: "il [le réalisme] choisit de préférence . . . ce qui justement ne vaut pas la peine d'être peint, les petits caractères, les petits hommes, les petites choses, les côtés bas et vils, vulgaires et mesquins de la nature humaine."[110] A multitude of other passages contain the same reproach, which is the most prominent of these three prominent censures.[111]

By 'ugliness' (in the third place) the critics obviously refer to the realists' preference for the repulsive and their disdain for the beautiful. The same charge appears, we remember, in the case of painting; there, however, it is much more prominent than in the case of the novel. 'Ugliness' itself is a term more applicable to the pictorial than to the literary, and for the latter the equivalent terms 'lowness' and 'triviality' are more apt to be used. Nevertheless, the realistic school in literature is called "l'école du laid," it is described as "celle qui outre le principe et qui recherche seulement la vérité dans la laideur."[112] Léon Gautier maintains that:

Le Réaliste est épris de la réalité laide, et enlaidit le beau pour le rendre réel. C'est la première fois peut-être que l'on voit toute une foule se passionner pour le laid, marcher, courir, voler à sa recherche, pousser des cris de joie à sa découverte, se prosterner devant lui et l'adorer.[113]

In an article entitled "Du laid dans les arts," Edouard L'Hôte characterizes the realistic method: "Introduire dans la pratique et l'exécution des œuvres d'art la représentation des choses vulgaires ou dépourvues d'élégance et de beauté, se passionner pour le commun, consacrer son ciseau, son pinceau ou sa plume à l'exaltation du laid . . ."[114] Thus we find a group of critics who insist on the realists' emphasis on the ugly; but it should be noted that they are comparatively few in number and that their reproach comes relatively late, appearing with frequency only after 1857.

One clause of the realistic credo, that which established the primacy of character among the components of the novel, was entirely ignored by the critics. They made no comment upon it. Rather did they indicate constantly, as we have seen, that the realists were preoccupied chiefly with external and accessory detail, with things, with the physical side of reality, and that they neglected what was essentially human.

The realists' attitude towards form, however, did elicit considerable comment. They held that arrangement and disposition of the materials was necessary, but that it must be guided always by the severest principle of simplicity. A few critics recognized this demand for simplicity as a part of realistic theory, and in general they approved of it heartily. "Les grandes inventions d'autrefois," said Charles de Mazade, "ont fait leur temps. Il y a un effort pour ressaisir un certain naturel, une certaine simplicité de conception et de style."[115] Pontmartin, wondering what was meant by "réalisme," asked: "Est-ce une bonne et franche haine contre la convention, la manière, la sensibilité factice, l'artificiel et le guindé? Alors nous ne pouvons qu'applaudir."[116] Similarly, Granier de Cassagnac declared: "Exprimer simplement une idée claire semble un secret perdu. Retrouver ce secret et protester, en le pratiquant, contre le verbiage et la boursouflure, est un dessein digne d'éloges."[117] Many more writers distinguished in realism a reaction against the conventional in form and in vocabulary; to this they raised no objection, although there are few statements of definite approval.[118]

But when the critics read the works of the new school, they discovered that those works were in direct contradiction to their own aesthetic notions. The realistic novels lacked beauty of form; "faisant fi du style, de la forme et de la couleur," says Cormenin, "les réalistes se rabattent sur les idées."[119] The various authors of the groups are similar in "la négligence du style";[120] a realist may even be defined as a *contempteur de la grammaire et du beau langage.*"[121] The realistic novels failed to arrange their materials; they tended to present objects in their natural juxtapositions—necessarily an unartistic arrangement.[122] Worst of all, the realistic writings neglected all principles of subordination, of perspective, of ensemble. Important and insignificant details were given the same attention—when the insignificant ones did not entirely outbalance the others—to such an extent that the work was confused and disproportionate. This was a fault. "Les réalistes manquent à cette loi de la perspective," says Rouquette. "Il est certains détails dont l'effet doit être amoindri, qui ne doivent paraître que dans l'enfoncement, avec les proportions que leur place demande."[123] According to Lataye, "Le grand défaut de cette école est de sacrifier l'ensemble au détail, et de là résulte une cause d'impuissance non moins grave que le culte exagéré de la forme."[124] I might cite, finally, the opinion of Arnould: "Ils se perdent dans le détail, et l'ensemble leur échappe. Or le détail est un fait brutal, sans portée et sans moralité, dès qu'on cesse de le rattacher à un ensemble qui lui donne sa signification vraie."[125] It should be noted, in conclusion,

that while this reproach on the basis of form was varied and well represented, it was nevertheless a minor reproach as compared with others
outlined above.

The claim of the realists to a moral function for their art was essentially an *ex post facto* manifestation; it came late and only after the
reproach of immorality had been frequently voiced. But this reproach
itself was of much later appearance than many others. To be sure, it was
very early applied to specific authors—especially Stendhal and Balzac—
but as a censure directed at the realistic school as a whole and at the
doctrine of that school, it does not occur with any regularity until the
publication of *Madame Bovary*. Before 1857, we find only isolated
assaults on realism as immoral—especially Caro's article (1854) on "Le
Sensualisme dans la littérature."[126] With the prosecution of *Madame
Bovary,* however, the cry of immorality enters definitely into the arsenal
of the adversaries. Pinard's accusation contains the elements:

Cette morale [la morale chrétienne] stigmatise la littérature réaliste,
non pas parce qu'elle peint des passions: la haine, la vengeance, l'amour;
le monde ne vit que là-dessus, et l'art doit les peindre; mais quand elle
les peint sans frein, sans mesure.[127]

Subsequently, the cry of immorality finds various expressions. The
critics blame realism for treating the "mauvais monde," that of the
prostitute, the "demi-monde";[128] for neglecting wholly "la vérité
morale" in its search for "la vérité toute matérielle";[129] for concentrating its attention on the sensual.[130] They see realism as seeking always
the scandalous subject, in the desire to "taquiner les bourgeois,"[131] and
as exposing aspects of life which should remain private and hidden:

Il y a des détails de notre existence qui se passent derrière la scène; je
demande par pure convenance qu'ils les laissent là, qu'ils ne retournent
pas cette arrière scène de la vie et ne la donnent pas pour le spectacle. Il
y a des séductions naturelles: qu'elles restent séductions; il y a des
entraînements terribles: que ces entraînements restent entraînements, et
qu'on les regarde passer comme on regarde passer la tempête.[132]

Several writers, on the contrary, do not admit that given subjects are in
themselves immoral; rather it is the manner in which the novelist
handles them that makes them immoral. Nor is a work moral because it
has a moral ending: it may indeed bear throughout the stamp of an
unmistakable immorality. Everything depends on the attitude of the
artist, on his possession of the "moral sense." Rigault and Vapereau give
the best statements of this point of view.[133]

These various types of immorality were, for the critics, inevitable
consequences of the realistic doctrine. The reasons adduced are the same
as those given for the inevitable appearance of the ugly: the realist,

seeking truth, soon discovers that common, every-day life is uninteresting; but he has a prejudice against depicting men as better than they are; hence he is obliged to treat exclusively of men as worse than they generally are. He becomes an apostle of the ugly and the immoral; and the farther he pushes his system, the more deeply he sinks into the distasteful and the repulsive.

The realists, in rebuttal, asserted that there could be no immorality in truth, that the only immorality was in falsification of the real by the ideal, by the fantastic, by the impossible.[134] But this was a feeble answer indeed, and was immediately rejected by the critics. The more closely we approach the end of the period, the more vigorous and constant becomes the assertion that realism is an immoral system of art.

For realistic doctrine as a whole, then, the critics had little sympathy. They were ready to accept a literature which would correct the excesses of romanticism and replace the dead conventions of classicism. But realism, either because it erred in its theory or because it failed to apply properly the acceptable parts of that theory, did not supply the desired corrective. It neglected the ideal and the immaterial, and hence it did not attain truth. It replaced the study of man by the study of things, and hence it did not achieve an adequate representation of human action. It chose, among the objects of imitation, those which were undesirable for art, and hence it did not achieve the universality of subject to which it pretended. It disdained form, style, proportion, and hence it did not attain artistic beauty. In a word, as reflected against the preconceived aesthetic notions of the critics, realism could not fail to be regarded as an affront to artistic principles, as a diminution of the artist's function, as a vicious step towards the complete annihilation of art. Thus it was rejected as a doctrine, rejected as a general practice, rejected as a method for the individual novelist. This we shall see, more clearly even than in the case of Balzac, of Mérimée, of Stendhal, when we examine the criticism of those realists who appeared during the years of formation and application of the realistic doctrine.

---

[1] *691a*, Fortoul.

[2] *691b* to *691f*, Planche. On realism in the *Revue des deux mondes*, see *22a*, Du Val.   [3] *691b*, Planche.   [4] *300*, Hains.   [5] *693*, Anon., p. 380.

[6] *585*, Fournier, p. 258.   [7] *435*, Castille, pp. 367-368.

[8] *695*, Houssaye.   [9] *799*, Thomas.

[10] Note that after Houssaye, the next writers to use the words in painting were also on the staff of *L'Artiste;* cf. *604*, Leboucher; *607*, Calemard de Lafayette; *611*, "Feu Diderot." For a time, the new terms were almost a monopoly of this journal.

[11] The earliest dictionary definition of the literary term that I have been able

to discover is in Bescherelle's dictionary of 1845-1847. There, *s. v. réalisme,* he says: "Se dit aussi dans le sens de réalité. Ces effrayants tableaux de martyrs sont très-nombreux en Espagne, où l'amour du réalisme et de la vérité dans l'art est poussé aux dernières limites. (Th. Gaut.)" I have been unable to find the passage quoted from Gautier. Under *réaliste,* Bescherelle gives only the philosophical meaning. A more complete definition is given by Larousse (of which, unfortunately, I have seen no edition before the eighteenth, of 1865); he defines *réalisme* as "tendance que manifestent certains artistes et certains littérateurs de nos jours, à représenter la nature sous son côté *réel* et purement matériel." He defines *réaliste* as "Partisan du réalisme," both as noun and adjective. Finally, in 1866, both words are defined in the *Complément du dictionnaire de l'Académie française publié sous la direction d'un membre de l'Académie française* (Paris: Firmin Didot, 1866): "*Réalisme.* s. m. (néol.) Système moderne qui paraît consister à peindre la nature telle qu'elle est, ou telle qu'on croit la voir: *Le réalisme dans les arts, en littérature.—Réaliste.* s. m. et adj. (néol.) Qui affecte le réalisme dans la littérature ou dans les arts: *Un réaliste. L'école réaliste.*"

[12] *697,* Janin; *704,* Champfleury, pp. 585, 588; *713,* Pontmartin; *746,* Vignon, p. 2; *749,* Barthet, p. 77; *757,* Reymond, p. 14; *792,* Lefrançais, p. 3; *794,* Laprade, p. 500.

[13] *747,* Cadoudal, p. 26; *761,* Bersot; *778,* Chesneau, p. 223; *794,* Laprade, p. 496.   [14] *413,* Babou, pp. 130-131.

[15] *704,* Champfleury, p. 588. Cf. (4) and (7) below for other statements by Champfleury; also Bouvier, *op. cit.,* pp. 297-312, for a full summary of Champfleury's standpoint. I cite only the most significant documents here.

[16] *709,* Caro, pp. 434-435.   [17] *710,* Champfleury, pp. 396-397, 569-586.

[18] *715,* Desnoyers.   [19] Cf. above, pp. 105-106.   [20] *719,* Assézat.

[21] *823,* Champfleury.   [22] *824,* Aubryet, p. 282.   [23] *723,* Duranty.

[24] *724, 726, 730, 733,* Thulié.   [25] *740,* Watripon.

[26] *750,* Sarcey. In 1864, à propos of *Salammbô,* Sarcey restated his conception of realism; cf. *918.*   [27] *779,* Feydeau.   [28] Cf. above, p. 70.

[29] *799,* Thomas, p. 51.   [30] *848,* Janin.   [31] *710,* Champfleury, pp. 567-574.

[32] *727,* Belloy, p. 559.   [33] *817,* Boiteau, p. 137.   [34] *750,* Sarcey, p. 3.

[35] *913,* Saint-René Taillandier.   [36] *806,* Pontmartin, p. 651.

[37] *709,* Caro, p. 446; *500,* Ulbach, p. 62.

[38] *717,* Chancel, p. 371; cf. *696,* Poincelot, p. 118; *485,* Ulbach, p. 379; *706,* Lenoir, p. 289; *707,* Cormenin, p. 831; *819,* Cuvillier-Fleury; *728,* Soulas, p. 57; *736,* Arnould, p. 2; *886,* Weiss, p. 146; *774,* Fournel, p. 372; *958a,* Pontmartin, p. 149; *793,* Mazade, p. 501; *794,* Laprade, p. 484.   [39] *691a, 691d,* Planche.

[40] Cf. above, pp. 20, 29, 70.

[41] Cf. *104,* Balzac, p. 275.   [42] Cf. above, p. 93.

[43] I give only the first appearance of each in this connection.

[44] *799,* Thomas.   [45] *848,* Janin.   [46] *697,* Janin.   [47] *698,* Champfleury.

[48] *806,* Pontmartin.   [49] *808,* Cuvillier-Fleury.   [50] *701,* Boiteau.

[51] *708,* Lerminier.   [52] *709,* Caro.   [53] *960,* Babou.   [54] *715,* Desnoyers.

[55] *717,* Chancel.   [56] *863,* Pinard.   [57] *870,* Sainte-Beuve.   [58] *886,* Weiss.

[59] *940,* Chasles.   [60] *751,* Bersot.   [61] *951,* Vapereau.   [62] *763,* Pontmartin.

[63] *768,* Claveau.   [64] *769,* Etienne.   [65] *780,* Fournel.

[66] *799,* Thomas, p. 51.   [67] *763,* Pontmartin.

[68] Cf. *742,* Woestyn. On anti-romanticism, cf. *692,* Chaudes-Aigues, p. 51; *701,* Boiteau; *818,* Cuvillier-Fleury; *960,* Babou, p. 406; *500,* Ulbach, p. 62; *820,*

Goudall, p. 2; *728*, Soulas, p. 56; *887*, Granier de Cassagnac, p. 26; *766*, Levallois, p. 321; *787*, Coligny, p. 44; *788*, Desonnaz, p. 563.

[69] *920*, Gautier, p. 183. Cf. *702*, Bovet, p. i; *739*, Sand, p. 289; *757*, Reymond, p. 15.   [70] *809*, Mazade, p. 1207.

[71] *709*, Caro, pp. 432-433; cf. *696*, Poincelot, pp. 119-120; *808*, Cuvillier-Fleury; *812*, Mazade, p. 1222; *707*, Cormenin, p. 827; *708*, Lerminier, p. 618; *817*, Boiteau, p. 137; *774*, Fournel, p. 371; *991*, Levallois, p. 330; *917*, Delaplace, pp. 140-144; *930*, Scherer, pp. 293-294, for other definitions.   [72] *443*, Aubert.

[73] *768*, Claveau, p. 544.   [74] *554*, Desraimes, p. 4.

[75] Cf. *115*, Aubert; *442*, Maron, p. 242; *808*, Cuvillier-Fleury; *496*, Nettement, p. 249; *717*, Chancel, p. 371; *822*, Chasles, p. 464; *516*, Poitou, p. 761; *727*, Belloy, p. 559; *739*, Sand, p. 293; *753*, Arnould, p. 901; *837*, Cherbuliez, p. 256; *769*, Etienne; *794*, Laprade, p. 500; *795*, Félix, p. 383; *936*, Pontmartin, p. 294. Cf. *788*, Desonnaz, pp. 562-563, for a defence.   [76] *765*, Goncourt.

[77] Cf. esp. *817*, Boiteau, p. 137; *718*, Goudall; *840*, Vapereau, p. 103; *777*, Rondelet, p. 537; *778*, Chesneau, p. 219; *789*, Barbey d'Aurevilly, p. iii, and numerous others.   [78] *775a*, Sainte-Beuve, pp. 137-138.

[79] *815*, Barbey d'Aurevilly, p. 22.

[80] *753*, Arnould, p. 901.   [81] *754*, Montégut, p. 972.

[82] Cf. *809*, Mazade, p. 1207; *874*, Cuvillier-Fleury; *964*, Boissière, p. 539; *968*, Chavesne, p. 638; *999*, Vapereau, p. 58; *790*, Guillemot, pp. 148-149; *931*, Sand, p. 421.

[83] *727*, Belloy, pp. 558-559; cf. *694*, Delacroix, p. 435; *870*, Sainte-Beuve, p. 179; *779*, Feydeau, pp. xliv-xlv.   [84] *883*, Baudelaire, p. 106.

[85] *931*, Sand, p. 421. Cf. *820*, Goudall, p. 2; *736*, Arnould, p. 3; *915*, Boutmy, p. 75; *790*, Guillemot, p. 144.   [86] *766*, Levallois, pp. 321-322.

[87] *951*, Vapereau, p. 124.

[88] *893*, Merlet, p. 709; cf. *413*, Babou, p. 135; *808*, Cuvillier-Fleury; *813*, Chasles, p. 1098; *820*, Goudall, p. 3; *516*, Poitou, p. 745; *887*, Granier de Cassagnac, p. 29; *753*, Arnould, p. 901; *764*, Mazade, p. 244; *967*, Barbey d'Aurevilly, p. 238; *776*, Laprade, p. 541; *790*, Guillemot, p. 148; *554*, Desraimes, p. 4; *794*, Laprade, p. 489.

[89] *706*, Lenoir, p. 289; cf. *806*, Pontmartin, p. 651; *705*, Rouquette, p. 313; *709*, Caro, p. 435; *874*, Cuvillier-Fleury; *892*, Monpont, p. 29; *785*, Nettement, pp. 110-111; *795*, Félix, p. 383.   [90] Cf. *754*, Montégut, p. 983; *858*, Merlet, p. 35.

[91] *775*, Clément de Ris, pp. 306-307.   [92] *736*, Arnould, p. 3.

[93] *696*, Poincelot, p. 118; *813*, Chasles, p. 1098; *815*, Barbey d'Aurevilly, p. 21; *707*, Cormenin, p. 827; *874*, Cuvillier-Fleury; *754*, Montégut, p. 966; *892*, Monpont, p. 28; *858*, Merlet, pp. 34-35; *954*, Cuvillier-Fleury; *764*, Mazade, p. 244; *768*, Claveau, p. 544; *990*, Vapereau, p. 77.

[94] In addition to the articles cited in the preceding note, cf. *705*, Rouquette, p. 313; *820*, Goudall, p. 3; *734*, Texier, p. 295; *875*, Pontmartin, p. 303; *876*, Habans, p. 4; *746*, Vignon, p. 2; *749*, Barthet, p. 77; *758*, Anon.; *760*, Gautier; *837*, Cherbuliez, p. 255; *765*, Goncourt; *774*, Fournel, p. 371; *788*, Desonnaz, p. 562; *794*, Laprade, p. 489.

[95] Cf. above, pp. 119-120.   [96] *727*, Belloy, p. 558.   [97] *761*, Bersot.

[98] Cf. *803*, Pontmartin; *807*, Prarond, p. 145; *500*, Ulbach, p. 62; *870*, Sainte-Beuve, p. 183; *735*, Limayrac; *835*, Duranty, p. viii; *759*, Pontmartin; *764*, Mazade, p. 244; *538*, Geoghegan, p. 489; *777*, Rondelet, p. 536; *794*, Laprade, pp. 485, 494.

[99] Cf. above, pp. 104-105; also *820*, Goudall, p. 2; *732*, Caro, p. 674; *878*, Donis, pp. 75-76; *740*, Watripon, p. 244.

[100] *766*, Levallois, p. 321; cf. *817*, Boiteau, pp. 136-137; *741*, Dziedzic, p. 435.

[101] *782*, Peytel, p. 98.

[102] *774*, Fournel, p. 371; cf. *442*, Maron, p. 242; *813*, Chasles, p. 1098; *751*, Bersot; *754*, Montégut, p. 983; *892*, Monpont, p. 38; *893*, Merlet, p. 709; *837*, Cherbuliez, p. 256; *930*, Scherer, p. 293.   [103] *858*, Merlet, p. 46.   [104] *707*, Cormenin, p. 833.

[105] *752*, Dubellay.   [106] *716*, Monselet.

[107] Cf. *806*, Pontmartin, p. 651; *709*, Caro, p. 435; *500*, Ulbach, p. 62; *819*, Cuvillier-Fleury; *717*, Chancel, p. 368; *826*, Babou, p. 427; *876*, Habans, p. 4; *741*, Dziedzic, p. 438; *746*, Vignon, p. 2; *754*, Montégut, p. 983; *967*, Barbey d'Aurevilly, p. 229; *958*, Peyronnet, p. 131; *780*, Fournel, p. 339; *792*, Lefrançais, p. 4.

[108] *744*, Scholl.   [109] *826*, Babou, p. 427.   [110] *774*, Fournel, p. 371.

[111] Cf. *442*, Maron, p. 242; *960*, Babou, p. 406; *500*, Ulbach, p. 64; *820*, Goudall, p. 2; *717*, Chancel, p. 371; *824*, Aubryet, p. 283; *736*, Arnould, p. 3; *875*, Pontmartin, p. 301; *519*, Aubineau; *886*, Weiss, p. 177; *742*, Woestyn; *940*, Chasles; *746*, Vignon, p. 2; *747*, Cadoudal, p. 26; *751*, Bersot; *892*, Monpont, p. 28; *758*, Anon.; *759*, Pontmartin; *763*, Pontmartin; *966*, Cherbuliez, p. 389; *967*, Barbey d'Aurevilly, p. 230; *767*, L'Hôte, p. 82; *768*, Claveau, p. 544; *990*, Vapereau, p. 77; *775*, Clément de Ris, p. 307; *912*, Clergier, p. 11; *777*, Rondelet, p. 536; *917*, Delaplace, p. 145; *784*, Heurle, p. 10; *846*, Laffite, p. 56; *554*, Desraimes, p. 4; *792*, Lefrançais, p. 4.

[112] *902*, Claveau, p. 648.   [113] *920*, L. Gautier, pp. 186-187.

[114] *767*, L'Hôte, p. 82; cf. *714*, Pontmartin; *874*, Cuvillier-Fleury; *742*, Woestyn; *747*, Cadoudal, p. 26; *944*, Janin, p. ix; *196*, Merlet, p. 141; *749*, Barthet, p. 77; *769*, Etienne; *775*, Clément de Ris, p. 308; *914*, Néantes; *958*, Peyronnet, p. 132; *782*, Peytel, p. 98; *846*, Laffite, p. 56; *1006*, Villetard, p. 523; *1009*, Roqueplan.

[115] *804*, Mazade.   [116] *714*, Pontmartin.

[117] *887*, Granier de Cassagnac, p. 29; cf. *799*, Thomas, p. 51; *701*, Boiteau; *702*, Bovet, p. iii; *874*, Cuvillier-Fleury; *773*, Pontmartin, p. 705.

[118] Cf. *705*, Rouquette, p. 313; *714*, Pontmartin; *822*, Chasles, p. 463; *878*, Donis, p. 75; *741*, Dziedzic, p. 436; *835*, Duranty, p. xxi; *765*, Goncourt; *774*, Fournel, p. 373; and on vocabulary, *702*, Bovet, p. ii; *819*, Cuvillier-Fleury.

[119] *707*, Cormenin, p. 833.   [120] *874*, Cuvillier-Fleury.

[121] *762*, Révillon, p. 4; cf. *968*, Chavesne, p. 638; *766*, Levallois, p. 321.

[122] Cf. *813*, Chasles, p. 1098; *774*, Fournel, p. 371.

[123] *705*, Rouquette, p. 313.   [124] *748*, Lataye.

[125] *753*, Arnould, p. 901; cf. *813*, Chasles, p. 1098; *822*, Chasles, p. 464; *727*, Belloy, p. 559; *875*, Pontmartin, p. 304; *749*, Barthet, p. 77; *764*, Mazade, p. 243; *914*, Néantes; *790*, Guillemot, p. 144.

[126] *709*, Caro; cf. *442*, Maron, p. 242; *696*, Poincelot, p. 118; *807*, Prarond, p. 133; *714*, Pontmartin.

[127] *863*, Pinard, pp. 577-578.   [128] *732*, Caro.   [129] *874*, Cuvillier-Fleury.

[130] *875*, Pontmartin, pp. 299-301; cf. *751*, Bersot; *892*, Monpont; *759*, Pontmartin; *783*, Fèvre.

[131] *940*, Chasles.   [132] *761*, Bersot; cf. *796*, David, p. 184.

[133] *941*, Rigault; *890*, Vapereau; cf. *846*, Laffite.

[134] *779*, Feydeau; *784*, Heurle; *930*, Scherer; cf. the Bibliography for answers to Feydeau.

CHAPTER VI

CHAMPFLEURY

Chronology

1847: *Feu Miette*
      Pauvre Trompette
      Chien Caillou
1848: *La Reine des carottes*
1851: *Contes*
1852: *Contes domestiques*
      Les Excentriques
1853: *Contes d'été*
      Les Oies de Noël
      Aventures de Mademoiselle Mariette
      Les Souffrances du Professeur Delteil
1854: *Contes d'automne*
1855: *Les Bourgeois de Molinchart*
1856: *M. de Boisdhyver*
1857: *Le Réalisme*
      La Succession Le Camus
1859: *Les Amis de la nature*
      Les Amoureux de Sainte-Périne
1862: *Les Frères Le Nain*
      Le Violon de faïence
1864: *Les Demoiselles Tourangeau*

WITH Champfleury, for the first time in our study of individual novelists, we come to a writer whose first work appeared after the realistic battle had begun. Balzac, Mérimée, Stendhal, had completed or almost completed their writing when the realistic 'movement' emerged, and that movement merely shed a new light on the interpretation of their work. But when Champfleury's first stories were published, critics had already begun to use the term *réaliste;* in painting and in literature there was already a definite set of reactions to the new system called realism. The discussion, in so far as it was literary, now crystallized about the novels of Champfleury, and continued to center about them for almost ten years. Hence the criticism of Champfleury, although it is limited in quantity (about fifty-five articles), is highly interesting as epitomizing an early phase in the criticism of realism viewed as a literary doctrine.[1] In the present chapter, I shall study first the critics' conception of Champfleury's realism and their response to it, and secondly their appreciation of Champfleury as an artist.

It should be noted, at the outset, that Champfleury was not always considered a realist. The first articles, to be sure, stressed his realistic qualities, but for some time he was classed with the *fantaisistes,* and some critics would admit no other designation. Patrice Rollet, when he calls Champfleury "le réaliste de la fantaisie" (1851), applies both terms to him for the first time.[2] Later (1854), Paul Boiteau remarks that "Champfleury est un fantaisiste, si vous appelez ainsi quiconque n'est pas ennuyeux; mais si un fantaisiste est un littérateur à la chasse des niaiseries soi-disant originales et des absurdités inutiles, il n'est pas un fantaisiste."[3] But these are rare exceptions, and after Rollet's article practically everybody refers to Champfleury as the chief exponent of realism.

If Champfleury is considered a realist, it is partly because he is anti-romantic. The earliest critics stress this point—among them André Thomas:

Champfleury ment à son nom comme un aubergiste à son enseigne. Ni champs ni fleurs dans sa littérature. La brise n'a rien qui lui chante à l'oreille; et en fait de feuilles et de fleurs il ne connaît que celles qui servent à préparer des cataplasmes ou des infusions. S'il trouvait un rossignol il le ferait cuire et il le mangerait. Il fait les contes les plus charmants avec des artistes pâles de faim, des vieilles femmes qui boivent du curaçao de Hollande, des filous, des bourgeois de Laon, un chat qui crève et un corbillard.[4]

Emile Chasles, speaking of *Les Oies de Noël,* advises: "Si vous désirez du raffinement, de grands coups d'estoc et de taille ou l'hystérisme de bonne compagnie, cherchez ailleurs."[5] Rather than participate in this false romanticism, Champfleury maintains a strict independence; he records only what he sees and what he feels; he is absolutely sincere. This sincerity constitutes a second element in his realism. Monselet, for example, discerns in *Les Aventures de Mademoiselle Mariette* the prejudices and preferences of the author. "Ce mérite," he says, "est assez rare, par nos temps de lâchetés convenues, pour qu'on le signale avec empressement."[6] Similarly, Prarond compliments Champfleury for his courage in attacking the "ridicules d'une petite ville qu'on a habitée pendant vingt années."[7] Obviously, this 'sincerity' welcomed by the critics was only indirectly related to the 'impersonality' demanded by the realists.[8]

But by far the principal claim of Champfleury to the title of realist is his constant preoccupation with truth. This the critics recognize from the very beginning, and they admit throughout that Champfleury concerns himself solely with reality, and that he succeeds in depicting it faithfully. As to the desirability of the reality portrayed, there were divers opinions: but that the depiction was truthful was rarely questioned. "Quel clair et courageux sentiment de la vérité!" exclaims Marc

Fournier.[9] "Voilà," says Baudelaire in applause, "ce que Champfleury osa pour ses débuts: se contenter de la nature et avoir en elle une confiance illimitée."[10] This attention to nature produces an accurate representation of it; "c'est bien là la vie réelle," says the Comte de Villedeuil, "avec ses drames mesquins et ses catastrophes exiguës;—c'est bien la vie réelle avec ses grandeurs et ses petitesses, ses misères et ses ridicules."[11] The partisans of realism, of course, were all the more enthusiastic in their praise of Champfleury's "impitoyable fidélité à la vérité,"[12] but even the professed opponents were obliged to concede his perseverance and his proficiency in the study of nature.[13]

So far, these have been general realistic traits. But a tendency related more especially to Champfleury's particular brand of realism is his preference for the humble, even the lowly, subject. Critics stress this more than any other point in connection with Champfleury. Essentially, they are opposed to such a preference. They find that the subjects chosen for treatment by Champfleury are hopelessly trivial and uninteresting; in life, they would pass unnoticed, and when magnified by lengthy description they are tedious if not absolutely disgusting. We have seen this preference parodied in the article by Scholl quoted above;[14] we find it caricatured again in a mock trial during which Champfleury is represented as constantly lying on the ground, studying bits of apple peel, of carrot, of cabbage.[15] Vapereau describes this manner much more overtly:

Quant aux scènes, prenez les plus vulgaires, des cancans de toute espèce, des rivalités de sacristie, des intrigues de comptoir, des exhibitions de guenilles, des bonnes fortunes de chiffoniers, des orgies d'étudiants . . .[16]

To this reproach of lack of interest is added the old reproach of materialism; Champfleury's attention to minute detail and trivial object cannot but preclude the ideal and the spiritual:

. . . il n'observe que le détail inutile, la particularité insignifiante, et ses minutieuses recherches, qui n'ont pour objet que l'extérieur des choses, que la surface et les apparences des personnages, laissent de côté le caractère, le sentiment, la virtualité des êtres qu'il croit faire agir et qu'il néglige de faire penser. Il ne connaît rien de l'âme humaine et n'a jamais pénétré dans les replis du cœur où s'agite la passion. Il observe des yeux, non de l'esprit. Il regarde avec opiniâtreté, il ne voit pas. Un grain de poussière n'échappe point à son binocle, mais les secrets de la conscience, que l'intuition seule surprend, ne lui sont jamais révélés. Observateur, tant que vous voudrez, mais observateur myope.[17]

On the other hand, a number of critics come to Champfleury's defence; some of them, such as Janin, maintain that these subjects have a certain respectability by virtue of their truth.[18] Others, such as Chasles, prefer them to the wild imaginings of the romanticists.[19] Still others, like Thulié, admit them because of the light they throw on the understanding of humanity.[20] These vindications, numerous though they be, do not however offset the opposition, which annihilates Champfleury with the crushing epithet of *bourgeois*.[21]

This does not mean, necessarily, that the critics found no virtue in the representation itself; indeed, many pointed to Champfleury's skill in the depiction of manners, especially of provincial manners. Even so severe an opponent as Mazade admits that "l'auteur . . . peint certaines souffrances obscures, certains côtés vulgaires de la vie provinciale avec une sagacité singulière parfois."[22] But he and others who made this admission[23] immediately asked, after it, whether it was worth-while to execute an exact imitation of such objects and such people.

One special phase of Champfleury's social portrayal, his characterization, often elicited the praise of the critics. They liked his technique of creating characters, of investing them with the traits of a type. Without calling upon the exaggerated praise of a Thulié or a Duranty, we find highly laudatory appreciations from such critics as Perrier, Chasles, Lambert, and Chavesne.[24] The last of these asserts that "Il a saisi dans leur vérité antipathique, mais réelle, certains types odieux . . . et il a su les faire agir, les maintenir dans un rôle difficile, à travers les monotonies d'un sujet sans action." Here, however, there were also objectors, who blamed Champfleury for treating exceptional rather than typical people, for presenting in his books individual men and not mankind in its more general manifestations.[25] It is to be noted, though, that several critics upheld this system of studying and analyzing the exceptional character, for the reason that any character so treated might serve as a document to the scientist or the historian. As Prarond says, "les livres du genre des *Excentriques* seront les traités spéciaux des maladies graves de notre intelligence, ou plus modestement, pour les critiques difficiles, de simples mémoires à consulter, des thèses de médecine."[26]

Champfleury's skill in presenting *tableaux de mœurs* and in drawing characters was, for the critics, the result of his aptitude for careful and accurate observation. This was the one talent accorded him with any degree of consistency. As we might expect, the critics challenged the choice of objects to which his observation was applied, they found that he sinned through excess; but they did admire the talent. "Il a," remarks Rollet, "un grain d'esprit observateur que n'aurait pas dédaigné Stendhal."[27] "Le côté remarquable de cette étude [*Mademoiselle Mariette*]," says the hostile Mazade, "c'est qu'il y a réellement, en dépit de tout, une rare faculté d'observation."[28] "M. Champfleury," according to Lambert, "est un homme d'observation, et ses ouvrages attachent par cela même."[29] And many other passages echo and reëcho the same notion. Frequently, however, Champfleury's use of this faculty is blamed. One critic will claim that he observes only external, 'superficial' details.[30] Another, that he studies too minutely the objects represented, and sins by a luxuriance of unessential details.[31] Still another, that he studies these objects too completely in the desire to approach, by his descriptions, the exactness of the photograph; but he produces only an effect of exaggeration and of *invraisemblance*.[32] These we recognize as the stock objections brought to bear on the observation practiced by the realists.

For several critics, in fact, it was Champfleury's realistic preoccupations that spoiled his work; he had, they said, estimable literary capacities which were vitiated by application of an erroneous system. Eugène Lataye states the case thus:

Pourquoi donc M. Champfleury, qui a de réelles qualités de conteur, se fait-il ainsi la victime d'une mauvaise thèse? Il est observateur, il peint avec délicatesse certaines affections, et il a parfois le sentiment du véritable comique. C'est la vanité d'un faux système qui l'a donc entraîné . . .[33]

For Dusolier, there are two distinct people in Champfleury: "l'écrivain spontané, l'homme de jet et de tempérament, qui est le *nouvelliste,*—et le serf, la victime d'un système, qui est le romancier."[34] What these talents were we have already seen in part. First, the aptitude for observation and characterization discussed above. Second, a certain delicacy in the treatment of the passions, which the critics called "le sentiment."[35] Third, a sense of humor which discerned and exploited the ridiculous in people and in things, and which in many cases explained Champfleury's choice of the trivial and the ugly.[36] Fourth, a simplicity, even a naïveté of presentation, of means and of effect, which were welcomed as an antidote to affected style and tone;[37] finally, though only for a few critics, a narrative manner which held the attention of the reader despite fallacies of method and of subject.[38]

Instead of producing satisfactory novels, however, these talents were wasted—said the critics—on a system which could only be sterile. For when the artist decides that reality serves adequately in art, when he commits himself to the exact reproduction of nature without the necessary falsification produced by selection and arrangement, he eliminates all possibility of creating an 'artistic' work. So it is with Champfleury. His novels, lacking as they do composition and perspective, choice and subordination, suffer from all the anarchy, the chaos, the confusion of life itself. Sarcey condemns him completely on this score:

Le champfleurisme dédaigne ce soin [i.e., of composition]. Comme en ce monde, les événements se poussent l'un l'autre d'un cours ininterrompu, sans qu'on puisse jamais savoir où l'un finit et où l'autre commence, il s'imagine qu'ils n'ont, en effet, ni commencement, ni fin; découpe, au hasard, une tranche de la réalité, et sert au public des histoires qui n'ont ni queue ni tête.[39]

But a still more complete statement of the critics' objections, and one which we may take as typifying their attitude, is formulated by Dusolier:

Romancier, il se compose, il *se* raisonne: il part de ce principe que, le lecteur moderne étant par éducation, par la fatalité des temps, curieux du détail et voulant se rendre compte de tout, il est tenu, lui, de retracer avec minutie les faits les plus insignifiants aussi bien que les plus dramatiques, et de donner à tous même importance. Du choix, de la composition, M. Champfleury ne montre nul souci. Il observe—et transcrit à mesure que la matière *observable* se présente. Dédaigneux d'arriver à un effet d'ensemble, il ne dirige pas les diverses parties de son œuvre vers une situation centrale, qui soudainement les éclairera toutes et fera voir d'un coup le roman. Non. L'observation, l'observation seule, et c'est assez! l'observation qui ne devrait être que la justification, la raison, l'appui du drame, et qui, au lieu de cela, le prime et le supprime.[40]

Not only did the realistic prepossession spoil Champfleury's general manner, but it was responsible for the weaknesses of his style as well. How, argued the critics, could the realist 'write' his works when he set out with the intent of excluding all 'literary' quality? Obviously, that was impossible; he must use only the language he heard about him, uncritically recorded. Stenography. But Champfleury's diction was worse even than realism would justify; for he did not know French. Babou told him so: "Il vous était impossible de saisir la valeur exacte d'un mot, de déterminer les rapports logiques de plusieurs mots entre eux, de couler la moindre pensée dans un moule de phrase irréprochable."[41] Sarcey proclaimed it abroad to the world: "Le réalisme écrit en français; le champfleurisme écrit dans la langue de Champfleury."[42] But even an ignorance of French would be pardonable; Babou goes still farther in his accusation: "Il serait injuste de soutenir que ses solécismes et ses barbarismes sont des fautes de français; ce seraient tout aussi bien des fautes d'anglais, d'allemand, d'indoustani et même d'iroquois, parce qu'elles portent atteinte à la syntaxe naturelle de tous les peuples."[43] The condemnation is severe. Against it there arose, especially in the early years, a group of critics who defended Champfleury's style on the basis of its clearness, its simplicity, its freedom from false graces.[44] But they were soon outnumbered by those who declared, repeatedly, that Champfleury had no style.

Furthermore, he had no ideas and no moral purpose. These, too, were precluded by the realistic point of view. The realist makes no comment on the facts presented, he refrains from indoctrinating the reader through interpretation of the facts; he merely gives the facts. This was Champfleury's method.[45] It is to be noted, however, that this reproach is relatively mild in the case of Champfleury; unlike Balzac, for example, he was not often accused of positive and wilful immorality. But by abstaining from all personal intervention in the novel, said the critics, he produced works of a cold and cynical character, works which discouraged or even disgusted the reader, and which—by counteracting Champfleury's native tendencies towards 'sentiment'—again demonstrated the evil results of his servitude to a system.[46]

Evidently, the total critical reaction to Champfleury as a novelist was unfavorable, and the case against him was stated quite clearly. In the earliest years, from 1847 to about 1852, the few scattered articles were largely sympathetic towards him. After that, the ratio of condemnatory to laudatory statements constantly increased. There were, nonetheless, critics who praised him highly throughout the entire period under consideration—Boiteau in 1854, Chasles in 1856, Thulié in 1857, Duranty in 1859, Fournel in 1863, Assézat in 1864, Laffite in 1865.[47] But these were, in large part, realists or advocates of the realistic movement. For others, it was precisely his realistic prejudices that were responsible for his lack of artistry, for the undistinguished, the monotonous, the humdrum character of his novels.

---

[1] Cf. 7, Bouvier, pp. 318-321, for a brief summary of criticism of Champfleury, based on a small number of articles.   [2] 801, Rollet, p. 391.

[3] 817, Boiteau, p. 137; cf. 827, Thulié, p. 50; 846, Laffite, p. 56.

[4] 799, Thomas, p. 52.

[5] 813, Chasles, p. 1097; cf. 797, Fournier; 798, Baudelaire, p. 169; 817, Boiteau, p. 137; 827, Thulié, p. 56; 835, Duranty, p. xii.   [6] 811, Monselet, p. 92.

[7] 807, Prarond, p. 136.

[8] Cf. 797, Fournier; 798, Baudelaire, p. 172; 817, Boiteau, p. 137; 652, Perrier, p. 85; 827, Thulié, p. 50.   [9] 797, Fournier.   [10] 798, Baudelaire, p. 169.

[11] 814, Villedeuil, p. 338.   [12] 835, Duranty, p. xxv.

[13] Cf. 799, Thomas, p. 52; 849, Janin; 802, Cuvillier-Fleury, 2nd art.; 809, Mazade, p. 1207; 811, Monselet, p. 91; 813, Chasles, p. 1097; 816, Mazade, p. 1050; 817, Boiteau, p. 137; 652, Perrier, p. 85; 822, Chasles, p. 464; 824, Aubryet, p. 282; 827, Thulié, p. 56; 832, Lambert, p. 916; 834, Merlet, p. 303; 836, Laurent-Pichat, p. 326; 837, Cherbuliez, p. 255; 840, Vapereau, p. 102; 839, Cherbuliez, p. 488; 846, Laffite, p. 56.   [14] Cf. p. 137.   [15] 830, Rousseau.

[16] 840, Vapereau, p. 102; cf. 801, Rollet, p. 391; 802, Cuvillier-Fleury, 2nd art.; 804, Mazade; 812, Mazade, p. 1222; 816, Mazade, p. 1050; 750, Sarcey, p. 3; 832, Lambert, p. 917; 836, Laurent-Pichat, p. 326; 837, Cherbuliez, p. 255; 838, Chavesne, p. 637; 839, Cherbuliez, p. 488; 841, Cherbuliez, p. 122.

[17] *833*, Duchesne, p. 6; cf. *808*, Cuvillier-Fleury; *809*, Mazade, p. 1207.
[18] *849*, Janin.   [19] *813*, Chasles, p. 1097.
[20] *827*, Thulié, p. 50; cf. *797*, Fournier; *798*, Baudelaire, p. 172; *799*, Thomas, p. 51; *811*, Monselet, p. 91; *883*, Baudelaire, p. 106; *835*, Duranty, p. viii; *846*, Laffite, p. 56, for defences.   [21] Cf. *824*, Aubryet, p. 281; *831*, Lataye, p. 248.
[22] *812*, Mazade, p. 1222.
[23] Cf. *798*, Baudelaire, p. 169; *804*, Mazade; *805*, Venet, p. 228; *822*, Chasles, p. 464; *823*, Anon., p. 3; *835*, Duranty, p. viii; *837*, Cherbuliez, p. 256; *845*, Laurent-Pichat.
[24] *827*, Thulié; *835*, Duranty, p. xxix; *652*, Perrier, p. 85; *822*, Chasles, p. 463; *832*, Lambert, p. 916; *838*, Chavesne, p. 636; cf. *823*, Anon., p. 3.
[25] *883*, Baudelaire, p. 106; *750*, Sarcey, p. 3; *834*, Merlet, p. 324.
[26] *807*, Prarond, p. 145; cf. *835*, Duranty, pp. xvi, xxvi; *843*, Assézat.
[27] *801*, Rollet, p. 391.   [28] *809*, Mazade, p. 1207.
[29] *832*, Lambert, p. 916; cf. *798*, Baudelaire, p. 172; *805*, Venet, p. 228; *807*, Prarond, p. 142; *812*, Mazade, p. 1222; *813*, Chasles, p. 1098; *819*, Cuvillier-Fleury; *820*, Goudall, p. 3; *827*, Thulié, p. 50; *828*, Anon., p. 330; *829*, Révillon; *831*, Lataye, p. 248; *835*, Duranty, p. xxiii; *845*, Laurent-Pichat; *846*, Laffite, p. 56.
[30] Cf. above, p. 147.
[31] *812*, Mazade, p. 1222; *819*, Cuvillier-Fleury; *833*, Duchesne, p. 6; *834*, Merlet; *846*, Laffite, p. 56.
[32] *802*, Cuvillier-Fleury, 2nd art.; *819*, Cuvillier-Fleury; *823*, Anon., p. 3; *831*, Lataye, p. 249.   [33] *831*, Lataye, p. 249.
[34] *842*, Dusolier, p. 28; cf. *813*, Chasles, p. 1098; *815*, Barbey d'Aurevilly, p. 21; *816*, Mazade, p. 1051; *840*, Vapereau, p. 104.
[35] Cf. *813*, Chasles, p. 1097; *827*, Thulié, p. 50.
[36] Cf. *801*, Rollet, p. 391; *831*, Lataye, p. 249; *835*, Duranty, p. xxii; and especially *846*, Laffite, p. 56.
[37] Cf. *798*, Baudelaire, p. 169; *799*, Thomas, p. 51; *813*, Chasles, p. 1097; *817*, Boiteau, p. 137; *822*, Chasles, p. 464; *827*, Thulié, p. 50; *835*, Duranty, p. xxii; *846*, Laffite, p. 56.
[38] Cf. *821*, Janin; *831*, Lataye, p. 249; *836*, Laurent-Pichat, p. 326; *846*, Laffite, p. 57.   [39] *750*, Sarcey, p. 3.
[40] *842*, Dusolier, p. 29; cf. *803*, Pontmartin; *813*, Chasles, p. 1098; *815*, Barbey d'Aurevilly, p. 21; *816*, Mazade, p. 1050; *820*, Goudall, p. 4; *821*, Janin; *828*, Anon., p. 330; *831*, Lataye, p. 249; *836*, Laurent-Pichat, p. 326; *840*, Vapereau, p. 103.
[41] *826*, Babou, p. 426.   [42] *750*, Sarcey, p. 3.
[43] *826*, Babou, p. 426; *807*, Prarond, p. 145; *812*, Mazade, p. 1222; *815*, Barbey d'Aurevilly, p. 20; *819*, Cuvillier-Fleury; *820*, Goudall, p. 4; *823*, Anon., p. 3; *825*, Bataille; *828*, Anon., p. 330; *830*, Rousseau, p. 5; *831*, Lataye, p. 248; *832*, Lambert, p. 917; *833*, Duchesne, p. 7.
[44] Cf. *798*, Baudelaire, p. 172; *811*, Monselet, p. 91; *813*, Chasles, p. 1097; *817*, Boiteau, p. 137; *822*, Chasles, p. 464; *835*, Duranty, pp. xxi-xxii.
[45] *815*, Barbey d'Aurevilly, p. 20; *816*, Mazade, p. 1050; *823*, Anon., p. 4; *833*, Duchesne, p. 6; *834*, Merlet, p. 317; *836*, Laurent-Pichat, p. 327
[46] *801*, Rollet, p. 391; *805*, Venet, p. 228; *815*, Barbey d'Aurevilly, p. 20; *819*, Cuvillier-Fleury; *830*, Rousseau; *832*, Lambert, p. 917. Also *817*, Boiteau, p. 137, for a defence.   [47] Nos. *817*, *822*, *827*, *835*, *780*, *843*, and *846* respectively.

CHAPTER VII

MURGER

Chronology
1849: *La Vie de Bohème* (drama)
1851: *Scènes de la Vie de Bohème* (novel)
Scènes de la Vie de jeunesse
1852: *Le Pays latin*
Le Bonhomme Jadis (drama)
1857: *Les Vacances de Camille*
1861: Murger's death

H ENRI MURGER was only to a very small extent a realist. He is more properly considered as a romantic with passing attempts at a modified realism.[1] But since some critics linked him with the realistic movement, it will be profitable for us to consider in what respects they thought him realistic. Here, as in Chapter III, I have made a selection among the materials available.

The primarily romantic quality of Murger's talent was remarked and emphasized by most of his reviewers. For them, he was distinguished from his contemporaries by his delicate treatment of passion, by his sentimentality, by his melancholy. His work sprang from his own life and embodied his own emotions; in this sense it was strictly personal. These ideas recur throughout criticism of Murger, from the earliest articles on *La Vie de Bohème* to the necrologic notices of 1861. Eyma, in 1849, speaks of "l'exquise délicatesse des sentiments,"[2] Janin of the "vif entraînement de passion."[3] Clément de Ris finds in Murger's first novel "une mélancolie affectueuse et douce, puisée dans son propre cœur"; this he regards as Murger's principal claim to originality.[4] And so on down through Aubryet, who ranks him among the "novelists of sentiment,"[5] to Claveau who speaks of "cette même facilité d'émotion, cette même tendresse exquise, enfin cette même fleur de sentiment qui embaume tous les ouvrages d'Henri Monnier."[6] Besides this manner of handling the passions, other qualities differentiate Murger from the realists and his works from the "romans d'observation."[7] These are best characterized by Merlet in his article on "Un Réaliste imaginaire," where he shows at length why Murger must not be considered as a realist. Merlet points especially to the presence of the author's personality in his work, to his sympathy with his characters, to the purely fictional nature of his

153

people and his plots, above all to the idealization of his heroines, as so many differences between Murger and his realistic contemporaries.[8]

Nevertheless other critics, and sometimes the same critics in other passages of their articles, gave indications as to why Murger might be classed with the realists. First and foremost, his works give to some the impression of having been based on real life; the phrase "la vie réelle" appears several times as a description of his subjects.[9] This reality, too, is essentially contemporary; according to Fournier, "Si un livre mérite de vivre parce qu'il est l'expression d'une époque, c'est celui-là [*Scènes de la Vie de Bohème*]."[10] Auguste Lireux goes still farther: "Chose assez digne de remarque . . . , et qui révèle l'observateur : les jeunes gens de M. Murger personnifient l'un des grands vices du temps; ils manquent de jeunesse, ils n'ont ni expansion, ni légèreté, ni enthousiasme, ils n'ont rien de bon." He calls attention, then, to the strong intermixture of sordid detail with Murger's sentimental stories, which he calls "tableaux assez honteux de la vie de bohème."[11] This treatment of Bohemian life was in itself sufficient, for some, to identify Murger with the realists. Nettement, for example, classes Murger and Champfleury together under the heading of "L'Elégie dans le roman," and characterizes the *Scènes de la Vie de Bohème* and its sequels as "les œuvres réalistes de Murger."[12] For a short time, at least, this association with Bohemian subjects was one mark of the realist; thus Pontmartin, in 1852, called Musset a precursor of the new movement because of such stories as *Mimi Pinson* and *Frédéric et Bernerette*.[13]

Secondly, Murger is a realist by his style, which in its simplicity departs from the manner of the *fantaisistes*. We may take the testimony of André Thomas to this effect:

. . . nous aimons cet accent de vérité qu'on y retrouve sous chaque mot; le style est un défi hardiment jeté à tous les écrivains excentriques et somptueux, qui depuis Théophile Gautier jusqu'à Duvert et Lausanne s'exercent à jongler avec des adjectifs et à avaler des verbes enflammés . . . Après M. Murger, nous ne voyons plus trop ce que l'on pourrait faire dans ce genre-là. Il a dépassé les colonnes d'Hercule de l'hyperbole et fait crier grâce à la rhétorique.[14]

Clément de Ris, too, welcomes this departure from the "oripeaux fanés de l'antithèse" and believes that it accounts for the favor of the public.[15] On the other hand, and very curiously, Pontmartin seems to think that it is because of his style that Murger is distinct from the realists; Pontmartin, in this passage, apparently conceives of realism as an overwrought and highly imaged style, of realists as "les maîtres les plus raffinés de la ciselure et de l'arabesque."[16] It was Pontmartin, too, who earlier had said of the *Vie de Jeunesse:*

Ses *Scènes de la Vie de Jeunesse* n'étaient, à vrai dire, qu'une seconde épreuve de son premier livre, épreuve poussée au noir, et où les tendances réalistes devenaient si excessives, que l'auteur, au lieu d'interpréter la nature ou même de la copier, semblait vouloir ne nous donner que des études d'amphithéâtre, d'après le cadavre ou l'écorché.[17]

One wonders, with Martino,[18] to what element in the harmless novel Pontmartin could possibly be referring here. Both passages are perhaps explained by the fact that Pontmartin was one of those critics who saw in every work they disliked a manifestation of realism, and who found realistic traits in every inferior writer. Finally, Murger was associated with the new movement through the "sincerity" of his work.[19]

It will be evident, even from this brief summary, that Murger's realism, in the eyes of the critics, was of a very tempered sort. It occasioned no great controversy and did not prevent many readers from enjoying in his work what was sentimental and romantic. Thus we may agree entirely with Martino that "l'école réaliste élabora sa doctrine et fit sa campagne tout à fait en dehors de Murger."[20]

---

[1] Cf. the characterization by Martino, *op. cit.*, pp. 26-50. [2] *848*, Eyma, 2nd art.
[3] *849*, Janin.   [4] *853*, Clément de Ris, p. 181.   [5] *857*, Aubryet, p. 111.
[6] *859*, Claveau, p. 710; cf. *861*, Nettement.   [7] *857*, Aubryet, p. 111.
[8] *858*, Merlet.   [9] Cf. *848*, Eyma, 2nd art.; *849*, Janin; *856*, Prarond, p. 163.
[10] *852*, Fournier, p. 28.   [11] *855*, Lireux; cf. *859*, Claveau, p. 710.
[12] *861*, Nettement, pp. 141, 151.   [13] *806*, Pontmartin.   [14] *851*, Thomas, p. 45.
[15] *853*, Clément de Ris, p. 180.   [16] *860*, Pontmartin, p. 702.
[17] *854*, Pontmartin, p. 194.   [18] *Op. cit.*, p. 32.   [19] Cf. *851*, Thomas, p. 46.
[20] *Op. cit.*, p. 50.

THE SCHOOL OF 1857

CHAPTER VIII

FLAUBERT

Chronology
1856: *Madame Bovary* (serial form)
1856-1857: *La Tentation de Saint-Antoine*
1857: *Madame Bovary*
1862: *Salammbô*
1869: *L'Education sentimentale*

W HEN Flaubert published *Madame Bovary,* the realistic battle had been in progress for almost fifteen years. For nearly ten years it had centered about the works of Champfleury, and for almost as long about the paintings of Courbet. It had involved, as well, the novels of the precursors of realism, and the paintings of many minor artists. But except in the case of Courbet the encounters had been mere skirmishes; the protest had been neither very persistent nor very violent, the defence had been mild. In the second half of 1856, however, Duranty and his group had published the first numbers of *Réalisme,* attracting considerable attention to the new movement. During the same period Flaubert published *Madame Bovary* in periodical form; the misgivings of the *Revue de Paris* and public indignation began to crystallize anti-realistic feeling about this novel, and this indignation reached its climax in the trial of Flaubert for immorality. As we have seen, the appearance of his novel had immediate repercussions on the criticism of Balzac and on the general conception of realism. We have now to examine the reception of the novel itself. The criticism of Flaubert centers about the three novels published during our period, *Madame Bovary, Salammbô,* and *L'Education sentimentale,* and I shall indicate separately the response to each of these novels.

In his arraignment of Flaubert before the imperial court, advocate Ernest Pinard brought essentially one charge, the immorality of *Madame Bovary.*[1] Critics of the novel, however, reiterated this charge only rarely; but they made frequent and adverse comments on Flaubert's attitude towards his subject-matter, which in the ensemble were equivalent to Pinard's accusation of immorality. Let us first examine the nature of these comments.

For much of this criticism, Sainte-Beuve himself unwittingly gave the

159

keynote: "Fils et frère de médecins distingués, M. Gustave Flaubert tient la plume comme d'autres le scalpel. Anatomistes et physiologistes, je vous retrouve partout!"[2] The remark was not new; we have encountered it in the criticisms of Balzac from the earliest years. But the critics of Flaubert now adopted it as one of the principal weapons against him. They indicated that his approach to his subject was mainly scientific, that he proceeded by analysis and dissection, that his method was that of the physiologist. Thus Vapereau entitled his review "Succès du roman physiologique"[3] and Merlet called his article "Le Roman physiologique."[4] From the literary standpoint, this method was highly undesirable. It accounted, for example, for Flaubert's indifference to moral considerations; as Texier says, "La physiologie est une science dont je fais le plus grand cas, mais à la condition qu'elle ne submerge pas le monde métaphysique, et, dans *Madame Bovary,* j'avoue que le carabin me cache un peu trop le moraliste."[5] Again, it explained the licentiousness of subject and treatment:

Son licencieux procède de sa physiologie. Etudiant l'homme comme un objet d'histoire naturelle et non comme une personne morale, il a envisagé dans la luxure un accident de sa constitution, et il s'est imposé le devoir d'en noter scrupuleusement les phases diverses.[6]

Above all, the scientific approach was responsible for Flaubert's "impassibilité," for his complete impersonality; thus Merlet called him "un chirurgien qui se trompe de vocation et applique à l'analyse des caractères le sang-froid cruel de l'anatomiste."[7]

To this impersonality, particularly, the critics objected violently; few would agree with Sainte-Beuve that it was "une grande preuve de force."[8] Rather did they see it as one of Flaubert's principal failings. For Duranty, despite his realistic convictions, the book was cold and devoid of life, a mathematical demonstration instead of a novel.[9] For Barbey d'Aurevilly, its real virtues were negatived by this very insensibility:

. . . l'auteur de *Madame Bovary* n'était point immoral. Il n'était qu'insensible. . . . Tel est le défaut radical d'un ouvrage qui se recommande par des qualités d'une grande force, mais que la critique devait signaler tout d'abord, avant tout détail et toute analyse, parce que ce défaut affecte l'ensemble et le fond du livre même,—parce que cette indigence de sensibilité, d'imagination, et je dirai plus, de sens moral et poétique, se retrouve à toute page et frappe l'œuvre entière de M. Flaubert d'une épouvantable sécheresse. Pour notre compte, nous ne connaissons pas de composition littéraire d'un talent plus vrai et qui soit en même temps plus dénuée d'enthousiasme, plus vide de cœur; d'un sang-froid plus cruel.[10]

One after another, the critics repeat the accusation, in extended passages like the above, in brief formulas such as Cuvillier-Fleury's "ni imagination, ni émotion, ni morale."[11]

On the other hand, the scientific approach plus the complete indifference to the implications of subject-matter leads—via physiological preoccupations—to an out-and-out sensualism. Madame Bovary is a voluptuary dominated completely by her senses; in his study of her, Flaubert emphasizes only these sensual aspects. Thus he must frequently present scabrous details and indiscreet "scènes d'alcove." "C'est par préméditation de sensualisme," says Weiss, "que M. Flaubert retrace si au long les révoltes furieuses, les savantes jouissances et les rassasiements de la volupté charnelle."[12] According to Monpont, "Son roman est plein de crudités et de sensualisme vulgaire; il a les allures érotiques des mauvais livres que cachent les écoliers au fond de leurs pupitres."[13] These are extreme criticisms; but more temperate and otherwise sympathetic critics made the same reproach.[14]

A final evidence of the vicious nature of Flaubert's approach to his subject—say the critics—is the scepticism, the cynicism, the fatalism which he displays in its treatment. He is disillusioned and hard, cruel and brutal; he sees in human action only the inevitable operation of implacable laws. For the best statement of this last point of view, we must again turn to Weiss:

. . . chaque degré [of character change] arrive avec les caractères de l'inévitable, chaque moment de la passion est engendré de celui qui précède et engendre celui qui suit comme le levier, mis en mouvement par une force quelconque, pousse une roue qui en pousse une autre. . . . Ce fatalisme, d'ailleurs, est savant. Il n'est pas d'instinct, comme il arrive souvent dans les livres passionnés. Il n'est pas non plus de fantaisie et seulement pour l'effet romanesque. Il couronne un système arrêté, dont le matérialisme est la base.[15]

All these alleged vices of Flaubert's attitude to his subject were, as we have seen, related; they might be reduced to a single failing such as 'impersonality' or 'scientific approach.' Their result, too, might be generally stated as 'moral indifference' or 'immorality.' In addition to the above discussion, I might indicate other passages which repeat the charge of immorality and vigorously condemn *Madame Bovary* on that account. Especially interesting is a passage of Merlet's in which he defines the whole attitude:

Quant à celui [le réalisme] qui tue l'éloquence et la poésie, sacrifie l'homme à la brute, se débarrasse de l'âme et du cœur, prétend nous plaire par le goût des choses dépravées, et calomnie la création et la société en affectant de n'y voir que la laideur physique et morale, celui-là je propose qu'on l'appelle désormais le *bovarisme*.[16]

On the other hand, a number of critics defended Flaubert against this very charge. They cited the retribution in the dénouement. They invoked the right of the novelist to treat such subjects as adultery and to refrain from any moral conclusion: the facts themselves contain their own lesson. They went so far as to declare that Flaubert's dénouement was itself an error, that the moral would have been sufficiently obvious without it.[17]

There were, too, some phases of the author's point of view which were acceptable to the critics. His irony was one of these—for those who discerned it.[18] Cuvillier-Fleury perceived and praised his humor in such episodes as the "comice agricole."[19] Baudelaire found in *Madame Bovary* the same lyricism he had discovered in the published fragments of *La Tentation de Saint-Antoine,* and Weiss—usually adverse—approved of Flaubert's "poésie native."[20] But these were thin, small voices ineffectual against a chorus of disapproval.

Having studied the attitude of the author towards his materials, we may now attempt to discover the nature of those materials themselves as they were seen and judged by the critics. Naturally enough, a number of remarks were made on the reality of the substance presented in *Madame Bovary;* Flaubert was immediately recognized as a seeker after truth and one who frequently attained it. He gave, said the critics, an adequate portrayal of provincial life and character, his rendition of setting was accurate, his treatment of landscape superior. Certain critics were particularly delighted by this "retour au vrai"; thus Donis, who saw in Madame Bovary an exception to the "catégorie ridicule et tant exploitée des *âmes veuves* et des *femmes incomprises.*"[21] So too Henry Denys, who foresaw the objections to the novel:

. . . il contient des pages éblouissantes d'audace et de vérité. Aussi les éternels amis de cette fiction aux doigts roses dont la tête repose dans le clair obscur, le reste du corps dans des flots de gaze, seront peut-être offensés par une lumière trop vive: le long usage de verres trompeurs leur a fait un regard faible, indécis et superficiel.[22]

But to foresee was not to forestall, and the "lovers of rosy-fingered fiction" were quick to raise the expected objections. Flaubert's materials were real, for them, only in so far as a world of trivial objects and trivial people, containing no ideal, no good to contrast with evil, might be considered real. First, the reproach of triviality: it amounted to saying that the people and things represented were uninteresting in themselves, and hence unworthy of artistic treatment. For example, the characters: "Autant de figures effacées," says Jean Rousseau, "parfaitement vulgaires et aussi nulles que possible, madame Bovary en tête."[23] Or material objects, which are "puerile, ugly, dirty."[24] Next, the lack of the ideal: Flaubert, said the critics, wilfully excluded the good, the beautiful, which, by their presence, would have thrown into higher relief the evil and the ugly so prominent in his book.[25] One evidence of this is his failure to include any sympathetic characters, any personages with whom the reader—or even the writer—might identify himself.[26]

Much of the discussion of subject-matter centered about Flaubert's use of detail. That he was an adept in the study and presentation of details—details of color, sound, form—was never contested; critics granted him an absolute virtuosity here.[27] But they concluded, almost without exception, that his use of such detail was excessive. As a result of his mania for describing everything within his field of perception, his novel became a confused mass of descriptions in which the significant was indistinguishable from the unimportant, the great from the small, the main action from the minute episode. An anarchy of bright, dazzling objects.[28] Besides being superabundant, these details were exclusively physical and material in nature; they never penetrated beneath the surface of things or people. Hence the critics blamed them for their externality. An example of this reproach may be selected from Monpont's book:

L'observation de M. Gustave Flaubert semble être toute physique, toute matérielle; elle ne paraît s'en tenir qu'à l'enveloppe des êtres et des choses; rarement elle entame l'écorce pour nous faire connaître d'abord ce qu'il y a dedans. Ainsi, lorsqu'il veut peindre le caractère d'un homme, il commencerait volontiers par indiquer comment sont noués ses cordons de souliers; des souliers, il passerait au pantalon, à l'habit, dont il parlerait de la coupe, de la couleur du drap, de sa qualité, en indiquant même le nom et l'adresse du fabricant d'où il sort; puis il passerait aux mains et au visage et s'arrêterait là.[29]

Thus Flaubert's skill in presenting reality was admitted; but his bias in the choice of the commonplace and his excessive use of external detail were reprehended. This skill was itself recognized as deriving from another faculty which, however, was praised by all: that of observation. Weiss remarks that "Il observe avec précision, il rend avec imprévu, et néanmoins au juste moment, les nuances minutieuses";[30] Sainte-Beuve calls him "un grand et véridique observateur";[31] Mazade grants him "un certain don d'observation vigoureuse et âcre."[32]

Given the attitude of the artist and the materials outlined above, what kind of novel will be produced? How will *Madame Bovary* fare when examined in the light of current aesthetic standards? It was on these questions of literary form that opinions were most controversial and that, on the whole, Flaubert was most favorably judged. For many of those who repudiated Flaubert's philosophy and the world he chose to treat were nevertheless willing to grant him a definite superiority of treatment. This was true, for example, with regard to 'composition,' to the general plan of the work. Such a critic as Weiss, whose objections we have already seen, was enthusiastic in his admiration of Flaubert's composition:

La composition générale de l'ouvrage est, en son genre, achevée. Elle offre les traits d'une œuvre classique: unité rigoureuse d'action, un petit nombre d'acteurs poussant avec des mouvements divers au même dénoûment, nulle péripétie à fracas, nul incident qui ne soit naturel et qui ne sorte uniment du cours journalier de la vie, l'intérêt renfermé dans l'analyse du caractère principal . . . Cette simplicité du plan et cette largeur du dessin sont déjà la marque d'une force d'esprit peu commune. . . . il connaît l'art difficile de produire des effets tragiques avec de petits moyens . . .[33]

These and similar qualities appealed to the taste of other critics: Champfleury, Sainte-Beuve, Roqueplan, Habans, Merlet.[34] On the other hand many (and sometimes the same) critics pointed to flaws in composition which definitely detracted from the artistic value of the novel:[35] the failure to establish a definite hierarchy of details and incidents and the consequent lack of perspective; the failure to attain the relief afforded by contrast; the excessive development of extraneous episodes such as Charles's youth and the famous history of the "pied-bot."

Among the elements of presentation, the one most generally lauded was Flaubert's handling of character. To the type of characters portrayed there was at times, as we have seen, an objection. But the purely novelistic technique of depicting them was found excellent. They were consistent, their actions were directed by a strict logical necessity, they were striking and alive. They had, for Weiss, an "epic solemnity": "Ils ont de l'épopée les manières et le geste amples."[36] Barbey d'Aurevilly saw in the delineation of Emma the great triumph of the novel:

Le grand mérite de ce roman est dans la figure principale, qui est toute la pensée du livre et qui, quoique commune, cesse de l'être par la profondeur avec laquelle elle est entendue et traitée. Madame Bovary, étudiée, scrutée, détaillée comme elle l'est, est une création supérieure, qui seul vaut à son auteur le titre conquis de romancier.[37]

Only rarely, as in the case of Sarcey, did a critic regard Flaubert's characters as exaggerated or unreal.[38]

Another technical excellence generally accorded Flaubert was that of description. The minuteness and delicacy of his observation would have been to no avail if he had not possessed, in his style, an instrument capable of rendering every subtlety of the object observed. This instrument, according to the critics, Flaubert did possess. He had a rare talent for choosing the right epithet, the *mot propre;* for giving, in a few words, a complete picture; for evoking in the reader every kind of sensation, visual or auditory.[39] But his descriptive passages labored under all the disadvantages of their subject-matter: they were too complete, and hence photographic;[40] they were too numerous, and hence confusing, dazzling; they were too long, and hence monotonous.

Description, of course, was only a part of the more general question of 'style' or diction; it was on this question that opinion was most divided. Sainte-Beuve, again, had precipitated the controversy: "Une qualité précieuse distingue M. Gustave Flaubert des autres observateurs plus ou moins exacts qui, de nos jours, se piquent de rendre en conscience la seule réalité, et qui parfois y réussissent; il a le *style*."[41] But while many agreed with Sainte-Beuve, almost as many took exception to the statement that Flaubert "had style." Those who agreed pointed to the directness and the firmness of Flaubert's language, to its variety of tone and color, its wealth of happy images; they singled out the sharp thrust of his dialogue and the incisiveness of his portraiture. Of these favorable opinions we may take Merlet's as an example:

Ajoutez . . . un style brusque, tourmenté, inculte, mais impérieux, s'abattant avec frénésie sur le mot propre, éclatant parmi des rages d'expressions originales, emportant l'idée d'assaut avec une vaillance téméraire qui rencontrerait plus d'une page définitive si, à l'ordonnance logique de l'ensemble, au fini du détail, à la justesse du trait, à sa virilité de touche, M. Flaubert daignait allier le respect de la langue et de la grammaire.[42]

This statement is typical, indeed, to the extent of including some of the major objections to Flaubert's style. For others, too, held that he was excessively disdainful of grammar, syntax, and usage. Still others declared that his style was hard, unharmonious, even dry; it was overwrought, heavy, confused.[43] In spite of these objections, however, the balance of opinion on style was in Flaubert's favor; even those who found fault conceded that the book was 'written,' that it showed a consistent and often successful effort at literary form, and that thereby it distinguished itself from other realistic productions.

This distinction was emphasized still further by a general, somewhat impalpable quality which the critics called "force." They designated by "force" the directness with which the principal theme was stated and developed, the clarity of profile of the characters, the vigor of the style, the frankness in the handling of situation.[44] It was this forcefulness that made *Madame Bovary* stand out from among the novels of the day, explained its success, and led many critics to condone the numerous faults they discovered. For on the whole the reception of *Madame Bovary* cannot be said to have been definitely unfavorable. The originality of the work, its aesthetic qualities, the merit it displayed in observation and in social depiction, tended to mitigate the severity of the criticism directed against Flaubert's materialism, his scientific attitude, the subject he chose to treat.

Whatever sympathy the world of criticism expressed for *Madame Bovary* was enhanced when, five years later, *Salammbô* made its appearance. No sooner had the critics read the Carthaginian novel than they looked back nostalgically to the days of the story of Normandy. As they compared the two books, point by point, the superiority of the first became increasingly clear to them; much of the new criticism consisted merely of such comparison. But even those critics who had not liked *Madame Bovary* found that *Salammbô* repeated and emphasized all its failings. Hence the old book, when compared with its successor, was more favorably judged than ever before, but the new received rarely a word of welcome; the opposition to it was united and strong.

For many critics *Salammbô* was an attempt to treat an impossible subject in an impossible way, and its failure was inevitable. Flaubert was a realist, whose merit lay in the observation and depiction of what he saw about him; for such as he the historical novel, presupposing the evocation of people, objects, and actions no longer observable, is a mistake. And to choose as subject for a historical novel ancient Carthage, whose civilization is preserved in only the most fragmentary form, is to condemn oneself to a hopeless pastiche.[45] The genre of *Salammbô* is uncertain: it is half realistic, half romantic; half history, half novel: the realistic bias spoils the romantic, imaginative evocation, just as the romantic effort invalidates the results of the realistic observation; the history is forever interfering with the progress of the novel, and the novel with the truth of the history.[46] Because of this imperfect definition of the approach, there is throughout a sense of effort, a feeling that the artist strives constantly to overcome a great difficulty, and as constantly falls short of the mark.[47]

With so different a problem at hand, the approach of the writer must needs undergo certain changes, although in other respects it will remain the same. For example, Flaubert will retain his scientific intention; but since he can no longer apply it to the analysis of characters and of actions which he sees, he will devote himself to the resurrection of a lost civilization, to a work of erudition. From analysis, he will pass to synthesis. Many critics doubt the validity of the synthesis he makes—considering the sparsity of available materials—when they do not call into question the very reliability of his erudition.[48] Again, he will display the impersonality, the lack of feeling, which is the fundamental principle of his art. Of this, critics disapprove just as much as when it manifested itself in his first book.[49] For it leads, even more than previously, to cynicism and scepticism, to fatalism and sensualism, and through them ultimately to immorality. The reproach of cynicism, especially, gains in prominence during this second period; the critics charge Flaubert with cruelty, with brutality, with inhumanity. "Cet orgueil du doute," says Boutmy, "se sent à chaque ligne dans les ouvrages de M. Flaubert; à la froideur dédaigneuse qui en est le ton général, à l'amertume de certains mots, parfois à la brutalité furieuse de la peinture."[50] So also the reproach of sensualism: Salammbô is merely a second Emma in her voluptuousness and Flaubert, now as before, merely a student of the flesh. Says Sainte-Beuve, thinking back to the first book:

... on aurait voulu ... que, sans renoncer à aucune hardiesse, à aucun droit de l'artiste sincère, il purgeât son œuvre prochaine de tout soupçon d'érotisme et de combinaison trop maligne en ce genre: l'artiste a bien des droits, y compris celui même des nudités; mais il est besoin qu'un certain sérieux, la passion, la franchise de l'intention et la force du vrai l'absolvent et l'autorisent.[51]

In this sensualism lies, according to several judges, the principal source of Flaubert's immorality.[52] Finally, in this critical survey of Flaubert's point of view, I might note the new opinions on his lyricism and his romanticism. A few critics of *Bovary* had singled out the lyric strain in Flaubert's talent; others now see in *Salammbô* a manifestation of that strain, of the romantic side of Flaubert's art. Opinions are about evenly divided as to the desirability of this turning away from the realistic to the romantic subject. Cuvillier-Fleury is on the affirmative side: "*Salammbô*, c'est la revanche de *Madame Bovary*, c'est la rançon que le réalisme essaie de payer à l'idéal."[53] Guillaume Froehner speaks for the negative:

... il nous semble que *Salammbô* est la fille naturelle des *Misérables* et du musée Campana. On y surprend, en effet, de ces phrases sublimes, de ces idées colossales qui sont la marque distinctive du talent de Victor Hugo. En revanche, la même diction forcée, le même penchant pour les atrocités, pour les scènes horribles, et une tendance fâcheuse à les rendre plus horribles encore. ... Rien de naturel dans ces escalades d'une imagination fébrile et surexcitée; tout est cherché, factice, outré au dernier point.[54]

From what has preceded, we might almost predict the reaction of the critics to the subject-matter of the new novel. Reality? Truth? But reality and truth, the undeniable virtues of a realistic study, are by definition excluded from a novel like *Salammbô*, a pure fiction. Now the critics remember with pleasure the presence of these virtues in *Madame Bovary*. Jules Levallois, for example, berates the public for the anxiety with which it had awaited the new novel:

Le rachat d'une peinture exacte par une composition artificielle, d'une
œuvre moderne par une composition inspirée de l'antique, d'une création
originale par un pastiche, c'est là ce que comportait et sous-entendait
l'anxieuse attente d'une partie du public. . . . Nous nous retrouvons
toujours en face de cette timidité d'intelligence—grosse de préjugés,
mortelle au goût,—qui n'accepte le vivant et le vrai qu'à la dernière
extrémité, et qui rougit de ses admirations lorsqu'il lui est impossible de
les étayer sur une idolâtrie quelconque.[55]

Others state the same preference for the world of the first novel—if
only because they deplore and reject that of the second.[56] There were,
of course, the habitual remarks on Flaubert's neglect of the ideal[57] and
on the triviality of his subject-matter,[58] but these were less prominent
than before. As for detail, critics still recognized his expertness in
discerning and presenting it, but they contended always that he used it
to excess: too much of it was irrelevant, and so irrelevant that it obscured the main lines of the novel.[59] In the same way, they contended
that in itself the detail merited blame because of its externality; Flaubert was a student of the 'superficial,' who never penetrated to the
essence of things or the souls of people.[60] All these we know as the
standard objections to the materials of the realists in general as well as
of Flaubert. A somewhat newer note is the attention called not only to
Flaubert's preference for the ugly, but to his definite penchant for the
horrible. To some critics, *Salammbô* appears as a bloody orgy of
slaughter and massacre; so Douhaire: "on n'y a trouvé que d'affreux
tableaux de guerre, de hideux massacres, d'abominables boucheries
humaines."[61] So, too, Cadoudal, who finds that "tout est sacrifié . . . à
la recherche complaisante et raffinée de l'horrible, du sanglant et de l'in-
fect."[62] Finally, one of the gravest faults of the subject was that it
precluded the exercise of one of Flaubert's principal merits, that of
observation. The skill so magnificently displayed in *Bovary* must necessarily be absent from *Salammbô,* since the objects of imitation are no
longer observable objects. The Carthaginian landscape alone will lend
itself to Flaubert's delicate observation.[63]

These vices of the subject extended even to the aesthetic aspects of
the work, and impaired the presentation. The mixture of the historical
and the fictional prevented any unity of composition; the book became a
series of unrelated episodes, inferior in that respect to the integrated
structure of *Bovary*.[64] The plot—in so far as the work may be said to
be a novel and thus to have a plot—is tenuous and uncertain; its thread
is lost in the mass of erudition and description.[65] The description itself,
while frequently excellent, is so superabundant as to outweigh all other
elements of the book.[66] Even Flaubert, in his answer to Sainte-Beuve's

articles, admitted that "Le piédestal est trop grand pour la statue."[67] Naturally so, thought the critics: for Flaubert, obliged to construct a whole civilization on the basis of a few texts, must heap colorful detail upon colorful detail, he must be violent and declamatory, he must exaggerate every trait in order to be convincing.[68] It is largely from this excessive vividness of coloring, from this overdescription, from page after page of bombast that the book derives its deadly monotony.[69] In spite of these failings a few—but very few—critics admire Flaubert's powers of historical evocation. Caro is one of these: "C'est toute une renaissance matérielle et morale; ce n'est rien moins que la résurrection d'une civilisation morte."[70] Gautier is another: "C'est la plus étonnante restauration architecturale qui se soit faite."[71] But for most of the commentators this restoration was unsatisfactory for the reasons already given; and even when they admitted an adequate reproduction of the physical aspects of Carthage, they refused to accept the characters as Carthaginians. For example, the statement of the Goncourts: "Quant à une restitution morale, le bon Flaubert s'illusionne, les sentiments de ses personnages sont les sentiments banaux et généraux de l'humanité, et non les sentiments d'une humanité particulièrement carthaginoise, et son Mathô n'est au fond qu'un ténor d'opéra dans un poème barbare."[72] Of the various opinions on character, most of the favorable ones referred back to *Madame Bovary*, although some few critics did approve of the personages as conceived in *Salammbô*.[73] Usually, however, the critics regarded the people in the latter work as unreal and unconvincing, as merely attempts to transport contemporary types into a remote period. As Sarcey says, "il a repris les personnages de son premier roman et . . . il les a tout simplement habillés en Carthaginois"; but they lose in the transformation, since they are no longer living people but erudite syntheses.[74]

Flaubert's style, too, suffers from its application to the new materials. Only two or three of the critics speak of it in terms reminiscent of the high praise accorded the diction in *Madame Bovary*.[75] The rest condemn it totally because they find it exaggerated, forced, bombastic. Delaplace's statement is representative:

La prose de M. Flaubert ressemble aux *Iambes* de Barbier: désespérant de trouver la force dans la simplicité, tous deux la cherchent dans l'enflure, dans une grossièreté brutale; de peur de rester en deçà, ils vont au delà; ils dépassent le but pour être sûrs de l'atteindre; enfin, suant, haletant, épuisés par cet excès continu, ils rencontrent quelque trait vigoureux, quelque image saisissante, mais on sent l'effort, on voit les muscles tendus, prêts à se rompre; ils ne touchent pas, ils étonnent, ils font presque peur.[76]

Thus the total impression on the artistic aspects, as well as on other elements, is unfavorable. Not that the critics denied Flaubert a real literary talent: on the contrary, nearly all admitted that he had a vigorous and a sure literary gift. But through an unfortunate choice of subject, through an untenable materialistic philosophy, through an excessive effort to make the unreal real, this talent was negated and misapplied; its product was deplorable.

In *L'Education sentimentale,* critics hailed a return to the manner and the subject-matter of *Madame Bovary*—a contemporary theme realistically treated. Not all, indeed, were ready to accept the book (opinion was about evenly divided upon it), but with few exceptions they welcomed a return to the contemporary world. Since the new novel was generally similar—in its study of modern society and in its realistic approach—to Flaubert's first, much of the reaction to its various elements was practically the same as that outlined for *Madame Bovary.* Hence I shall indicate only briefly the opinion on such points as reality of subject, observation, description, characterization, and style, and dwell more at length on several more fervently contested issues.

I have already said that most critics welcomed, in *L'Education sentimentale,* the portrayal of nineteenth-century French society; I might add that many of them found the depiction eminently true. Banville's comment was brief but conclusive:

Si l'*Education sentimentale* est pour tout le monde un beau livre, il faut avoir vécu, comme nous, en 1840, pour savoir avec quelle puissance d'évocation vous avez ressuscité cette époque de transition avec ses défaillances et avec ses aspirations impuissantes. Tout cela est vrai jusque dans la moelle des os, et exprimé dans une forme immortelle.[77]

Levallois, in a more extended discussion, marvels at the hard, brilliant light in which every person and every object is seen, at their immediacy to the spectator. This impression of truthfulness is largely responsible for the interest of the book: "Vérité dans la peinture du monde extérieur, dans le langage et la conduite des personnages, dans l'analyse de leurs sentiments, il n'en faut pas plus pour retenir, enchaîner l'attention."[78] Only a few commentators held that Flaubert's presentation was unsatisfactory or untrue.[79] The faculty for observation responsible for the impression of reality was, as in the preceding years, again highly lauded; André Lefèvre's remarks are typical: "nous estimons à son prix . . . l'excellence de ses yeux, qui saisissent jusqu'au moindre reflet d'une goutte de rosée sur une feuille de rose, et, brusquement, sans s'éblouir, fixent leur regard sur les lustres en feu, sur le ruissellement des étoffes éclatantes ou les féeries du soleil couchant."[80] It was above all in the perception and the rendering of minute detail that this faculty

produced admirable results; Flaubert, for many, was incomparable as
a student of physical detail, and as an observer of the influence of
ostensibly unimportant objects on the emotions of his heroes.[81] Contrariwise, the characters placed in this background failed to gain the
approval of the reviewers, who thought they were unrepresentative or
incompletely realized; Frédéric Moreau especially aroused the indignation of readers.[82]

Considering it from the moral standpoint, critics saw in *L'Education
sentimentale* a satire of an entire period. This in itself was not reprehensible; but where Flaubert sinned was in failing to display any
indignation at the state of affairs he portrayed, in maintaining his cold
impersonality. Of this objection Cuvillier-Fleury gives the best statement:

Il touche à tout et il flétrit tout. Il a la rage d'abaisser ce qui s'élève,
d'éteindre ce qui brille, la science, le talent, le patriotisme, l'indépendance,
la noblesse, la pudeur, la fortune bien acquise, l'élégance courtoise, les
grandes vertus comme les petites. . . .
. . . c'est la satire, la satire froide, impersonnelle, nullement gaie, mais
nullement railleuse, la satire réaliste sans un cri du cœur, sans une
émotion, sans une leçon. Eh bien! c'est à cette impartialité navrante que
je m'attaque dans le moraliste, comme je m'attaquais autrefois à "l'im-
personnalité" dans le romancier et dans l'artiste. . . . Un moraliste,
étroitement borné à la peinture du vice, trahit la vertu.[83]

The same objection is made notably by Paul de Léoni, André Lefèvre,
Francisque Sarcey (who calls Flaubert "le néo-parnassien de la prose"),
Saint-René Taillandier.[84] With it goes always the additional reproach
that the author misrepresents the period of the Revolution of 1848, that
he portrays only its more trivial and more ignoble aspects, that he fails
to seize its greatness.

To the artistry of the novel there was also one essential objection: it
failed to attain any unity. Episodes, scenes, people, all were unrelated.
They were, individually, finely observed and admirably presented; but
they were linked to one another only by the arbitrary decision of the
author. "Ce ne sont," said Amédée de Cesena, "que des esquisses de
caractères ou des ébauches de passions, des commencements d'aventures
ou des velléités de volontés."[85] Cuvillier-Fleury made a fuller condemnation: "Le livre de M. Gustave Flaubert n'est pas un roman, c'est une
satire composée de récits, de tableaux, d'épisodes qu'on pourrait croire
détachés les uns des autres, de personnages qui se rassemblent sans se
joindre, de pièces de rapport qui ne s'emboîtent pas, d'événements sans
cause et sans issue."[86] For Pontmartin, *Bovary* and *L'Education sentimentale* shared this same weakness: "Ce sont exactement les mêmes
effets, les mêmes séries de tableaux, ou, pour parler plus juste, de

morceaux, juxtaposés au récit, au lieu d'en faire partie essentielle, comme chez les vrais maîtres."[87]

Both of these reproaches, the moral and the artistic, were answered by other critics. Asselineau, especially, held a brief for Flaubert's novelistic technique. This technique, he believed, was disconcerting for the French reader since it departed from the French "heroic" tradition and attempted a closer approximation to life.[88] Jules Levallois had already remarked that Flaubert deserted the "unité à la mode française" for the method of the English novelists, especially Thackeray.[89] That Flaubert failed to draw a moral conclusion from his investigation was merely a result of his literary theory, and hence entirely justifiable. Léon Dommartin, Taine, Asselineau approved of this method.[90] I might quote the appreciation of Taine, who summarizes what he believes to have been Flaubert's principle:

"Jetons un filet sur le boulevard et ramassons les individus qui passent. Les types très francs et très absolus sont faux, ils n'existent que dans l'esprit. Tout homme réel et vivant n'est qu'un à peu près, un hybride, un mélange de velléités et d'inconséquences. Faire vrai, c'est faire le monsieur que voici, et non le personnage énergique et grandiose que mon imagination aurait du plaisir à contempler. Cela posé, promenons ces spécimens de la moyenne humaine parmi des événements et des paysages rigoureusement réels, que j'ai vus un à un, à travers l'histoire et la nature que j'ai observées de plus par moi-même et de plus près. J'aurai donné le plus exact spécimen du bourgeois parisien, au dix-neuvième siècle, dans un cadre qui sera comme lui un document."

These defences, of course, were supplemented by the praise for Flaubert's style, the merits of which annulled, for many critics, any defects the work might have; as Scherer decided, the book was an "acte d'écrivain":

En fin de compte et pour parler franc, il n'y a que deux classes de romans: ceux qui sont écrits et ceux qui ne le sont pas; et les premiers sont les seuls qui comptent. . . . On sent partout chez lui le souci de la ligne, le sentiment de la couleur, le besoin de la lumière. C'est quelque chose, c'est beaucoup. Prenez garde: pour peu que vous me pressiez, je dirai que c'est tout![91]

Whatever these critics might deny Flaubert in the way of philosophical purpose or social study, they could not go so far as to deny him the qualities of the literary artist: excellent diction, a rare talent for description, a sense of style.

In conclusion, the criticism of Flaubert's three novels might be summarized thus: (1) the response to *Madame Bovary*, coming at the crucial moment in the criticism of realism, epitomizes the arguments for and against the new movement. (2) Critical impatience with *Salammbô* is symptomatic of the growing dislike for the historical novel and for high romantic coloring. (3) The reception of *L'Education sentimentale* reveals an increased willingness on the part of the critics to tolerate the contemporary subject and the new, realistic type of structure; at the same time, it shows the persistence of the standard objections to realism: impersonality, immorality, the tendency to portray society as worse than it really is. Throughout, it is notable that the admiration for Flaubert's diction, for his skill in observation and characterization, for his superior treatment of detail, leads many critics to accept works which they otherwise would have rejected. The case is exactly the opposite to that of Balzac: with him, the portrayal of society justified the inferiority of style; with Flaubert, the style justified the faults of subject-matter and of general approach.

---

[1] *863*, Pinard.   [2] *870*, Sainte-Beuve, p. 183.   [3] *890*, Vapereau.
[4] *893*, Merlet.   [5] *734*, Texier, p. 295.   [6] *886*, Weiss, p. 177.
[7] *893*, Merlet, p. 722; cf. *869*, Mazade, p. 218; *880*, Castelnau, p. 155; *882*, Barbey d'Aurevilly, p. 63; *890*, Vapereau, p. 53; *957*, Barbey d'Aurevilly, p. 238, for various objections.   [8] *870*, Sainte-Beuve, p. 167.   [9] *865*, Duranty.
[10] *882*, Barbey d'Aurevilly, pp. 64, 65.
[11] *874*, Cuvillier-Fleury; cf. *875*, Pontmartin, pp. 300-301; *877*, Denys, p. 39; *878*, Donis, p. 85; *886*, Weiss, p. 167; *890*, Vapereau, p. 53; *893*, Merlet, pp. 709, 723.   [12] *886*, Weiss, p. 177.   [13] *892*, Monpont, p. 38.
[14] Cf. *863*, Pinard, p. 562; *870*, Sainte-Beuve, p. 179; *734*, Texier, p. 295; *875*, Pontmartin, p. 299; *893*, Merlet, p. 736.
[15] *886*, Weiss, p. 162; cf. *866*, Champfleury, p. 313; *874*, Cuvillier-Fleury; *879*, Sainte-Beuve; *887*, Granier de Cassagnac, p. 26; *890*, Vapereau, p. 53; *891*, Chevalet, p. 193; *945*, Vapereau, p. 64.
[16] *893*, Merlet, p. 740; cf. *863*, Pinard; *874*, Cuvillier-Fleury; *875*, Pontmartin, p. 303; *519*, Aubineau; *880*, Castelnau, p. 153; *886*, Weiss, p. 159; *890*, Vapereau, p. 49; *891*, Chevalet, p. 193; *957*, Barbey d'Aurevilly, p. 238.
[17] *888*, Rousseau, p. 5; cf. *864*, Sénard, p. 581; *870*, Sainte-Beuve, p. 167; *873*, Desdemaines; *877*, Denys, pp. 35-36; *882*, Barbey d'Aurevilly, p. 64.
[18] *864*, Sénard, p. 581; *867*, Sainte-Beuve, p. 315; *872*, Roqueplan; *883*, Baudelaire, p. 109; *886*, Weiss, p. 157; *893*, Merlet, p. 726.   [19] *874*, Cuvillier-Fleury.
[20] *883*, Baudelaire, p. 108; *886*, Weiss, p. 157.   [21] *878*, Donis, p. 85.
[22] *877*, Denys, p. 35; cf. *864*, Sénard, p. 581; *867*, Sainte-Beuve, p. 314; *870*, Sainte-Beuve, p. 166; *874*, Cuvillier-Fleury; *880*, Castelnau, p. 155; *885*, About, p. 525; *887*, Granier de Cassagnac, p. 29. On landscape, cf. *878*, Donis, p. 84; *879*, Sainte-Beuve; *886*, Weiss, p. 157.   [23] *888*, Rousseau, p. 4.
[24] *876*, Habans, p. 4; cf. *882*, Barbey d'Aurevilly, p. 73; *887*, Granier de Cassagnac, p. 29; *890*, Vapereau, p. 52; *892*, Monpont, p. 30; *893*, Merlet, pp. 707, 728.
[25] *870*, Sainte-Beuve, p. 180; *874*, Cuvillier-Fleury; *880*, Castelnau, p. 153; *884*, Sandeau.
[26] *867*, Sainte-Beuve, p. 315; *870*, Sainte-Beuve, p. 181; *734*, Texier, p. 295; *882*, Barbey d'Aurevilly, p. 75.
[27] Cf. *864*, Sénard, p. 584; *957*, Barbey d'Aurevilly, p. 232; *893*, Merlet, p. 709.

[28] Cf. *865*, Duranty; *869*, Mazade, p. 218; *870*, Sainte-Beuve, p. 169; *734*, Texier, p. 295; *871*, Deschamps, p. 281; *875*, Pontmartin, p. 304; *876*, Habans, p. 4; *877*, Denys, p. 39; *882*, Barbey d'Aurevilly, p. 75; *888*, Rousseau; *890*, Vapereau, p. 56; *945*, Vapereau, p. 67; *892*, Monpont, p. 31; *893*, Merlet, pp. 715-717.

[29] *892*, Monpont, p. 31; cf. *869*, Mazade, p. 218; *734*, Texier, p. 295; *874*, Cuvillier-Fleury; *887*, Granier de Cassagnac, p. 29.   [30] *886*, Weiss, p. 157.

[31] *879*, Sainte-Beuve.

[32] *869*, Mazade, p. 218; cf. *864*, Sénard, p. 585; *867*, Sainte-Beuve, p. 314; *870*, Sainte-Beuve, p. 169; *876*, Habans, p. 4; *878*, Donis, p. 85; *882*, Barbey, p. 67; *893*, Merlet, p. 709.   [33] *886*, Weiss, p. 156.

[34] *866*, Champfleury, p. 313; *867*, Sainte-Beuve, p. 314; *870*, Sainte-Beuve, p. 183; *872*, Roqueplan; *876*, Habans, p. 4; *890*, Vapereau, p. 59; *893*, Merlet, p. 712.

[35] *862*, Du Camp; *867*, Sainte-Beuve, p. 315; *734*, Texier, p. 295; *871*, Deschamps, p. 281; *875*, Pontmartin, p. 303; *888*, Rousseau, p. 5; *892*, Monpont, p. 30; *893*, Merlet, pp. 712-713.

[36] *886*, Weiss, p. 156; cf. *864*, Sénard, p. 585; *867*, Sainte-Beuve, p. 314; *868*, Gozlan, p. 313; *870*, Sainte-Beuve, p. 172; *872*, Roqueplan; *876*, Habans, p. 4; *888*, Rousseau, p. 5; *890*, Vapereau, p. 58; *893*, Merlet, p. 709.

[37] *882*, Barbey d'Aurevilly, p. 73.   [38] *521*, Sarcey, p. 3.

[39] Cf. *864*, Sénard, p. 584; *888*, Rousseau, p. 5; *890*, Vapereau, p. 55; *893*, Merlet, p. 711.

[40] Cf. *874*, Cuvillier-Fleury; *876*, Habans, p. 4; *888*, Rousseau, p. 5; *892*, Monpont, p. 31.   [41] *870*, Sainte-Beuve, p. 169; cf. *867*, Sainte-Beuve, p. 314.

[42] *893*, Merlet, p. 709; cf. *864*, Sénard, p. 585; *734*, Texier, p. 295; *872*, Roqueplan; *878*, Donis, p. 84; *881*, Aubryet, p. 47; *882*, Barbey d'Aurevilly, p. 75; *884*, Sandeau; *885*, About, p. 526; *886*, Weiss, p. 156; *887*, Granier de Cassagnac, p. 26; *888*, Rousseau, p. 5.

[43] *865*, Duranty; *869*, Mazade, p. 218; *871*, Deschamps, p. 281; *874*, Cuvillier-Fleury; *875*, Pontmartin, p. 305; *876*, Habans, p. 4; *886*, Weiss, p. 155; *888*, Rousseau, p. 3; *892*, Monpont, p. 31.

[44] Cf. *870*, Sainte-Beuve, p. 183; *734*, Texier, p. 295; *872*, Roqueplan; *873*, Desdemaines; *875*, Pontmartin, p. 305; *876*, Habans, p. 4; *878*, Donis, p. 77; *882*, Barbey d'Aurevilly, pp. 62, 65; *890*, Vapereau, p. 58; *893*, Merlet, p. 707.

[45] *898*, Sainte-Beuve, p. 228; *901*, Levallois; *911*, Cadoudal; *917*, Delaplace, p. 159; *918*, Sarcey, p. 500.

[46] *906*, Jouvin, p. 1; *907*, Douhaire, p. 803; *908*, Pontmartin, p. 102; *911*, Cadoudal; *912*, Clergier, p. 11; *916*, Fournel, p. 353.

[47] *898*, Sainte-Beuve, p. 230; *910*, Dusolier, p. 122; *911*, Cadoudal; *915*, Boutmy, p. 77; *916*, Fournel, p. 353.

[48] *896*, Mérimée, p. 209; *898*, Sainte-Beuve, p. 234; *902*, Claveau, p. 652; *906*, Jouvin, p. 1; *909*, Froehner; *911*, Cadoudal; *913*, Saint-René Taillandier, p. 855.

[49] *898*, Sainte-Beuve, p. 220; *900*, Caro, p. 267; *902*, Claveau, p. 650; *905*, Gautier, p. 317; *915*, Boutmy, p. 82.

[50] *915*, Boutmy, p. 83; cf. *898*, Sainte-Beuve, p. 192; *902*, Claveau, p. 644; *904*, Scherer; *913*, Saint-René Taillandier, p. 855; *919*, Nettement, p. 118.

[51] *898*, Sainte-Beuve, p. 185; *900*, Caro, p. 267; *902*, Claveau, p. 651; *904*, Scherer; *906*, Jouvin, p. 2; *912*, Clergier, p. 8; *913*, Saint-René Taillandier, p. 855; *919*, Nettement, p. 121.

[52] *916*, Fournel, p. 351; Cuvillier-Fleury, *899*, disagrees.

[53] *899*, Cuvillier-Fleury; cf. *895*, Calmels, p. 3; *897*, Calmels, p. 6; *905*, Gautier, p. 283.

[54] *909*, Froehner, p. 855; cf. *896*, Mérimée, p. 209; *902*, Claveau, p. 644; *913*, Saint-René Taillandier, p. 855; *920*, Gautier, p. 194. [55] *901*, Levallois.

[56] *898*, Sainte-Beuve, p. 184; *909*, Froehner, p. 855; *910*, Dusolier, p. 116; *915*, Boutmy, p. 84; *917*, Delaplace, p. 144; *918*, Sarcey, p. 500. Gautier, *905*, approves of both subjects. [57] *902*, Claveau, p. 652; *917*, Delaplace, p. 144.

[58] *902*, Claveau, p. 648; *912*, Clergier, p. 10; *913*, Saint-René Taillandier, p. 843. Cuvillier-Fleury, *899*, disagrees.

[59] *902*, Claveau, p. 650; *903*, Laffite, p. 267; *904*, Scherer; *910*, Dusolier, p. 116; *912*, Clergier, p. 6; *913*, Saint-René Taillandier, p. 843; *915*, Boutmy, p. 78; *916*, Fournel, p. 351; *918*, Sarcey, p. 500.

[60] *902*, Claveau, p. 648; *903*, Laffite, p. 268; *911*, Cadoudal; *912*, Clergier, p. 11; *915*, Boutmy, p. 81; *916*, Fournel, p. 350. [61] *907*, Douhaire, p. 802.

[62] *911*, Cadoudal; cf. *898*, Sainte-Beuve, p. 236; *902*, Claveau, p. 644; *906*, Jouvin, p. 2; *909*, Froehner, p. 855; *910*, Dusolier, p. 118; *911*, Cadoudal; *912*, Clergier, p. 10; *916*, Fournel, p. 352; *917*, Delaplace, p. 159.

[63] *903*, Laffite, p. 267; *904*, Scherer; *910*, Dusolier, p. 117; *918*, Sarcey, p. 500; *919*, Nettement, p. 118. On landscape, cf. especially *910*, Dusolier, p. 121.

[64] *906*, Jouvin, p. 2; *910*, Dusolier, pp. 116, 120; *912*, Clergier, p. 7; *917*, Delaplace, p. 161. Cf. *903*, Laffite, p. 267, and *913*, Saint-René Taillandier, p. 843, for favorable opinions.

[65] *902*, Claveau, p. 646; *903*, Laffite, p. 267; *906*, Jouvin, p. 2; *909*, Froehner, p. 856; *910*, Dusolier, p. 120; *916*, Fournel, p. 351; *920*, Gautier, p. 192.

[66] *894*, Goncourt, p. 289; *898*, Sainte-Beuve, p. 235; *899*, Cuvillier-Fleury; *902*, Claveau, p. 646; *904*, Scherer; *905*, Gautier, p. 282; *909*, Froehner, p. 857; *910*, Dusolier, p. 120; *912*, Clergier, p. 7; *916*, Fournel, p. 351.

[67] Letter of December, 1862; cf. *60*, II, 249.

[68] *894*, Goncourt, p. 289; *896*, Mérimée, p. 209; *899*, Cuvillier-Fleury; *913*, Saint-René Taillandier, p. 858; *915*, Boutmy, p. 79; *918*, Sarcey, p. 502.

[69] *898*, Sainte-Beuve, p. 229; *900*, Caro, p. 269; *906*, Jouvin, p. 2; *908*, Pontmartin, p. 94; *910*, Dusolier, p. 120; *912*, Clergier, p. 11; *916*, Fournel, p. 353; *918*, Sarcey, p. 502; *920*, Gautier, p. 194. [70] *900*, Caro, p. 263.

[71] *905*, Gautier, p. 318; cf. *897*, Calmels, p. 6; *899*, Cuvillier-Fleury.

[72] *894*, Goncourt, p. 289.

[73] *897*, Calmels, p. 6; *905*, Gautier, p. 319; *909*, Froehner, p. 855; *915*, Boutmy, pp. 80, 88.

[74] *918*, Sarcey, p. 500; cf. *899*, Cuvillier-Fleury; *900*, Caro, p. 266; *901*, Levallois; *910*, Dusolier, p. 120; *911*, Cadoudal.

[75] *897*, Calmels, p. 6; *903*, Laffite, p. 267; *919*, Nettement, p. 120.

[76] *917*, Delaplace, p. 159; cf. *894*, Goncourt, p. 289; *898*, Sainte-Beuve, p. 238; *900*, Caro, p. 269; *901*, Levallois; *902*, Claveau, p. 652; *906*, Jouvin, p. 2; *909*, Froehner, p. 855; *913*, Saint-René Taillandier, p. 843; *916*, Fournel, p. 350.

[77] *933*, Banville.

[78] *926*, Levallois; cf. *927*, Léoni; *931*, Sand, p. 415; *935*, Taine, p. 703; *937*, Asselineau, p. 37. [79] *923*, Gayet de Cesena; *930*, Scherer, p. 293.

[80] *928*, Lefèvre, p. 343; cf. *926*, Levallois; *929*, Sarcey; *930*, Scherer, p. 299; *934*, Hugo.

[81] *923*, Gayet de Cesena; *925*, Dommartin; *926*, Levallois; *931*, Sand, p. 421; *937*, Asselineau, p. 41.

[82] *923*, Gayet de Cesena; *925*, Dommartin; *929*, Sarcey; *930*, Scherer, p. 299; *932*, Saint-René Taillandier, p. 1004.   [83] *924*, Cuvillier-Fleury, 2nd art.

[84] *927*, Léoni; *928*, Lefèvre, p. 343; *929*, Sarcey; *932*, Saint-René Taillandier, p. 989.   [85] *923*, Gayet de Cesena.

[86] *924*, Cuvillier-Fleury, 2nd art.; cf. *928*, Lefèvre, p. 343; *930*, Scherer, p. 295; *932*, Saint-René Taillandier, p. 1004.

[87] *936*, Pontmartin, p. 289.   [88] *937*, Asselineau.   [89] *926*, Levallois.

[90] *925*, Dommartin; *935*, Taine; *937*, Asselineau.

[91] *930*, Scherer, pp. 300-301; cf. *925*, Dommartin; *926*, Levallois; *927*, Léoni; *928*, Lefèvre, p. 343; *929*, Sarcey; *931*, Sand, p. 423; *932*, Saint-René Taillandier, p. 1002; *933*, Banville; *934*, Hugo; *937*, Asselineau, p. 42.

CHAPTER IX

FEYDEAU; ABOUT, DURANTY, DUMAS *FILS*

Chronologies

[Ernest Feydeau]

1858: *Fanny*
1859: *Daniel*
1860: *Catherine d'Overmeire*
1863: *Un Début à l'Opéra*

[Edmond About]

1855: *Tolla*
1856: *Les Mariages de Paris*
1857: *Germaine*
1864: *Madelon*

[Edmond Duranty]

1860: *Le Malheur d'Henriette Gérard*
1862: *La Cause du Beau Guillaume*

[Alexandre Dumas *fils*]

1866: *Affaire Clémenceau*

IN THE wake of *Madame Bovary* came a group of novelists who, more or less independently of Flaubert's example, carried on what had definitely become the tradition of the realistic novel. Of these writers the most important were undoubtedly the Goncourts, whom I shall discuss in the following chapter. The most vigorously criticized novel of the period, however, was Feydeau's *Fanny*, and next after it came Alexandre Dumas *fils' Affaire Clémenceau;* about both of these the realistic battle raged vigorously. The response to About's and to Duranty's novels was less considerable; yet they, too, were unmistakably associated with the cause of the realists. It is these four minor novelists that I propose to treat briefly in the present chapter.

For about five years Feydeau was the storm-center of the realistic quarrel. His first novel, *Fanny*, was published in the midst of the controversy over *Madame Bovary;* it was immediately interpreted as an imitation of the latter, as an intensification of all of Flaubert's undesirable practices. Hence the opponents of realism now shift their attention from Flaubert to Feydeau, and each new novel of the latter calls forth

177

more insistent censure. *Daniel, Catherine d'Overmeire, Un Début à l'Opéra,* are regarded as successive heightenings of a vicious manner— the realistic manner—and the reviews contain long discussions of that manner. Finally, as we have already seen,[1] the preface to the last novel reopens the whole question of morality in literature and leads to a long debate. Thus from the beginning to the end, criticism of Feydeau is intimately connected with the history of the reaction to realism.

During this controversy, Feydeau had but one defender of note, Sainte-Beuve. For *Fanny,* as for *Madame Bovary* the year before, it was Sainte-Beuve who directed attention to the new work by writing a highly laudatory review. He admired, in the novel, the sense of life and vitality, the poetic inspiration, the originality. He found that it combined—as so few books did—a delicate psychological analysis with a minute description of external details; this made it a convincing novel, one adapted to the needs of contemporary life. At the same time, Sainte-Beuve foresaw the objections that would be made to the work: questions regarding the genuineness of Roger's love and the exceptional nature of his jealousy; or the "cruelty" of the treatment and the feverish tone of the expression.[2] But what he did not foresee was the objection that would be raised to his own article, the attack upon his own person as a result of his two defences of the two most daring contemporary novels. Both novels, in fact, were accused of immorality, and the wrath they excited was continuously visited upon the head of Sainte-Beuve. Therefore, in 1860, he wrote another article on Feydeau, in which he discussed the general question of morality and art, and gave brief appreciations of *Daniel* and *Catherine d'Overmeire.* These, he thought, were superior to their predecessor and showed a steady gain in artistry; they had the same unity of conception, the same superior portrayal of character, the same dramatic handling of episode. Besides, they had broader and more fruitful subjects.[3] With these appraisals several other critics agreed: Lataye and Emile Chasles on the unity and sobriety of composition,[4] Cuvillier-Fleury on the dramatic qualities,[5] a few others on the excellence of the psychological analysis,[6] still others on the vividness of style.[7] But the rest of the criticism was adverse.

By the time that *Fanny* appeared (June, 1858) "realism" itself was a term of opprobrium, and this term was immediately invoked as sufficient condemnation of the new novel. Critics had only to say "réaliste" to suggest to the public the complex of errors that had been so much discussed in connection with *Madame Bovary.* So it was with *Fanny* and with Feydeau's subsequent novels. Emile Chasles, speaking of the first book, summarized the tendencies in which Feydeau participated:

Il y a une école qui s'est bien permis de braver le sens public, de taquiner ce qu'elle appelle les bourgeois, de risquer des situations, de violenter froidement la langue, les lecteurs et la vérité. Un livre pour elle est un défi: que la donnée scandalise, que le ton blesse, que les mots fassent l'effet d'un breuvage inconnu et vertigineux, c'est à merveille. Toute brutalité dans le sujet, toute affectation dans la forme, est une bonne fortune. La phrase surtout exige une architecture spéciale: sous une apparence de force musculaire, elle se cambre, elle se fait anguleuse; ou bien elle se tord en volutes massives qui n'appartiennent à aucun ordre connu.[8]

If we add to this Henry de la Madelène's judgment of *Daniel*,[9] we shall have a fairly complete summary of the general conception of Feydeau's realism:

M. Feydeau ne compose pas, il étudie.—Les longueurs parasites de son récit: étude;—la minutie puérile des détails: étude;—l'exactitude niaise et, pour ainsi dire, photographique: étude;—la distillerie quintessenciée des sentiments: étude encore;—la torture des phrases et l'alambicage des mots: étude encore,—étude de style sans doute?

Realism, for the critics of Feydeau's work, is thus composed of a fundamental immorality, of an unsuccessful attempt at reproducing reality, of an excessive use of minute detail, of an exaggerated analysis of character, of an affected style. On immorality, opinion is little short of unanimous: many articles discuss the works exclusively from this point of view. In *Fanny,* for example, the whole situation is deemed immoral, and the balcony scene particularly is indicated as an evidence of the author's scandalous intention. Merlet calls his manner *"le réalisme de la corruption fashionable."*[10] This immorality resides in the undeniable sensualism of the subject and of the characters, and this in turn is embodied in the materialism of the presentation. On the purely physical nature of Feydeau's analysis the critics are again insistent; we might take another passage of Chasles as typical:

Personne ne sait, comme lui, étudier la mort, traduire la matière, donner un nom à tout ce qui n'a pas de vie morale. Il connaît mieux qu'un médecin tous les tons de la chair, vivante ou éteinte; il entend mieux qu'un sculpteur le grain de la pierre; il sait dire la forme, le contour, le relief de ce qu'il a si bien examiné.[11]

At the same time, these external details—furniture, hangings, clothing, trinkets—are multiplied in such abundance and evoked with such minuteness that they soon crowd out all other elements of the novel; Feydeau attempts deliberately to substitute the plastic arts for literature, and his work remains suspended, vague and confused, between the two forms.[12] In spite, however, of this use of detail in the effort to create

an illusion of reality, Feydeau's books do not give the impression of
being reflections of real life. Their situations are usually far-fetched,
wilful twistings and distortions of the normal events of life. Their
people (Roger, for example) are either exceptional, torn by strange
passions and indulging in curious self-analysis;[13] or they represent so
common and humdrum a humanity as to be entirely uninteresting.[14]
Finally, Feydeau's style reflects all the vices of the realistic approach; it
multiplies metaphors and epithets in the effort to describe accurately; it
becomes bombastic and confused in the attempt to reflect completely
every nuance of feeling.[15]

In the later books, especially *Catherine d'Overmeire* and *Un Début
à l'Opéra,* the critics discerned a modification of Feydeau's realism by
a new lyricism or "Byronism." Sainte-Beuve himself had suggested the
phrase "un passionné et un byronien";[16] others soon turned it to ridicule
—Merlet who wrote an article called "Le Réalisme byronien,"[17] Barbey
d'Aurevilly who dubbed Feydeau "ce Byron d'épiderme, mais qui a le
réalisme sous la peau."[18] This new, hybrid system of writing was all to
Feydeau's disadvantage; it was worse than his 'pure' realism. As Merlet
said:

L'habit d'Arlequin est moins bariolé que le réalisme de M. Feydeau. . . .
Nous le voyons osciller tour à tour entre un système ennemi acharné de
l'idéal, et de vagues instincts qui l'emportent à travers les nuages, sur
les ailes du dithyrambe, dans les régions de l'impossible.[19]

Hence Feydeau produced a strange mixture of the real and the ideal;
he passed from the exaggerated to the improbable, and from the improbable to the vulgarly melodramatic. Of this cheap, melodramatic
manner *Un Début* was the ultimate expression: Feydeau no longer de-
served consideration as a literary artist.[20] Thus both as realist and as
romantic Feydeau was rejected by the critics, and had it not been for
the support of Sainte-Beuve and the attention he called to Feydeau by
the *Lundis,* the novelist's reputation would probably have been very
limited.

As early as 1854 About's *Grèce contemporaine* brought him fame as
a wit and a satirist. It was not until the following year, however, that
he became associated with the realistic movement through *Tolla.* Hippolyte Babou established the connection on the basis of the contemporaneity of the subject, which was derived from a recent *cause célèbre;*
he also analyzed About's style as derivative from Balzac, George Sand,
Mérimée, Stendhal, and the novels of Dumas *fils.*[21] In 1856, again, *Les
Mariages de Paris* was criticized for similar tendencies. Fournel, especially, used the book as an excuse for attacking the whole tendency to

mingle contemporary facts with purely fictional materials; this, he believed, produced the very opposite of the effect desired:

... un peu plus de vague, ou du moins l'absence de ces renseignements détaillés, de ces noms, de ces numéros, de ces dates, qui ouvrent les voies à un contrôle facile et qui l'appellent même, aurait permis de croire à la vérité de l'histoire, tandis qu'en précisant les choses à ce point, vous forcez le lecteur à se dire qu'elle ne peut être vraie, parce qu'il est certain que rien de pareil ne s'est passé dans les circonstances indiquées par l'auteur.[22]

But it was not until the appearance of *Germaine,* contemporary with *Bovary,* that About's realism was violently opposed. The opposition came chiefly from Pontmartin, who treated the novels of About and of Flaubert in a single article called "Le Roman bourgeois et le roman démocrate." For him, About's work represented the very worst effects of the bourgeois spirit in literature; it glorified material and technical details, new inventions, current events and preoccupations; its characters, even when they were artists or aristocrats, acted and thought on a bourgeois level. "Comme on sent que le roman où se meuvent de semblables héros est bien d'accord avec une époque où l'imagination se met au service de l'industrie, où la littérature et la presse tendent à s'absorber dans la finance!" *Germaine* added to these reprehensible practices the further sin of a physiological, medical approach. This and About's other novels were merely pale imitations of Balzac, reducing the splendor of the *Comédie humaine* to the level of the dominating class in contemporary France, the bourgeoisie.[23] Jouvin, speaking of the same novel, remarked on the indebtedness to Balzac in the technique of characterization, and on About's Voltairian style.[24] A few years later, in 1860, Boissière designated his lack of poetry, enthusiasm, and emotion as a "first symptom" of realism.[25] Finally, Mazade writing on *Madelon* in 1864 found in it "un réalisme d'une crudité sinistre."[26] These few articles give various reasons for connecting About with the realistic movement: contemporaneity, material detail, reduction to the bourgeois scale, the medical approach, impersonality. Most other criticisms, however, put these considerations aside and discussed only About's political ideas, his wit, or his satirical intention; they thus make no contribution to the history of the criticism of realism in our period.

With Duranty we may be brief, as were his contemporaries. For whereas he was much discussed, in 1856-1857, as the editor of *Réalisme,* his novels of a few years later inspired very little interest. On *Le Malheur d'Henriette Gérard* there were only three articles of value for our study. The first, by Cherbuliez, criticized Duranty for presenting uninteresting characters and unattractive scenes, and concluded: "Ne nous présenter que des caractères ignobles et des scènes repoussantes, ce n'est pas reproduire la vie telle qu'elle est; c'est être aussi faux, dans son genre, que le sont, dans le leur, ceux qui veulent tout embellir et tout idéaliser."[27] The second review, by Chavesne, declared that the novel was spoiled by its realistic prejudice, which was manifested in the strange dénouement and in the stylistic search for triviality.[28] The third discussion of *Henriette Gérard,* by Barbey d'Aurevilly, was the most extended and the most penetrating. Barbey, too, thought that the book was harmed by Duranty's systematic realism, which was evident in his disdain for stylistic elegance and in his neglect of the ideal. In both of these failings he resembled Stendhal and Flaubert.[29] The single article on *La Cause du Beau Guillaume,* by Lataye, again found realism to blame, since Duranty described everything without making a choice and made no attempt to impose a superior harmony upon the chaos of life.[30]

The novels of Dumas *fils* written before the middle of the century passed practically unnoticed; of them, as of his dramas, I shall say nothing here. But in 1866, towards the end of our period, he momentarily abandoned the stage for the novel and published *Affaire Clémenceau.* In it he continued the practices of his theater: a concern with contemporary social problems, a close attention to detail, a truthful presentation of character and episode. Hence the book was recognized as another manifestation of realism in the novel, with its own originality and its own contribution.

The newness of *Affaire Clémenceau* consisted precisely in its treatment of social problems; and here it made several innovations. For one thing (according to Pradal) it applied for the first time in fiction the theory of transmission of personality from one generation to another as elaborated by Darwin and Herbert Spencer; Pradal found this a courageous and a meritorious step.[31] Most other critics, however, took exception to it, either because they thought the theory itself invalid or commonplace (compare Sarcey, who says that it proves only that "les chiens ne font pas les chats"),[32] or because they felt that it was out of place in a literary work. The latter objection was the most prominent: as had been the case with Balzac's philosophical and social novels, so now the commentators felt that such materials were inappropriate to a work of art, particularly when they were allowed to overbalance the fictional elements.[33] In the second place, the work made a plea for illegitimate children—a favorite theme with Dumas—and devoted long discussions to the legal and social aspects of the problem; once again, these discussions were regarded as too long and as intrinsically unde-

sirable.[34] Finally, *Affaire Clémenceau,* by its very title, announced itself
as a legal document; it was merely the exact story of a *cause célèbre,*
such as one might find in any issue of the *Gazette des tribunaux.* As a
result, it could have only the passing interest that such documents have—
after all, one does not go back to reread the crime stories in his daily
newspaper.[35]

On the other hand, the novel had definite literary qualities which
distinguished it from a "memento de Palais." These were summarized
by Merlet:

. . . on y reconnaît dès l'abord la conscience d'une étude approfondie, le
coup d'œil pénétrant d'un observateur, la sûreté d'une plume virile, les
combinaisons d'une industrie consommée, la discipline d'une force qui se
possède, se ménage, se dirige, prémédite ses intentions et ne livre rien
au hasard. Je rends donc pleine justice à la facture d'un style souple et
vigoureux, à la dextérité parfois magistrale de l'exécution, à cet art
ingénieux d'animer l'intérêt par le choix des détails, enfin à la distinction
d'un peintre qui entend à merveille les ressources du dessin et de la
couleur.[36]

Practically all the critics were willing to admit these merits.[37] Some of
them discerned, besides, an excellence in the delineation of character
and a sobriety in the conduct of the plot which tempted them to pardon
the philosophical failings and the realistic excesses. As a matter of fact,
and despite the adverse comments summarized in the preceding pages,
the qualities of the book were generally judged as outweighing its defects, and the total impression in reading these criticisms is one of
sympathy rather than of antagonism. It would seem that here again,
as in other cases we have studied, the critics were prone to take lightly
any errors an author might make (provided they were not too prominent) on condition that he conform to their literary standards of unity,
order, and moderation in style.

---

[1] Cf. above, p. 126.   [2] *938,* Sainte-Beuve.   [3] *953,* Sainte-Beuve.
[4] *939,* Lataye, p. 969; *940,* Chasles.   [5] *950,* Cuvillier-Fleury.
[6] *939,* Lataye, p. 969; *940,* Chasles; *941,* Rigault; *942,* O. L.
[7] *942,* O. L.; *944,* Janin, p. ix.   [8] *940,* Chasles.   [9] *947,* La Madelène.
[10] *955,* Merlet, p. 691; cf. *941,* Rigault; *943,* Montégut, pp. 198, 201; *946,* Delord; *948,* Lataye, p. 243; *956,* Barbey d'Aurevilly; *958a,* Pontmartin, p. 152;
959, Nettement, p. 140.
[11] *949,* Chasles; cf. *941,* Rigault; *943,* Montégut, p. 201; *946,* Delord; *948,*
Lataye, p. 240; *951,* Vapereau, p. 126; *952,* Claveau, p. 547; *955,* Merlet, p. 671;
959, Nettement, p. 131.
[12] *943,* Montégut, p. 201; *951,* Vapereau, p. 126; *956,* Barbey d'Aurevilly, pp.
123, 127, 139; *958,* Peyronnet, pp. 142-144.
[13] *941,* Rigault; *942,* O. L.; *955,* Merlet, p. 698.

[14] *943*, Montégut, p. 204; *955*, Merlet, p. 670; *956*, Barbey d'Aurevilly, p. 135; *957*, Vapereau, p. 72; *958*, Peyronnet, p. 140.

[15] *939*, Lataye, p. 970; *941*, Rigault; *948*, Lataye, p. 241; *950*, Cuvillier-Fleury; *951*, Vapereau, p. 126; *955*, Merlet, p. 683; *957*, Vapereau, p. 73.

[16] *953*, Sainte-Beuve, p. 352.   [17] *955*, Merlet.

[18] *956*, Barbey d'Aurevilly, p. 126.   [19] *955*, Merlet, p. 668.

[20] Cf. *950*, Cuvillier-Fleury, 2nd art.; *951*, Vapereau, p. 126; *952*, Claveau; *954*, Cuvillier-Fleury; *955*, Merlet, p. 683; *958a*, Pontmartin, pp. 153 ff.

[21] *960*, Babou.   [22] *961*, Fournel, p. 363.   [23] *963*, Pontmartin, pp. 289-298.

[24] *962*, Jouvin.   [25] *964*, Boissière.   [26] *965*, Mazade.

[27] *966*, Cherbuliez, p. 389.   [28] *968*, Chavesne.   [29] *967*, Barbey d'Aurevilly.

[30] *969*, Lataye.   [31] *971*, Pradal.   [32] *975*, Sarcey, p. 536.

[33] *970*, Jouvin; *972*, Bernard, p. 29; *973*, Landrol; *977*, Claveau, p. 561; *978*, Merlet, pp. 117 ff.   [34] *972*, Bernard, p. 28; *973*, Landrol; *977*, Claveau, p. 563.

[35] *973*, Landrol; *974*, Pontmartin, p. 66; *976*, Werner, p. 295; *977*, Claveau, p. 560; *979*, Vapereau, pp. 56 ff.   [36] *978*, Merlet, pp. 116-117.

[37] Cf. *970*, Jouvin, 2nd art.; *972*, Bernard, p. 29; *973*, Landrol; *975*, Sarcey, pp. 540-548; *976*, Werner, p. 300; *977*, Claveau, p. 563; *979*, Vapereau, p. 61.

CHAPTER X

THE GONCOURTS

Chronology

1860: *Les Hommes de lettres (Charles Demailly)*
1861: *Sœur Philomène*
1864: *Renée Mauperin*
1865: *Germinie Lacerteux*
1867: *Manette Salomon*
1869: *Madame Gervaisais*
1870: Death of Jules de Goncourt

AFTER almost a decade of collaboration as journalists and as historians of the eighteenth century, Edmond and Jules de Goncourt published, in 1860, their first important novel of contemporary life, *Les Hommes de lettres*. During the next ten years, until the death of Jules, they published five more novels. It is with the criticism of these six works, which alone concern the history of realistic fiction in our period, that we shall have to deal. That criticism is, on the whole, very restricted in scope; the works were apparently discussed in only forty articles, many of which were short notices. On the majority of the novels opinion was almost evenly divided; it was preponderantly unfavorable to *Charles Demailly* and *Madame Gervaisais*, and favorable to *Renée Mauperin*. Since there were so few judgments concerning the individual works, I shall be able here to indicate the reaction towards each successive novel before summarizing the general tendencies to be discerned in the whole body of criticism.

The antagonism towards *Charles Demailly* is easily understood. For, like Balzac's *Grand Homme de province à Paris*, it was recognized as an attack on the press and the literati, unfair since it portrayed only the seamy side of the literary world. Janin, who had sounded the alarm in 1839, likewise leads the assault on the Goncourts in 1860; his principal objection, now as before, is that they misrepresent contemporary journalism:

. . . jamais, que je sache, il n'y eut, livre ou drame, un spectacle à la fois plus triste et plus déshonorant que le spectacle d'une littérature en proie à ces trahisons, à ces perfidies, à ces monstruosités. MM. de Goncourt, voulant frapper fort, ont oublié de frapper juste. Ils ont inventé des crimes inconnus, des orgies impossibles, des monstres en morale![1]

The same charge is brought by Duchesne, Barbey d'Aurevilly, and Vapereau. Duchesne, however, gives a much fuller judgment, condemning the book as well for its lack of unity and composition, for its precious, affected style, and praising it for the fine psychological study of Charles in the second part.[2] Barbey, too, finds that the brothers abuse language and rhetoric, that the novel is poorly put together; he quarrels with the materials, however, not because he would defend the press, not because the subject itself is "low," but because the writers have failed to discover "l'idéal dans le laid et dans le mauvais."[3] There are few defences of the book: Chasles likes it because it is striking and alive;[4] Chavesne, because he believes Marthe Demailly to be a new and remarkable creation;[5] Pontmartin, because he finds in it an expression of his own animosity for the press, and merely uses it as a point of departure for a savage attack on contemporary writers.[6]

With *Sœur Philomène*, in 1861, the principal difficulty was again one of subject-matter. To take as heroine a sister of charity was in itself a desecration.[7] To study her passion for an unworthy medical student was again reprehensible. But by far the worst offence was in mingling constantly this psychological analysis with the detailed description of the hospital which served as setting.[8] These technical, medical details were repulsive to the critics, and considered as unworthy of art; in any case, they spoiled this novel entirely. Says Pontmartin: "A côté d'une étude où le sentiment moral domine, les auteurs ne nous font pas grâce des plis d'un rideau d'hôpital, de la moiteur affadissante d'un dortoir, d'un cadavre dessinant sous les draps ses formes rigides, des détails d'une opération ou d'un amphithéâtre."[9] Naturally, the realistic bias behind the choice of such materials led inevitably, in the view of judges, to that other vice of over-description. On the other hand, *Sœur Philomène* was to be commended for the reality of certain characters, the vividness of certain scenes, the style of certain pages.[10] The only really notable praise of the novel came from Jules Levallois, who answered all of the critical objections. Considering that literature must afford a direct contact with life, not an escape from it, he thinks the subject completely justified. There is no attempt to shock or disgust the reader; rather are the "incidents and accidents purified by the purity of the basic conception." If anything, the authors have sinned by timidity rather than by boldness. Finally, their style is excellent:

Ceux qui goûtent la délicatesse du tour, la finesse de l'expression, l'harmonie de la phrase, cet indéfinissable arrangement des paroles, charme et autorité du langage, auront senti un petit frisson de joie et de délectation, auront applaudi, salué le don le plus envié, l'un des plus enviables, le talent. . . . MM. de Goncourt sont des écrivains de race.[11]

After two and a half years of silence, the Goncourts published *Renée Mauperin* (April, 1864), which was greeted immediately by the enthusiastic appraisals of Banville and of Paul de Saint-Victor. Other favorable reviews followed, and the praise became almost unanimous. The great virtue of the book, for the critics, was the character of the heroine, fresh, alive, entirely original: a *new* heroine.[12] Other characters, too, were admirably portrayed; the book was well composed; the sense of contrast and of pathos was commendable. The whole attitude is best expressed by Saint-Victor:

Toutes les qualités d'écrivains et d'observateurs de MM. de Goncourt s'y sont resserrées et comme exaltées. Pas une langueur et pas un hors-d'œuvre. Un souffle poétique anime le récit: les chapitres se succèdent courts et rapides comme des strophes. Des figures toujours en mouvement, des caractères que leur action fait saillir, des causeries qui sont des comédies de mœurs esquissées au vol. Le style, déjà d'une qualité si rare dans *Sœur Philomène,* a gagné encore en justesse et en concision; il peint d'une touche; il dessine d'une ligne; il abonde en expressions senties et vivantes. Cette brièveté dans le rendu des détails laisse plus de jeu à l'intérêt et au sentiment. L'art du récit s'efface sous les émotions qu'il excite: on s'attendrit avant d'admirer.

However, there were some adverse criticisms: A. D. condemns the novel in terms which might apply to any realistic work;[13] Cuvillier-Fleury finds the general tone affected, and takes special exception to the strange *argot* spoken by Renée;[14] Vapereau blames the realistic system for concentrating the attention upon an exceptional heroine ("plus vraie que vraisemblable"), for emphasizing the picturesque aspects of reality to the detriment of the emotional.[15] But this time the negative opinions are decidedly in the minority.

Over *Germinie Lacerteux,* the most extensively discussed of the Goncourt novels, a veritable controversy was waged during 1865. While numerically the groups of the defendants and the plaintiffs were about even, the case of the latter was so much more vehemently stated that the general impression is one of a victory for the opposition. It was in connection with this novel, too, that the question of realism was most persistently raised; hence the criticism is doubly interesting. Let us first examine the defence. A few critics—Dauriac, Jules Claretie, Zola—boldly declared themselves partisans of realism; therefore they were willing to accept a novel treating of the very lowest class of society. For Dauriac, literature must not attempt to escape from life and especially from vice, but it must depict evil in order to inspire a hatred of evil.[16] Similarly, Claretie maintained that truth was never immoral,[17] and Zola that one could not go too far in portraying the real: "il ne saurait en principe y avoir de limite dans l'étude de la vérité."[18] Even the materialistic, the purely physiological is thus fully justified. In the present novel, the Goncourts have been so courageous, so painstaking in their search for truth, so frank, so energetic, so fearless in the description of what they found, that their book must command the interest and the admiration of the reader.[19] In two respects especially their observation and their artistry have given excellent results: in the subtle psychological study of Germinie herself and in the numerous descriptive passages.[20] The style is of course superior.

But against these critics there were the intransigent enemies of realism. They attacked first the preface and its program for a *roman populaire:* the people, they said (misunderstanding the intention of the authors), had no desire to see itself portrayed, but wanted rather an escape from life in literature.[21] Even were the thesis of a popular (or proletarian) novel tenable, it was indubitable that the Goncourts had failed to produce one here. For they had chosen so low and so ugly a milieu, their characters were so exceptional, that the 'people' was everywhere misrepresented and calumniated. Jules Claretie summarizes thus their conception of the populace: "De l'argot, une senteur d'eau-de-vie et de mauvais lieux, des vices et encore des vices, le Mont-de-Piété, la Bourbe, l'hôpital, et c'est là le peuple!"[22] Merlet calls the book "une insulte faite aux classes populaires, et une excitation au mépris des petits et des pauvres."[23] As for the heroine, far from being a representative of her class, she was a pathological case, a rare exception, and hence untrue generally speaking. It was this pathological aspect, this medical type of analysis, that the critics found most objectionable. "MM. de Goncourt," to quote Claretie again, "n'ont pas fait autre chose, ce semble, que puiser dans leur répertoire de connaissances médicales; ils ont écrit leur roman à la pointe du bistouri."[24] This medical bias, for one thing, leads to a frank materialism, and thence to a vulgar sensualism; as Claveau says, "ils ont, dans *Germinie Lacerteux,* glorifié, illuminé la bête, ils ont méprisé, oublié la femme et l'humanité."[25] These sins, of course, were all to be laid at the door of realism, of a "réalisme outré," a "réalisme brutal." It was the realistic system (here strangely coupled with an eighteenth-century affectation) which led to a complete disdain for moral considerations, to the choice of the low subject, to the wallowing in useless material detail.[26]

Manette Salomon, in 1865, passed practically unnoticed by the critics; I have found only two reviews of it, one (consisting of two articles) by Chesneau in the *Constitutionnel,* the other (a brief notice) by E. C. in the *Revue contemporaine.* We need examine only the first of these. Chesneau declares that the book must not be considered as a novel centering about Manette, since then it will appear badly constructed, slow, full of digressions. Considered, however, as a study of the artist Coriolis and of artists in general, the book becomes significant down to the last word. In this study, the Goncourts have excelled in psychological analysis, in pictorial presentation, in the rendering of the speech of the ateliers. They have erred in selecting an unrepresentative artist for their hero, in displaying a certain animosity towards artists, and in stressing the physical instead of the moral aspects of their subject.[27]

The last joint effort of the Goncourts, *Madame Gervaisais,* was again unanimously rejected by the critics. Such of its phases as the truthful observation, the descriptions, certain episodes, the style, were given the customary praise. But the basic conception underlying the work was regarded as false: the writers set out to study a disease, an abnormal case, an exception, and hence their novel could have no general interest. Roqueplan puts it thus: "ils semblent avoir voulu écrire l'histoire d'une intelligence, et ils n'ont guère écrit, en réalité, que l'histoire d'une maladie."[28] And Barbey thus: "on n'y trouve, en définitive, qu'une description psychique et physiologique d'un cas d'organisation très particulier."[29] Their effort to demonstrate, scientifically, the influence of milieu upon Madame Gervaisais, and to deduce rigorously each stage of her malady from the preceding stage, has led them to an unreal and an unjustified dénouement.[30] Again, their literary convictions cause them to devote excessive care to the study of external details, to lose sight of the broader aspects of the subject, to fall into exaggeration. Barbey d'Aurevilly comments on this exaggeration:

MM. de Goncourt ont regardé à la loupe ce phénomène dans tous ces détails, et ils nous l'ont rendu avec cette saillie de style qui est une autre loupe fixée sur l'objet regardé et déjà grossi. Vous comprenez alors le degré d'énormité, et même de difformité, que les choses prennent sous ces deux espèces de verres grossissants.[31]

Barbey's attack, however, springs essentially from his own religious disposition: he finds the novel materialistic and anti-Catholic.

From the preceding pages it will be evident that certain criticisms recur constantly in reviews of the Goncourts. The objections tend to center about a few points. First, subject-matter. The critics find, in one novel after another, that the milieu chosen by the authors is undesirable: in *Charles Demailly,* the world of "la petite presse"; in *Sœur Philomène,* the hospital; in *Germinie Lacerteux,* the lowest reaches of Parisian society. Secondly, the hero or heroine detached from the milieu is always an exceptional case. This reproach extends even to novels in which the environment itself is not objectionable, to the characters of Renée Mauperin and Madame Gervaisais. Hence each of these novels is in a sense a pathological study, an investigation centered upon a curious but rare specimen. In the third place, the Goncourts very definitely portray their society and their personages as worse than they really are in life. They see everything through a black veil. This misrepresentation results from the fact (and this is the fourth point) that they tend to see only externals, only the 'accidents,' and to ignore the spiritual and the ideal. Finally, from a purely literary standpoint, this emphasis on the external produces an exaggerated attention to detail, a carelessness of plot and composition, a tendency to overdescription. Most of these failings were attributed, by the critics, to the realistic system of the writers, whose native talent was recognized by nearly all the commentators.

That native talent, according to the reviewers, was manifold, and it produced excellent results in certain phases of these novels. For one thing, the Goncourts had a real gift for observation, for close and subtle study of reality, and many a passage of their work was indisputably true. Again, they had a genius for description: time after time they were likened to painters, to etchers, to engravers, and their Parisian scenes were regarded as prodigious transferences of pictorial technique to the literary art. More strikingly still, they were experts in the delineation of character: their people (no matter how exceptional they might be) were always alive, real, delicately apprehended and set forth with a rare sureness of touch. Finally, they had a superior style, contested by some, but admired by most for its richness and color, for its capacity to render the most tenuous of sensations. These qualities, plus a certain vigor and conviction, made their works fascinating, even for the reader who objected to them on moral or literary grounds. They explain the modicum of praise which was always mingled with the most devastating censure, as well as the concessions made by the most adverse critics.

---

[1] *980,* Janin.   [2] *983,* Duchesne.
[3] *985,* Barbey d'Aurevilly, p. 192; cf. *986,* Vapereau.   [4] *982,* Chasles.
[5] *984,* Chavesne.   [6] *981,* Pontmartin.   [7] Cf. *992,* Fournel, p. 351.
[8] *988,* Cherbuliez, p. 469; *989,* Pontmartin, p. 708; *990,* Vapereau, p. 78; *992,* Fournel, p. 351.   [9] *989,* Pontmartin, p. 708.
[10] *987,* Arnould; *992,* Fournel, p. 351; *993,* Ernouf.   [11] *991,* Levallois.
[12] *994,* Saint-Victor; *995,* Banville; *998,* Cuvillier-Fleury; *1011,* Claveau, p. 575.
[13] *996,* A. D.   [14] *998,* Cuvillier-Fleury; cf. *1011,* Claveau, p. 575.
[15] *999,* Vapereau.   [16] *1000,* Dauriac, p. 71.   [17] *1002,* Claretie, p. 171.
[18] *1008,* Zola, p. 81.
[19] *1000,* Dauriac, p. 71; *1002,* Claretie, p. 171; *1004,* Banville; *1006,* Villetard, p. 523; *1008,* Zola, pp. 79, 82.
[20] *1000,* Dauriac, p. 71; *1002,* Claretie, pp. 171, 175; *1003,* Pontmartin, p. 111;

1004, Banville; *1006*, Villetard, p. 523; *1008*, Zola, p. 82; *1007*, Merlet, p. 82; *1011*, Claveau, p. 577.

[21] *1002*, Claretie, p. 168; *1003*, Pontmartin, p. 109; *1005*, Duchesne, p. 3; *1007*, Merlet, p. 85; *1011*, Claveau, p. 576.

[22] *1002*, Claretie, p. 172; cf. *1003*, Pontmartin, p. 113; *1005*, Duchesne, p. 3; *1006*, Villetard, p. 523; *1007*, Merlet, p. 91; *1011*, Claveau, p. 576.

[23] *1007*, Merlet, p. 91.

[24] *1002*, Claretie, p. 173; cf. *1003*, Pontmartin, p. 111; *1005*, Duchesne, p. 3.

[25] *1011*, Claveau, p. 576; cf. *1002*, Claretie, p. 175.

[26] Cf. especially *1001*, Lagenevais; *1003*, Pontmartin, pp. 104, 109; *1005*, Duchesne, p. 3; *1007*, Merlet, p. 89; *1011*, Claveau, p. 577.   [27] *1013*, Chesneau.

[28] *1016*, Roqueplan.

[29] *1018*, Barbey d'Aurevilly, p. 40; *1020*, Asselineau, p. 125.

[30] *1016*, Roqueplan; *1019*, Ebelot, p. 509; *1020*, Asselineau, p. 124.

[31] *1018*, Barbey d'Aurevilly, p. 40; cf. *1017*, Villarceaux; *1019*, Ebelot, pp. 508, 511.

CONCLUSIONS

IN THE Introduction, the reader may remember, I announced as the purpose of this study the answering of a given set of questions relevant to the criticism of realism between 1830 and 1870. Some of these questions have been treated directly in one or another of the preceding chapters. The meanings attached to the words *réalisme* and *réaliste,* the elements considered as constituents of the realistic method, the reaction (in the abstract) to these elements, have been studied in Chapters IV and V. The reaction to each of the authors included has been discussed in the appropriate chapter. But there still remain a number of points which could not be examined prior to the completion of the individual studies. Essentially, they are these:

(1) What elements of literary attitude or technique are indicated, by the critics, as recurring constantly in the various authors treated?

(2) Which of these elements are specifically associated with realistic theory and practice? Which seem merely accidental features of realistic novels?

(3) What is the attitude towards the definitely realistic elements? Towards the others?

(4) Which of the authors embodying these elements were accepted by the critics, and which rejected?

(5) What are the general literary standards applied by the critics in these judgments?

(6) Can we discern any change, from one decade to another, in the total response to realistic traits and authors?

I shall attempt to answer these questions briefly in the remaining pages.

One would expect that critics of a definite period, studying the works of authors who wrote for the tastes of that period and who represented its society, would discover a certain number of traits common to those works. If, besides, the authors were associated through a common purpose—the endeavor to portray contemporary life as it was—and if the critics saw in them individual manifestations of a single literary method—realism—one would expect these common traits to be very numerous. Such is indeed the case with the works and the critics included in the present study. On the other hand, those authors would be differentiated among themselves by a host of purely personal qualities: their techniques, their conceptions of literary method, their philosophies, their personalities—all of the factors which make an individual of the artist. These personal characteristics would be reflected

192

in the works produced, and would explain to a large degree their differences. These too we should expect the critics to note, but as isolated phenomena rather than as recurrent elements. Hence they would be of little service in any attempt we might make to characterize the authors as a group or the attitude of the critics towards these authors. We must therefore fall back upon the common traits and their reception by the critics.

The critics, as we have seen, constantly repeat certain words, certain phrases, certain ideas in connection with the realists. These I might summarize thus :[1]

List I

(a) The authors attempt a truthful representation of the real world (Ia, Ib, II, IIIa, VI, VII, VIII, IXa, X).

(b) The real world, for them, consists of contemporary life and manners (Ia, Ib, II, IIIa, IIIb, VI, VII, VIII, IXb, X).

(c) It must be approached through the faculty of observation, not through that of imagination (Ia, Ib, II, IIIa, IIIb, VI, VIII, IXa, IXd, X).

(d) Since observation can be applied only to what is immediately observable, these authors are most concerned with the study of objective reality and the description of external details (II, IIIa, IIIb, VI, VIII, IXa, X).

(e) Hence they neglect the "ideal" and everything that escapes observation (Ia, II, VI, VIII, X).

(f) In their anxiety to reproduce the physical world, they tend to indulge in excessive minute detail (Ia, II, VI, VIII, IXa, X).

(g) When they treat character and the inner world of the mind, they apply the same method of minute analysis (Ia, Ib, II, IIIb, VIII, IXa, X).

(h) The result is frequently comparable to a medical dissection, to a scientific experiment (Ia, II, VIII, IXb, X).

(i) This entire approach results from a philosophical bias which is eminently materialistic or positivistic (Ia, Ib, II, VI, VIII, IXa, X).

(j) The authors' impersonality is a reflection of this materialism (Ib, II, IIIa, VI, VIII, IXb).

(k) So are their scepticism and their cynicism (Ia, Ib, II, VI, VIII).

(l) So, also, is the complete indifference to moral considerations which is responsible for the immorality of their works (Ia, Ib, II, VIII, IXa, X).

(m) In its worst form, this positivism appears as an out-and-out sensualism and ultimately as fatalism (VIII, IXa, X).

(n) As a consequence of the study of contemporary life from this materialistic bias, the world of the authors is false (Ia, II, VIII, IXc, X).

(o) It is limited exclusively to the ugly and the trivial and hence it is incomplete (Ia, Ib, II, IIIa, VI, VIII, IXc, X).

(p) Its people are exceptional, and their actions may not be taken as representing those of humanity in general (Ia, II, VI, IXa, X).

(q) These practices lead, on the formal side, to digressions and *longueurs* (II, VIII) ;
(r) to a lack of unity (II, VI, VIII, IXc, X) ;
(s) and to an involved style (II, IXa, X).

If now we compare this list with the formulation of realistic theory given above (pages 126-127), we shall discover immediately which of these recurrent elements were essential parts of the realistic doctrine as set forth by contemporary spokesmen for the movement. They are, in brief, the following:

List II

(a) A truthful representation of the real world.
(b) The study of contemporary life and manners.
(c) The approach through observation.
(g) The analytical method in character study.
(j) The impersonality of the author's attitude.

It will be evident that this list includes but a very small number of the elements commonly found by the critics in the novels of the realists. In other words, there is a notable discrepancy between the theory of realism as stated by the novelists (or their champions) and the practice of realism as described by the critics. On the other hand, the few elements contained in List II were the very basis of realistic theory: they were the indispensable features of the new literary movement, those which made it distinct from antecedent or contemporary traditions. Apparently, then, the critics, in their discussions of individual writers, discerned in them the fundamental qualities of realism, but they perceived as well many additional traits.

From the standpoint of the critics, however, most of these additional traits did belong, definitely, to realism. This we may ascertain by comparing List I with the materials found in Chapters IV and V which, it will be remembered, deal with realism in the abstract, and as related to both painting and literature. The materials are of two types: the formal definitions of realism given by critics and their general discussions, in both chapters, of realistic theory. A comparison of this body of opinion with List I (i.e., of traits said to be generally realistic with traits discovered in the particular writers) shows that the following recurrent elements were commonly regarded by the critics as pertaining directly to the new literary method:

List III

(a) A truthful representation of the real world.
(b) The study of contemporary life and manners.
(c) The approach through observation.
(d) The emphasis on external detail.

(e) The neglect of the ideal.
(f) Excessive minute detail.
(g) The analytical method in character study.
(h) The scientific method of analysis.
(i) The materialistic (or positivistic) bias.
(j) Impersonality.
(l) Moral indifference and immorality.
(m) Sensualism and fatalism.
(o) The limitation to the ugly and the trivial.

From this comparison it is clear that all except a few of the recurrent elements (in List I) were considered as directly related to realism; and these few seem to have been incidental concomitants of the realistic method: (k) Scepticism and cynicism; (n) Falseness of the world portrayed; (p) Exceptional people; (q) Digressions and *longueurs;* (r) Lack of unity; (s) Involved style.

We may now ask what the reaction of the critics was to the two groups of elements (Lists II and III) as they found them in the different authors. In the first place, what did they think of the points admitted by the realists themselves as part of their doctrine? They approved of the desire for a truthful representation of the real world: examples are their admiration for Balzac's social portrayal, their preference for *Madame Bovary* over *Salammbô,* their frequent endorsement of anti-romantic tendencies. This approbation they extended to the contemporaneity of subject-matter: almost universally (in literature at least) they welcomed the change from the historical subjects of the classicists and the romanticists. The approach through observation was again almost always accepted. For although the absence of imagination was often decried, the application of a subtle technique of observation to the materials studied found favor constantly, and the skill of the observer was in nearly every case distinguished as the dominant quality of the author. The same was true of the analytical method in character study: the process of penetrating deep within the soul of the personage, of studying his actions with respect to their causes and as reflected in their effects, was applauded as endowing him with a reality he had never had before. On the question of impersonality, however, opinion was divided: for while in some authors it was found responsible for the truthfulness of the portrayal, in others it was blamed for the coldness of general impression. Nevertheless, had the writings of the realists been characterized only by the traits set forth in their theory, these writings would almost certainly have been acceptable to the critics.

But we must ask, in the second place, what the critics thought of the additional traits which they themselves considered as part and parcel of the realistic method. It is here that we discover why the realistic movement was so often condemned. For each of these additional traits—repudiated by the realists—was regarded by the critics as a major objection to the writers they were studying. The critics included in their conception of realism the emphasis on external detail: this was generally denounced since it was regarded as taking the attention from the proper subject of art, the soul of man, and as placing all the stress on inanimate or purely material objects. They likewise included the neglect of the ideal as an inevitable attribute of realism; and I need hardly insist on the opposition which this neglect everywhere met. So too for the reproach of excessive minute detail—always a reproach—and the idea that the realistic method was primarily scientific. There were few commentators who would admit this scientific method in literature; for nearly all, it was incompatible with art. The materialistic philosophy at the basis of this scientific approach was, for many judges, an unpardonable error. But by far the most objectionable element included here by the critics was that of moral indifference and immorality, with the cognate vices of sensualism and fatalism. The drastic condemnation of immorality informs discussion of realism throughout, from the very beginning to the very end; that of sensualism and fatalism appears only after 1857. Finally, the critics conceived of realism as exploiting the trivial and the ugly and refused to tolerate such a falsification of the world as they saw it. Hence it will be evident that in the current conception of realism were comprised a number of elements which were entirely incompatible with the artistic or philosophical ideals of the time, as stated by representative critics. A system of writing embodying these elements was doomed on the whole to disapproval.

How, then, may we explain the fact that the authors whose work embodied these objectionable traits were not wholly rejected by the literary world? For that they were not is obvious from the individual chapters. Mérimée, for example, was readily accepted. Balzac emerged victorious from a long and heated struggle, but definitely victorious. Flaubert won the suffrage of about half of those who reviewed his two realistic novels. The Goncourts, while not so successful, nevertheless had staunch defenders. On the contrary, Stendhal was appreciated by only a very few; Champfleury fought throughout a losing battle; the minor realists, in so far as they were realists, were all condemned in no uncertain terms. Why these differences of reception?

A complete answer to this question (if indeed such an answer be possible) would demand a much more subtle analysis of literary merit and of public taste than it is here possible to give. But I believe that a partial answer, at least, has from time to time been suggested in the foregoing chapters: the critics were willing to accept writers who conformed to their own artistic standards, and to forgive almost any philosophical misdemeanors if the artistry was in sufficient agreement with those standards. Mérimée is the best case in point: for in spite of his treatment of low subjects, his impersonality and his cynicism, his immorality and his materialism, he received the highest praise; and this was because his works had "unity" and "composition," "clarity" and "sobriety," "order" and "select diction." The same might be said for Flaubert: he incarnated all the realists' vices; but "il avait le style," his first book presented a single action, a unified approach, one sensed in it a definite and a superior artistry. So too for the Goncourts: each of their works was an "acte d'écrivain," each showed a mastery of style and an effort at composition, each presented a single and unified action. With Balzac the case was somewhat different, but none the less revealing. For while much of the opposition to his work was on the basis of its philosophical and social aspects, a good deal of it was directed against Balzac's artistic practices. Balzac was admired, it will be remembered, largely for the excellence of his portrayal of contemporary society, and it seems reasonable to suppose that, had he coupled this portrayal with the "classical" literary traits demanded by the critics, his acceptance would have been more immediate and more complete.

Stendhal supplies the best example of an author rejected because his philosophical vices were not compensated, in the opinion of the critics, by sufficient literary merit. They discerned in his works no arrangement, no plan; his style was choppy and inelegant; he passed abruptly from one development to another with no apparent reason; in a word, he did not "compose." Champfleury, again, in spite of admitted qualities (personal rather than technical) was hardly considered seriously as a novelist, and this was because the critics would not admit that he was an artist. The same held true for the other minor realists.

From these cases it is clear what the aesthetic standards of the critics were. We have already seen, in Chapters IV and V, that they demanded that art be an idealization of nature, a reflection of nature against the personality of the artist. We now learn, besides, how this idealization was to be effected. The artist was to choose a single and unified subject, all the parts of which he was to dispose in a clear and logical order. He was to avoid excess or exaggeration of any one of the parts, and to keep the whole in proportion. In his diction, he was to maintain the same sobriety, the same severity in the choice of elements and in their disposition. The reader will immediately identify this attitude as "classical" or "traditional" rather than as "romantic." Why the realists, setting out with a different artistic purpose, failed to fulfil (partly or completely, in the given case) these requirements has been indicated time and again in the preceding chapters.

Finally, we may ask if there was any change discernible in the attitude of the critics from one decade to another. This is difficult to ascertain. For were not the same objections brought against Balzac in the first years as in the last? Was not a similar condemnation called down upon *Le Rouge et le Noir* in 1830 and upon *Madame Gervaisais* in 1869? Did not *L'Education sentimentale* elicit the same comments in 1869 as did *Les Aventures de Mademoiselle Mariette* in 1853? These similarities would seem to indicate the persistence of one attitude throughout the forty-year period. Nevertheless, there was some change, some progress. On the one hand, and taking the authors individually, we note that towards some of them the public attitude is progressively more sympathetic; this is perhaps true with Stendhal, and definitely so with Balzac. On the other hand, it is clear that elements which aroused considerable discussion in the earlier years were, later on, accepted without comment. It would seem that, despite protesting critics, the movement made steady headway in the direction of acceptance, and that even the most persistent objectors were obliged to abandon trench after trench in their retreat before the increasing onslaught of realistic novels. As these novels became more daring and more extreme in their tendencies, earlier writings appeared mild by comparison. In certain cases, these earlier writings were themselves taken as standards of comparison for the new works; witness the case of *Madame Bovary,* so much discussed when first published, and which increased in favor as first *Salammbô* and then *L'Education sentimentale* confronted the public. Or the case of Balzac who, as the realists outstrip him in boldness, becomes more and more distinct from them in critical conception, and more and more admirable. The same change is to be noted in the cases of individual critics: Pontmartin, for example. His animosity towards Balzac (in 1857) is increasingly mollified as first Flaubert, then Feydeau, then the Goncourts extend the limits of realism, and in the end (1869) he is all but an apologist of the *Comédie humaine. Madame Bovary,* after all, was much more drastic in its tendencies than *Père Goriot* had been, and *Germinie Lacerteux* more so than *Madame Bovary.* In spite of the fact that such new reproaches as "sensualism" and "fatalism" were formulated for the later works, the mere willingness of the critics to condone some of their failings—and in some instances even to defend them—is an indication that the mass of opinion was not entirely intransigent. *Le Rouge et le Noir,* had it appeared in the '60's, would probably

have met with very little opposition. The materials set forth above in
the individual chapters do not, I believe, warrant any further generaliza-
tions with respect to the change of attitude towards realism from one
decade to another.

---

[1] References are to chapter only. Where several authors are treated in a
single chapter, they are designated by a, b, c, or d, respectively. Chapters IV and V,
devoted to theory and abstract discussion, are not included.

APPENDIX I

PERIODICALS EXAMINED

B ELOW are listed the periodicals examined in which pertinent materials were found, with the years for which they were examined. In nearly all cases, these years indicate the entire duration of the periodical. Publications of less than one-year duration were excluded, as were all provincial journals.

Abeille artistique et littéraire. 1854.
Abeille littéraire. 1844-1848.
Appel. 1855.
Art et progrès, revue du théâtre. 1834-1838.
Artiste. 1831-1870.
Athenaeum français. 1852-1856.
Avenir. 1841-1842.
Avenir. 1855-1856.
Bagatelle. 1832-1833.
Bibliothèque universelle. 1830-1835.
Boulevard. 1861-1863.
Bourgeois de Paris. 1859-1860.
Bulletin du bibliophile. 1834-1870.
Chérubin. 1834-1835.
Chronique. 1841-1845.
Chronique de Paris. 1834-1837.
Chronique de Paris. 1850-1852.
Chronique littéraire. 1862.
Constitutionnel. 1830-1870.
Correspondance littéraire. 1856-1865.
Correspondant. 1843-1870.
Courrier de Paris. 1850-1851.
Critique (le). 1835-1836.
Critique (le). 1866-1867.
Critique française. 1861-1864.
Dilettante. 1838-1839.
Echo de la Jeune France. 1833-1837.
Echo de la littérature et des beaux-arts. 1840-1849.
Eclair. 1852-1853.
Estafette. 1855-1856.
Europe littéraire. 1833-1834.
Feuilleton mensuel. 1841-1842.
Figaro. 1826-1833.
Figaro. 1839-1840.

Figaro. 1856-1866.
France littéraire. 1832-1843.
Franchise. 1862-1863.
Gaulois. 1857-1861.
Gazette littéraire. 1830-1831.
Gazette littéraire. 1864.
Indépendant. 1830-1848.
Jeunesse. 1868-1869.
Journal des débats politiques et littéraires. 1830-1870.
Journal du dimanche. 1846-1847.
Littérateur universel. 1834-1839.
Magasin de librairie. 1858-1860.
Mémorial de la littérature et des beaux-arts. 1840-1841.
Mercure de France. 1835-1836.
Messager des théâtres et des arts (éd. bis-hebdomadaire). 1848-1850.
Monde artistique et littéraire. 1853-1854.
Monde dramatique. 1835-1841.
Moniteur des arts. 1845-1846.
Musée des familles. 1833-1862.
Nouvelle bibliothèque des romans. 1833-1835.
Nouvelle revue encyclopédique. 1846-1847.
Panorama littéraire de l'Europe. 1833-1834.
Phalange. 1836-1843.
Présent. 1857.
Province et Paris. 1841-1844.
Réalisme. 1856-1857.
Révolution littéraire. 1851-1852.
Revue britannique. 1830-1865.
Revue contemporaine. 1852-1870.

Revue de France. 1835-1836.
Revue de l'année religieuse, philosophique et littéraire. 1861-1864.
Revue de Paris. 1830-1844.
Revue de Paris. 1851-1857.
Revue de Paris. 1864-1870.
Revue des cours littéraires. 1863-1870.
Revue des deux mondes. 1830-1870.
Revue du dix-neuvième siècle. 1836-1840.
Revue du dix-neuvième siècle. 1854-1855.
Revue du dix-neuvième siècle. 1866-1867.
Revue du progrès. 1863-1864.
Revue encyclopédique. 1830-1833, 1835.
Revue européenne. 1831-1835.
Revue européenne. 1859-1861.
Revue française. 1830.
Revue française. 1855-1859.

Revue française. 1861-1869.
Revue française et étrangère. 1837-1838.
Revue gauloise. 1866-1867.
Revue indépendante. 1841-1848.
Revue indépendante. 1862-1866.
Revue littéraire et critique. 1842-1845.
Revue moderne. 1857-1858.
Revue nationale et étrangère. 1860-1867.
Revue nouvelle. 1845-1847.
Revue parisienne. 1853-1861.
Revue philosophique et religieuse. 1855-1858.
Siècle. 1833.
Spectateur. 1838-1839.
Tam-Tam. 1835-1839.
Varia. 1860-1863.
Vérité. 1834-1835.

Note. The following periodicals were examined and found to contain no pertinent materials:

Album universel. 1853-1855.
Annuaire des lettres. 1846-1847.
Bulletin de la Société des gens de lettres. 1845-1846.
Bulletin littéraire. 1862-1864.
Cabinet littéraire. 1841-1845.
Causeur. 1852-1854.
Chronique française. 1837.
Chronique théâtrale et littéraire. 1862-1863.
Chronique théâtrale et littéraire de Paris. 1831.
Correspondant littéraire, 1843-1844.
Courrier de l'union littéraire et bibliographique, 1839-1840.
Critique (la). 1840-1841.
Critique (la). 1850.
Critique au dix-neuvième siècle. 1835.
Echo de la littérature. 1832.
Echo des deux mondes. 1857-1858.
Fanfare. 1842-1843.

Foyer. 1833-1835.
Gringoire. 1865-1866.
Gymnase poétique et littéraire. 1845-1846.
Homme de lettres. 1836-1837.
Journal des journaux. 1840-1845.
Liberté de pensée. 1847-1849.
Magazine français. 1833-1835.
Mois littéraire. 1866-1867.
Monde littéraire. 1856-1857.
Revue critique parisienne et départementale. 1859-1866.
Revue des lettres et des arts. 1867-1868.
Revue du monde catholique. 1861-1870.
Revue française. 1837-1839.
Revue parisienne. 1830-1839.
Revue pittoresque. 1844-1847.
Revue universelle, 1837-1838.
Revue universelle, 1848-1849.
Spectateur universel. 1838.
Union des arts. 1846-1847.

APPENDIX II

BIBLIOGRAPHY

THE following bibliography includes only the items which contain pertinent materials, and which were actually used in the preparation of the various chapters. It is divided into two sections. The first, arranged alphabetically, consists of general works, especially those containing bibliographical materials, and of collections of essays, etc., in which two or more items of interest were printed. The second section comprises the individual critical articles consulted; it is divided into a number of parts, each of which corresponds to a chapter of the study; these parts follow the order of the chapters themselves. Within each part, the items are arranged in precise chronological order, except where uncertain dating made this arrangement impossible. In many cases, the item appeared or was reprinted in one of the works included in the general bibliography; in these cases, the index number of the general work is given as a cross-reference. In cases where more than one printing or edition is given for a single item, an asterisk [*] is used to indicate the edition to which reference is actually made in the present study. When, as frequently occurred, articles contained references to the subject of more than one chapter, the cross-references are given in the bibliographies of the appropriate chapters; in this manner all the sources of information on any given writer will be found in the part of the bibliography devoted to that writer.

In referring to the *Revue des deux mondes,* no attempt has been made to indicate the various series and volume numbers. I merely give the number of the volume within the year in question: thus "1843, III" refers to the third volume of 1843.

A. GENERAL BIBLIOGRAPHY

1. Babou, Hippolyte. *Lettres satiriques et critiques.* Paris: Poulet-Malassis, 1860.

2. Balzac, Honoré de. *Revue parisienne.* Paris: Revue parisienne, 1840.

3. Barbey d'Aurevilly, Jules. *Le Roman contemporain.* 3d ed. Paris: Lemerre, 1902.

4. ———. Les Œuvres et les hommes: 1ʳᵉ série, IVᵉ partie, *Les Romanciers.* Paris: Amyot, 1865.

5. ———. *Romanciers d'hier et d'avant-hier.* 3d ed. Paris: Lemerre, 1904.

6. Baudelaire, Charles. *L'Art romantique.* Paris: Conard, 1925.

7. Bouvier, Emile. *La Bataille réaliste (1844-1857)*. Paris: Fontemoing et Cie, 1914.

8. Caro, Elme-Marie. *Poètes et romanciers*. Paris: Hachette, 1888.

9. Champfleury (Pseudonym of Jules François F. Fleury). *Le Réalisme*. Paris: Michel Lévy Frères, 1857.

10. Cherbuliez, Joël. *Revue critique des livres nouveaux*. Paris: Ab. Cherbuliez et Cie, 1835-1840, 1858-1863.

11. Clément de Ris, Comte Louis. *Critiques d'art et de littérature*. Paris: Didier, 1862.

12. ———. *Portraits à la plume*. Paris: Didier, 1853.

13. Cordier, Auguste. *Comment a vécu Stendhal*. Paris: Villerelle, 1900.

14. Cordier, Henri. *Bibliographie stendhalienne*. Paris: Champion, 1914.

15. Cuvillier-Fleury, Alfred Auguste. *Dernières Etudes historiques et littéraires*. 2 vols. Paris: Calmann Lévy, 1859.

16. ———. *Etudes et portraits*. 2 vols. Paris: Michel Lévy Frères, 1865-1868.

17. ———. *Historiens, poètes et romanciers*. 2 vols. Paris: Michel Lévy Frères, 1863.

18. Delacroix, Eugène. *Journal d'Eugène Delacroix*. 3 vols. Paris: Plon, 1932.

19. Descharmes, René, and Dumesnil, René. *Autour de Flaubert*. 2 vols. Paris: Mercure de France, 1912.

20. Dumesnil, René. *La Publication de "Madame Bovary."* Amiens: Edgar Malfère, 1928. ("Les Grands Evénements littéraires.")

21. ———. " 'Madame Bovary' et son temps (1857)," *Mercure de France,* 16 novembre, 1er décembre 1911, pp. 291-316, 466-491.

22. Duquesnel, Amédée. *Du travail intellectuel en France depuis 1815 jusqu'à 1837*. 2 vols. Paris: Coquebert, 1839.

22a. Du Val, Thaddeus Ernest, Jr. *The Subject of Realism in the "Revue des Deux Mondes" (1831-1865)*. Philadelphia: 1936. (University of Pennsylvania Dissertation.)

23. Flaubert, Gustave. *L'Education sentimentale*. Paris: Conard, 1910.

24. ———. *Madame Bovary*. Paris: Conard, 1910.

25. ———. *Salammbô*. Paris: Conard, 1910.

26. Forest, H. U. " 'Réalisme,' Journal de Duranty," *Modern Philology,* XXIV (1927), 463-479.

27. Girault de Saint-Fargeau, Eusèbe. *Revue des romans:* Recueil d'analyses raisonnées des productions remarquables des plus célèbres romanciers français et étrangers. 2 vols. Paris: Firmin-Didot, 1839.

28. Gobineau, Joseph-Arthur, Comte de. *Etudes critiques (1844-1848)*. Paris: Kra, 1927.

29. Goncourt, Edmond et Jules de. *Journal des Goncourt*. Vols. I-III. Paris: Flammarion-Fasquelle, 1935-36.

30. Hatin, Eugène. *Bibliographie historique et critique de la presse périodique française*. Paris: Firmin-Didot, 1866.

31. Lanson, Gustave. *Manuel bibliographique de la littérature française moderne*. Vol. IV, *Révolution et XIXᵉ siècle*. Paris: Hachette, 1921.

32. Levallois, Jules. *Critique militante:* Etudes de philosophie littéraire. Paris: Didier, 1863.

33. Lumet, Louis. *Honoré de Balzac, critique littéraire*. Paris: Messein, 1912.

34. Martino, Pierre. *Le Roman réaliste sous le Second Empire*. Paris: Hachette, 1913.

35. Maynial, Edouard. *L'Epoque réaliste.* "Le XIX⁰ Siècle. Sous la direction de René Lalou." Paris: Les Œuvres représentatives, 1931.

36. Mélia, Jean. *Stendhal et ses commentateurs.* Paris: Mercure de France, 1911.

37. Mérimée, Prosper. *Carmen. Arsène Guillot. L'Abbé Aubain.* Paris: Champion, 1927.

38. ———. *Mosaïque.* Paris: Champion, 1933.

39. ———. *Portraits historiques et littéraires.* Paris: Champion, 1928.

40. Merlet, Gustave. *Hommes et livres.* Paris: Didier, 1869.

41. ———. *Portraits d'hier et d'aujourd'hui.* Vol. IV, *Réalistes et fantaisistes.* Paris: Didier, 1863.

42. Nettement, Alfred. *Histoire de la littérature française sous le gouvernement de juillet.* 2 vols. Paris: Jacques Lecoffre et Cie, 1854.

43. ———. *Le Roman contemporain.* Paris: Jacques Lecoffre et Cie, 1864.

44. Palfrey, Thomas R. *L'Europe littéraire (1833-1834).* Paris: Champion, 1927.

45. Paupe, Adolphe. *Histoire des œuvres de Stendhal.* Paris: Dujarric et Cie, 1903.

46. ———. *La Vie littéraire de Stendhal.* Paris: Champion, 1914.

47. Planche, Gustave. *Portraits littéraires.* 2 vols. Paris: Werdet, 1836.

48. Pontmartin, Armand de. *Causeries du samedi.* Paris: Michel Lévy Frères, 1875.

49. ———. *Causeries littéraires.* Paris: Michel Lévy Frères, 1854.

50. ———. *Nouveaux samedis.* Vols. II, IV, VII. Paris: Michel Lévy Frères, 1866-1870.

51. ———. *Nouvelles Causeries du samedi.* Paris: Michel Lévy Frères, 1859.

52. ———. *Nouvelles Causeries littéraires.* Paris: Michel Lévy Frères, 1859.

53. ———. *Nouvelles Semaines littéraires.* Paris: Michel Lévy Frères, 1863.

54. Prarond, Ernest. *De quelques écrivains nouveaux.* Paris: Michel Lévy Frères, 1852.

55. Prod'homme, J. G. *Vingt Chefs-d'œuvre jugés par leurs contemporains: Opinions, critiques; Correspondances choisies et annotées.* Paris: Librairie Stock, 1930.

56. Royce, William Hobart. *A Balzac Bibliography:* Writings relative to the life and works of Honoré de Balzac. Vol. I. Chicago: University of Chicago Press, 1929.

57. Sainte-Beuve, Charles-Augustin. *Causeries du lundi.* 15 vols. Paris: Garnier Frères, 1851-1862.

58. ———. *Nouveaux Lundis.* 13 vols. Paris: Calmann Lévy, 1868-1878.

59. ———. *Portraits contemporains.* 5 vols. Paris: Michel-Lévy, 1870-1871.

59a. ———. *Premiers Lundis.* 3 vols. Paris: Michel Lévy Frères, 1874-1875.

60. ———. *Les Grands Ecrivains français:* Etudes des *Lundis* et des *Portraits* classées selon un ordre nouveau et annotées par Maurice Allem. *XIXe Siècle: Les Romanciers.* 2 vols. Paris: Garnier Frères, 1927.

61. Sand, George. *Questions d'art et de littérature.* Paris: Calmann Lévy, 1878.

62. Sarcey, Francisque. *Quarante Ans de théâtre.* Vol. IV. Paris: Bibliothèque des Annales, 1901.

63. Scherer, Edmond. *Etudes critiques sur la littérature contemporaine.* Vol. IV. Paris: Michel-Lévy, 1873.

64. Spoelberch de Lovenjoul, Vicomte Charles de. *Histoire des œuvres de H.*

de Balzac. 3d ed. Paris: Calmann Lévy, 1888.

65. Taine, Hippolyte. *Nouveaux Essais de critique et d'histoire.* Paris: Hachette, 1930.

66. Talvart, Hector, and Place, Joseph. *Bibliographie des auteurs modernes de langue française (1801-1927).* Vols. i-iv. Paris: Chronique des lettres françaises, 1928-1933.

67. Thieme, Hugo P. *Bibliographie de la littérature française de 1800 à 1930.* 3 vols. Paris: E. Droz, 1933.

68. Trahard, Pierre, and Josserand, Pierre. *Bibliographie des œuvres de Prosper Mérimée.* Paris: Champion, 1929.

69. Ulbach, Louis. *Causeries du dimanche.* Paris: Delahaye, 1857.

70. Vapereau, Gustave. *L'Année littéraire et dramatique.* 11 vols. Paris: Hachette, 1858-1868.

71. Zola, Emile. *Mes Haines.* Paris: Faure, 1866.

B. BIBLIOGRAPHY BY CHAPTERS

STENDHAL

[1830]

77. Anon. "'Le Rouge et le Noir, chronique du dix-neuvième siècle,' par M. de Stendhal," *Revue de Paris,* 28 novembre 1830, 1ʳᵉ série, xx, 258-260.

78. ———. "'Le Rouge et le Noir,'" *Gazette littéraire,* 2 décembre 1830, ii, 3-4. Reprinted in *Le Rouge et le Noir,* ed. Marsan, pp. lvii-lviii n.

79. ———. "'Le Rouge et le Noir,'" *Figaro,* 20 décembre 1830.

80. Janin, Jules [signed J. J.]. "'Le Rouge et le Noir,'" *Journal des débats,* 26 décembre 1830.

[1831]

81. Balzac, Honoré de. "Lettres sur Paris," *Voleur,* 8 janvier 1831. *Reprinted in *Œuvres complètes,* xxiii (Paris: Michel-Levy, 1873), pp. 168-169.

82. Anon. "'Le Rouge et le Noir,'" *Correspondant,* 14 janvier 1831.

83. ———. "'Rouge et Noir,' par M. de Stendhall [*sic*]," *Artiste,* 1831, i, 13.

84. Pichot, Amédée [signed A. P.]. "'Le Rouge et le Noir,'" *Revue encyclopédique,* février 1831, xlix, 350-359.

85. Anon. "Revue littéraire et politique: 'Le Rouge et le Noir,'" *Gazette de France,* 16 février 1831. Reprinted in *27,* Girault de Saint-Fargeau, i, 67.

86. Béranger, Pierre Jean de [attributed to]. "'Le Rouge et le Noir.' Chanson. Air: Ce magistrat irréprochable." Dated mars 1831. In *46,* Paupe, pp. 49-51.

87. Mérimée, Prosper. [Letter to Stendhal, 1831]. In Stryienski, Casimir. "Lettres de Mérimée à Stendhal," *Revue de Paris,* 15 juillet 1898, p. 413.

88. Saint-Priest, Alexis de. "Les deux Saint-Simoniens," *Paris, ou Le Livre des Cent-et-un.* Paris: Ladvocat, 1831, ii, 275. *Reprinted Bruxelles: Méline, 1831, ii, 277.

[1833]

Cf. *245,* Anon., p. 244.

[1835]

Cf. *287,* Berthoud, p. 143.

[1838]

89. Forgues, Emile Daurand [signed Old Nick]. " 'Mémoires d'un Touriste,' " *Commerce*, 8 juillet 1838.

90. Wey, Francis. " 'Mémoires d'un Touriste,' " *Presse*, 10 juillet 1838.

91. M. B.[1] " 'Mémoires d'un Touriste," *Gazette de France*, 27 juillet 1838.

92. Briffault, Eugène [signed E. B.]. " 'Mémoires d'un Touriste,' " *Temps*, 9 août 1838.

93. Frémy, Arnould. "Critique littéraire: 'Les Mémoires d'un Touriste,' " *Revue de Paris*, 19 août 1838, 2e série, LVI, 207-217.

94. Chaudes-Aigues, J.-G. "Revue littéraire," *Artiste*, 1838, 2e série, I, 260-262.

95. Guinot, Eugène. " 'Mémoires d'un Touriste,' " *Courrier français*, 28 décembre 1838.

[1839]

96. Duquesnel, Amédée. In *22*, II, 200-201.

97. Balzac, Honoré de. [Letter to Stendhal, 20 mars 1839]. *Correspondance*, Paris: Calmann Lévy, 1876, p. 328.

98. Cherbuliez, Joël. " 'La Chartreuse de Parme.' " In *10*, avril 1839, VII, 111-113.

99. Frémy, Arnould. "Critique littéraire: 'La Chartreuse de Parme,' par l'auteur de 'Rouge et Noir,' " *Revue de Paris*, mai 1839, 3e série, V, 51-63.

100. Muret, Théodore. "Revue littéraire. 'La Chartreuse de Parme,' " *Quotidienne*, 24 juillet 1839.

101. Anon. "Bulletin," *Revue de Paris*, novembre 1839, 3e série, XI, 284.

[1840]

102. Forgues, Emile Daurand [signed Old Nick]. " 'L'Abbesse de Castro,' " *Commerce*, 4 janvier 1840.

103. Balzac, Honoré de. "Lettres sur la littérature, le théâtre et les arts. 1re. A Madame la comtesse E." In *2*, 25 juillet 1840, p. 82.

104. ———. "Etude sur M. Beyle. (Frédéric Stendalh [*sic*])." In *2*, 25 septembre 1840, pp. 273-342.

[1842]

105. Forgues, Emile Daurand [signed Old Nick]. "Une Erreur de nom," *National*, 1er avril 1842.

106. Anon. [No title.] *Feuilleton mensuel*, 15 avril 1842. 2e année, II, 48-50.

107. Bussière, Auguste. "Poètes et romanciers modernes de la France. XLVIII. Henri Beyle (M. de Stendhal)," *Revue des deux mondes*, 15 janvier 1843, I, 250-299.

108. Crozet, Louis. [Letter to R. Colomb, 10 avril 1844]. In *13*, Cordier, pp. 103-105.

109. Béranger, Pierre Jean de. [Letter to R. Colomb, 20 novembre 1844]. In *46*, Paupe, pp. 115-116.

110. Aubert de Vitry, F.-J.-P. "Beyle," *Dictionnaire de la conversation*, LV, 172-174. (Paris: Garnier, 1844.)

[1845]

111. Gobineau, Joseph-Arthur de. "Essai de critique. Œuvre de M. de Stendhal (M. Beyle)," *Commerce*, 14 janvier 1845. *Reprinted by Charles Simon, *Stendhal par Gobineau*, Editions du Stendhal-Club.—No. 20. Paris, 1926.

---

[1] Is this Mathurin-Joseph Brisset, as Royer suggests in his edition of the *Touriste*, p. lxxiv?

112. Crozet, Louis. [Letter to R. Colomb, 17 octobre 1845.] In *13*, Cordier, pp. 118-123.

113. Colomb, Romain. *Notice sur la vie et les ouvrages de M. Beyle (de Stendhal)*, Paris: Schneider et Langrand, 1845.

[1846]

114. Balzac, Honoré de. [Letter to R. Colomb, 30 janvier 1846.] *Correspondance*, Paris: Calmann Lévy, 1876, pp. 491-492.

115. Aubert, Albert. "Œuvres de Stendhal (Henri Beyle)," *Constitutionnel*, 23 février 1846.

116. Babou, Hippolyte. "Du caractère et des écrits de Henri Beyle," *Revue nouvelle*, 1ᵉʳ novembre 1846, xi, 341-380.

[1847]

117. Ducoin, Amédée. "Rapport sur 'Le Rouge et le Noir,'" *Bulletin de l'Académie delphinale*, 15 janvier 1847, ii, 186-193.

118. ———. "Rapport sur 'La Chartreuse de Parme,'" *Bulletin de l'Académie delphinale*, 6 août 1847, ii, 343-353.
Cf. *443*, Aubert.

[1853]

119. Ratisbonne, Louis. "'De l'amour,'" *Journal des débats*, 29 septembre 1853.

120. Chasles, Emile. "'De l'amour,'" *Athenaeum français*, 22 octobre 1853, ii, 1001-1003.

121. Monselet, Charles. "Préface," *Armance*, Paris: D. Giraud, 1853, pp. i-viii.

122. Ulbach, Louis [signed Jean Verdun]. "L''Armance' de Stendhal," **Revue de Paris*, 15 novembre 1853, xix, 662-665. Reprinted in *Ecrivains et hommes de lettres*, Paris: A. Delahaye, 1857, pp. 92-96.
Cf. *488*, Barbey d'Aurevilly, p. 14; *490*, Castille, p. 314.

[1854]

123. Sainte-Beuve, C.-A. "M. de Stendhal. Ses 'Œuvres complètes,'" *Moniteur universel*, 2, 9 janvier 1854. Reprinted in **57*, ix, 301-341 and in *60*, i, 88-132.

124. Boiteau, Paul [signed Paul d'Ambly]. "Critique," *Artiste*, 15 janvier 1854, 5ᵉ série, xi, 191.

125. Mazade, Charles de. "Chronique de la quinzaine," *Revue des deux mondes*, 15 janvier 1854, i, 429-430.

126. Anon. "'Promenades dans Rome,'" *Athenaeum français*, 25 février 1854, iii, 168.

127. Babou, Hippolyte [signed Hip. B.]. "'Racine et Shakespeare,'" *Athenaeum français*, 3 juin 1854, iii, 504.

128. Chasles, Emile. "'La Chartreuse de Parme.—Le Rouge et le Noir.— Romans et nouvelles,'" *Athenaeum français*, 10 juin 1854, iii, 524-526.

[1855]

130. Despois, Eugène. "De Stendhal.—'Correspondance inédite,'" *Avenir*, 13 mai 1855, i, 14-16.

131. Caro, Elme-Marie. "Stendhal. (Deuxième partie). Romans, voyages, critiques d'art," **Revue contemporaine*, 30 juin 1855, xx, 209-241. Re-

printed in *Etudes morales sur le temps présent,* Paris: Hachette, 1856, pp. 281-333.

132. Barbey d'Aurevilly, Jules. [June, 1855.][1] In *4,* pp. 43-59.

[1856]

133. Taine, Hippolyte. "Les Philosophes français au dix-neuvième siècle," *Revue de l'instruction publique,* 4 septembre 1856. *Extract in *36,* Mélia, p. 280. Cf. *724,* Thulié, p. 23.

[1857]

Cf. *522,* Poitou, pp. 113-114; *740,* Watripon, p. 249; *882,* Barbey d'Aurevilly, p. 62.

[1859]

Cf. *749,* Barthet, p. 76.

[1860]

Cf. *967,* Barbey d'Aurevilly, p. 231.

[1862]

134. Sainte-Beuve, C.-A. " 'Souvenirs de soixante années,' par M. Etienne-Jean Delécluze," *Constitutionnel,* 18 août 1862. *Reprinted in *58,* iii, 111-118.

[1863]

135. Taine, Hippolyte. "Introduction," *Histoire de la littérature anglaise,* 2d ed., Paris: Hachette, 1866, i, xlv-xlvi.

[1864]

136. ———. "Etude sur Stendhal," *Nouvelle Revue de Paris,* 1er mars 1864, i, 193-216. Reprinted in *65,* pp. 223-257. Cf. *918,* Sarcey, p. 498.

[1865]

Cf. *198,* Barbey d'Aurevilly, p. 329; *1002,* Claretie, p. 172.

[1866]

137. Bougy, Alfred de. [Letter of Uriage, 3 septembre 1866]. In *46,* Paupe, p. 65. Cf. *970,* Jouvin, 1st article; *971,* Pradal; *972,* Bernard, p. 27.

MÉRIMÉE

[1829]

138. Anon. " '1572. Chronique du temps de Charles IX,' " *Revue française,* mars 1829, viii, 319-321.

139. ———. " 'Scènes féodales. La Jacquerie,' " *Revue française,* juillet 1829, x, 293-295.

---

[1] Cf. *Lettres à Trébutien,* Paris: Bernouard, 1927, iii, 275; letter of 20 or 21 (?) juin 1855: "Cet article *composé et retardé* doit chaque jour paraître et je retire chaque jour . . ."

[1830]

140. Anon. " 'Théâtre de Clara Gazul,' " *Figaro,* 14 octobre 1830.
141. ———. " 'Théâtre de Clara Gazul,' nouvelle édition," *Revue de Paris,* 17 octobre 1830, 1re série, xix, 165-167.
142. Ampère, Jean-Jacques. "Littérature. 'Théâtre de Clara Gazul,' " *National,* 23 octobre 1830. *Reprinted in *Théâtre de Clara Gazul,* ed. Trahard, Paris: Champion, 1927, pp. 531-536.
143. Anon. " 'Théâtre de Clara Gazul,' " *Gazette littéraire,* 28 octobre 1830, i, 742-744.
144. H. P. " 'Théâtre de Clara Gazul,' " *Revue encyclopédique,* décembre 1830, xlviii, 768-770.

[1831]

145. Sainte-Beuve, C.-A. " 'Théâtre de Clara Gazul,' " *Globe,* 24 janvier 1831. Reprinted in *59,* pp. 196-199 n., and *60, ii, 282, n. 2.
146. Cs. " 'Théâtre de Clara Gazul,' " *Journal des débats,* 22 mars 1831.

[1832]

147. G. P. " 'Chronique de Charles IX.'—(2e édition)," *Journal des débats,* 1er septembre 1832.
148. Planche, Gustave. "Poètes et romanciers modernes de la France. iii. Prosper Mérimée," *Revue des deux mondes,* 1er septembre 1832, iii, 576-591. Reprinted in *47,* i, 213-236, and in *38,* Mérimée, pp. 488-493.

[1833]

149. Anon. " 'Mosaïque,' recueil de contes et nouvelles," *Figaro,* 28 juin 1833.
150. Rémusat, Charles de [signed C. R.] " 'Mosaïque.' Recueil de contes et nouvelles, par P. Mérimée," *Artiste,* 1833, 2e semestre, vi, 106-107. *Reprinted in *38,* Mérimée, pp. 497-499.
151. Pichot, Amédée. " 'La Double Méprise.' M. Pr Mérimée," *Revue de Paris,* août 1833, 1re série, liii, 224-226.
152. Anon. " 'Une Double Méprise,' " *Figaro,* 11 septembre 1833.
153. Saint-Michel, H.-C. de. "Revue critique. 'La Double Méprise,' " *Revue de Paris,* septembre 1833, 1re série, liv, 185-187.
154. Anon." 'Une Double Méprise,' " *Panorama littéraire de l'Europe,* septembre 1833, i, 307-308.
155. ———. " 'La Double Méprise,' " *Bagatelle,* 3 octobre 1833, ii, 21-22.
156. Desessarts, Alfred. " 'La Double Méprise,' " *France littéraire,* octobre 1833, ix, 411-412.
157. Anon. " 'Une Double Méprise,' " *Revue européenne,* novembre 1833, vii, 370-371.
158. Planche, Gustave. " 'La Double Méprise,' " *Revue des deux mondes,* septembre 1833, iii, 710-718. Reprinted in *47,* i, 236-249.

[1835]

159. Anon. " 'Notes d'un voyageur dans le midi de la France,' " *Revue des deux mondes,* 1er septembre 1835, iii, 627-628.
160. Legoyt, Alfred. "Bulletin," *Littérateur universel,* 25 septembre 1835, ii, 223.

[1836]

161. Anon. "Chronique de la quinzaine," *Revue des deux mondes,* 15 novembre 1836, ıv, 512.

[1837]

162. Delécluze, Etienne-Jean. "'Notes d'un voyage dans le midi de la France,'" *Journal des débats,* 11 juin 1837.

[1838]

Cf. *321,* Anon., p. 129.

[1839]

163. Merle, Jean-Toussaint [signed J. T.]. "Revue dramatique: 'La Vendetta,'" *Quotidienne,* 16 septembre 1839.

164. Girault de Saint-Fargeau, Eusèbe. In *27,* ıı, 89-93.

[1840]

165. Anon. "Bulletin," *Revue de Paris,* juillet 1840, 3ᵉ série, xıx, 144.

[1841]

166. Stein, T. de. "'Colomba. Les Ames du purgatoire,'" *Mémorial de la littérature,* 25 juillet 1841, ıı, cols. 324-326.

167. Cherbuliez, Joël. "'Colomba.'" In *10,* août 1841, ıx, 264.

168. Sainte-Beuve, C.-A. "'Essai sur la guerre sociale,' par M. Prosper Mérimée.—'Colomba,'" *Revue des deux mondes,* 1ᵉʳ octobre 1841, ıv, 77-90. Reprinted in *59,* ııı, 470-492, and in *60,* ıı, 1-21.

[1844]

169. Asseline, Alfred. "'Arsène Guillot,'" *Echo de la littérature,* avril 1844, v, 107-109.

170. Cherbuliez, Joël. "'Etudes sur l'histoire romaine.'" In *10,* mai 1844, xıı, 157-160.

171. Cassou, Charles. "'Etudes sur l'histoire romaine,'" *Revue indépendante,* 25 juin 1844, xıv, 542-564.

172. Rémusat, Charles de. "'Etudes sur l'histoire romaine,'" *Constitutionnel,* 22 juillet 1844.

173. Al. D. "'Etudes sur l'histoire romaine,'" *Revue de Paris,* 17 août 1844, ı, 548-550.

174. Molènes, Paul Gaschon de. "M. Mérimée.—'Etudes sur l'histoire romaine' et 'Arsène Guillaut [*sic*],'" *Journal des débats,* 14 septembre, 8 octobre 1844.

[1845]

175. Etienne, Charles Guillaume. "Réponse de M. Etienne" [to Mérimée's reception speech at the Académie française], *Constitutionnel,* 7 février 1845.

176. Anon. "Académie française. Réception de M. Mérimée," *Constitutionnel,* 7 février 1845.

177. ———. "Académie française. Séance du 7 février.—Réception de M. Mérimée," *Journal des débats,* 8 février 1845.

178. Anon. "Académie française. Réception de M. Mérimée," *Moniteur des arts,* 9 février 1845, ɪ, 11-12.

179. D. "Académie française. Réception de M. Mérimée.—M. Etienne," *Echo de la littérature et des beaux-arts,* 1845, pp. 49-50. *Reprinted in *39,* Mérimée, pp. 340-341.

180. Labitte, Charles. "Académie française. Réception de M. Mérimée," **Revue des deux mondes,* 15 février 1845, ɪ, 737-748. Reprinted in *Etudes littéraires,* Paris, 1846, ɪɪ, and in *39,* Mérimée, pp. 326-340.

181. Sainte-Beuve, C.-A. "Revue littéraire," **Revue des deux mondes,* 1ᵉʳ décembre 1845, ɪᴠ, 884. Reprinted in *59a,* ɪɪɪ, 260.

[1846]

Cf. *435,* Castille, p. 367.

[1847]

182. Pontmartin, Armand de. "Revue littéraire," **Revue des deux mondes,* 30 avril 1847, ɪɪ, 574. Reprinted in *37,* Mérimée, p. 244.

[1848]

183. ———. "Revue littéraire et dramatique," *Revue des deux mondes,* 31 mai 1848, ɪɪ, 811.

[1852]

184. Wailly, Léon de. " 'Nouvelles,' par M. Prosper Mérimée," **Athenaeum français,* 3 juillet 1852, ɪ, 5-6. Reprinted in *37,* Mérimée, pp. 246-251.

185. Pontmartin, Armand de. " 'Nouvelles,' " *Revue contemporaine,* août 1852, ɪɪɪ, 168-171.

[1853]

186. Enault, Louis. "M. Prosper Mérimée. ɪ. 'Nouvelles,' " **Gazette de France,* 12 janvier 1853. Reprinted in *37,* Mérimée, pp. 251-258.

187. Sainte-Beuve, C.-A. " 'Les Faux Démétrius' : Episode de l'histoire de Russie," *Moniteur universel,* 7 février 1853. Reprinted in **57,* ᴠɪɪ, 371-388; *60,* ɪɪ, 22-41. Also in part in *37,* Mérimée, pp. 258-260 and *38,* Mérimée, pp. 500-501.

188. Cuvillier-Fleury, A. A. " 'Les Faux Démétrius,' " *Journal des débats,* 20 février 1853.

189. Pontmartin, Armand de. "M. Prosper Mérimée. 'Les Faux Démétrius,' " *Assemblée nationale,* 2 avril 1853.

190. Delessert, Edouard. " 'Les Deux Héritages,' " *Athenaeum français,* 30 juillet 1853, ɪɪ, 714-715.

191. Ulbach, Louis [signed Jean Verdun]. " 'Les Deux Héritages,' " *Revue de Paris,* 1ᵉʳ septembre 1853, xᴠɪɪɪ, 790-791.

192. Clément de Ris, Comte L. "Prosper Mérimée." In *12,* pp. 99-119.

[1854]

193. Planche, Gustave. "Ecrivains modernes de la France. Prosper Mérimée," **Revue des deux mondes,* 15 septembre 1854, ɪɪɪ, 1207-1232. Reprinted in *Etudes littéraires,* Paris: Michel Lévy, 1855, pp. 75-114. Also in part in *37,* Mérimée, pp. 260-263 and *38,* Mérimée, pp. 501-506.

[1855]

195. Pelletan, Eugène. "'Nouvelles,' par M. P. Mérimée," *Estafette*, 24 mai 1855.
Cf. *500*, Ulbach, p. 62.

[1859]

196. Merlet, Gustave. "Ecrivains contemporains. M. Prosper Mérimée, de l'Académie française," *Revue contemporaine*, 15 janvier 1859, 2ᵉ série, VII, 212-260.

[1861]

197. Vattier, Gustave. "Galerie des académiciens. IV. M. Mérimée," *Correspondance littéraire*, 25 décembre 1861, VI, 38-44.

[1862]

Cf. *902*, Claveau, p. 648.

[1864]

Cf. *918*, Sarcey, p. 498.

[1865]

198. Barbey d'Aurevilly, Jules. "M. Prosper Mérimée," *Figaro*, 17 août 1865. Reprinted in **4*, pp. 323-336.

BALZAC

[First Period]

[1830]

200. Latouche, Hyacinthe de. "'Physiologie du mariage,'" *Figaro*, 14 janvier 1830.
201. Janin, Jules [signed J. J.]. "'Physiologie du mariage,'" *Journal des débats*, 7 février 1830.
202. Pichot, Amédée. "'La Physiologie du mariage,'" *Revue encyclopédique*, février 1830, XLV, 434-436.
203. ———. "'Le Dernier Chouan,'" *Revue encyclopédique*, mars 1830, XLV, 720-722.
204. Anon. "'Scènes de la Vie privée,'" *Figaro*, 23 mai 1830.

[1831]

205. Anon. "Une Débauche," *Revue des deux mondes*, mai 1831, II, 287 n.
206. Latouche, Hyacinthe de. "'La Peau de chagrin,'" *Figaro*, 8 août 1831.
207. R. . . . n. "'La Peau de chagrin,'" *Gazette littéraire*, 11 août 1831, II, 569-571.
208. Anon. "'La Peau de chagrin,' par M. de Balzac," *Revue de Paris*, 12 août 1831, 1ʳᵉ série, XXIX, 128-131.
209. Bernard, Charles de. "'La Peau de chagrin,' par M. de Balzac," *Gazette de Franche-Comté*, 13 août 1831. Reprinted in **64*, Lovenjoul, pp. 355-357.
210. Pichot, Amédée [signed X. X. X.]. "'La Peau de chagrin,'" *Revue encyclopédique*, août 1831, LI, 325-336.
211. N. "'La Peau de chagrin,'" *Journal des débats*, 30 août 1831.
212. Anon. "'La Peau de chagrin,'" *Revue européenne*, septembre 1831, I, 92-94.

213. Deschamps, Emile. "M. de Balzac," *Revue des deux mondes*, 1ᵉʳ novembre 1831, IV, 313-322.

214. Janin, Jules. " 'La Peau de chagrin,' par M. de Balzac," *Artiste*, 1831, II, 18-21.

215. E. C. " 'La Peau de chagrin,' " *Bibliothèque universelle*, 1831, XLVIII, 260-288.

216. Chasles, Philarète. "Introduction" to Balzac, *Romans et contes philosophiques*, Paris: Gosselin, 1831, pp. 5-48. Reprinted in *64*, Lovenjoul, pp. 171-177.

217. Anon. " 'Romans et contes philosophiques,' par M. de Balzac," *Revue de Paris*, 13 octobre 1831, 1ʳᵉ série, XXXI, 194-195.

218. ———. " 'Romans et contes philosophiques,' par M. de Balzac," *Constitutionnel*, 28 octobre 1831.

219. ———. " 'Romans et contes philosophiques,' par M. de Balzac," *Artiste*, 1831, II, 95-97.

220. Bernard, Charles de. " 'Romans et contes philosophiques,' par M. de Balzac," *Gazette de Franche-Comté*, 21 décembre 1831. *Reprinted in *64*, Lovenjoul, pp. 357-358.

[1832]

221. Buchey, Jules. " 'Contes bruns,' " *Revue encyclopédique*, janvier 1832, LIII, 189-192.

222. Anon. " 'Contes bruns,' " *France littéraire*, février 1832, I, 404.

223. ———. " 'Contes bruns,' par une tête à l'envers," *Revue de Paris*, février 1832, 1ʳᵉ série, XXXV, 185-189.

224. ———. " 'Contes bruns,' par une tête à l'envers," *Revue des deux mondes*, 1ᵉʳ mars 1832, I, 634-635.

225. ———. " 'Contes bruns,' par [une tête à l'envers]," *Artiste*, 1832, III, 16-17.

226. Charton, Edouard. " 'Les Cent Contes drolatiques,' " *Revue encyclopédique*, mars 1832, LIII, 683-688.

227. Anon. " 'Les Cent Contes drolatiques,' " *Revue des deux mondes*, 15 avril 1832, II, 253-255.

228. A. " 'Les Cent Contes drolatiques,' " *Revue de Paris*, avril 1832, 1ʳᵉ série, XXXVII, 265-267.

229. Anon. " 'Contes drolatiques,' " *Artiste*, 1832, III, 192-193.

230. ———. "Chronique de la quinzaine," *Revue des deux mondes*, 15 juin 1832, II, 717-718.

231. ———. " 'Scènes de la Vie privée,' " *Quotidienne*, 29 juin 1832.

232. ———. "Chronique de la quinzaine," *Revue des deux mondes*, 15 octobre 1832, IV, 244.

233. Desessarts, Alfred. " 'Contes philosophiques,' de Balzac," *France littéraire*, octobre 1832, IV, 216-217.

234. Anon. " 'Nouveaux Contes philosophiques,' " *Revue européenne*, novembre 1832, V, 368-369.

235. Comte de C. " 'Nouveaux Contes philosophiques,' " *Bagatelle*, [3 novembre?] 1832, I, 42-45.

236. Anon. " 'Nouveaux Contes philosophiques,' par M. de Balzac," *Revue des deux mondes*, 1ᵉʳ décembre 1832, IV, 607-608.

237. Saint-C. " 'Nouveaux Contes philosophiques,' par M. de Balzac," *Artiste*, 1832, IV, 282-283.

[1833]

238. Anon. "'Histoire intellectuelle de Louis Lambert,'" *Revue européenne,* février 1833, v, 768.

239. ———. "'Louis Lambert,'" *Bagatelle,* [6 février?] 1833, i, 184.

240. ———. "'Louis Lambert,' par M. de Balzac," *Revue de Paris,* février 1833, 1ʳᵉ série, xlvii, 155.

241. H. de V. "'Le Médecin de campagne,'" *Bagatelle,* 12 septembre 1833, i, 543-545 [incorrectly numbered "343-345"].

242. M. F. "'Le Médecin de campagne,'" *Echo de la Jeune France,* septembre 1833, i, 232-235.

243. Anon. "'Le Médecin de campagne,'" *Panorama littéraire de l'Europe,* septembre 1833, i, 307.

244. ———. "'Le Médecin de campagne,' par M. de Balzac," *Revue de Paris,* septembre 1833, 1ʳᵉ série, liv, 124.

245. ———. "Chronique de la quinzaine," *Revue des deux mondes,* 15 octobre 1833, iv, 244-245.

246. Desessarts, Alfred. "'Le Médecin de campagne,'" *France littéraire,* octobre 1833, ix, 412-414.

247. Anon. "Jugement de la Revue d'Edinbourg sur la littérature française contemporaine," *Revue britannique,* octobre 1833, 3ᵉ série, v, 214-215.

[1834]

248. Janin, Jules. "Manifeste de la jeune littérature," *Revue de Paris,* janvier 1834, 2ᵉ série, i, 5-30.

249. Anon. "Œuvres de M. de Balzac," *Revue de Paris,* janvier 1834, 2ᵉ série, i, 255-56.

250. ———. "'Etudes de mœurs au dix-neuvième siècle . . . Scènes de la Vie de province,'" *Nouvelle Bibliothèque des romans,* janvier-février 1834, i, 260-267.

251. Desessarts, Alfred. "Revue littéraire," *France littéraire,* février 1834, xi, 454-455.

252. Mennechet, Edouard [signed E. M.]. "Ma Revue," *Panorama littéraire de l'Europe,* février 1834, ii, 178-179.

253. A. "'Etudes de Mœurs au XIXᵉ siècle . . . Scènes de la Vie parisienne,'" *Nouvelle Bibliothèque des romans,* mars-avril 1834, ii, 121-130.

254. A. D. L. "Mouvement littéraire: 'Eugénie Grandet,'" *Echo de la Jeune France,* 5 mai 1834, ii, 48.

255. I. C. T. "Revue littéraire. 'Etudes de mœurs au dix-neuvième siècle,' par M. de Balzac," *Constitutionnel,* 5 juin 1834.

256. ———. "Revue littéraire. 'Le Médecin de campagne,' par M. de Balzac," *Constitutionnel,* 24 juillet 1834.

257. Lecler, F. "Revues," *France littéraire,* juillet 1834, xiv, 114.

258. Anon. "'Les Chouans,'" *Indépendant,* 21 août 1834.

259. I. C. T. "Revue littéraire. De la terminologie scientifique appliquée à la littérature," *Constitutionnel,* 11 septembre 1834.

260. ———. "Revue littéraire. 'La Recherche de l'absolu,' par M. de Balzac," *Constitutionnel,* 9 octobre 1834.

261. Anon. "'De la recherche de l'absolu, Scènes de la vie privée . . . ,'" *Chronique de Paris,* 19 octobre 1834, i, 183-184.

262. Anon. "'L'Ami Grandet,'" *Chronique de Paris,* 26 octobre 1834, I, 199-200.

263. Desessarts, Alfred. "Ouvrages," *France littéraire,* novembre 1834, XVI, 188-189.

264. A. "'Etudes de Mœurs au XIXᵉ siècle . . . Scènes de la Vie privée,'" *Nouvelle Bibliothèque des romans,* novembre 1834, III, 254-266.

265. Sainte-Beuve, C.-A. "M. de Balzac, 'La Recherche de l'Absolu,'" *Revue des deux mondes,* 15 novembre 1834, IV, 440-58. Reprinted in *59,* II, 327-357, and in *60,* I, 139-165.

266. Anon. "'La Revue de Paris.' M. H. de Balzac.—'Le Père Goriot," *Vérité,* 31 décembre 1834.

[1835]

267. Anon. "'La Fille de l'Avare,'" *Vérité,* 10 janvier 1835.

268. Janin, Jules. "'La Fille de l'Avare,' vaudeville en deux actes, par MM. Paulin et Bayard," *Journal des débats,* 12 janvier 1835.

269. Muret, Théodore. "Galerie contemporaine. M. de Balzac," *Voleur,* 15 janvier 1835, 2ᵉ série, IV, 33-35. [Reprinted from *La Mode.*]

270. Desessarts, Alfred. "'Etudes philosophiques,'" *France littéraire,* janvier 1835, XVII, 186-187.

271. Al. de C. "Chronique littéraire," *Chronique de Paris,* 8 février 1835, II, 23-24.

272. Anon. "Histoire littéraire," *Voleur,* 15 février 1835, 2ᵉ série, IV, 140. [Reprinted from *Vert-Vert.*]

273. Al. de C. "Chronique littéraire," *Chronique de Paris,* 22 février 1835, II, 55.

274. D. "'Le Père Goriot,'" *Nouvelle Bibliothèque des romans,* février 1835, 2ᵉ année, I, 85-88.

275. Béranger, Pierre Jean de. [Letter to Madame Cauchois-Lemaire, 1835.] *Amateur d'autographes,* avril-mai 1876, 14ᵉ année, 56-57.

276. I. C. T. "Revue littéraire: 'Le Père Goriot,' par M. de Balzac," *Constitutionnel,* 23 mars 1835.

277. Anon. "'Le Père Goriot.' Comédie-Vaudeville en trois actes, de MM. Jaime, Comberousse, et Théaulon," *Art et progrès,* 6-11 (?) avril 1835, III, 394-395.

278. ———. "'Le Père Goriot,'" *Indépendant,* 9 avril 1835.

279. J. "Revue dramatique. 'Le Père Goriot,'" *Voleur,* 10 avril 1835, 2ᵉ série, IV, 318.

280. Muret, Théodore. "'Le Père Goriot,'" *Quotidienne,* 11 avril 1835.

281. Anon. "'Le Père Goriot.' Vaudeville en deux actes par M. Ancelot," *Chronique de Paris,* 12 avril 1835, II, 169.

282. Janin, Jules. "'Le Père Goriot,' vaudeville en trois actes, par MM. Jaime, Comberousse et Théaulon," *Journal des débats,* 13 avril 1835.

283. Anon. "Balzac. A. Dumas. Lamartine," *Littérateur universel,* 25 avril 1835, II, 63.

284. Cherbuliez, Joël. "'Le Père Goriot.'" In *10,* avril 1835, III, 80-81.

285. Gonzalès, Emmanuel [signed Emmanuel G.]. "'La Fille aux yeux d'or,'" *Revue de France,* juillet 1835, I, 70-71.

286. Guéroult, Adolphe. "'La Fille aux yeux d'or': Lettre à un ami de province," *Revue de Paris,* août 1835, XX, 188-190.

287. Berthoud, Samuel-Henry. "Gazette du mois," *Mercure de France,* 1835, 1ʳᵉ année, 143.

288. Carné, Louis de. "Etudes sur la littérature contemporaine," *Revue européenne,* octobre 1835, Nouvelle série, II, 394-395.

289. Al. de C. "Chronique littéraire," *Chronique de Paris,* 29 novembre 1835, III, 279.

290. Guinot, Eugène [signed L. (E.?) G.; E. G.]. "Etudes littéraires. Œuvres de M. de Balzac.—'La Fleur des pois,'" *Charivari,* 12, 22 décembre 1835.

291. Al. de C. "Chronique littéraire," *Chronique de Paris,* 13 décembre 1835, III, 312-313.

292. "The Reviewer." "Bulletin littéraire. 'Le Livre mystique,' par M. de Balzac. 'Les Proscrits.—Louis Lambert.—Séraphita,'" *Revue de Paris,* décembre 1835, 2ᵉ série, XXIV, 51-58.

293. Y. "'Le Livre mystique. Séraphita,'" *Le Critique,* 27 décembre 1835, 1ʳᵉ année, No. 1, pp. 2-3.

294. Accarias, Louis. "Budget littéraire de 1835," *France littéraire,* décembre 1835, XXII, 354-355.

[1836]

295. Lassailly, Charles. "Revue littéraire," *Indépendant,* 3 janvier 1836.

296. Juin, Abbé Jean-Augustin [signed Juin d'Allas]. "'Le Livre mystique,'" *Epoque,* janvier 1836, III, 692-714.

297. Y. "'Valentine,' Vaudeville en deux actes, De MM. Scribe et Mélesville," *Constitutionnel,* 18 janvier 1836.

298. Legoyt, Alfred. "Bulletin," *Littérateur universel,* 25 janvier 1836, II, 347, 349-352.

299. Anon. "Revue bibliographique," *Revue de France,* janvier 1836, II, 188.

300. Hains. "M. de Balzac," *Echo de la Jeune France,* 1ᵉʳ février 1836, IV, 105-112.

301. Gonzalès, Emmanuel. "M. de Balzac," *Art et progrès,* février 1836, VII, 243-245.

302. Nettement, Alfred [signed N.]. "Les Modernes.—M. de Balzac," *Gazette de France,* 9 février 1836. Second article: "M. de Balzac.—Sa poétique," *Ibid.,* 16 février 1836. Third article: *Ibid.,* 23 février 1836 [for this article, missing in the B. N. copy, reference is made to Spoelberch de Lovenjoul, *Un Roman d'amour,* Paris: Calmann Lévy, 1896, pp. 227-248].

303. Bernard, Charles de. "'France et Marie,' par M. de Latouche," *Chronique de Paris,* 14 février 1836, Nouvelle série, I, 166.

304. Chaix d'Est-Ange, Mᵉ Gustave. "Affaire de *la Revue de Paris* contre M. de Balzac [3 juin 1836]," *Discours et plaidoyers* . . . , publiés par Edmond Rousse, 2ᵉ éd. rev. et aug. par Charles Constant, Paris: Durant et Pedone-Lauriel, 1877, III, 37-55.

305. Pichot, Amédée [signed Pickersghill Junior]. "Fin d'une histoire qui ne devait pas finir. Lettre à une femme qui n'a pas trente ans," *Revue de Paris,* juin 1836, 2ᵉ série, XX, 209-227. *Reprinted in *64,* Lovenjoul, pp. 68-80.

306. M. B.[1] "'Le Lys dans la vallée,'" *Gazette de France,* 21 juillet 1836.

307. Cherbuliez, Joël. "'Le Lis dans la vallée.'" In *10,* juillet 1836, IV, 200-204.

308. A. C. T. "Revue littéraire," *Revue des deux mondes,* 1ᵉʳ septembre 1836, III, 621-622.

309. Second, Albéric. "'Le Lys dans la vallée,'" *Art et progrès,* 10 septembre 1836, IX, 376-378.

---

[1] Cf. *91* for a possible identification.

310. Souvestre, Emile. "Du roman," *Revue de Paris,* octobre 1836, 2e série, xxxiv, 116-128.

311. Chaudes-Aigues, J.-G. "M. de Balzac," *Revue du dix-neuvième siècle,* 29 octobre 1836, i, 411-415.

312. Izalguier, Eugène d'. " 'La Vieille Fille,' " *Phalange,* 20 novembre 1836, i, cols. 433-439.

[1837]

313. Brucker, Raymond [signed P. Delafronde]. " 'Argow le pirate,' " *Tam-Tam,* 15 janvier 1837.

314. Ozenne, Louis [signed Camille Baxton]. "Jules Janin, Balzac," *Revue française et étrangère,* avril 1837, ii, 53-61.

315. Gaudin, P. " 'Scènes de la Vie de province,' " *France littéraire,* mai 1837, 2e série, iii, 108-112.

316. "L'Indépendant." " 'La Femme supérieure,' " *L'Indépendant,* 16 juillet 1837.

317. Fontaney, A. [signed . . . Y]. "Revue littéraire," *Revue des deux mondes,* 15 août 1837, iii, 505-507.

318. Janin, Jules [signed J. J.]. " 'A x Mz = O x X,' ou 'le Rêve d'un Savant,' vaudeville en un acte, par MM. Bayard et Biéville," *Journal des débats,* 13 novembre 1837.

319. Anon. "A un élève de l'Ecole des beaux-arts, à Rome. (Deuxième lettre)," *Artiste,* 1837, xiii, 218-222.

320. Lecomte, Jules-François [signed Van Engelgom de Bruxelles]. *Lettres sur les écrivains français,* Bruxelles: 1837, pp. 19-24.

[1838]

321. Anon. "A un élève de l'Ecole des beaux-arts, à Rome. (Sixième lettre)," *Artiste,* 1838, xv, 127-130.

322. Beyle, Henri [signed Stendhal]. *Mémoires d'un Touriste,* Paris: Champion, 1932, p. 72.

323. Anon. " 'A trente ans, ou la femme raisonnable,' Vaudeville en trois actes, de M. Rosier," *Constitutionnel,* 29 janvier 1838.

324. Cherbuliez, Joël. " 'Histoire de la grandeur et de la décadence de César Birotteau.' " In *10,* janvier 1838, vi, 12-14.

325. Bourjot, Auguste. " 'César Birotteau,' " *France littéraire,* janvier 1838, 2e série, v, 107-110.

326. Chasles, Philarète. " 'Histoire de la grandeur et de la décadence de César Birotteau,' " *Journal des débats,* 30 janvier 1838. Second article: *Ibid.,* 5 mars 1838. Third article: "Romans de M. de Balzac," *Ibid.,* 16 août 1838.

327. Boniface. "Honoré de Balzac," *Littérateur universel,* 25 février 1838 (?), iv, 365-366.

328. Ozenne, Louise [signed Camille Baxton]. " 'César Birotteau,' " *Revue française et étrangère,* avril 1838, vi, 80-88.

329. Ed. O. " 'Le Médecin de campagne,' vaudeville en deux actes, par MM. Courcy et Théaulon," *Constitutionnel,* 6 juillet 1838.

330. M. B.[1] " 'Histoire de la grandeur et de la décadence de César Birotteau,' " *Gazette de France,* 23 septembre 1838.

331. Beaufort, Léon. "M. de Balzac," *Dilettante,* 13 september 1838, i, 73-75.

---

[1] Cf. *91* for a possible identification.

332. Lacroix, Paul [signed P.-L. Jacob, Bibliophile]. *Les Aventures du grand Balzac,* Paris: Dumont, 1838, 1, 8-14. Reprinted as *"Les Deux Balzac" in *Constitutionnel,* 30 septembre 1838, supplément, and in *64,* Lovenjoul, pp. 471-473.

333. Sainte-Beuve, C.-A. "Charles de Bernard," *Revue des deux mondes,* 15 octobre 1838, vi, 253-257. *Reprinted in *59a,* ii, 350-359.

334. Pichot, Amédée [signed Pickersghill]. " 'La Maison Nucingen, Une préface,' de M. de Balzac," *Revue de Paris,* 21 october 1838, Nouvelle série, lviii, 226-229.

335. Cherbuliez, Joël. " 'La Femme supérieure; La Maison Nucingen; La Torpille.' " In *10,* octobre 1838, vi, 309-311.

336. Bourjot, Auguste. " 'La Femme supérieure,' " *France littéraire,* octobre 1838, 2ᵉ série, vii, 201-208.

337. Sainte-Beuve, C.-A. "H. de Balzac. 'Etudes de mœurs au dix-neuvième siècle. La Femme supérieure, La Maison Nucingen, La Torpille,' " *Revue des deux mondes,* 1ᵉʳ novembre 1838, iv, 366-369. *Reprinted in *59a,* ii, 360-367.

[1839]

338. Duquesnel, Amédée. In *22,* ii, 175-177.
339. Girault de Saint-Fargeau, Eusèbe. In *27,* i, 32-44.
340. Cherbuliez, Joël. " 'Le Cabinet des Antiques.' " In *10,* mai 1839, vii, 144-145.
341. "De Blanzac." "L'Epicier," *Indépendant,* 30 juin 1839.

[Second Period]

342. Janin, Jules. " 'Un Grand Homme de province à Paris,' par M. de Balzac," *Revue de Paris,* juillet 1839, 3ᵉ série, vii, 145-178. Reprinted in Spoelberch de Lovenjoul, *Un Dernier Chapitre de l'Histoire des œuvres de H. de Balzac,* Paris: Dentu, 1880, pp. 26-51.

343. Granier de Cassagnac, Adolphe. " 'Un Grand Homme de province à Paris,' " *Presse,* 15, 25 juillet 1839.

344. Anon. " 'Un Grand Homme de province à Paris,' " *Indépendant,* 18 juillet 1839.

345. Dumartin, Adolphe. " 'Un Grand Homme de province à Paris,' par M. de Balzac," *Artiste,* 21 juillet 1839, 2ᵉ série, iii, 201-204.

346. Second, Albéric. "Le Dernier Livre de M. de Balzac," *Figaro,* 28 juillet 1839.

347. Reybaud, Louis [signed L. R.]. " 'Un Grand Homme de province à Paris.' Par M. de Balzac," *Constitutionnel,* 24 août 1839.

348. Anon. "Bulletin," *Revue de Paris,* août 1839, 3ᵉ série, viii, 148.

349. Cherbuliez, Joël. " 'Un Grand Homme de province à Paris. Berthe la repentie.' " In *10,* août 1839, vii, 237-238.

350. Sainte-Beuve, C.-A. "De la littérature industrielle," *Revue des deux mondes,* 1ᵉʳ septembre 1839. *Reprinted in *59,* ii, 444-471.

351. Lucas, Hippolyte. "Une Conversation à propos de M. de Balzac," *Artiste,* 22 septembre 1839, 2ᵉ série, iv, 54-56.

352. Cherbuliez, Joël. " 'Une Fille d'Eve.' " In *10,* octobre 1839, vii, 309-310.

353. Janin, Jules. " 'L'Ecole des journalistes.' Lettre à Madame Emile de Girardin," *Artiste,* 17 novembre 1839, 2ᵉ série, iv, 181-191.

354. Chaudes-Aigues, J.-G. "M. de Balzac. 'Une Fille d'Eve,' " *Revue de Paris,* novembre 1839, 3ᵉ série, xi, 20-38.

355. Muret, Théodore. "Revue littéraire. 'Un Grand Homme de province à Paris,'" *Quotidienne*, 10 décembre 1839.

[1840]

356. Reybaud, Louis [signed L. R.]. "'Les Français peints par eux-mêmes,' édités par M. L. Curmer," *Constitutionnel*, 28 février 1840.
357. Sainte-Beuve, C.-A. "Dix ans après en littérature," *Revue des deux mondes*, 1ᵉʳ mars 1840. *Reprinted in *59*, ii, 472-494.
358. Janin, Jules. "'Vautrin,'" *Journal des débats*, 16 mars 1840.
359. Y. "'Vautrin,' Drame en cinq actes, de M. de Balzac," *Constitutionnel*, 16 mars 1840.
360. Lucas, Hippolyte. "'Vautrin,' par M. de Balzac," *Artiste*, 22 mars 1840, 2ᵉ série, v, 214-216.
361. Anon. "Porte-Saint-Martin," *Mémorial de la littérature et des beaux-arts*, 25 mars 1840, i, 81-82.
362. A - - - e. "'Vautrin,' Drame en cinq actes et en prose, par M. de Balzac," *Constitutionnel*, 28 mars, 1ᵉʳ et 9 avril 1840.
363. Karr, Alphonse. *Les Guêpes*, 1ʳᵉ année, VIᵉ livraison, Paris: "Figaro," avril 1840, pp. 28-32.
364. Reybaud, Louis [signed L. R.]. "Œuvres de M. de Balzac," *Constitutionnel*, 8 mai, 15 juin 1840.
365. Cherbuliez, Joël. "'Vautrin.'" In *10*, mai 1840, viii, 141-144.
366. Anon. "'Revue parisienne,'" *Figaro*, 23 août 1840.
367. Sainte-Beuve, C. A. "M. Eugène Sue," *Revue des deux mondes*, 15 septembre 1840. *Reprinted in *59*, iii, 89.
368. Montigny, Gabriel. "'La Revue parisienne,' par M. de Balzac," *Artiste*, 1840, 2ᵉ série, vi, 171-173, 289.
369. Eyma, Louis-Xavier, and Lucy, A. de. "De Balzac," *Ecrivains et artistes vivants, français et étrangers*, i, 8ᵉ livraison, Paris: Libraire universelle, 1840, pp. 189-220.

[1841]

370. Anon. [No title]. *Feuilleton mensuel*, 15 mai 1841, i, 102-104.
371. Girault, Francis. "Les Romanciers. Honoré de Balzac" *Bibliographe*, 25 avril, 2, 13 mai, 1ᵉʳ juillet 1841. *Reprinted in Spoelberch de Lovenjoul, *Une Page perdue de H. de Balzac*, Paris: Ollendorff, 1903, pp. 227-259.
372. Anon. "'Les Lecamus,' étude philosophique," *Feuilleton mensuel*, 15 mai 1841, iii, 67-77.
373. Chaudes-Aigues, J.-G. "Critique littéraire," *Revue de Paris*, mai 1841, 3ᵉ série, xxix, 342-346.
374. Ladet, Ulysse. "'Les Ecrivains modernes de la France,' par J. Chaudes-Aigues," *Artiste*, juin 1841, 2ᵉ série, vii (24ᵉ livraison), 403-404.
375. Nicolle, Henri. "Les Romans et les revues: 'Ursule Mirouet,'" *Musée des familles*, octobre 1841, ix, 28.
376. Berthoud, Samuel-Henry. "Etudes littéraires. M. Honoré de Balzac," *Musée des familles*, octobre 1841, ix, 31-32.
377. Barthélémy Lanta, A. de. "'Le Curé de village,'" *Mémorial de la littérature*, 25 novembre 1841, ii, cols. 560-563.
378. Loménie, Louis de. "M. de Balzac," *Galerie des contemporains illustres*, Paris: Au bureau central, 1841, iii (no. 9), 36 pp.

[1842]

379. Anon. [No title: on the collection *Le Fruit défendu*]. *France littéraire*, 9 janvier 1842, 3ᵉ série, VIII, 46.

380. Molènes, Paul Gaschon de. "Revue littéraire: 'Mémoires de deux jeunes mariées,'" *Revue des deux mondes*, 15 mars 1842, I, 979-986.

381. Merruau, Paul. "'Quinola,'" *Courrier français*, 21 mars 1842.

382. D - - - y. "'Les Ressources de Quinola,'" *Constitutionnel*, 21 mars 1842.

383. X. "'Les Ressources de Quinola,'" *National*, 21 mars 1842.

384. Janin, Jules. "'Les Ressources de Quinola,'" *Journal des débats*, 21 mars 1842.

385. La Boullaye, Ferdinand de. "'Les Ressources de Quinola,'" *Indépendant*, 24 mars 1842.

386. Forgues, Emile Daurand [signed Old Nick]. "'Mémoires de deux jeunes mariées,'" *National*, 26 mars 1842.

387. Laverdant, Gabriel-Désiré. "'Les Ressources de Quinola,'" *Phalange*, 27 mars 1842, 3ᵉ série, V, no. 37, cols. 595-606.

388. M. . . "Chronique théâtrale," *Journal des artistes*, 27 mars 1842, XXXII, 205.

389. AE. "'Les Ressources de Quinola,'" *Avenir*, 31 mars 1842, pp. 281-283.

390. Anon. "'Les Ressources de Quinola,'" *Revue de Paris*, mars 1842, 4ᵉ série, III, 301-303.

391. Molènes, Paul Gaschon de. "Revue dramatique: 'Les Ressources de Quinola,'" *Revue des deux mondes*, 1ᵉʳ avril 1842, II, 136-151.

392. Thierry, Edouard. "Simples lettres," *France littéraire*, 3 avril 1842, Nouvelle (3ᵉ) série, IX, 41-48.

393. Anon. "Chronique théâtrale," *Feuilleton mensuel*, 15 avril 1842, 2ᵉ année, II, 88-90.

394. Janin, Jules. "La Préface de Quinola," *Journal des débats*, 18 avril 1842.

395. L. O. "'Les Ressources de Quinola,'" *Constitutionnel*, 20 avril, 11 juin, 17 juin 1842.

396. F. G. "'Les Ressources de Quinola,'" *Revue indépendante*, avril 1842, III, 248-249.

397. Cherbuliez, Joël. "'Les Ressources de Quinola.'" In *10*, mai 1842, X, 133-137.

398. Anon. [No title; on *Albert Savarus*]. *Feuilleton mensuel*, 15 juin 1842, 2ᵉ année, IV, 78-79.

399. Molènes, Paul Gaschon de. "Simples essais d'histoire littéraire: M. de Balzac," *Revue des deux mondes*, 1ᵉʳ novembre 1842, IV, 390-411.

400. Gandonnière, Almire [signed A. Philibert de Loué]. "M. H. de Balzac," *Chronique, revue universelle*, 15 novembre 1842, 2ᵉ année, II, 133-138.

[1843]

401. Asseline, Alfred. "'Un Ménage de garçon en province,' par M. de Balzac," *Revue de Paris*, janvier 1843, 4ᵉ série, XIII, supplément, 61-67.

402. Janin, Jules. "Réponse à M. de Balzac, à propos de sa 'Monographie de la presse parisienne,'" **Journal des débats*, 20 février 1843. Reprinted in *Variétés littéraires*, Paris, s. d. [1857], pp. 106-115.

403. Cormenin, Louis de [signed Louis de C.]. "Portraits littéraires. M. de Balzac," *Unité*, 6 mai 1843, II, 146-151.

404. Molènes, Paul Gaschon de. "Revue littéraire," *Revue des deux mondes*, 15 juin 1843, II, 990-998.

405. Forest, Prudent. "Critique littéraire. . . . M. de Balzac," *Phalange,* 12 juillet 1843, 3ᵉ série, VI (2), cols. 2667-2668.

406. Anon. " 'Le Curé de village,' " *Revue littéraire et critique,* septembre 1843, II, 429-432.

407. Foucher, Paul-Henri [signed Paul Fouché]. "Revue des théâtres," *Echo de la littérature,* septembre 1843, IV, 277.

408. Berru, Camille, " 'Paméla Giraud,' " *Indépendant,* 28 septembre 1843.

409. Janin, Jules. " 'Paméla Giraud,' " *Journal des débats,* 2 octobre 1843.

410. Babou, Hippolyte. " 'La Muse du département,' par M. de Balzac," *Revue de Paris,* 1ᵉʳ octobre 1843, Nouvelle (4ᵉ) série, XXII, 52-61.

411. Belenet, Ernest de. " 'Mystères de province.—Rosalie,' " *Echo de la littérature,* novembre 1843, IV, 323-327.

412. Molènes, Paul Gaschon de [signed F. de Lagenevais]. "Les Derniers Romans de M. de Balzac et de M. Frédéric Soulié," *Revue des deux mondes,* 1ᵉʳ décembre 1843, IV, 810-829.

413. Babou, Hippolyte. "Le Roman de mœurs. 'Un Homme sérieux,' par M. Charles de Bernard," *Revue de Paris,* 10 décembre 1843, 4ᵉ série, XXIV, 126-138.

414. Saint-Marc Girardin. "Ch. X. De l'ingratitude des enfants. . . . —'Le Père Goriot' de M. de Balzac," *Cours de littérature dramatique,* Paris: Charpentier, 1843, I, 241-255.

415. Ottavi, Joseph. " 'La Confession générale,' par Frédéric Soulié," *L'Urne,* Paris: Paulin, 1843, pp. 454-457.

[1844]

416. Berru, Camille. "Reprise de 'la Fille de l'Avare,' " *Indépendant,* 10 mars 1844.

417. Fournier, Marc. "Notes pour les annales littéraires de ce temps. I. Les Pêcheurs à la ligne," *Artiste,* 14 avril 1844, 3ᵉ série, V, 235-237.

418. Forgues, Emile Daurand. " 'Les Deux Frères,' " *National,* 18 avril 1844.

419. ———. " 'Ursule Mirouet,' " *National,* 28 avril 1844.

420. Asseline, Alfred. " 'Modeste Mignon,' par M. de Balzac," *Revue de Paris,* 4 mai 1844, I, 11-12.

421. Gobineau, Joseph-Arthur de. " 'Modeste Mignon.' " In *28,* pp. 27-37.

422. Limayrac, Paulin. "Simples Essais d'histoire littéraire. V. De l'esprit de désordre en littérature," *Revue des deux mondes,* 1ᵉʳ juin 1844, II, 808-809.

423. ———. "Revue littéraire. . . . Romans," *Revue des deux mondes,* 1ᵉʳ juillet 1844, III, 135-136.

424. Thomas, Alexandre. " 'Un Début dans la vie,' par M. de Balzac," *Revue de Paris,* 25 juillet 1844, I, 430-431.

425. Asseline, Alfred. "Sur M. de Balzac, à propos de son nouveau roman: 'Splendeurs et misères des courtisanes,' " *Artiste,* 29 septembre 1844, 4ᵉ série, II, 75-76.

426. Gobineau, Joseph-Arthur de. " 'Esther.' " In *28,* pp. 11-25.

427. Cherbuliez, Joël. " 'Catherine de Médicis expliquée: Le Martyr calviniste.' " In *10,* octobre 1844, XII, 325-330.

428. Limayrac, Paulin. "De la littérature improvisée," *Revue de Paris,* 5 décembre 1844, II, 488-491.

429. Thomas, Alexandre. "'Les Paysans,' de M. de Balzac," *Revue de Paris,* 28 décembre 1844, II, 609-611.

430. Chasles, Philarète [signed V. Caralp]. "Balzac," *Dictionnaire de la conversation,* LIV (2° du supplément), Paris: Garnier, 1844, 413-415.

[1845]

431. Limayrac, Paulin. "Du roman actuel et de nos romanciers," *Revue des deux mondes,* 1ᵉʳ septembre 1845, III, 955-956.

432. Anon. "Des nouvelles générations littéraires," *Artiste,* 21 décembre 1845, 4° série, V, 113.
   Cf. *180,* Labitte, p. 739.

[Third Period]

[1846]

433. Achard, Amédée. "M. H. de Balzac," *Epoque,* 9 mai 1846.

434. Maron, Eugène. "Revue des derniers romans-feuilletons," *Revue indépendante,* 10 août 1846, 2° série, IV, 326-342.

435. Castille, Hippolyte. "M. H. de Balzac," *Semaine,* 4 octobre 1846. Reprinted in *L'Abeille littéraire,* février 1847, V, 108-113, and in *64,* Lovenjoul, pp. 362-368.

436. Anon. "'La Comédie humaine,'" *Journal du dimanche,* 8 novembre 1846, I, no. 7, p. 9.

437. Pelletan, Eugène. "Balzac. 'La Comédie humaine,'" *Presse,* 30 novembre 1846. *Reprinted in *Heures de travail,* Paris: Pagnerre, 1854, I, 98-107.

438. Weill, Alexandre. "'Les Parents pauvres,'" *Démocratie pacifique,* 27 décembre 1846.

439. Chavigny, C. "'La Lune de miel,'" *Echo de la littérature,* 30 décembre 1846, VII, 377-381.

440. Nettement, Alfred. "G. Sand et Balzac," *Etudes critiques sur le feuilleton roman,* 2° série, Paris: Perrodel, 1846, pp. 26-33.

441. Sainte-Beuve, C.-A. [Additions to article of 1834, Item *265,* as reprinted in the *Portraits contemporains,* II, 337n., 341.]
   Cf. *585,* Fournier, pp. 257-258.

[1847]

442. Maron, Eugène. "Critique littéraire. Année 1846," *Revue indépendante,* 25 janvier 1847, 2° série, VII, 237-244.

443. Aubert, Albert. "Œuvres complètes de M. de Balzac. Edition nouvelle," *Constitutionnel,* 27 janvier 1847.

444. Babou, Hippolyte. "Petites Lettres confidentielles à M. de Balzac par une femme du monde, un diplomate et un pédant," *Revue nouvelle,* février 1847, XIII, 94-124. Reprinted in *1,* pp. 75-117.

445. Lerminier, J.-L.-E. "De la peinture des mœurs contemporaines," *Revue des deux mondes,* 15 avril 1847, II, 151-167.

446. Janin, Jules. "La Semaine dramatique. 'Les Paysans,' . . . par MM. Dennery, Cormon, et Grangé," *Journal des débats,* 22 novembre 1847.

447. Champfleury. *Feu Miette. Fantaisies d'été,* Paris: Martinon, Sartorius, 1847.

[1848]

448. Chavigny, C. "Panorama littéraire. Nos romanciers," *Echo de la littérature,* 30 avril 1848, IX, 123.

449. Rolle, Hippolyte [signed R.]. " 'La Marâtre,' " *Constitutionnel,* 29 mai 1848.
450. Janin, Jules. "La Semaine. 'La Marâtre,' " *Journal des débats,* 29 mai 1848.
451. Pontmartin, Armand de. "Revue littéraire et dramatique," *Revue des deux mondes,* 31 mai 1848, II, 812-815.
452. Champfleury. " 'La Reine d'Espagne,' . . . par M. H. Delatouche," *Messager des théâtres et des arts* [éd. bis-hebdomadaire], 8 décembre 1848, supplément.
453. Roux, Gabriel. "Avant-propos," *Le Provincial à Paris* [*Les Comédiens sans le savoir*], Paris: Roux, 1848. *Reprinted in *64,* Lovenjoul, pp. 134-138. Cf. *798,* Baudelaire, p. 171.

[1849]

454. Janin, Jules. "La Semaine dramatique. 'Mme Marneffe,' . . . par M. Clairville," *Journal des débats,* 15 janvier 1849.
455. Rolle, Hippolyte [signed R.]. " 'Madame Marneffe, ou le Père prodigue,' comédie-vaudeville en cinq actes, de M. Clairville," *Constitutionnel,* 15 janvier 1849.
456. Sainte-Beuve, C.-A. " 'Les Confidences,' par M. de Lamartine," *Constitutionnel,* 8 octobre 1849. *Reprinted in *57,* I, 20-34.

[1850]

457. Janin, Jules. " 'Vautrin' et M. de Balzac," *Journal des débats,* 29 avril 1850.
458. Hugo, Victor. "Funérailles de Balzac, 20 août 1850," *Actes et paroles.— Avant l'exil,* Paris: Hetzel, Quantin, s. d., I, 191-193.
459. Janin, Jules. [Conversation of August 21, 1850], in Lemer, Julien. *Balzac, Sa vie—son œuvre,* Paris: Sauvaitre, 1892, pp. 1-6.
460. Chasles, Philarète. [No title.] *Journal des débats,* 24 août 1850.
461. Achard, Amédée. "Lettres parisiennes," *Assemblée nationale,* 25 août 1850.
462. Mazade, Charles de. "Revue littéraire. M. de Balzac," *Revue des deux mondes,* 1er septembre 1850, III, 912-917.
463. Aubryet, Xavier. "Quelques mots sur M. de Balzac," *Artiste,* 1er septembre 1850, 5e série, v, 110.
464. Lecomte, Jules [signed Jules du Camp]. "H. de Balzac," *Artiste,* 1er septembre 1850, 5e série, v, 107-109.
465. Sainte-Beuve, C.-A. "M. de Balzac," *Constitutionnel,* 2 septembre 1850. *Reprinted in *57,* II, 443-463.
466. Desnoiresterres, Gustave. "Etudes contemporaines. M. H. de Balzac," *Ordre,* 11, 12, 13 septembre 1850. Reprinted as *M. Honoré de Balzac,* Paris: Paul Permain, 1851.
467. Guinot, Eugène. "Revue de Paris," *Ordre,* 6 octobre 1850. Cf. *800,* D—yes.

[1851]

468. Janin, Jules. " 'Mercadet le faiseur,' " *Journal des débats,* 25 août 1851.
469. Lireux, Auguste. " 'Mercadet,' " *Constitutionnel,* 25 août 1851.
470. Jouvin, Benoît. " 'Mercadet ou le faiseur,' " *Chronique de Paris,* 4 septembre 1851, III, 249-250.
471. Janin, Jules. " 'La Peau de chagrin,' mélodrame . . . par M. Judicis," *Journal des débats,* 8 septembre 1851.
472. Lireux, Auguste. " 'La Peau de chagrin,' " *Constitutionnel,* 15 septembre 1851.

473. Jolly, Jules. *De l'influence de la littérature et du théâtre sur l'esprit public et les mœurs pendant les vingt dernières années.* Mémoire qui a obtenu une médaille d'or à l'Académie de Châlons-sur-Marne dans sa séance publique du 25 septembre 1851. Paris: Amyot, 1851.

474. Loisne, Charles Menche de. *Influence de la littérature française de 1830 à 1850 sur l'esprit public et les mœurs.* Ouvrage couronné par l'Académie de Châlons-sur-Marne dans sa séance solennelle du 25 septembre 1851. Paris: Garnier, 1852.

475. Planche, Gustave. "'Mercadet,'" *Revue des deux mondes,* 30 septembre 1851, III, 1135-1138.

476. Cuvillier-Fleury, A. A. "Le Roman français en 1851," *Etudes historiques et littéraires,* Paris: Michel Lévy, 1854, I, 259-293. [Article dated 5 octobre 1851.]

477. Sand, George. "Notice" [dated 23 octobre 1851], *Le Compagnon du tour de France,* Paris: Calmann Lévy, 1885, p. 2.

478. Anon. "Maximes et pensées de Balzac," *Illustration,* 6 décembre 1851, XVIII, 363.

479. Lacroix, Paul. "Notice biographique sur M. de Balzac," *Les Femmes de H. de Balzac,* Paris: Janet, 1851, pp. i-xii.
    Cf. *853,* Clément de Ris, p. 181.

[1852]

480. Baschet, Armand. *Honoré de Balzac,* essai sur l'homme et sur l'œuvre, avec notes historiques par Champfleury, Paris: Giraud et Dagneau, 1852.

481. Champfleury. "Physionomies littéraires: M. de Balzac, par Armand Baschet," *Pays,* 14 avril 1852.

482. Boyer, Philoxène, and Banville, Théodore de. *Le Feuilleton d'Aristophane,* comédie satirique . . . représentée pour la première fois, à Paris, sur le théâtre de l'Odéon, le 26 décembre 1852. Paris: Michel Lévy Frères, 1853.

[1853]

483. Dufaï, Alexandre. "'Maximes et pensées,'" *Athenaeum français,* 5 février 1853, II, 113-115.

484. L'Hôte, Edouard. "De l'influence de la littérature et du théâtre sur l'esprit public et les mœurs, depuis vingt ans," *Artiste,* 15 février 1853, 5ᵉ série, X, 27.

485. Ulbach, Louis. "La Liquidation littéraire," *Revue de Paris,* mars 1853, XVI, 377-401.

486. Lireux, Auguste. "'Le Lys dans la Vallée,' drame en cinq actes, par MM. Amédée de Beauplan et Théodore Barrière," *Constitutionnel,* 20 juin 1853.

487. Barbey d'Aurevilly, Jules. "Balzac," *Pays,* 22 juin et 10 mai 1853, 15 et 26 février 1856. *Reprinted in *5,* pp. 16-61.

488. ———. "Stendhal et Balzac," *Pays,* 13 juillet 1853. *Reprinted in *5,* pp. 1-16.

489. Sand, George. "Honoré de Balzac," *Autour de la table,* Paris: Michel Lévy, 1876, pp. 197-213. [Reprint of the "Notice" to Houssiaux's edition of Balzac's works, 1855; dated October 1853.]

490. Castille, Hippolyte. *Les Hommes et les mœurs en France sous le règne de Louis-Philippe,* Paris: Henneton, 1853, pp. 313-316, 320.

491. Hippeau, Célestin. "Balzac (Honoré de)," *Nouvelle Biographie universelle,* IV (1853), cols. 328-330.

492. Clément de Ris, Comte L. "Honoré de Balzac." In *12,* pp. 291-333.
Cf. *808,* Cuvillier-Fleury; *119,* Ratisbonne; *121,* Monselet, p. vi; *122,* Ulbach, p. 663; *706,* Lenoir, p. 289.

[1854]

493. Pontmartin, Armand de. "Honoré de Balzac à propos de MM. Clément de Ris et Armand Baschet." In *49,* pp. 292-303.

494. Delacroix, Eugène. [Items dated Dieppe, 3 septembre, 7 septembre 1854.] In *18,* II, 251-252, 255.

495. Lucas, Hippolyte. "Pages oubliées.—Balzac moraliste," *Annales romantiques,* mai-août 1913, x, 228-231. [Undated; *ca.* 1854?].

496. Nettement, Alfred. "Balzac." In *42,* II, 238, 242-254.
Cf. *123,* Sainte-Beuve, p. 337; *128,* E. Chasles, p. 526; *707,* Cormenin, p. 832; *708,* Lerminier, pp. 613-618.

[1855]

497. Pontmartin, Armand de. "Charles de Bernard," *Revue des deux mondes,* 1er février 1855. *Reprinted in *52,* pp. 294-325.

498. Forgues, Emile Daurand [signed Old Nick]. "Œuvres complètes de Charles de Bernard," *Athenaeum français,* 31 mars 1855, IV, 253-255.

499. Planche, Gustave. "La Littérature française de 1830 à 1848," *Revue des deux mondes,* 1er mai 1855, II, 558-559.

500. Ulbach, Louis. "Du roman moderne. Préface de 'Suzanne Duchemin,'" **Artiste,* 3 juin 1855, 5e série, IV, 60-64. Reprinted in *Revue de Paris,* 1er et 15 janvier 1856, and in *Suzanne Duchemin,* Paris: Didier, 1855.

501. Fournel, Victor. " 'Suzanne Duchemin,' par Louis Ulbach," *Avenir,* 14 octobre 1855, I, 186-188.

502. Mazade, Charles de. "Chronique de la quinzaine," *Revue des deux mondes,* 15 novembre 1855, IV, 922.

503. Pontmartin, Armand de. "M. Alfred Nettement." In *52,* p. 196.

504. Sand, George. *Histoire de ma vie, 1854-1855,* Paris: Calmann Lévy, 1893, pp. 126-137, 294-295.
Cf. *820,* Goudall, pp. 2-3.

[1856]

505. Cauvain, Henri. " 'Les Contes drolatiques,' " *Constitutionnel,* 10 mars 1856.

506. Anon. "Bulletin bibliographique. 'Les Contes drolatiques,' de Balzac," *Revue de Paris,* 1er avril 1856, XXXI, 157-158.

507. ———. "Bulletin bibliographique: 'Le Père Goriot,' par H. de Balzac," *Revue de Paris,* 1er mai 1856, XXXI, 473.

508. ———. "Balzac: 'Le Cousin Pons,' " *Revue de Paris,* 1er mai 1856, XXXI, 474.

509. Lurine, Louis. "Concours de la Société des Gens de Lettres. Discours prononcé par M. Louis Lurine, Vice-président de la Société [17 avril 1856]. Etude sur Balzac," **Semaine,* 4 mai 1856, no. 16, pp. 273-283. Reprinted in *Société des gens de lettres de France: Discours, 17 avril 1856,* Paris: Imprimerie de Brière, 1856, and in Spoelberch de Lovenjoul, *Une Page perdue de H. de Balzac,* Paris: Ollendorff, 1903, pp. 279-327.

510. Champfleury. "Lettre à M. Veuillot" [dated Vichy, 2 juillet 1856], *Figaro,* 10 juillet 1856, pp. 3-4.
511. Limayrac, Paulin. "Les Livres nouveaux. . . . 'Balzac en pantoufles,' de M. Léon Gozlan. 'Les Femmes de Balzac,' " *Constitutionnel,* 27 juillet 1856.
512. Jouvin, Benoît. "Comédie française," *Figaro,* 14 septembre 1856, p. 6.
513. Champfleury. "La Jeunesse d'Honoré de Balzac," *Gazette de Champfleury,* 1ᵉʳ novembre 1856, I, 81-106.
   Cf. *824,* Aubryet, p. 282.

[Fourth Period]
[1856]

514. Pontmartin, Armand de. "M. de Balzac," *Correspondant,* 25 novembre et 25 décembre 1856. *Reprinted in *48,* pp. 32-103.
515. Duranty, Edmond. "Le Remarquable Article de M. de Pontmartin sur Balzac," *Réalisme,* 15 décembre 1856, No. 2, pp. 28-29.
516. Poitou, Eugène. "M. de Balzac, étude morale et littéraire," *Revue des deux mondes,* 15 décembre 1856, VI, 713-767. Reprinted in *Portraits littéraires et philosophiques,* Paris: Charpentier, 1868, pp. 91-169.

[1857]

517. Barbey d'Aurevilly, Jules. "Honoré de Balzac," *Pays,* 1ᵉʳ janvier 1857. *Reprinted in *4,* pp. 1-14.
518. Mazade, Charles de. "Chronique," *Revue des deux mondes,* 1ᵉʳ mai 1857, III, 217-220.
519. Aubineau, Léon. "Variétés. D'un roman nouveau [*Madame Bovary*]," *Univers, union catholique,* 26 juin 1857.
520. Goncourt, Edmond et Jules de. [Item dated septembre 1857]. In *29,* I, 163.
521. Sarcey, Francisque [signed Satané Binet, Provincial]. "La Première aux Parisiens. Lettres d'un provincial," *Figaro,* 1ᵉʳ novembre 1857, pp. 2-3.
522. Poitou, Eugène. *Du roman et du théâtre contemporains et de leur influence sur les mœurs,* Paris: A. Durand, 1857. *Second edition, 1858, pp. 19-20, 55-58, 113-115, 172 n., 179-181, 188-189, 272.
   Cf. *578,* Aubryet, p. 242; *579,* Desdemaines, p. 4; *827,* Thulié, p. 56; *878,* Donis, p. 77; *882,* Barbey d'Aurevilly, p. 62; *883,* Baudelaire, p. 106; *963,* Pontmartin, pp. 294-298.

[1858]

523. Taine, Hippolyte. "Honoré de Balzac," *Journal des débats,* 3, 4, 5, 23, 25 février, 3 mars 1858. *Reprinted in *65,* pp. 1-94.
524. Gautier, Théophile. "Galerie du XIXᵉ siècle. III. Honoré de Balzac," *Artiste,* 21, 28 mars, 4, 18, 25 avril, 2 mai 1858. *Reprinted as *Honoré de Balzac,* Paris: Poulet-Malassis et De Broise, 1859.
525. Delacroix, Eugène. [Item dated Plombières, 27 juillet 1858.] In *18,* III, 207.
526. Babou, Hippolyte. "Le Noviciat de Balzac. Lettre à Madame Surville," *Revue française,* 1ᵉʳ septembre 1858,' XIV, 235-244. Reprinted in *1,* pp. 55-74.
527. Goncourt, Edmond et Jules de. [Item dated octobre 1858]. In *29,* I, 198-199.
528. Ancelot, Mme Marguerite L. Virginie. "Le Salon de la Duchesse

d'Abrantès," *Les Salons de Paris:* foyers éteints, Paris: Tardieu, 1858, p. 97.
Cf. *829,* Révillon; *886,* Weiss, pp. 145, 161.

[1859]

528a. Baudelaire, Charles. "Théophile Gautier," *Artiste,* 13 mars 1859. *Reprinted in *6,* pp. 168-169.

529. Fiorentino, Pier-Angelo. " 'La Marâtre' . . . (reprise)," *Constitutionnel,* 12 septembre 1859.

530. Sarcey, Francisque. " 'La Marâtre' " [article dated 12 septembre 1859]. Reprinted in *62,* IV, 187-193.

531. Jouvin, Benoît. "Balzac dramaturge," *Figaro,* 17 septembre 1859, pp. 1-3.

532. Caro, Elme-Marie. "Le Roman contemporain. M. de Balzac, son œuvre et son influence," *Revue européenne,* 1, 15 octobre 1859, v, 5-36, 225-267. Reprinted in *8,* pp. 271-369.

533. Gautier, Théophile. "Œuvres complètes de Balzac," *Moniteur universel,* 10 décembre 1859.

534. Sirtema de Grovestins, Baron Charles Frédéric. *Les Gloires du romantisme,* appréciées par leurs contemporains et recueillies par Un Autre Bénédictin, II, Paris: Dentu, 1859, pp. 95-133.

[1860]

535. Anon. "Aperçus littéraires," *Varia,* Paris: Michel Lévy, février 1860, I, 191-195.

536. Delacroix, Eugène. [Item dated Champrosay, 27 juillet 1860]. In *18,* III, 300-301.

537. Mouy, Charles de. " 'Honoré de Balzac,' par M. Théophile Gautier," *Magasin de librairie,* 25 septembre 1860, XII, 317-319.

538. Geoghegan, Edward. "Causeries: De l'influence de Balzac sur le mouvement littéraire actuel," 6 ou 7 octobre 1860 [source unknown]. *Reprinted in *64,* Lovenjoul, pp. 488-491.

[1861]

539. Sainte-Beuve, C.-A. "M. Louis Veuillot," *Constitutionnel,* 30 septembre 1861. *Reprinted in *58,* I, 59.

[1862]

540. Goncourt, Edmond et Jules de. [Item dated 21 mai 1862]. In *29,* II, 28-29.

541. Mazade, Charles de. "Les Romans nouveaux," *Revue des deux mondes,* 1ᵉʳ juillet 1862, IV, 242-251.

542. Avond, Auguste. "Le Roman moderne en France et Madame George Sand," *Critique française,* novembre 1862, IV, 321-338.
Cf. *904,* Scherer.

[1863]

543. Goncourt, Edmond et Jules de. [Item dated 11 mai 1863.] In *29,* II, 90-91.

544. Delaborde, Henri. "La Lithographie en France," *Revue des deux mondes,* 1ᵉʳ octobre 1863, v, 589.

545. Sainte-Beuve, C.-A. "Gavarni," *Constitutionnel,* 12 octobre 1863. *Reprinted in *58,* VI, 160-161.

546. Roqueplan, Nestor. "'Les Ressources de Quinola,'" *Constitutionnel,* 19 octobre 1863.
547. Vapereau, Gustave. "'Les Ressources de Quinola.'" In *70,* vi, 235-238.
    Cf. *842,* Dusolier, p. 31.

[1864]

548. Barbey d'Aurevilly, Jules. "Shakespeare et . . . Balzac," *Pays,* 10 mai 1864.
    *Reprinted in *Portraits politiques et littéraires,* Paris: Lemerre, 1898, pp. 1-17.
549. Sainte-Beuve, C.-A. "M. Taine," *Constitutionnel,* 30 mai 1864. *Reprinted in *58,* viii, 66-137.
550. Dollfus, Paul. "Sur les systèmes littéraires," *Artiste,* 15 octobre 1864, pp. 178-183.
551. Lamartine, Alphonse de. "Balzac et ses œuvres," *Cours familier de littérature,* xviii, Paris: Michel Lévy Frères, 1864, pp. 273-527.
    Cf. *919,* Nettement, p. 118; *136,* Taine, pp. 197, 214.

[1865]

552. Reynald, Hermile. "'Nouveaux Essais de critique et d'histoire,' par H. Taine," *Revue française,* 1ᵉʳ décembre 1865, xii, 629-630.
553. Gastineau, Benjamin. "Balzac," *Les Génies de la liberté,* Paris: Librairie internationale, 1865, pp. 119-136.

[1866]

554. Desraimes, Maria. "L'Influence du roman," *Nain jaune,* 31 mars 1866, pp. 4-5.
    Cf. *974,* Pontmartin, p. 66.

[1867]

555. Luzarche, Robert. "Un Livre immoral, S. V. P.," *Le Critique,* 3 août 1867, p. 3.

[1868]

556. Ampère, Jean-Jacques. [Opinion on Balzac, quoted by Sainte-Beuve, "Jean-Jacques Ampère," *Constitutionnel,* 1ᵉʳ septembre 1868. *Reprinted in *58,* xiii, 264.]
557. Roqueplan, Nestor. "'Mercadet,'" *Constitutionnel,* 26 octobre 1868.
558. Asselineau, Charles. "'Mercadet,'" *Bulletin du bibliophile,* 1868, pp. 623-630.
559. Vapereau, Gustave. "'Mercadet.'" In *70,* xi, 89-90.
560. Féval, Paul. "Romans," *Rapport sur les progrès des lettres,* Paris: Imprimerie impériale, 1868, pp. 50-51.

[1869]

562. Pontmartin, Armand de. "Balzac." In *50,* vii, 74-89. [Article dated avril 1869.]
563. Boulé, Alphonse. "Une Préface à la 'Comédie humaine' de Balzac, contenant un ordre de lecture," *Illustration,* 10 et 17 juillet 1869. *Reprinted in *64,* Lovenjoul, pp. 382-389.
564. Lucas, Hippolyte. "Œuvres complètes de H. de Balzac," *Siècle,* 23 juillet 1869.

565. Cuvillier-Fleury, A. A. "Œuvres complètes de H. de Balzac," *Journal des débats,* 10 octobre 1869.
Cf. *926,* Levallois; *927,* Léoni; *931,* Sand, p. 423.

[1870]

566. Scherer, Edmond. "Balzac," *Temps,* 1er mars 1870. *Reprinted in *63,* iv, 63-73.

MONNIER

[1830]

567. Anon. " 'Scènes populaires,' " *Figaro,* 5 juin 1830.

[1831]

568. ———. " 'Scènes populaires dessinées à la plume,' " *Figaro,* 7 août 1831.
569. Balzac, Honoré de. " 'Recréations,' album par Henry Monnier," *Caricature,* 3 novembre 1831. *Reprinted in *33,* Lumet, pp. 139-140.
570. L. B. " 'Scènes populaires,' dessinées à la plume; par Henri Monnier," *Artiste,* 1831, ii, 43-44.

[1838]

Cf. *335,* Cherbuliez, p. 311.

[1840]

Cf. *104,* Balzac, p. 276.

[1841]

571. Cherbuliez, Joël. " 'Scènes de la ville et de la campagne.' " In *10,* octobre 1841, ix, 334-335.
572. Nicolle, Henri. "Les Revues et les romans," *Musée des familles,* novembre 1841, ix, 61.

[1843]

Cf. *403,* Cormenin, p. 147.

[1848]

573. Thoré, Théophile. "Revue des arts," *Constitutionnel,* 9 janvier 1848.

[1849]

574. Eyma, Louis-Xavier [signed L. X. E.]. " 'Les Compatriotes,' scènes populaires en un acte, par M. Henri Monnier," *Messager des théâtres* [ed. bis-hebdomadaire], 14 août 1849.
575. Janin, Jules. "La Semaine. 'Les Compatriotes,' un acte, par Henri Monnier," *Journal des débats,* 13 août 1849.

[1852]

576. Dufaï, Alexandre. " 'La Grandeur et la décadence de M. Prudhomme,' " *Athenaeum français,* 4 décembre 1852, i, 368-369.

[1855]

577. Gautier, Théophile. "Henri Monnier," *Presse,* 20 février 1855.

[1857]

578. Aubryet, Xavier. "Monsieur Prudhomme. Histoire d'une idée," *Artiste*, 22 mars 1857, 6ᵉ série, III, 241-244.

579. Desdemaines, Emile. "M. Henri Monnier et les 'Mémoires de Joseph Prudhomme,'" *Rabelais*, 16 mai 1857, I, No. 1, pp. 4, 6.

[1858]

Cf. *888*, Rousseau, pp. 4-5.

CHARLES DE BERNARD

[1838]

580. C. "'Le Nœud gordien,'" *Revue du dix-neuvième siècle*, 18 février 1838, V, 421-425.
Cf. *321*, Anon., p. 129; *333*, Sainte-Beuve, pp. 352-359.

[1839]

581. Anon. "Revue littéraire," *Artiste*, 3 février 1839, 2ᵉ série, II, 168-170.

582. Alloury, Louis. "'Le Nœud gordien. Le Paravent,'" *Journal des débats*, 20 et 21 mai 1839.

583. Girault de Saint-Fargeau, Eusèbe. "'Le Nœud gordien.'" In *27*, I, 63-65.

[1843]

Cf. *413*, Babou.

[1844]

584. Lamarque, Jules de. "Bernard," *Dictionnaire de la conversation*, Paris: Garnier, 1844, LV (IIIᵉ du supplément), 134-135.

[1846]

585. Fournier, Marc. "La Semaine littéraire. Du loisir dans les travaux de l'esprit," *Artiste*, 21 juin 1846, 4ᵉ série, VI, 257-258.

[1854]

Cf. *708*, Lerminier, pp. 614-616.

[1855]

586. Forgues, Emile Daurand. "'Œuvres complètes de Charles de Bernard,'" *Athenaeum français*, 31 mars 1855, IV, 253-255.

CRITICISM OF REALISTIC PAINTING

[1841]

587. Rolle, Hippolyte [signed R.]. "Salon de 1841," *Constitutionnel*, 12 avril 1841.

588. Gautier, Théophile. "Salon de 1841," *Revue de Paris*, avril 1841, 3ᵉ série, XXVIII, 268-269.

589. Luthereau, Jean [signed Jacques Le Normand]. "Salon de 1841. Deuxième lettre. A M. le Vicomte Fritz de C***," *Province et Paris*, 15 mai 1841, I, 193.

[1842]

590. Delécluze, Etienne Jean. "Salon de 1842," *Journal des débats,* 28 et 29 mars 1842.

591. Robert, H. "Salon de 1842. (6ᵉ article)," *National,* 8 mai 1842.

592. Luthereau, Jean. "Lettres sur le salon de 1842. II," *Revue de la province et de Paris,* mai 1842, III, 90-97.

[1843]

593. Anon. "Salon de 1843. (Deuxième article)," *Unité,* 26 mars-1ᵉʳ avril 1843, II, 32-34.

[1844]

594. La Faloise, F. de. "Salon de 1844," *Revue de Paris,* avril 1844, 4ᵉ série, XXVIII, 351.

595. Thoré, Théophile. "Salon de 1844," *Constitutionnel,* 12 mai 1844.

596. Viardot, Louis. "De la peinture allemande contemporaine," *Artiste,* 1ᵉʳ septembre 1844, 4ᵉ série, II, 5.

[1845]

597. Thoré, Théophile. "Salon de 1845," *Constitutionnel,* 23 mars 1845.

598. Anon. "Salon de 1845," *Moniteur des arts,* 20 avril, 27 avril, 23 mai 1845, I, 89-91, 97-100, 129-131.

599. Janin, Jules. " 'Œuvres choisies de Gavarni,' " *Journal des débats,* 11 août 1845.

600. Houssaye, Arsène. "Naissance de l'art en Hollande," *Artiste,* 28 septembre 1845, 4ᵉ série, IV, 194.

601. X. " 'Œuvres choisies de Gavarni,' " *Journal des débats,* 21 décembre 1845.

[1846]

602. Houssaye, Arsène. *Histoire de la peinture flamande et hollandaise,* Paris: Hetzel, 1866 [*sic* for 1846], 224 pp. and 100 engravings.

603. Mantz, Paul. "Le Salon. Les Coloristes," *Artiste,* 12 avril 1846, 4ᵉ série, VI, 90.

604. Leboucher, Emmanuel [signed Emmanuel de Lerne]. "Le Salon. Les Tableaux de genre," *Artiste,* 26 avril 1846, 4ᵉ série, VI, 125.

605. Guillot, Arthur. "Salon de 1846. Troisième article," *Revue indépendante,* 25 mai 1846, 2ᵉ série, II, 427-453.

606. Houssaye, Arsène. "Les Peintres de la vie privée," *Artiste,* 20 décembre 1846, 4ᵉ série, VIII, 97-101. [Extract from *602.*]

[1847]

607. Calemard de Lafayette, Charles. "Généralités sur l'art," *Artiste,* 28 février 1847, 4ᵉ série, VIII, 257.

608. Vaines, Maurice de. "Salon de 1847," *Revue nouvelle,* 15 avril 1847, XIV, 236-276.

609. Thoré, Théophile. "Salon de 1847," *Constitutionnel,* 17 avril 1847.

609a. Gautier, Théophile. "Du beau dans l'art," *Revue des deux mondes,* 31 avril 1847, III, 886-908.

    Cf. *447,* Champfleury, p. 18.

[1848]

610. Mercey, Frédéric [signed Lagenevais]. "Salon de 1848," *Revue des deux mondes,* 15 avril 1848, II, 298.

[1849]

611. "Feu Diderot." "Salon de 1849," *Artiste,* 1ᵉʳ juillet 1849, 5ᵉ série, III, 97-98.
612. Peisse, Louis. "Salon de 1849," *Constitutionnel,* 15 juillet 1849.
613. Lagenevais. "Le Salon de 1849," *Revue des deux mondes,* 15 août 1849, III, 559-593.

[1850]

614. Champfleury. "Mouvement des arts," *Ordre,* 21 septembre 1850.

[1851]

615. Delécluze, Etienne Jean. "Exposition de 1850," *Journal des débats,* 7 janvier 1851.
616. Peisse, Louis. "Salon de 1850," *Constitutionnel,* 8 janvier 1851.
617. Clément de Ris, Comte L. "Le Salon. III," *Artiste,* 1ᵉʳ février 1851, 5ᵉ série, VI, 3-9.
618. Enault, Louis. "Salon de 1850. (Deuxième article)," *Chronique de Paris,* 16 février 1851, II, 120.
619. Geofroy, Louis de. "Le Salon de 1850," *Revue des deux mondes,* 1ᵉʳ mars 1851, I, 928-931.
620. Clément de Ris, Comte L. "Salon de 1851. V," *Artiste,* 1ᵉʳ mars 1851, 5ᵉ série, VI, 33-37.
621. Richard, Fleury. "A M. le directeur de 'L'Artiste,'" *Artiste,* 1ᵉʳ mars 1851, 5ᵉ série, VI, 47.
622. Bonnassieux, Eugène. "Salon de 1850-1851," *Courrier de Paris,* 1ᵉʳ mars 1851, pp. 17-18.
623. Clément de Ris, Comte L. "Salon de 1851. VII," *Artiste,* 16 avril 1851, 5ᵉ série, VI, 81-83.

[1852]

624. Enault, Louis. "Le Salon de 1852. II," *Chronique de Paris,* 1ᵉʳ mai 1852, IV, 233-234.
625. Clément de Ris, Comte L. "Le Salon," *Artiste,* 1ᵉʳ mai 1852, 5ᵉ série, VIII, 99-100.
626. Decazes, Baronne [signed Elisa de Mirbel]. "Le Salon de 1852," *Révolution littéraire,* 10 mai 1852, III, 75.
627. Peisse, Louis. "Salon. V," *Constitutionnel,* 12 mai 1852.
628. Planche, Gustave. "Le Salon de 1852," *Revue des deux mondes,* 15 mai 1852, II, 670-672.
629. Peisse, Louis. "Salon. VI," *Constitutionnel,* 19 mai 1852.
630. Du Camp, Maxime. "Salon de 1852," *Revue de Paris,* mai 1852, VII, 83-84.
631. Delécluze, Etienne Jean. "Exposition de 1852. De l'état présent de la peinture en France," *Journal des débats,* 8 juillet 1852.
632. Boyer, Philoxène, and Banville, Théodore de. *Le Feuilleton d'Aristophane,* [cf. *482*], pp. 13-15.

[1853]

633. Delacroix, Eugène. [Items dated Paris, 15 avril 1853 and Champrosay, 17 octobre 1853]. In *18*, II, 18-19, 91-92.

634. Cham, Comte Henry de Noé, *dit.* "Première promenade à l'exposition," *Charivari*, 29 mai 1853.

635. Clément de Ris, Comte L. "Salon de 1853," *Artiste*, 1ᵉʳ juin 1853, 5ᵉ série, x, 129-133.

636. Gautier, Théophile. "De l'art moderne," *Artiste*, 1ᵉʳ juin 1853, 5ᵉ série, x, 135-136.

637. Mazade, Charles de. "Chronique de la quinzaine," *Revue des deux mondes*, 1ᵉʳ juin 1853, II, 1070.

638. Viel Castel, Comte Horace de. "Salon de 1853," *Athenaeum français*, 4 juin 1853, II, 534-535.

639. Delaborde, Henri. "Salon de 1853," *Revue des deux mondes*, 15 juin 1853, II, 1142-1144.

640. Du Pays, Augustin Joseph. "Salon de 1853. (4ᵉ article)," *Illustration*, 18 juin 1853, XXI, 391-394.

641. Cham, Comte Henry de Noé, *dit.* "Troisième promenade à l'exposition," *Charivari*, 19 juin 1853.

642. Calonne, Alphonse de. "Salon de 1853," *Revue contemporaine*, juin 1853, VIII, 131-134.

643. Peisse, Louis. "Salon. VII. Tableaux de genre et paysages," *Constitutionnel*, 22 juillet 1853.

644. Clément de Ris, Comte L. "Salon de 1853," *Artiste*, 1ᵉʳ août 1853, 5ᵉ série, XI, 6-7.

645. La Madelène, Henry de Collet, baron de. "Le Salon de 1853. Quatrième article," *Eclair*, 1853, III (No. 24), 279.

[1854]

646. L'Hôte, Edouard. "De l'idéalisme et du réalisme," *Artiste*, 15 juillet 1854, 5ᵉ série, XII, 184-185.

[1855]

647. Cham, Comte Henry de Noé, *dit.* "Promenades à l'Exposition," *Charivari*, 19 et 23 juin 1855.

648. Mantz, Paul. "Salon de 1855. III. Angleterre," *Revue française*, 1ᵉʳ juillet 1855, II, 122-134.

649. Champfleury. "Du réalisme. Lettre à madame Sand," **Artiste*, 2 septembre 1855, 5ᵉ série, XVI, 1-5. Reprinted in *9*, pp. 270-285.

650. Deleutre, Paul [signed Paul d'Ivoy]. "Exposition universelle. . . . Les Français," *Estafette*, 7 septembre 1855.

651. Dubosc de Pesquidoux, Clément. "Beaux-Arts. Etudes critiques. (6ᵉ article). Ecole française.—MM. Flandrin, Lhemann, etc.," *Appel*, 9 septembre 1855.

652. Perrier, Charles. "Du réalisme. Lettre à M. le Directeur de 'L'Artiste,' " *Artiste*, 14 octobre 1855, 5ᵉ série, XVI, 85-90.

653. Dubosc de Pesquidoux, Clément. "Beaux-Arts. Etudes critiques. (12ᵉ article). Ecole française.—Le Réalisme," *Appel*, 11 novembre 1855.

654. About, Edmond. "Chapitre V. XI. Les Réalistes," *Voyage à travers l'Exposition des Beaux-Arts*, Paris: Hachette, 1855, pp. 201-208.

[1856]

655. Banville, Théodore de. "Bonjour, monsieur Courbet!!!" *Figaro,* 7 février 1856, p. 5.
656. Ratisbonne, Louis. " 'La Peinture contemporaine en France,' par Anatole de Laforge," *Journal des débats,* 10 juillet 1856.
657. Duranty, Edmond. "Notes sur l'art," *Réalisme,* 10 juillet 1856.
658. Planche, Gustave. "L'Art grec et la sculpture réaliste," *Revue des deux mondes,* 1ᵉʳ octobre 1856, v, 530-555.

[1857]

659. Gautier, Théophile. "Salon de 1857," *Artiste,* 14 juin 1857, Nouvelle série, i, 189-192.
660. Nadar, Gustave-Félix Tournachon, *dit.* [Caricature of Courbet's 'Demoiselles de la Seine']. *Rabelais,* 24 juin 1857, i, No. 12, p. 4.
661. Rousseau, Jean. "Salon de 1857. ii. Les Indépendants," *Figaro,* 28 juin 1857.
662. Gautier, Théophile. "Salon de 1857. iv," *Artiste,* 5 juillet 1857, Nouvelle série, i, 245-249.
663. Cham, Comte Henry de Noé, *dit.* "Promenades à l'Exposition," *Charivari,* 8 juillet, 4 août 1857.
664. Du Camp, Maxime. "Salon de 1857," *Revue de Paris,* 15 juillet 1857, xxxviii, 161-224.
665. Gautier, Théophile. "Salon de 1857," *Artiste,* 20 septembre 1857, Nouvelle série, ii, 33-36.
666. Perrier, Charles. "x. Le Réalisme. M. Courbet et M. Biard," *L'Art français au Salon de 1857,* Paris: Michel Lévy Frères, 1857, pp. 121-128.

[1858]

667. Clément de Ris, Comte L. "Les Notabilités de l'art depuis dix ans. ii," *Artiste,* 27 juin 1858, Nouvelle série, iv, 118-119.
668. Delaborde, Henri. "Les Préraphaélites à propos d'un tableau de Raphael," *Revue des deux mondes,* 15 juillet 1858, iv, 241-260.
669. About, Edmond. "M. Courbet," *Nos Artistes au Salon de 1857,* Paris: Hachette, 1858, pp. 141-155.

[1859]

670. Belloy, Marquis Auguste de. "Salon de 1859. iii," *Artiste,* 1ᵉʳ mai 1859, Nouvelle série, vii, 4-6.
671. ———. "Salon de 1859. iv," *Artiste,* 7 mai 1859, Nouvelle série, vii, 17-18.
672. Cantrel, Emile. "Salon de 1859. Les Paysagistes. ii," *Artiste,* 22 mai 1859, Nouvelle série, vii, 52-53.
673. Baudelaire, Charles. "Lettre à M. le Directeur de la 'Revue française' sur le Salon de 1859," *Revue française,* 10, 20 juin, 1ᵉʳ, 20 juillet 1859; xvii, 257-266, 321-334, 385-398, 512-534.
674. Perrin, Emile. "Salon de 1859. iv. Les Réalistes," *Revue européenne,* 30 juin 1859, iii, 650-57.
675. Cairon, C.-A. [signed Jules Noriac]. [Advertisement for a celebration at the realists' cafe], *Figaro,* 4 octobre 1859, p. 5.
676. Houssaye, Arsène. "Les Peintres du laid," *Artiste,* 1ᵉʳ novembre 1859, Nouvelle série, viii, 97-100.

677. Pérignon, Alexis-Joseph. "Les Peintres du laid. A M. Arsène Houssaye," *Artiste,* 15 novembre 1859, Nouvelle série, VIII, 121-122.

[1860]

678. Delacroix, Eugène. [Item dated Paris, 22 février 1860]. In *18,* III, 266-272.
679. Fillonneau, Ernest. "L'Exposition de Peinture du Boulevart des Italiens," *Chronique littéraire,* mai 1862, p. 24.

[1862]

680. L'Hôte, Edouard. "De l'idéal au point de vue moderne," *Artiste,* 1ᵉʳ octobre 1862, pp. 145-147.
681. Pelloquet, Théodore. "L'Ecole moderne," *Artiste,* 15 décembre 1862, pp. 260-261.

[1863]

682. Cordier, Auguste. "Le Salon de 1863," *Critique française,* 15 mai 1863, V, 404-411.
683. Viollet-le-Duc, Ad. "De l'imitation exacte dans les arts. 'Le Réalisme,' par M. Champfleury . . . ," *Journal des débats,* 7 août 1863.
684. Proudhon, Pierre Joseph. *Du principe de l'art et de sa destination sociale,* Paris: Garnier, 1865 [Posthumous; written in 1863 on the Exposition].

[1864]

685. Chesneau, Ernest. "Un Peintre naturaliste," *Constitutionnel,* 30 mars 1864.

[1865]

686. Chesneau, Ernest. "Salon de 1865. Les Peintres de la vie contemporaine," *Constitutionnel,* 23 mai 1865.
687. Du Camp, Maxime. "Salon de 1865," *Revue des deux mondes,* 1ᵉʳ juin 1865, III, 648-679.
688. Zola, Emile. "Proudhon et Courbet," *Salut public* (Lyon), 1865. *Reprinted in *71,* pp. 21-40.

[1866]

689. "Un Flaneur." "Le Salon," *Revue de Paris,* 15 mai 1866, II, 142-143.
690. Du Camp, Maxime. "Salon de 1866," *Revue des deux mondes,* 1ᵉʳ juin 1866, III, 687-719.

[1867]

691. Goncourt, Edmond et Jules de. [Item dated 18 septembre 1867]. In *29,* III, 124-125.

THEORY AND OPPOSITION

[1834]

691a.[1] Fortoul, Hippolyte. "Revue littéraire du mois," *Revue des deux mondes,* 1ᵉʳ novembre 1834, IV, 339.

[1835]

691b. Planche, Gustave. "Histoire et philosophie de l'art. VI. Moralité de la poésie," *Revue des deux mondes,* 1ᵉʳ février 1835, I, 250.

---

[1] For references to items *691a* to *691f* I am indebted to *22a,* Du Val, Ch. I.

691c. Planche, Gustave. "'Chatterton' de M. Alfred de Vigny," *Revue des deux mondes,* 15 février 1835, I, 438.

[1836]

Cf. *300,* Hains, p. 111.

[1837]

691d. ———. "Du théâtre moderne en France. I," *Revue des deux mondes,* 15 février 1837, I, 446-448.
691e. ———. "Du théâtre moderne en France. II," *Revue des deux mondes,* 15 mai 1837, II, 499-516.
691f. ———. "Poètes et romanciers modernes de la France. xxv. M. Auguste Barbier," *Revue des deux mondes,* 1ᵉʳ juillet 1837, III, 70-71.

[1840]

692. Chaudes-Aigues, J.-G. "Etat présent de la littérature," *Artiste,* 26 janvier 1840, 2ᵉ série, v, 49-52.
693. Anon. "'Idéalisme et réalité,' par M. Eugène Villard," *Semeur,* 25 novembre 1840, IX, No. 48, 380-381.

[1843]

Cf. *413,* Babou, pp. 130-131.

[1845]

694. Delacroix, Eugène. [Undated item; *ca.* 1845]. In *18,* Supplément, III, 435-436.

[1846]

Cf. *115,* Aubert; *435,* Castille, pp. 367-368; *585,* Fournier, p. 258.

[1847]

695. Houssaye, Arsène. "Post-face. Les écoles en littérature," *Artiste,* 21 novembre 1847, 4ᵉ série, XI, 34.
Cf. *442,* Maron, p. 242; *443,* Aubert.

[1848]

Cf. *799,* Thomas, p. 51.

[1849]

Cf. *849,* Janin.

[1851]

696. Poincelot, Achille. "La Réaction littéraire," *Révolution littéraire,* 10 mai 1851, I, 114-122.
Cf. *468,* Janin; *801,* Rollet, p. 392; *802,* Cuvillier-Fleury.

[1852]

697. Janin, Jules. "'La Dame aux camélias,'" *Journal des débats,* 9 février 1852.
698. Champfleury. "'La Forge.' Traduction inédite d'Hebel," *Artiste,* 1ᵉʳ mai 1852, 5ᵉ série, VIII, 104-106.
699. Nerval, Gérard de. "Les Nuits d'octobre. Paris—Pantin—Meaux. I. Le Réalisme," *Illustration,* 9, 23, 30 octobre, 6, 13 novembre 1852. Reprinted

in *La Bohème galante, Paris: Michel Lévy Frères, 1855, pp. 177-179, and in Petits Châteaux de Bohème, Paris: Champion, 1926, pp. 127-182.

Cf. 480, Baschet, pp. 83, 90; 803, Pontmartin; 804, Mazade; 806, Pontmartin, p. 651; 807, Prarond, p. 133.

[1853]

700. Champfleury. "Préface," Les Aventures de Mademoiselle Mariette, Paris: Charpentier, 1874, pp. iii-ix.

701. Boiteau, Paul [signed Paul d'Ambly]. "La Littérature militante," Artiste, 1er avril 1853, 5e série, x, 74.

702. Bovet, F. [Preface to] Poésies complètes de J. P. Hébel, traduites et suivies de Scènes champêtres par Max. Büchon, Paris: Borrani et Droz, 1853, pp. i-viii. [Dated juillet 1853].

703. Anon. " 'Poésies complètes de J. P. Hébel,' " Athenaeum français, 1er octobre 1853, ii, 940-941.

704. Champfleury. "Lettre à M. Ampère touchant la poésie populaire," *Revue de Paris, 15 novembre 1853, xix, 585-592. Reprinted in 9, pp. 184-197.

705. Rouquette, Jules. "De l'exclusivisme dans les arts (Suite)," Monde artistique et littéraire, 1853, i, 313-314.

706. Lenoir, Jules. "Influence du matérialisme sur la littérature," Monde artistique et littéraire, 1853, i, 289-290.

Cf. 485, Ulbach, p. 378; 808, Cuvillier-Fleury; 809, Mazade, p. 1207; 810, Pontmartin; 812, Mazade; 813, Chasles, p. 1098; 814, Villedeuil, p. 338.

[1854]

707. Cormenin, Louis de. "Du vrai dans l'art," Revue de Paris, 1er mars 1854, xx, 826-834.

708. Lerminier, J.-L.-E. "Lettres critiques sur la littérature contemporaine, iii," Revue contemporaine, 31 mars 1854, xii, 613-629.

709. Caro, Elme-Marie. "Etudes morales sur le xixe siècle. ii. Le sensualisme dans la littérature," Revue contemporaine, avril 1854, xiii, 427-462.

710. Champfleury. "L'Aventurier Challes," *Revue de Paris, 1er et 15 mai 1854, xxi, 385-412, 559-586. Reprinted in 9, pp. 23-115.

711. Monnier, Marc. "Jérémias Gotthelf: 'Nouvelles bernoises.' . . . B. Auerbach: 'Scènes villageoises de la Forêt noire . . . ,' " Athenaeum français, 9 septembre 1854, iii, 833-834.

712. Dupont, Pierre. [Note sur la chanson 'Le Pâturage']. Chants et chansons, iv, Paris: Houssiaux, 1854, p. 161.

Cf. 496, Nettement, p. 249; 815, Barbey d'Aurevilly, pp. 21-22; 817, Boiteau; 818, Cuvillier-Fleury.

[1855]

713. Pontmartin, Armand de. "Charles de Bernard," Revue des deux mondes, 1er février 1855, i, 541.

714. ———. "Le Roman en 1855," Revue contemporaine, 30 juin 1855, xx, 249.

715. Desnoyers, Fernand. "Du réalisme," Artiste, 9 décembre 1855, 5e série, xvi, 197-200.

Cf. 500, Ulbach; 819, Cuvillier-Fleury; 820, Goudall, pp. 2-3; 821, Janin; 960, Babou, p. 406.

[1856]

716. Monselet, Charles. "Poème réaliste," *Figaro*, 24 janvier 1856, p. 7.
717. Chancel, Camille de. "La Courtisane dans le théâtre contemporain," *Revue de Paris*, 1ᵉʳ mars 1856, xxx, 362-378.
718. Goudall, Louis. "Revue littéraire," *Figaro*, 20 avril 1856, p. 3.
719. Assézat, Jules. " 'Profiles et grimaces.' Par Auguste Vacquerie," *Réalisme*, 10 juillet 1856.
720. Rolland, Amédée. "Béranger," *Diogène*, 10 août 1856, I, No. 1.
721. Duranty, Edmond. "Les Jeunes," *Figaro*, 13 novembre 1856, pp. 4-6.
722. Rolland, Amédée. "Chronique," *Diogène*, 23 novembre 1856, I, No. 16.
723. Duranty, Edmond. "Pour ceux qui ne comprennent jamais. Résumé du numéro précédent," *Réalisme*, 15 décembre 1856, No. 2, pp. 17-18.
724. Thulié, Henri. "Le Roman. Du caractère," *Réalisme*, 15 décembre 1856, No. 2, pp. 23-24.
     Cf. *510*, Champfleury, p. 3; *515*, Duranty, p. 29; *516*, Poitou, pp. 734, 756, 761-762; *822*, Chasles; *823*, Champfleury, p. 4; *824*, Aubryet, pp. 282-283.

[1857]

725. Soulas, Jean-Baptiste [signed Bonaventure Soulas]. "Le Réalisme et les réalistes," *Figaro*, 11 janvier 1857, pp. 2-3.
726. Thulié, Henri. "Du roman (suite). Description," *Réalisme*, 15 janvier 1857, No. 3, pp. 37-39.
727. Belloy, Marquis Auguste de. "L'Année 1856. —Le Réalisme. —Le Romantisme," *Revue française*, 20 janvier 1857, VII, 557-62.
728. Soulas, Jean-Baptiste [signed Bonaventure Soulas]. "Lettre sur le réalisme. A. M. Edmond Duranty," *Réalisme*, 15 février 1857, No. 4, pp. 56-58.
729. Duranty, Edmond. "Réalisme et réalistes. Réponse à M. Soulas," *Réalisme*, 15 mars 1857, No. 5, pp. 68-69.
730. Thulié, Henri. "Du roman. L'action," *Réalisme*, 15 mars 1857, No. 5, pp. 70-71.
731. Champfleury. "Quelques notes pour servir de préface," *Le Réalisme* [cf. *9*], pp. 1-21. (Preface dated 25 mars 1857].
732. Caro, Elme-Marie. "Les Mœurs contemporaines au théâtre," *Revue contemporaine*, 31 mars 1857, xxx, 649-695.
733. Thulié, Henri. "Du roman. Le style," *Réalisme*, avril-mai 1857, No. 6, pp. 86-87.
734. Texier, Edmond. "Chronique littéraire," *Illustration*, 9 mai 1857, XXIX, 294-295.
735. Limayrac, Paulin. "Des causes et des effets dans notre situation littéraire," *Constitutionnel*, 10 mai 1857.
736. Arnould, Arthur. "Le Réalisme. Conte satirique," *Figaro*, 14 mai 1857, pp. 2-3.
737. Limayrac, Paulin. "Causerie littéraire à travers champs," *Constitutionnel*, 7 juin 1857.
738. Aubryet, Xavier. "Revue parisienne," *Artiste*, 7 juin 1857, Nouvelle série, I, 184-188.
739. Sand, George. "Le Réalisme." In *61*, pp. 287-294. [Article dated 8 juillet 1857].
740. Watripon, Antonio. "De la moralité en matière d'art et de littérature," *Présent*, 16 août 1857, I, 242-249.

741. Dziedzic, Lucien. " 'Le Réalisme,' par M. Champfleury," *Revue philosophique et religieuse,* octobre 1857, VIII, 433-443.

Cf. *519,* Aubineau; *522,* Poitou, pp. 20, 189; *578,* Aubryet, p. 242; *826,* Babou, p. 427; *827,* Thulié, p. 56; *863,* Pinard, pp. 574, 577-578; *864,* Sénard, p. 581; *870,* Sainte-Beuve, p. 181; *871,* Deschamps, p. 281; *874,* Cuvillier-Fleury; *875,* Pontmartin, pp. 300-301, 303-304; *876,* Habans, p. 4; *878,* Donis, p. 76; *883,* Baudelaire, pp. 106-108.

[1858]

742. Woestyn, Eugène. "Le Réalisme," *Figaro,* 21 janvier 1858, p. 5.

743. Perret, Paul. " 'Du roman et du théâtre contemporains et de leur influence sur les mœurs,' par M. Eugène Poitou," *Artiste,* 28 février 1858, Nouvelle série, III, 147-149.

744. Scholl, Aurélien. "Un Trio de romans," *Figaro,* 21 mars 1858, p. 8.

745. Chasles, Emile. "La Léthargie du roman," *Revue contemporaine,* 31 juillet 1858, 2e série, IV, 241-274.

746. Vignon, Madame Claude. "Préface," *Récits de la vie réelle,* Paris: Dentu, 1861, pp. 1-4. [Preface dated La Spouze, septembre 1858.]

747. Cadoudal, Georges de. "Revue littéraire," *Semaine des familles,* 9 octobre 1858, I, 25-27.

Cf. *526,* Babou, p. 237; *886,* Weiss, pp. 147-148; *887,* Granier de Cassagnac, pp. 26-29; *888,* Rousseau; *890,* Vapereau, pp. 52-55; *940,* Chasles; *941,* Rigault; *944,* Janin, pp. viii-ix.

[1859]

748. Lataye, Eugène. "Revue dramatique," *Revue des deux mondes,* 15 janvier 1859, I, 508.

749. Barthet, Armand. " 'Récits de la vie réelle,' par M. Claude Vignon," *Artiste,* 30 janvier 1859, Nouvelle série, VI, 76-77.

750. Sarcey, Francisque [signed Sarcey de Suttières]. "Réalisme et champfleurisme," *Figaro,* 6 février 1859, pp. 3-4.

751. Bersot, Ernest. "Littérature réaliste. 'Le Sabot Rouge,' par M. Murger.— 'Les Amoureux de Sainte-Périne,' par M. Champfleury," *Journal des débats,* 20 février 1859.

752. Dubellay, Henry. "Réalisme," *Gaulois,* 3 avril 1859, p. 6. [Extract from *Rimes buissonnières,* Paris: Poulet-Malassis et De Broise, 1858, pp. 35-38.]

753. Arnould, Arthur. " 'Souvenirs des Funambules,' par M. Champfleury," *Revue européenne,* 15 juillet 1859, III, 900-902.

754. Montégut, Emile. "Le Théâtre et la nouvelle littérature dramatique," *Revue des deux mondes,* 15 décembre 1859, VI, 965-983.

755. Champfleury. [Passage from 'Les Amis de la nature,' cited by Jules Troubat, *Souvenirs sur Champfleury et le réalisme* (Conférence faite le 23 novembre 1905, à l'Association polytechnique), Paris: L. Duc, 1905, pp. 7-8.]

756. ———. "XIII. Le Réalisme montre ses cornes," *Souvenirs des Funambules,* Paris: Michel Lévy, 1859, pp. 97-98.

Cf. *196,* Merlet, pp. 142, 150; *835,* Duranty; *892,* Monpont, pp. 27, 29; *951,* Vapereau, p. 124.

[1860]

757. Reymond, William. "Sur le réalisme," *Artiste*, 15 janvier 1860, Nouvelle série, IX, 14-15.

758. Anon. "Aperçus littéraires," *Varia*, Paris: Michel Lévy, février 1860, I, 206.

759. Pontmartin, Armand de. "M. Ernest Feydeau. 'Catherine d'Overmeire,'" *Union*, 25 février 1860.

760. Gautier, Théophile. "'Un Parvenu,' comédie . . . de M. A. Rolland," *Moniteur universel*, 5 mars 1860.

761. Bersot, Ernest. "De l'application de la médecine à la littérature," *Journal des débats*, 20 avril 1860.

762. Révillon, Tony [signed H. Clément de Chaintré]. "La Belle Langue française," *Figaro*, 6 mai 1860, pp. 3-5.

763. Pontmartin, Armand de. "Le Réalisme en mains propres. MM. Paul Perret et Paul Deltuf," *Union*, 18-19 mai 1860.

764. Mazade, Charles de. "Les Romans d'hier et d'aujourd'hui," *Revue des deux mondes*, 1ᵉʳ septembre 1860, V, 237-248.

765. Goncourt, Edmond et Jules de. *Charles Demailly*, Paris: Flammarion, Fasquelle, 1926, p. 38.

766. Levallois, Jules. "M. Ernest Feydeau." In *32*, pp. 321-323.

Cf. *538*, Geoghegan, pp. 489, 491; *837*, Cherbuliez; *838*, Chavesne; *840*, Vapereau, p. 103; *858*, Merlet, pp. 34-35, 46; *893*, Merlet, pp. 707, 709, 712-714; *954*, Cuvillier-Fleury; *964*, Boissière, p. 539; *966*, Cherbuliez, p. 389; *967*, Barbey d'Aurevilly, pp. 230-233; *968*, Chavesne.

[1861]

767. L'Hôte, Edouard. "Du laid dans les arts, à propos du dernier livre de Michelet," *Artiste*, 15 février 1861, Nouvelle série, XI, 82-83.

768. Claveau, Anatole. "Les romans: le roman réaliste," *Revue contemporaine*, 15 avril 1861, 2ᵉ série, XX, 540-544.

769. Etienne, Louis. "Bibliographie hebdomadaire," *Constitutionnel*, 26 avril 1861.

770. Blot, Alfred. "'Le Réalisme et la fantaisie dans la littérature,' par Gustave Merlet," *Critique française*, mai 1861, I, 491-493.

771. Lemercier de Neuville, Louis. "Les Réalistes. Scènes de la vie de convention," *Figaro*, 15 septembre 1861, pp. 1-3.

772. Leroy, Louis. "Bucolique réaliste," *Figaro*, 19 septembre 1861, pp. 5-6.

773. Pontmartin, Armand de. "Le Roman et les romanciers de 1861," *Revue des deux mondes*, 1ᵉʳ décembre 1861, VI, 700-717.

774. Fournel, Victor. "Les Romans en 1860," *Revue de l'année*, Paris: J. Lecoffre, 1861, I, 370-378.

Cf. *197*, Vattier, p. 42; *990*, Vapereau, p. 77; *991*, Levallois, pp. 325, 329-330.

[1862]

775. Clément de Ris, Comte L. "Les Notabilités littéraires depuis dix ans— 1848-1859." In *11*, pp. 306-313.

Cf. *898*, Sainte-Beuve, pp. 185-186; *902*, Claveau, p. 648.

[1863]

775a. Sainte-Beuve, C.-A. "'Les Frères Le Nain . . . ,' par M. Champfleury," *Constitutionnel*, 5 janvier 1863. *Reprinted in *58*, IV, 116-139.

776. Laprade, Victor de. "Les Origines du réalisme," *Correspondant,* 25 mars 1863, Nouvelle série, XXII, 541-557.

777. Rondelet, Antonin. "De la moralité dans la littérature et dans l'art," *Revue contemporaine,* 15 avril 1863, 2ᵉ série, XXXII, 531-554.

778. Chesneau, Ernest. "Le Réalisme et l'esprit français dans l'art," *Revue des deux mondes,* 1ᵉʳ juillet 1863, IV, 218-237.

779. Feydeau, Ernest. "Préface que pourra passer le lecteur, l'auteur ne l'ayant écrite que pour lui-même et quelques-uns de ses intimes," *Un Début à l'Opéra,* Paris: Michel Lévy Frères, 1863, pp. iii-lxxii.

780. Fournel, Victor. "Le Réalisme: 'Antoine Quérard,' par M. Bataille . . . ," *Revue de l'année,* Paris: A. Vaton, 1863, III, 336-340.
Cf. *842,* Dusolier, p. 28; *911,* Cadoudal; *912,* Clergier, pp. 10-11; *913,* Saint-René Taillandier, pp. 840-842; *914,* Néantes; *915,* Boutmy, pp. 74-76; *958,* Peyronnet, pp. 129-132, 144-146; *958a,* Pontmartin, pp. 149-151, 157.

[1864]

781. Desprez, Adrien. "La Nouvelle Génération littéraire," *Gazette littéraire,* 30 avril 1864, pp. 9-12.

782. Peytel, A. "Le Roman réaliste en Amérique," *Gazette littéraire,* 25 juin 1864, pp. 97-100.

783. Fèvre, Abbé Justin. *Du réalisme dans la littérature.* Discours présenté au congrès scientifique de France à la session de 1864, Paris: V. Palmé, 1865.

784. Heurle, Victor de. *Le Réalisme dans la littérature et dans les arts,* Paris: Germer-Baillière, 1865. [Extrait du Congrès scientifique de France, 31ᵉ session.]

785. Nettement, Alfred. "Le Sensualisme et le réalisme dans le roman." In *43,* pp. 109-159.

786. Goncourt, Edmond et Jules de. [Item dated 24 octobre 1864.] In *29,* II, 183.
Cf. *843,* Assézat; *917,* Delaplace, pp. 140-145; *918,* Sarcey, p. 499; *959,* Nettement, p. 140; *999,* Vapereau, pp. 58-59.

[1865]

787. Coligny, Charles. "Les Nouveaux Romans et les nouveaux venus.—'Contes à Ninon,' par Emile Zola," *Artiste,* 15 janvier 1865, pp. 43-44.

788. Desonnaz, A. "Ecoles et mœurs littéraires," *Revue française,* 1ᵉʳ août 1865, XI, 556-570.

789. Barbey d'Aurevilly, Jules. "Préface," *Les Romanciers* [cf. *4*], pp. i-vi.
Cf. *846,* Laffite; *920,* L. Gautier, pp. 183, 186-187; *1006,* Villetard, p. 523; *1008,* Zola, pp. 79-81; *1009,* Roqueplan; *1012,* Vapereau, pp. 133-134.

[1866]

790. Guillemot, Jules. "Le Théâtre contemporain. Le Réalisme au théâtre," *Revue contemporaine,* 15 janvier 1866, 2ᵉ série, XLIX, 135-156.

791. Hours, Eugène. "Théâtres," *Revue de Paris,* 1ᵉʳ février 1866, I, 87.
Cf. *554,* Desraimes, p. 4.

[1867]

792. Lefrançais, G. "Du roman populaire," *Le Critique,* 25 mai 1867, pp. 3-4.

793. Mazade, Charles de. "Le Réalisme dans la critique," *Revue des deux mondes,* 15 juillet 1867, IV, 499-515.

[1868]

794. Laprade, Victor de. "Du réalisme dans la poésie et dans les arts," *Le Sentiment de la nature chez les modernes,* Paris: Didier, 1868, pp. 483-501.
795. Félix, Le Père Joseph. "Des causes de la décadence dans les arts," *Artiste,* 1ᵉʳ septembre 1868, pp. 382-403.

[1869]

796. David, Mme Marie [signed Raoul de Navery]. "L'Adultère dans le roman et dans le drame," *Artiste,* 1ᵉʳ mai 1869, pp. 174-194.
   Cf. *922,* Barbey d'Aurevilly, p. 97; *930,* Scherer, pp. 293-297; *931,* Sand, p. 421; *936,* Pontmartin, p. 301.

CHAMPFLEURY

[1847]

797. Fournier, Marc. "Histoire littéraire. Variations sur des motifs nouveaux," *Artiste,* 14 février 1847, 4ᵉ série, VIII, 235.

[1848]

798. Baudelaire, Charles. "Les Contes de Champfleury. 'Chien-Caillou, Pauvre Trompette, Feu Miette,'" *Corsaire-Satan,* 18 janvier 1848. *Reprinted in *Œuvres posthumes,* Paris: Mercure de France, 1908, pp. 169-172.
799. Thomas, André. "Théâtres," *Artiste,* 1ᵉʳ octobre 1848, 5ᵉ série, II, 51-52.

[1849]

Cf. *849,* Janin.

[1850]

800. D—yes, Ad. "'Essai sur la vie et l'œuvre des Lenain,'" *Messager des théâtres* [éd. bis-hebdomadaire], 14 mai 1850.

[1851]

801. Rollet, Patrice. "Revue littéraire," *Revue des deux mondes,* 15 avril 1851, II, 391-392.
802. Cuvillier-Fleury, A. A. "Romanciers et conteurs," *Journal des débats,* 21 septembre, 5 octobre 1851.

[1852]

803. Pontmartin, Armand de. "'Les Excentriques,'" *Revue contemporaine,* avril 1852, I, 159.
804. Mazade, Charles de. "Chronique de la quinzaine," *Revue des deux mondes,* 1ᵉʳ août 1852, III, 619.
805. Venet. "'Contes domestiques,'" *Athenaeum français,* 9 octobre 1852, I, 228-229.
806. Pontmartin, Armand de. "Le Roman et la poésie. I," *Revue contemporaine,* novembre 1852, IV, 644-654.
807. Prarond, Ernest. "Champfleury." In *54,* pp. 131-151.

[1853]

808. Cuvillier-Fleury, A. A. "Revue littéraire de la quinzaine," *Journal des débats,* 9 janvier 1853.

809. Mazade, Charles de. "Revue.—Chronique," *Revue des deux mondes,* 15 mars 1853, I, 1207-1208.

810. Pontmartin, Armand de. "Les Jeunes Conteurs . . . Choufleury [*sic*]," *Assemblée nationale,* 26 mars 1853.

811. Monselet, Charles. "La Quinzaine littéraire," *Artiste,* 15 avril 1853, 5ᵉ série, x, 91-92.

812. Mazade, Charles de. "Chronique de la quinzaine," *Revue des deux mondes,* 15 septembre 1853, III, 1221-1222.

813. Chasles, Emile. "'Contes de printemps, Contes d'été. . . . Les Oies de Noël,'" *Athenaeum français,* 19 novembre 1853, II, 1097-1098.

814. Villedeuil, Comte Charles de. "'Contes d'été,'" *Eclair,* 1853, III (No. 37), 337-338.

[1854]

815. Barbey d'Aurevilly, Jules. "'Contes d'été,'" *Pays,* 14 janvier 1854. *Reprinted in *Voyageurs et romanciers,* 3d ed., Paris: Lemerre, 1908, pp. 19-23.

816. Mazade, Charles de. "Chronique de la quinzaine," *Revue des deux mondes,* 1ᵉʳ juin 1854, II, 1050-1051.

817. Boiteau, Paul [signed Paul d'Ambly]. "'Contes d'automne,'" *Artiste,* 1ᵉʳ juin 1854, 5ᵉ série, XII, 136-137.

818. Cuvillier-Fleury, A. A. "Conteurs français et flamands," *Journal des débats,* 2 juillet 1854.

[1855]

819. ———. "'Les Bourgeois de Molinchart,'" *Journal des débats,* 21 août 1855.

820. Goudall, Louis. "L'Ecole réaliste.—M. Champfleury," *Figaro,* 7 octobre 1855, pp. 2-4.

821. Janin, Jules. "Histoire littéraire et dramatique de l'année," *Almanach de la littérature,* etc., Paris, 1855, III, 26.
Cf. *652,* Perrier, p. 85.

[1856]

822. Chasles, Emile. "'Les Excentriques. . . . Les Bourgeois de Molinchart,'" *Athenaeum français,* 31 mai 1856, v, 463-464.

823. Anon. "Encore quelques mots à propos de 'M. de Boisdhyver,'" *Figaro,* 7 août 1856, pp. 3-4. [Followed by an answer by Champfleury, with a statement of his theory.]

824. Aubryet, Xavier. "Revue parisienne. M. Champfleury," *Artiste,* 9 novembre 1856, 6ᵉ série, II, 281-283. Reprinted in *Les Jugements nouveaux:* Philosophie de quelques œuvres, Paris: Librairie nouvelle, 1860.

825. Bataille, Charles. "La Semaine littéraire et artistique," *Diogène,* 7 décembre 1856, I, No. 18.

[1857]

826. Babou, Hippolyte. "La Vérité sur le cas de M. Champfleury," *Revue française,* 1ᵉʳ janvier 1857, VII, 421-431. Reprinted under the same title, Paris: Poulet-Malassis, 1857.

827. Thulié, Henri. "M. Champfleury," *Réalisme,* 15 février 1857, No. 4, pp. 49-56.

828. Anon. " 'Le Réalisme,' " *Revue de Paris,* 15 septembre 1857, XXXIX, 330-331.
  Cf. *883,* Baudelaire, p. 106.

[1858]

829. Révillon, Tony. "Personnalités artistiques et littéraires. IV. Champfleury," *Gaulois,* 10 mars 1858.

830. Rousseau, Jean. "Septième chambre du 'Figaro.'—Audience du 23 mars 1858.—Le Sieur Champfleury et 'Les Amoureux de Sainte-Périne.'—Excitation à la débauche de vieillards au-dessus de soixante ans," *Figaro,* 25 mars 1858, pp. 4-5.

[1859]

831. Lataye, Eugène. "Revue littéraire," *Revue des deux mondes,* 1er mars 1859, II, 248-250.

832. Lambert, Louis Eugène [signed Paul Dhormoys]. " 'Les Amoureux de Sainte-Périne,' par Champfleury," *Revue européenne,* 15 mars 1859, I, 916-917.

833. Duchesne, Alphonse. "La Mascarade de M. Champfleury," *Figaro,* 20 septembre 1859, pp. 6-7.

834. Merlet, Gustave. "Le Roman contemporain. Les Réalistes. M. Champfleury," **Revue européenne,* 15 décembre 1859, VI, 298-325. Reprinted in *41,* pp. 3-44.

835. Duranty, Edmond. "Caractéristique des œuvres de M. Champfleury (1847-1858)," in Champfleury, *Les Amis de la nature,* Paris: Poulet-Malassis et De Broise, 1859, pp. i-xl.
  Cf. *750,* Sarcey; *753,* Arnould, p. 902.

[1860]

836. Laurent-Pichat, Léon. " 'Mascarade de la vie parisienne,' " *Correspondance littéraire,* 25 mai 1860, IV, 326-327.

837. Cherbuliez, Joël. " 'M. de Bois-d'Hyver.' " In *10,* juin 1860, Nouvelle série, III, 255-256.

838. Chavesne, C. "Les Romans nouveaux," *Revue européenne,* 1er octobre 1860, XI, 636-637.

839. Cherbuliez, Joël. " 'La Succession Lecamus.' " In *10,* novembre 1860, Nouvelle série, III, 488-489.

840. Vapereau, Gustave. "M. Champfleury." In *70,* III, 102-104.

[1861]

841. Cherbuliez, Joël. " 'Les Souffrances du professeur Delteil.' " In *10,* mars 1861, Nouvelle série, IV, 121-122.

[1863]

842. Dusolier, Alcide. "M. Champfleury," *Nos gens de lettres,* Paris: Faure, 1864, pp. 27-47. [Dated 20 janvier 1863.]
  Cf. *780,* Fournel, p. 339.

[1864]

843. Assézat, Jules, " 'Les Demoiselles Tourangeau,' " *Journal des débats*, 10 février 1864.

844. Lavoix, Henri. " 'Les Demoiselles Tourangeau,' " *Moniteur universel*, 3 mars 1864.

845. Laurent-Pichat, Léon. " 'Les Demoiselles Tourangeau,' " *Correspondance littéraire*, 25 mars 1864, VIII, 149.

[1865]

846. Laffite, Paul [signed Victor Luciennes]. "La Caricature à coups de plume.— M. Champfleury," *Artiste*, 1er février 1865, pp. 56-57.

[1870]

847. Houssaye, Arsène, *or* Coligny, Charles [signed X. de Villarceaux]. "Les Livres d'étrennes," *Artiste*, 1er janvier 1870, pp. 115-117.

MURGER

[1849]

848. Eyma, Louis-Xavier. " 'La Vie de Bohème,' vaudeville en cinq actes . . . ," *Messager des théâtres* [éd. bis-hebdomadaire], 24 et 27 novembre 1849.

849. Janin, Jules. "La Semaine dramatique. 'La Vie de Bohême,' " *Journal des débats*, 26 novembre 1849.

850. Pontmartin, Armand de. "Revue littéraire," *Revue des deux mondes*, 30 novembre 1849, IV, 911-912.

851. Thomas, André. "Théâtre des Variétés," *Artiste*, 1er décembre 1849, 5e série, IV, 45-46.

[1851]

852. Fournier, Edouard. "Le Monde parisien et le monde littéraire," *Artiste*, 16 février 1851, 5e série, VI, 26-28.

853. Clément de Ris, Comte L. "Henri Murger et la vie de Bohème," *Artiste*, 15 juillet 1851, 5e série, VI, 180-183.

[1852]

854. Pontmartin, Armand de. [On 'Le Pays Latin.'] *Revue des deux mondes*, 1er janvier 1852, I, 194-195.

855. Lireux, Auguste. " 'Le Bonhomme Jadis,' " *Constitutionnel*, 26 avril 1852.

856. Prarond, Ernest. "Henry Murger." In *54*, pp. 153-189.

[1857]

857. Aubryet, Xavier. "Revue parisienne. 'Les Vacances de Camille,' " *Artiste*, 18 octobre 1857, Nouvelle série, II, 110-111.

[1860]

858. Merlet, Gustave. "Un Réaliste imaginaire. M. Henry Murger," *Revue européenne*, 1er mars 1860, VIII, 34-63. Reprinted in *41*, pp. 45-90.

[1861]

859. Claveau, Anatole. "Nécrologie: Henry Murger," *Revue contemporaine,* 28
février 1861, 2ᵉ série, xix, 709-711.

860. Pontmartin, Armand de. "Un Jeune Ecrivain. Etude morale. Henri Murger
et ses œuvres," *Revue des deux mondes,* 1ᵉʳ octobre 1861, v, 700-717.
Reprinted in *53,* pp. 131-161.

[1864]

861. Nettement, Alfred. "L'Elégie dans le réalisme.—Henry Murger." In *43,*
pp. 141-150.

FLAUBERT

[1856]

862. Du Camp, Maxime. [Letter to Flaubert, dated 14 juillet 1856.] In Maupas-
sant, *Etude sur Gustave Flaubert.* Œuvres complètes, t. 29; Œuvres
posthumes, t. 2, Paris: Conard, 1910, p. 93.

[1857]

863. Pinard, Ernest. "Le Ministère public contre G. Flaubert. Réquisitoire de
M. l'avocat impérial . . ." In *24,* Flaubert, pp. 558-578. [Dated 31 janvier
1857.]

864. Sénard, A.-J. "Plaidoirie du défenseur Mᵉ Sénard." In *24,* Flaubert, pp.
579-627.

865. Duranty, Edmond. "Nouvelles diverses," *Réalisme,* 15 mars 1857, No. 5,
p. 79.

866. Champfleury. [Letter to Flaubert, dated 22 avril 1857.] In *21,* Dumesnil,
pp. 313-314.

867. Sainte-Beuve, C.-A. [Letter to Flaubert, dated 25 avril 1857.] In *21,* Dumesnil, pp. 314-315.

868. Gozlan, Léon. [Letter to Flaubert, dated avril 1857.] In *21,* Dumesnil,
pp. 312-313.

869. Mazade, Charles de. "Chronique de la quinzaine," *Revue des deux mondes,*
1ᵉʳ mai 1857, iii, 217-219.

870. Sainte-Beuve, C.-A. " 'Madame Bovary,' " *Moniteur universel,* 4 mai 1857.
Reprinted in *57,* xiii, and in **60,* ii, 164-183.

871. Deschamps. [Article on 'Madame Bovary.'] *Revue des deux mondes,* 15
mai 1857, supplément. *Extracts in *55,* Prod'homme, pp. 280-282.

872. Roqueplan, Nestor. "Courrier de Paris," *Presse,* 16 mai 1857.

873. Desdemaines, Emile. "Les Jeunes. MM. Gustave Flaubert et Paul Deltuf,"
Rabelais, 23 mai 1857, i, No. 3, p. 7.

874. Cuvillier-Fleury, A. A. " 'Madame Bovary,' " *Journal des débats,* 26 mai
1857.

875. Pontmartin, Armand de. "Le Roman bourgeois et le roman démocrate.
MM. Edmond About et Gustave Flaubert," **Correspondant,* 25 juin 1857,
Nouvelle série, v, 289-306. Reprinted in *51,* pp. 299-326.

876. Habans, J. " 'Madame Bovary,' Roman par M. Gustave Flaubert," *Figaro,*
28 juin 1857, pp. 3-4.

877. Denys, Henry. " 'Madame Bovary, mœurs de province,' par M. Gustave
Flaubert," *Présent,* 9 juillet 1857, i, 34-39.

878. Donis, J.-B. "La Tradition littéraire et le roman moderne. 'Madame Bovary,' par M. Gustave Flaubert," *Revue moderne*, juillet 1857, i, 73-86.

879. Sainte-Beuve, C.-A. [Letter to Mme du Gravier, dated 5 août 1857.] In *20*, Dumesnil, p. 113.

880. Castelnau, Albert. "Le Roman réaliste. 'Madame Bovary,' par M. Gustave Flaubert," *Revue philosophique et religieuse*, août 1857, viii, 152-155.

881. Aubryet, Xavier. "Revue parisienne. Les niaiseries de la critique," *Artiste*, 20 septembre 1857, Nouvelle série, ii, 46-48.

882. Barbey d'Aurevilly, Jules. "M. Gustave Flaubert," *Pays*, 6 octobre 1857. *Reprinted in *4*, pp. 61-76.

883. Baudelaire, Charles. "M. Gustave Flaubert. 'Madame Bovary.—La Tentation de Saint Antoine,' " *Artiste*, 18 octobre 1857, Nouvelle série, ii, 105-109. Reprinted in *6*, pp. 393-408.

884. Sandeau, Jules. [Letter to Du Camp, dated "Dimanche matin" (1857).] In *21*, Dumesnil, p. 300.

885. About, Edmond. [Letter to Flaubert, undated (1857).] In *24*, Flaubert, pp. 525-526.

Cf. *519*, Aubineau; *521*, Sarcey, p. 3; *734*, Texier, p. 295.

[1858]

886. Weiss, Jean-Jacques. "La Littérature brutale. 'Les faux Bonshommes . . . , Madame Bovary . . . , Les Fleurs du Mal . . . ,' " *Revue contemporaine*, 15 janvier 1858, 2ᵉ série, i, 144-185.

887. Granier de Cassagnac, Adolphe. "La Bohème dans le roman. 'Madame Bovary,' " *Réveil*, 16 janvier 1858, I, 26-29.

888. Rousseau, Jean. "Les Hommes de demain. ii. M. Gustave Flaubert," *Figaro*, 27 juin 1858, pp. 3-5.

889. Dumas, Alexandre (*fils*). [Letter dated 17 juillet 1858.] *Intermédiaire des chercheurs et curieux*, 20 mars 1909, lix, cols. 438-440.

890. Vapereau, Gustave. "Succès du roman physiologique: M. G. Flaubert." In *70*, i, 47-59.

891. Chevalet, Emile. " 'Madame Bovary,' " *Les 365*, Annuaire de la littérature et des auteurs contemporains, par le dernier d'entre eux, Paris: Havard, 1858, pp. 192-194.

Cf. *945*, Vapereau, pp. 64, 67.

[1859]

892. Monpont. "Gustave Flaubert. 'Madame Bovary,' " *Les Chantres de l'adultère*, Paris: Ledoyen, 1859, pp. 27-38.

[1860]

893. Merlet, Gustave. "Le Roman physiologique. 'Madame Bovary,' par M. Gustave Flaubert," *Revue européenne*, 15 juin 1860, ix, 707-740. Reprinted in *41*, pp. 91-141.

Cf. *967*, Barbey d'Aurevilly, pp. 231-233, 238.

[1861]

894. Goncourt, Edmond et Jules de. [Item dated 6 mai 1861.] In *29*, i, 288-289.

[1862]

895. Calmels, Fortuné "La Nouvelle Œuvre de G. Flaubert," *Boulevard*, 30 novembre 1862, pp. 3-4.

896. Mérimée, Prosper. [Letter dated Cannes, 5 décembre 1862.] In *Lettres à une inconnue*, Paris: Michel Lévy, 1874, ii, 208-209. [Letter cclviii.]

897. Calmels, Fortuné. "'Salammbô,' par Gustave Flaubert," *Boulevard*, 7 décembre 1862, pp. 4, 6.

898. Sainte-Beuve, C.-A. "'Salammbô,'" *Constitutionnel*, 8, 15, 22 décembre 1862. Reprinted in *58*, iv, and **60*, ii, 184-241.

899. Cuvillier-Fleury, A. A. "'Salammbô,'" *Journal des débats*, 9, 13 décembre 1862.

900. Caro, Elme-Marie. "Gustave Flaubert," *France*, 9 décembre 1862. *Reprinted in *8*, pp. 260-270.

901. Levallois, Jules. "'Salammbô,'" *Opinion nationale*, 14 décembre 1862.

902. Claveau, Anatole. "'Salammbô,'" *Revue contemporaine*, 15 décembre 1862, 2ᵉ série, xxx, 643-652.

903. Laffite, Paul [signed Victor Luciennes]. "'Salammbô,'" *Artiste*, 15 décembre 1862, pp. 266-268.

904. Scherer, Edmond. "M. Gustave Flaubert," *Temps*, 16 décembre 1862.

905. Gautier, Théophile. "'Salammbô,'" *Moniteur universel*, 22 décembre 1862. *Reprinted in *L'Orient*, Paris: Charpentier, 1877, ii, 281-322.

906. Jouvin, Benoît. "M. Gustave Flaubert. 'Salammbô,'" *Figaro*, 28 décembre 1862, pp. 1-3.

907. Douhaire, Pierre-Paul. "Revue critique. 'Salammbô,'" *Correspondant*, décembre 1862, Nouvelle série, xxi, 801-804.

908. Pontmartin, Armand de. "M. Gustave Flaubert. 'Salammbô.'" In *53*, pp. 93-106. [Dated décembre 1862.]

909. Froehner, Guillaume. "Le Roman archéologique en France," *Revue contemporaine*, 31 décembre 1862, 2ᵉ série, xxx, 853-870.

[1863]

910. Dusolier, Alcide. "'Salammbô,'" *Revue française*, 1ᵉʳ janvier 1863, iv, 115-122.

911. Cadoudal, Georges de. "'Salammbô,'" *Union*, 8 janvier 1863.

912. Clergier, Albéric. "'Salammbô,' par Gustave Flaubert," *Critique française*, 15 janvier 1863, v, 1-11.

913. Saint-René Taillandier, R. G. E. "Le Réalisme épique dans le roman. 'Salammbô,'" *Revue des deux mondes*, 15 février 1863, i, 840-860.

914. Néantes, S. A. de. "Histoire courante: 'Salammbô,'" *Revue du progrès*, mars 1863, i, 46.

915. Boutmy, Emile. "Le Roman moderne et M. Gustave Flaubert," *Revue nationale et étrangère*, 10 mai 1863, xiii, 72-90.

916. Fournel, Victor. "'Salammbô,'" *Revue de l'année*, Paris: Vaton, 1863, iii, 349-356.

[1864]

917. Delaplace, Eugène. "Le Roman contemporain. . . . 'Salammbô,'" *Revue contemporaine*, 15 mars 1864, 2ᵉ série, xxxviii, 138-167.

918. Sarcey, Francisque. "Les Livres de l'An 1863: 'Salammbô,'" *Nouvelle Revue de Paris*, 15 mars 1864, I, 497-502.

919. Nettement, Alfred. "Gustave Flaubert." In *43*, pp. 118-129.

[1865]

920. Gautier, Léon. "M. Gustave Flaubert," *Etudes littéraires pour la défense de l'Eglise*, Paris: Vᵉ Poussielgue et fils, 1865, pp. 183-195.

[1868]

921. Levallois, Jules. "Les Romanciers de ce temps.—Air: 'A la façon de Barbari,'" *Les Contemporains chantés par eux-mêmes.—Chansons*, Paris: Librairie internationale, 1868, pp. 3-8.

[1869]

922. Barbey d'Aurevilly, Jules. "'L'Education sentimentale,'" *Constitutionnel*, 19 novembre 1869. *Reprinted in *3*, pp. 91-105.

923. Gayet de Cesena, Amédée. "'L'Education sentimentale,'" *Figaro*, 20 novembre 1869.

924. Cuvillier-Fleury, A. A. [No title.] *Journal des débats*, 20 novembre 1869. Second article: "'L'Education sentimentale . . .' La Satire dans le roman," *Journal des débats*, 14 décembre 1869.

925. Dommartin, Léon. "'L'Education sentimentale,' par Gustave Flaubert," *Gaulois*, 21 novembre 1869.

926. Levallois, Jules. "'L'Education sentimentale,'" *Opinion nationale*, 22 novembre 1869.

927. Léoni, Paul de. "Petite gazette. 'L'Education sentimentale,'" *Pays*, 26 novembre 1869.

928. Lefèvre, André. "'L'Education sentimentale,'" *Illustration*, 27 novembre 1869, LIV, 342-343.

929. Sarcey, Francisque. "'L'Education sentimentale,'" *Gaulois*, 3 décembre 1869. Second article: "Encore M. Flaubert," *Ibid.*, 4 décembre 1869.

930. Scherer, Edmond. "Un Roman de M. Flaubert," *Temps*, 7 décembre 1869. *Reprinted in *63*, IV, 291-301.

931. Sand, George. "'L'Education sentimentale,' par Gustave Flaubert." In *61*, pp. 415-423. [Dated Nohant, 10 décembre 1869.]

932. Saint-René Taillandier, R. G. E. "Le Roman misanthropique. 'L'Education sentimentale,'" *Revue des deux mondes*, 15 décembre 1869, VI, 987-1004.

933. Banville, Théodore de. [Letter to Flaubert, dated 15 décembre 1869.] In *23*, Flaubert, p. 702.

934. Hugo, Victor. [Letter to Flaubert, dated 20 décembre 1869.] In *23*, Flaubert, p. 704.

935. Taine, Hippolyte. [Letter to Flaubert, undated.] In *23*, Flaubert, pp. 703-704.

936. Pontmartin, Armand de. "M. Gustave Flaubert." In *50*, VII, 289-302.

[1870]

937. Asselineau, Charles. "'L'Education sentimentale,' par Gustave Flaubert," *Bulletin du bibliophile*, 1870-1871, pp. 35-42.

FEYDEAU

[1858]

938. Sainte-Beuve, C.-A. " 'Fanny.' Etude, Par M. Ernest Feydeau," *Moniteur universel*, 14 juin 1858. *Reprinted in *57*, xiv, 163-178.

939. Lataye, Eugène. "Les Livres nouveaux. 'Fanny,' " *Revue des deux mondes*, 15 juin 1858, iii, 968-971.

940. Chasles, Emile. " 'Fanny,' " *Constitutionnel*, 22 juillet 1858.

941. Rigault, Hippolyte. " 'Fanny,' " *Journal des débats*, 5 août 1858. Reprinted in *Conversations littéraires et morales*, Paris: Charpentier, 1859, pp. 310-324.

942. Lacroix, Octave [?] [signed O. L.]. " 'Fanny,' " *Gaulois*, 29 août 1858. [The preceding item in the same issue is a poem by Octave Lacroix; is he the same as the O. L. of the review?]

943. Montégut, Emile. "Le Roman intime de la littérature réaliste. 'Fanny . . . ,' " *Revue des deux mondes*, 1er novembre 1858, vi, 196-213.

944. Janin, Jules. "Préface" to *Fanny*, 2e édition, Paris: Amyot, 1858, pp. i-xvi.

945. Vapereau, Gustave. "Encore le roman physiologique. Recrudescence de succès. M. Ernest Feydeau." In *70*, i, 60-70.

    Cf. *889*, Dumas *fils*, col. 440.

[1859]

946. Delord, Taxile. "L'Année littéraire. 'Fanny,' " *Magasin de librairie*, 5 janvier 1859, ii, 145.

947. La Madelène, Henri Collet, baron de. " 'Daniel,' " *Gaulois*, 12 juin 1859, p. 6.

948. Lataye, Eugène. "Les Romans nouveaux," *Revue des deux mondes*, 1er juillet 1859, iv, 239-243.

949. Chasles, Emile. " 'Daniel,' " *Constitutionnel*, 19 juillet 1859.

950. Cuvillier-Fleury, A. A. " 'Daniel,' " *Journal des débats*, 29 et 30 octobre 1859.

951. Vapereau, Gustave. "Les Suites de 'Madame Bovary' et 'Fanny.' MM. H. Malot, Ed. Gourdon et E. Feydeau." In *70*, ii, 120-126.

[1860]

952. Claveau, Anatole. " 'Catherine d'Overmeire,' " *Revue contemporaine*, 15 février 1860, 2e série, xiii, 538-549.

953. Sainte-Beuve, C.-A. "A Monsieur le directeur gérant du 'Moniteur,' " *Moniteur universel*, 20 février 1860. *Reprinted in *57*, xv, 345-355.

954. Cuvillier-Fleury, A. A. " 'Catherine d'Overmeire,' " *Journal des débats*, 1er avril 1860.

955. Merlet, Gustave. "Le Réalisme byronien. M. Ernest Feydeau," *Revue européenne*, 15 août 1860, x, 609-703. Reprinted in *41*, pp. 143-196.

956. Barbey d'Aurevilly, Jules. "M. Ernest Feydeau." In *4*, pp. 105-143.

[1861]

957. Vapereau, Gustave. "Anciennes connaissances. Le réalisme impénitent. M. Ernest Feydeau." In *70*, iv, 71-74.

[1863]

958. Peyronnet, Comtesse de [signed Horace de Lagardie]. "Romanciers con-temporains. I.—M. Ernest Feydeau," *Revue nationale et étrangère*, 10 novembre 1863, xv, 129-147.

958a. Pontmartin, Armand de. "M. Ernest Feydeau. 'Un Début à l'Opéra,' etc." In *Dernières semaines littéraires*, Paris: Michel Lévy, 1864, pp. 146-158.

[1864]

959. Nettement, Alfred. "Ernest Feydeau.—'Fanny.'" In *43*, pp. 129-141.

ABOUT

[1855]

960. Babou, Hippolyte. "'Tolla,'" *Athenaeum français*, 19 mai 1855, iv, 405-406.

[1856]

961. Fournel, Victor. "'Les Mariages de Paris,'" *Revue contemporaine*, 1er septembre 1856, xxvii, 361-364.

[1857]

962. Jouvin, Benoît. "M. Edmond About.—'Germaine,'" *Figaro*, 19 avril 1857, pp. 3-4.

963. Pontmartin, Armand de. "Le Roman bourgeois et le roman démocrate. MM. Edmond About et Gustave Flaubert," *Correspondant*, 25 juin 1857, Nou-velle série, v, 289-306. Reprinted in *51*, pp. 299-326.

[1860]

964. Boissière, Emile. "Le Roman contemporain. M. Edmond About," *Revue européenne*, 1er août 1860, x, 534-553.

[1864]

965. Mazade, Charles de. "Les idées libérales et la littérature nouvelle. Deux publicistes," *Revue des deux mondes*, 1er avril 1864, ii, 736-741.

DURANTY

[1860]

966. Cherbuliez, Joël. "'Le Malheur d'Henriette Gérard.'" In *10*, septembre 1860, Nouvelle série, iii, 387-390.

967. Barbey d'Aurevilly, Jules. "M. Duranty." In *4*, pp. 227-238.

968. Chavesne, C. "'Le Malheur d'Henriette Gérard,'" *Revue européenne*, 1er octobre 1860, xi, 637-638.

[1862]

969. Lataye, Eugène. "Revue littéraire," *Revue des deux mondes*, 15 septembre 1862, v, 492-494.

DUMAS *FILS*

[1866]

970. Jouvin, Benoît. "M. Dumas fils romancier. 'L'Affaire Clémenceau,'" *Figaro*, 15 juillet 1866, pp. 1-3; 19 juillet 1866, pp. 1-2.
971. Pradal, Gabriel. "'L'Affaire Clémenceau,'" *Le Critique*, 19 juillet 1866.
972. Bernard, Jules. "'L'Affaire Clémenceau,'" *Revue gauloise*, 20 juillet 1866, No. 1, pp. 26-31.
973. Landrol, Gustave. "'Affaire Clémenceau, Mémoire de l'accusé,' par Alexandre Dumas fils," *Constitutionnel*, 23 juillet 1866.
974. Pontmartin, Armand de. "La Réalité dans le roman. 'Affaire Clémenceau,'" *Revue des deux mondes*, 1er août 1866, IV, 744-757. *Reprinted in *50*, IV, 50-75. [Signed F. de Lagenevais in the *Revue des deux mondes*.]
975. Sarcey, Francisque. "Romans et romanciers contemporains. M. Alexandre Dumas fils. 'L'Affaire Clémenceau,'" *Revue française*, 1er août 1866, XIV, 535-548.
976. Werner, Georges. "Le Roman contemporain. 'Affaire Clémenceau, Mémoire de l'accusé,' par M. Alexandre Dumas fils," *Revue du dix-neuvième siècle*, 1er août 1866, II, 295-301.
977. Claveau, Anatole. "'Affaire Clémenceau, Mémoire de l'accusé,'" *Revue contemporaine*, 15 août 1866, 2e série, LII, 556-563.
978. Merlet, Gustave. "M. Alexandre Dumas fils. 'Affaire Pierre Clémenceau.'" In *40*, pp. 115-131.
979. Vapereau, Gustave. "Les romans d'affaires criminelles et judiciaires. Les artistes assassins. M. Alexandre Dumas fils." In *70*, IX, 56-61.

EDMOND ET JULES DE GONCOURT

[1860]

980. Janin, Jules. "Théâtre des misères parisiennes.—'Les Hommes de lettres,' drame et roman, par MM. Edmond et Jules de Goncourt," *Journal des débats*, 30 janvier 1860.
981. Pontmartin, Armand de. "'Les Hommes de lettres,'" *Union*, 4 février 1860.
982. Chasles, Emile. "'Les Hommes de lettres,'" *Constitutionnel*, 30 mai 1860.
983. Duchesne, Alphonse. "Lettres critiques. 'Les Hommes de lettres.' A MM. Edmond et Jules de Goncourt," *Figaro*, 5 août 1860, pp. 2-3.
984. Chavesne, C. "'Les Hommes de lettres,'" *Revue européenne*, 1er novembre 1860, XII, 200-201.
985. Barbey d'Aurevilly, Jules. "MM. Jules et Edmond de Goncourt." In *4*, pp. 189-201.
986. Vapereau, Gustave. "'Les Hommes de lettres.'" In *70*, III, 118-119.

[1861]

987. Arnould, Arthur. "'Sœur Philomène,'" *Revue nationale et étrangère*, 23 septembre 1861, VI, 320.
988. Cherbuliez, Joël. "'Sœur Philomène.'" In *10*, novembre 1861, Nouvelle série, IV, 468-469.
989. Pontmartin, Armand de. "Le Roman et les romanciers en 1861," *Revue des deux mondes*, 1er décembre 1861, VI, 700-717.

990. Vapereau, Gustave. "Anciennes connaissances. Le réalisme impénitent. MM.
    . . . Edmond et Jules de Goncourt." In *70*, iv, 74-77.
991. Levallois, Jules. "MM. Edmond et Jules de Goncourt." In *32*, pp. 324-337.

[1862]

992. Fournel, Victor. "'Sœur Philomène,'" *Revue de l'année*, Paris: Lecoffre,
    1862, ii, 350-352.

[1864]

993. Ernouf, Baron Alfred-Auguste. "'Renée Mauperin,'" *Revue contemporaine*,
    15 mars 1864, 2ᵉ série, xxxviii, Bulletin bibliographique, p. 52.
994. Saint-Victor, Paul de. "'Renée Mauperin,'" *Presse*, 11 avril 1864.
995. Banville, Théodore de. "'Renée Mauperin,'" *Artiste*, 15 avril 1864, pp.
    186-187.
996. Desprez, Adrien [?] [signed A. D.]. "'Renée Mauperin,'" *Gazette lit-
    téraire*, 30 avril 1864 (fly leaf).
997. Polo, Auguste. "'Renée Mauperin,'" *Nouvelle Revue de Paris*, 1ᵉʳ juin
    1864, iii, 426-428.
998. Cuvillier-Fleury, A. A. "Les Mœurs parisiennes dans le roman moderne.
    'Renée Mauperin,'" *Journal des débats*, 19 octobre 1864.
999. Vapereau, Gustave. "Le réalisme impénitent. MM. Edmond et Jules de
    Goncourt." In *70*, vii, 56-59.

[1865]

1000. Dauriac, Philippe. "'Germinie Lacerteux,'" *Monde illustré*, 4 février 1865,
    xvi, 71, 74.
1001. Lagenevais. "Le Petit roman," *Revue des deux mondes*, 15 février 1865,
    i, 1061-1069.
1002. Claretie, Jules. "Romanciers du dix-neuvième siècle. Edmond et Jules de
    Goncourt. 'Germinie Lacerteux,'" *Revue de Paris*, 26 février 1865, x,
    166-177.
1003. Pontmartin, Armand de. "MM. Edmond et Jules de Goncourt. 'Germinie
    Lacerteux.'" In *50*, ii, 102-115. [Dated 27 février 1865.]
1004. Banville, Théodore de. "'Germinie Lacerteux,'" *Artiste*, 1ᵉʳ mars 1865,
    p. 105.
1005. Duchesne, Alphonse. "Le Roman pathologique. 'Germinie Lacerteux,'"
    Figaro, 30 mars 1865, pp. 3-4.
1006. Villetard, Edmond. "'Germinie Lacerteux,'" *Revue nationale et étrangère*,
    10 avril 1865, xx, 518-525.
1007. Merlet, Gustave. "Un Roman réaliste. 'Germinie Lacerteux,' par MM. de
    Goncourt." In *40*, pp. 81-96.
1008. Zola, Emile. "'Germinie Lacerteux,'" *Salut public* (Lyon), 1865. *Re-
    printed in *71*, pp. 67-84.
1009. Roqueplan, Nestor. "'Henriette Maréchal,'" *Constitutionnel*, 11 décembre
    1865.
1010. Janin, Jules. "'Henriette Maréchal,'" *Journal des débats*, 11 décembre 1865.
1011. Claveau, Anatole. "'Renée Mauperin.—Germinie Lacerteux,'" *Revue con-
    temporaine*, 15 décembre 1865, 2ᵉ série, xlviii, 574-578.
1012. Vapereau, Gustave. "'Henriette Maréchal.'" In *70*, viii, 126-135.

[1867]

1013. Chesneau, Ernest. " 'Manette Salomon,' " *Constitutionnel,* 26 novembre, 3 décembre 1867.

1014. Foucher, Paul-Henri. "Publicistes et moralistes au théâtre. . . . 'Henriette Maréchal,' " *Entre cour et jardin,* Paris: Amyot, 1867, pp. 340-348.

[1868]

1015. E. C. " 'Manette Salomon,' " *Revue contemporaine,* 30 avril 1868, 2ᵉ série, LXII, Bulletin bibliographique, p. 8.

[1869]

1016. Roqueplan, Nestor. " 'Madame Gervaisais,' " *Constitutionnel,* 1ᵉʳ mars 1869.

1017. Houssaye, Arsène *or* Coligny, Charles [signed X. de Villarceaux]. "Histoire littéraire. 'Madame Gervaisais,' " *Artiste,* 1ᵉʳ mars 1869, p. 388.

1018. Barbey d'Aurevilly, Jules. " 'Madame Gervaisais,' " *Nain Jaune,* 7 mars 1869. *Reprinted in *3,* pp. 39-46.

1019. Ebelot, Alfred. " 'Madame Gervaisais,' " *Revue des deux mondes,* 15 mai 1869, III, 507-511.

1020. Asselineau, Charles. " 'Madame Gervaisais,' " *Bulletin du bibliophile,* 1869, pp. 116-125.

[1870]

1021. ———. "Chronique littéraire. Jules de Goncourt," *Bulletin du bibliophile,* 1870-71, pp. 325-332.

INDEX OF AUTHORS AND CRITICS

Arabic numbers refer to pages; italics to items in the Bibliography